BECOMING A SUBJECT
Political Prisoners during the Greek Civil War

Polymeris Voglis

Berghahn Books
New York • Oxford

Published in 2002 by
Berghahn Books
www.berghahnbooks.com

Copyright © 2002 Polymeris Voglis

All rights reserved. Except for the quotation of short passages for the purpose of criticism and review, no part of this book may be reproduced in any form or by any means, electronic or mechanical, including photocopying, recording, or any information storage and retrieval system now known or to be invented, without written permission of the publisher.

Library of Congress Cataloguing-in-Publication Data

Voglis, Polymeris.
 Becoming a subject : political prisoners during the Greek Civil War / Polymeris Voglis.
 p. cm.
 Includes bibliographical references and index.
 ISBN 1-57181-308-X (alk. paper) -- ISBN 1-57181-309-8 (pbk. : alk. paper)
 1. Greece--History--Civil War, 1944-1949--Prisoners and prisons. 2. Political prisoners--Greece--History--20th century. I. Title.

DF849.53.P75 V64 2001
949.507'4—dc21   2001035619

British Library Cataloguing in Publication Data

A catalogue record for this book is available from the British Library.

Printed in the United States on acid-free paper.

Contents

Acknowledgments viii

Abbreviations x

Introduction 1

Part One
From Political Repression to Political Exclusion

Chapter 1: The Phenomenon of Political Prisoners 19
    Political Prisoners in the Interwar Authoritarian Regimes, 22
    Political Prisoners under Socialism, 26

Chapter 2: Legacies 33
    The First Signs of Political Exclusion, 33
    The Dictatorship of Ioannis Metaxas, 39
    Occupation and Resistance, 44

Chapter 3: The Civil War: A Case of "Nation-State Rebuilding" 52
    1945-1946: The "White Terror", 54
    1946-1949: Institutionalized Exclusion, 58
    The Elusive Subject, 64

Chapter 4: Emblems of the Civil War: Declarations of Repentance 74
    The Misguided, 75
    The Renegades, 79
    The Public Topos, 83

Part Two
The Body and the Psyche in Pain

Chapter 5: A Confined Life — 91
Exile, 92
Prisons, 96
Camps, 100

Chapter 6: The Domain of Deprivation — 116
Presence, 117
Absence, 120
"Send Us your Body in a Picture", 124

Chapter 7: Probing the Limits of the Other — 130
Torture, 131
Solitary confinement, 138

Chapter 8: "Everything Comes to an End" — 145
Dying Slowly, 146
Unexpected Death, 148
Executions, 151

Part Three
Prison as a Field of Conflict

Chapter 9: Transforming Prison — 163
Activities, 164
Feasts, 169
Tearing Down the Walls, 173

Chapter 10: Forms of Resistance — 182
"Not Struck by the Enthusiasm of the Audience", 184
Protests in Prisons, 187
Hunger Strikes, 192

Chapter 11: The Politics of Counterpower — 199
Becoming Communist, 201
Constructing Power: The Party Mechanism, 208
Us and Them: The Dissidents, 212

Epilogue: After Prison — 223

Bibliography — 237

Index — 246

To my parents

Acknowledgments

When I began the research for this book my intention was to study political prisoners from the Metaxas dictatorship until the end of the Greek Civil War. I realized, however, that there were enormous differences between these two periods despite their chronological proximity. I decided to focus on political prisoners in the Civil War, although with a certain reluctance. My initial reluctance had to do with the puzzle concerning the place the resistance and the Civil War occupied in the public life of Greece in the 1980s and 1990s. After decades of prohibition and repression (which I didn't experience), the "National Resistance" was celebrated on every occasion and became part and parcel of the official discourse of the Socialist Party in power. In my eyes as a student at the university in the 1980s, the resistance was incorporated into the new political establishment. However, I could see that if the resistance had found its place in a newly reconstructed national narrative, the same had not happened with the Greek Civil War. There were no public debates about the Civil War, only silence or truisms about fratricidal tragedies. This awkward situation was also reflected in the Greek historiography. Until very recently the academic interest in the Greek Civil War was limited to the study of the British and the United States intervention in Greece. It is not a coincidence that the first scholarly history of the Greek Civil War, written by a Greek historian, was published in 2001, more than half of a century after its end. Be that as it may, I started studying foreign archives, the press, writings of political prisoners, and talked to a number of them. After a while I was confused; I did not find what I expected and what I found challenged my preconceptions. I realized that the "National Resistance" of the 1980s had a remote only relation with what was at stake in the 1940s, the society and the subjects of the time. I realized that Greece, only half a century ago, was in fact a different country. Once my assumptions wavered, the questions multiplied. Most importantly, categories that I took for granted in the beginning of my research, even the very category "political prisoner," became more fluid and contested. After some time, I had many questions, perhaps too many. What was the impact of occupation upon the postwar Greece? What were the experience and the memory of imprisonment, and what was the relation between the two? What did it mean to be communist in the 1940s? How is a subject made? If this book gives some answers to these questions, then also some other people should be credited for helping me to do so.

The book is based on my dissertation. Antonis Liakos encouraged me to embark upon this study and, then, helped me to tackle problems that seemed insoluble to me. His comments were particularly insightful, perhaps because they stem from personal experience as well. Luisa Passerini introduced me to concepts and categories (of subjectivity in particular) which were crucial for the argumentation of this book. Her methodological considerations balanced the freedom I enjoyed working with her. Mark Mazower's thorough knowledge of this historical era, helped me to think in a broader and comparative perspective and to see the importance of issues that I considered secondary. I greatly benefited from the many and long discussions we had when I was revising the manuscript for publication. I would like also to thank David H. Close, Katherine Fleming, Steve Kotkin, Arno J. Mayer, Claudio Pavone, Stanley Payne, and Bo Stråth, for their comments and suggestions.

The director of the Contemporary Social History Archives in Athens Philippos Iliou, together with Vagelis Karamanolakis and Ioanna Papathanasiou created a unique working environment and provided invaluable information. The group of historians which publishes the *Historein* journal has been an important source of friends and feedback, especially Effi Gazi, Pothiti Hantzaroula, Ioanna Laliotou and Dimitra Lambropoulou. I would like also to thank Dawn Lyon for her remarkable help while I was finishing my dissertation, and Federico Palomo, Christos Papastylianos and Sabine Schweitzer.

The *Idryma Kratikon Ypotrofion* and the European University Institute provided the necessary financial resources for this research. I had the opportunity to further work on this book while I was the Ted and Elaine Athanassiades Postdoctoral Fellow in the Program in Hellenic Studies at Princeton University, and I would like to thank its director Dimitri Gondicas for his genuine interest and support. The final revisions of the manuscript were made while I was visiting scholar in the Program in Hellenic Studies at Columbia University.

Former political prisoners did not trust me only with their memories, but also with photographs, books, and notes. I thank all of them, and Takis Benas in particular whose patience with me was inexhaustible. I would like to express my gratitude to the staff of the library at the European University Institute, the Firestone Library at Princeton University, the ministry of Justice in Athens, the National Archives and Records Administration in College Park, Maryland, the Public Records Office in Kew, the Modern Greek Archives at King's College, and the United Nations Archives in New York.

From our first contact Marion Berghahn showed an unreserved interest in publishing my study, and the task of making my text more friendly to native speakers was assigned to Jaime Taber who did an excellent job. Myrto Bolota and Alekos Lytras processed the illustrations published in this book.

With Kathrin Zippel I shared my life and thoughts when I was writing this book. She helped me to clarify my ideas, challenged my assumptions and her relentless energy lightened up my prison world. Finally, this book is dedicated to my parents. Without their love and support this book would not have been written —I thank them once more.

Abbreviations

ASKI	*Archeia Synchronis Koinonikis Istorias* (Contemporary Social History Archives), Athens
BMM	British Military Mission
BPPM	British Police and Prisons Mission
EA	*Ethniki Allilegyi* (National Solidarity)
EAM	*Ethniko Apeleftherotiko Metopo* (National Liberation Front)
EDA	*Eniaia Dimokratiki Aristera* (Unified Democratic Left)
EDES	*Ethnikos Dimokratikos Ellinikos Syndesmos* (National Republican Greek League)
EKKA	*Ethniki kai Koinoniki Apeleftherosi* (National and Social Liberation)
ELAS	*Ethnikos Laikos Apeleftherotikos Stratos* (National People's Liberation Army)
EPON	*Eniaia Panelladiki Organosi Neon* (United Panhellenic Organization of Youth)
FO	Foreign Office, Public Records Office, Kew
KKE	*Kommounistiko Komma Elladas* (Communist Party of Greece)
MGA/LDG	Modern Greek Archives/League for Democracy in Greece, King's College
NARA	National Archives and Records Administration, College Park, MD
OSPE	*Omada Symviosis Politikon Exoriston* (Political Exiles' Cohabitation Group)
PEOPEF	*Panellinia Enosi Oikogeneion Politikon Exoriston (Fylakismenon* (Panhellenic Union of Political Exiles' (Prisoners' Families)
SK-ELD	*Sosialistiko Komma - Enosi Laikis Dimokratias* (Socialist Party (Union of People's Democracy)
UNRRA	United Nations Relief and Rehabilitation Administration, and United Nations Archives, New York

Introduction

This is a study of political prisoners in Greece in the Civil War that is, the relation between a specific subject, political prisoners, and certain practices of punishment in the context of a polarization that led to a civil war (1946-1949). The book addresses a number of questions: What is the impact of an exceptional situation, such as a civil war, on practices of punishment? How is the category of political prisoners constructed? How is a social and political subject made? How did political prisoners experience their internment?

The literature on prisons is voluminous and has flourished since the 1970s in particular. A wave of revisionist studies in the 1970s challenged the established ideas in the literature on prison, namely that the birth of prison was a result of the initiatives of enlightened philanthropists and reformers who fought against the brutality of the *ancien regime* for more humane punishment or that the history of prisons was a history of successive failures of well-intended prison reforms.[1] Instead of reviewing the arguments and new perspectives that these studies put forward, I shall discuss some questions in relation to the book at hand. I shall begin this introductory chapter with a discussion of the practices of punishment, in order to argue that cutting-edge events such as wars and civil wars have a grave impact on the realm of punishment. Then I shall turn to the discussion of the political prisoner as a subject to argue that the concept of subjectivity can enrich the analysis of agents in the fields of social and cultural history.

Practices of Punishment

One may write the history of punishment starting from the spectacle of the scaffold (the hanging, mutilation, whipping, branding of the convict), then moving to the penitentiary, and finally arriving at the development after the Second World War of non custodial forms of punishment (fines, probation,

---

Notes for this section can be found on page 14.

parole) or alternative modes of imprisonment (communal-based sentencing and "prisons without walls"), and arguing for the decline of prison as a dominant form of punishment.[2] One may also detect a "civilizing process" of people's sensibilities in the history of punishment: from retribution to rehabilitation, from the body to the psyche of the wrongdoer, from the spectacle of an execution to punishment "behind the scenes."[3] Although such a hypothesis seems reasonable, is it realistic? Some of the developments in the United States, such as the tripling of the prison population in the last fifteen years (it currently stands at over two million individuals, the highest number ever) and the alarming number of executions of prisoners on death row, cast doubt on this optimistic version of history.[4] Or were the Nazi concentration camps, the Soviet and Chinese gulags, the "disappeared" during Latin American dictatorships, to cite just a few examples, just aberrations in this process? The linear and developmental course that the "civilizing process" implies needs to be critically examined.

The practices of punishment used against political opponents in the Greek Civil War varied. Some were already dominant in the interwar era (exile), while some that had been secondary became equally important (prison). New forms of internment were improvised (mass internment camps), new forms of punishment were introduced (executions), and other practices that in the past had been employed against specific social groups (e.g., decapitation of brigands and public display of their heads) were employed against guerillas in the Civil War. Greece in the second half of the 1940s was an archipelago of punishment. The most modern practices of punishment, such as the mass internment camps, coexisted with the most obsolete, the spectacle of punishment. There was evolution in the practices of punishment, but at the same time all these practices resembled a genealogy of punishment. The continuity of some practices of punishment, the introduction of new ones, and the reemergence of old practices at the same time, constitute the genealogy of punishment, the enactment of the history of punishment in a very short period of time; afterwards, many of these practices—executions or mass internment camps for instance—ceased to exist. This short period of time is the Civil War years, and to a large extent the explanation for the genealogy of punishment lies therein, rather than in the degree of modernization of Greece or the brutality of the peoples in the Balkans.

If, after half of a century of relative peace in Western Europe, we are apt to think of war as an exceptional phenomenon, this was not the case in the recent past. The two world wars in general, and the history of Greece in the first half of the century in particular, seem to speak for the opposite. Both war and peace were regularities. Greek society was mobilized in the Balkan Wars (1912-1913), World War I (which also resulted in a civil strife), the expedition to Asia Minor (1920-1922), the Greek-Italian War (1940-1941), was under the occupation of the Axis forces (1941-1944), and, finally, after the liberation underwent the Civil War (1946-1949). War was as regular as peace and had its impact upon society. Moreover, war in general has a structural impact that profoundly changes societal practices and therefore marks the experience of individuals.

Pitirim Sorokin, a Russian sociologist who migrated to the United States after the Bolshevik revolution, wrote a book, during the Second World War on the impact of what he called "calamities upon societies." He argued that cutting-edge events, such as war, revolution, famine, and pestilence produce societal polarization due to the diversified effects they have on individuals and social groups. He pointed out that due to the drastic disruption of social relations and institutions, social processes become "sudden, violent, chaotic, largely involuntary" and they bring "more profound social transformations than normal agents of change operating over a period of many decades."[5] The concepts of polarization and rupture as structural effects of war and revolution, will reoccur in my analysis of the practices of punishment and the individual experience of the Civil War. To argue that changes in practices of punishment may be construed in the framework of changes in cultural practices, state organization, and the sociopolitical constellation I shall put forward three themes to explain the practices of punishment in the Civil War: the violence generated during the occupation, the reconstruction of state authority, and the peculiarity of the civil war situation.

The Second World War and the Nazi occupation put forward structural and social changes that Jan Gross aptly described as revolution with regard to Central and Eastern European countries. He argued that this complex process of changes during the war facilitated the etatization of the economy that would be implemented a few years later in the "people's republics."[6] In the case of the Axis occupation of Greece the structural impact was the collapse of the state authority and the development in the countryside and towns of protostate institutions, and of a political mobilization network that engendered the communist-led resistance in Greece.[7] Conflicts developed between the leftist and the nationalist resistance organizations on the one hand, and between the leftist resistance organizations and the collaborationist Greek armed units on the other. Moreover, these conflicts took place in the larger context of the resistance against the German, Italian, and Bulgarian occupation forces. They generated an unparalleled degree of violence in the forms of executions, mass killings, reprisals, round ups and arrests of suspects, taking hostages, and the public exhibition of corpses. One might say that the degree and forms of violence that the society accepted were enhanced due to the occupation. The legacy of occupation was not only polarization but also a culture of violence and its agents altogether, which would be embodied in the practices of punishment in the Civil War.

In acute sociopolitical crises like civil war, the state, in order to regain and establish its power, rediscovers the whole arsenal of punishments at its disposal. To understand better the realm of punishment of the years 1945-1950, one has to consider the impact of the war upon the state mechanism. The state mechanism collapsed after the invasion of the Axis forces in Greece and was replaced by one loyal to the occupation forces. The official state and the collaborationist government were discredited in the eyes of the population because of their incompetence during the famine of 1941/42, and their alignment with the occupiers against the resistance. After the liberation, the prime concern of the ruling strata and political elites was to reconstitute a state authority loyal to the established order, against the challenge of the leftist resistance organizations. Thus, the rediscovery of the history of punishment in the case of the Greek Civil War is connected to the reconstruction of a disputed state authority, in two ways in particular. First, the state mechanism was staffed on the basis of the anticommunist beliefs of the recruits (many wartime collaborators were recruited perpetuating the polarization of the occupation). Second, in the different phases of the process of reconstruction different agents were involved for different purposes. The agents of punishment were diverse: the National Guard, the police, the gendarmerie, the army and the paramilitary rightist bands. Each of these agents brought its own mentality and practices into the realm of punishment. In fact, it may be argued that the penal realm is not singular, but is "a complex network composed of a variety of different institutions, practices and relations supported by a number of agencies, capacities and discourses."[8] All these agents, whether or not invested with state authority, were actively involved in the reconstruction of a state authority, a constituent feature of which was the repression of the leftist resistance organizations.

If the violence generated during the occupation, and the multitudinous punitive practices of a variety of agents incorporated into the policies of a state under reconstruction, were sufficient conditions for the practices of punishment in postwar Greece, then the necessary condition was the very fact of the Civil War. For the purposes of this research two peculiar features of the Civil War will be addressed: first the consequences of the revolt against the state, and second, the irreparable societal rupture it produced.

"Crimes against the state" are a chapter of their own in the history of punishment. They were occasions for demonstrating the sovereign's power and representing the political criminal as the utter "other" of the community.[9] However, it was in the first half of twentieth-century Europe, an era of wars, revolutions, and nationalism, that political opponents were *en masse* ruthlessly persecuted, imprisoned, and executed. It was in this era that political prisoners reached unprecedented numbers and not only in Greece but in Fascist Italy, Nazi Germany, Franco's Spain, and interwar Hungary and Finland, as well as the Soviet Union and the postwar "people's republics." From this point of view the punishment of "enemies of the nation" or "counterrevolutionaries" denoted broader and significant changes in modern European states. If we focus on practices of punishment of political opponents, then we see that their salient features are sheer terror and violence. The legacy of the occupation does not suffice to explain the state terror and violence during the Civil War. The hypothesis that I put forward is that civil wars are cases of "nation-state rebuilding," in the sense of a radical reorganization of social relations, values and practices. The task of taking or maintaining political power after a civil war is coupled with the establishment of a new societal constellation, the reconfiguration of social and political relations. The terror and violence against tens of thousands of suspected leftists in camps, prisons and police stations, went hand in hand with the emergency laws that made possible the inexorable suppression, the numerical increase and enhanced role of the army and the police, and the energetic intervention of Great Britain and the United States in the postwar reconstruction. The nation-state rebuilding during the Greek Civil War (and, in a more subtle form, after the war as well) aimed at reversing the social, cultural, and political changes that the resistance had set off; the policy that underpinned the process of rebuilding was the political exclusion of the Communist Party and the leftists. Thus, political prosecution and practices of punishment were part and parcel of the reconfiguration of social and political relations, namely the construction of an anticommunist state in Greece.

On the other hand, civil wars bring deep division upon societies. They disrupt the social fabric on every level, on the macro- as well as on the micro-level, from the relations between civil society and the state to family ties. The polarization leads to a rupture in the society, in the sense that the social and cultural bonds or rules that had held a society together are pushed, disputed, negated or replaced by new ones. The rules, norms, and values that prevailed in Greece before the war were challenged during the occupation, and the resistance set new standards.[10] After the liberation and in the Civil War years, the rules set by the resistance waned and came under attack by the state; meanwhile, the new rules were not yet established. To a large extent, the 1940s in Greece were a liminal phase. The practices of punishment during the Civil War were not placed beyond rules (the "no rules" scenario is always met with certain restrictions),[11] but they questioned and tested the old rules and traced the boundaries of the new ones. In this sense these practices epitomized the "civilizing process" through the genealogy of punishment. Societal processes and human action are not necessarily developmental, accumulative, linear, and rational; they may well be reversed, diverted, punctuated, contingent, and ambiguous.

The Subject

Prisoners in the historiography of prison are depicted as the object of the rehabilitative discourses and practices, and at the same time as the site for the construction of the category of "delinquence." Nevertheless, little attention has been paid to the prisoners themselves. This is partly due to the fact that, especially before the twentieth century, the prisoner was an "obscure" subject; his/her "voice" was neither registered in the available prison archives nor able to leave any testimonies behind.[12] The other reason was that revisionist historiography focused on the prison as an institution rather than on prisoners. Against the background of a liberal or humanitarian historiography of prison, the focus of study was on prison as an institution that becomes the dominant form of punishment amidst the sweeping social, economic and cultural changes brought about by the industrial revolution and nation-state formation.[13]

Although these studies profoundly changed our view on prisons, they were not without problems. The first problem is that the historiography of prison to a large extent focused on the birth of the prison—that is, how and why the penitentiary became the dominant form of punishment—, and its evolution in the eighteenth and nineteenth centuries. The study of prison in the twentieth history was left out of the scope of historical study—with the exception of the Nazi concentration camps, which are a distinct case. The second problem is that the historiography of prison, although it soundly connected the new forms of regulation and control of social "disorder" with the new forms of criminality and new conceptualizations of what crime is, did not insist on defining their political aspects and implications. All these changes appeared together with new forms of sociopolitical organization and protest, which were considered punishable; the latter, however, were left out of the scope of the study of practices of punishment, as topics of political or working-class history.[14] These problems are multiplied when one comes to the study of political prisoners. Political persecution and imprisonment were seen as derivative of authoritarian regimes, and thus of little heuristic value. The awesome increase of political prisoners' populations in twentieth-century Europe notwithstanding, almost no attention was paid to the new categories and practices of punishment that state policies introduced concerning the suppression of political opponents. Moreover, in the case of political prisoners, historians can not claim that the social subject was obscure. Political prisoners' memoirs and autobiographical writings amount to thousands of volumes, constituting a literary genre per se, and give invaluable insights to the experience of imprisonment, everyday life in prison, and the memory of prison life. However, the abundance of material in this case did not stimulate any scholarly interest. Despite the fact that large scores of political opponents were interned in almost every European country, we know very little about political prisoners.[15]

Michel Foucault's *Discipline and Punish* has by far the greatest influence in the study of prison, despite heavy criticism of the book. To review the debate on this book or Foucault's ideas on the themes he developed in *Discipline and Punish* (such as body, discipline, power, and knowledge) is a task that lies beyond the scope of this book, so I will try to outline his most important arguments. Foucault did not study the history of prison, but rather why certain practices of punishment became salient and converged on the prison as an indispensable part of the penal system.[16] He viewed prison as an emblematic form and mechanism in the production of individuals in the modern era, as a metaphor and site of the disciplinary society. The great transformation in punishment was that public retribution upon the body of the criminal was replaced by the institutionalized disciplining of individuals, the "docile bodies." In the new technologies of the power to punish, there was a shift of interest, from the body of the criminal to his mind or soul, that marks the change.[17] The institution of prison was designed on the principle of surveillance of prisoners. At this point lies Foucault's argument, the power/knowledge couplet: the ability to exercise power over a certain group of people is dependent on knowledge about the individuals of that group and vice versa. In his words "there is no power relation without the correlative constitution of a field of knowledge, nor any knowledge that does not presuppose and constitute at the same time power relations."[18] Foucault's analysis of power and prison was groundbreaking because he did not focus only on their negative aspects (like the exclusion of criminals), but on their constitutive aspects in relation to the subject as well. The subject was produced by power. In his words again: "Discipline 'makes' individuals; it is the specific technique of a power that regards individuals both as objects and as instruments of its exercise."[19] The subject is inscribed in the power relations as object and/or vehicle, and these relations are constitutive of the subject. In his analysis, the subject cannot be an autonomous agent, since it has internalized the power norms and therefore power has a hold on the subject in the process of its self-constitution. Foucault's conceptualization of power and subject were criticized on the grounds, that he did not have any normative criteria of distinction between different forms of power, and, by feminist scholars particularly, because he dismissed the possibility of the subject's resistance.[20] Toward the end of his life, especially when he published the unfinished *History of Sexuality*, he redefined the concept of the subject. He acknowledged the double meaning of the word subject: "subject to someone else by control or dependence, and tied to his own identity by a conscience or self-knowledge"[21]—the subject, therefore, also as the relation to the self.

Foucault's analysis of the subject may serve as a starting point for the discussion of political prisoners. Political prisoners as subjects are constituted by the discourses and practices of the various agents involved in political prosecution and imprisonment. On the one hand, legislation, the press, official discourse, and reports of foreign officials construct the concept of political crime, that is, of a certain type of illegality. Law produces illegality, in the sense that certain ideas, acts, or behavior are prescribed as punishable and become the object of new definitions and areas of control and regulation. In the Greek case, the line between legality and illegality was drawn along the lines of nationalism versus communism. Ideas, intentions, and even family relations during the Civil War were labeled as "antinational" and thus became new forms of illegality and new objects of punitive practices. However, as we will see, at the same time the government denied that there were political prisoners in Greece. For the regime, the category of political prisoners did not exist.

On the other hand, practices like mass arrests, imprisonment, hard labor, torture, indoctrination, and deprivation became constitutive of the subject of political prisoners. Thousands of men and women became the objects of old and new techniques of disciplining individuals; the token of the disciplining was the inmates' conversion, that is, the recantation of their political beliefs (in the form of declarations of repentance). Moreover, a number of these political prisoners were not only objects but became also instruments of the prison administration. They were incorporated in the propaganda mechanisms of the prisons or the government, or, even worse, they became the guards and tormentors of their fellow inmates. However, for the analysis of the subject this Foucauldian approach is far from satisfactory, because the subject is presented as passive, "made," and unitary.[22]

In this study I argue that subjects are not simply made once and for all, but they are situated in contested relationships and processes of making. First of all, the subject is situated, it is the point of suture, as Stuart Hall wrote, between different and antagonistic discourses and practices.[23] The subject is formed not only by state agencies but also by countervailing discourses and practices inside and outside prison. The Communist Party and resistance organizations outside prisons challenged and questioned the official discourse and provided a radically different narrative of the policies of prosecution and the experience of imprisonment. Moreover, the political prisoners' collectivity inside prisons, through the informal organization of their everyday life reconstituted the political prisoners as a subject antagonistic to prison authorities. Last but not least, the prisoners themselves, with their different subject-positions in these relations (positions related to their cultural and social background, position in the prisoners' hierarchy, and gender), enacted different aspects of prisoners' subjectivity. The political prisoner as a subject is the meeting point and the site of contest between all these different and diverse discourses, practices and positions.

The subject is also in the process of making. Although the main features of political prisoners as a subject are already formed in 1945—the experience of internment in the prewar years and, mainly, their past participation in resistance organizations as constitutive of their identity—it is not a subject in inertia, but one that undergoes successive unmakings and remakings. These are two different and interrelated processes. The first process is that of unmaking the subject.[24] The authorities, through the ordeal of imprisonment, aim at the deconstruction of prisoners' individuality and the shattering of their collectivity. The second process is that of remaking the subject. The prisoners' collectivity, through the organization of everyday activities, undertakes to reconstruct prisoners' individuality within the framework of sustaining the collectivity. In addition, changing conditions in prisons (lax discipline in 1945, a strict regime between 1946 and 1949, more humane conditions again in the 1950s) provide different opportunities and bring to the fore different aspects of prisoners' collectivity. From this point of view the subject is "made" in 1945, and once "made," undergoes changes in the following years.[25]

If the subject is constituted by relations and processes, and is situated within the interplay of structure and agent, objective and subjective realities, then its study should combine the synchronic and diachronic approaches. The diachronic approach is to a certain degree restricted because of the short period of time I study. However, the real question, I think, is the different temporalities that the synchronic and diachronic approaches enclose, always in relation to the subject. The "thin" and "short" temporality of events seems to be contrasted to the "deep" and "longer" temporality of people's experience of these events and the indelible mark that the experience of incarceration leaves in the memory.

It goes without saying that the dangers of a *histoire événementielle*, or of an abstract and ahistorical analysis of the subject, are obvious in the two approaches. In the book I have tried to combine these two temporalities. The first reason is that the political events of the era mark and are closely connected to the experience of the political prisoners. Changes in legislation or in the course of the Civil War had a direct impact on the life of political prisoners. What was happening outside prison was not just the context, so a historical analysis should reconstitute the relation between what happened outside and inside prison. A second reason is that prison as an institution creates its own temporality, its own sense of time. Prison time is organized around an everyday set of routines, a set that is repeated infinitely. Repetition and monotony are the quintessence of prison time. For this reason events that interrupt the sameness of prison time and life, such as holidays, correspondence, or visits, gain a different significance as the subjective markers of time in prison. Third, certain experiences or extreme situations have a deep impact upon the human body and psyche. Torture and physical pain, for instance, or dying for a cause, are context-specific but at the same time their impact or importance exceeds the Civil War years. In these cases the short temporality may not be helpful in understanding how people made sense of their experiences. One must resort to the longer temporality of memory or of cultural patterns according to which people act, think or imagine themselves.

Moreover, I have tried to combine these two temporalities by focusing on cases and events. This choice resulted from the nature of the sources and certain methodological considerations. The sources were diverse (official reports, letters, newspaper clippings, interviews, and autobiographical writings, to name the most important) and were generated by various agents (Greek and foreign officials, the press, the Communist Party, and individual prisoners). Any attempt to homogenize them into a continuous narrative would impose on the events a teleological historical continuity and neutralize their merit, that they reveal the different dimensions and aspects of the same event.[26] Events may also serve as cases for a deeper analysis, as examples to discuss relations or processes taking place. William H. Sewell, Jr., commenting on E.P. Thompson's "synchronic" narrative style, pointed out the historian's need to "stop time", "by abstracting some pattern, structure or relationship out of the flow of events in order to contemplate, categorize, anatomize or construct it in her mind or in her text."[27] In this way, events lose their momentary character but not their singularity as they become emblematic, revealing the difference and the interplay between the contingent and the determined, the individual and the collective experience, the agent and the structure.

So far I have argued for the study of the subject as the meeting point of different and antagonistic discourses, practices and positions, "made" by relations and processes inside and outside prisons. I have also argued for an analysis that combines a "thin" and a "deep" temporality as adequate to correlate the events and the subjective experience of them. The image of the subject that emerges from this analysis is not one of a stable, unified, conclusively "made" subject. Yet, there is a common understanding of what a political prisoner is. I shall address the question of these two intertwined aspects, and the smouldering tension between them, in the last section of the introduction.

Beyond Identity

The literature on identity has flourished enormously in the last two decades, and the concept of identity has become dominant category of analysis in the field of social sciences, from the social constructionist viewpoint in particular. At the same time, the deconstructionist and postmodern critique has problematized the concept of a unified and stable identity. Moreover, there is a contradiction between the constructionist approach to identity and identity politics' claims which often essentialize identities. Instead of addressing all these issues, I shall examine critically the constructionist approach to identity to argue that the concept of subjectivity as a category of analysis may be more insightful and fruitful for the study of social agents.

The starting point for the discussion of identity can be Stuart Hall's formulation that identification is "a construction, a process never completed" and therefore identities "are subject to a radical historicization, and are constantly in the process of change and transformation."[28] This approach discards any naturalistic or essentialist conception of identity and addresses some problems in the use of identity as concept that I shall discuss further. The first is the problem of construction with respect to the agent, and the second, the normative and exclusionary aspects of identity.

Constructionist theory was built upon the split between society and the individual. It emphasized the production of the subject by social structures, relations, mechanisms, and discourses, against the liberal argument of the individual's free will. The problem with constructionist theory, however, is that it became deterministic through the disappearance of the agent. By stressing omnipresent and monolithic social institutions and discourses, it denied or minimized the subject as an agent.[29] As Judith Butler suggests, instead of theorizing constructions, as the necessary setting for the agent and the very terms by which an agent becomes intelligible, the constructionist approach was trapped in the binary between determinism and free will.[30] Theorizing the subject as a process and relationship, as active and present in its making, we may understand why identities are not fixed but changing, and why the subject is not simply determined but may have different subject-positions.

The second, interrelated problem with the concept of identity is that social subjects are viewed as homogeneous. The concept and category of identity is a relatively recent term in the social sciences—a term "borrowed" from the field of psychology. It resulted, on the one hand, from the criticism of previous theories and models (mainly the Marxian and the Althusserian), as one-dimensional and deterministic, and, on the other, from what have been called "new social movements," that is, the emergence of social subjects hitherto repressed and silenced by the dominant discourses and politics. The relevance of these theoretical developments to the present study is that the identity of a subject cannot be separated from politics in the construction of such an identity. Craig Calhoun connects these identity politics to the recognition of the subject, to the reclamation of a suppressed identity.[31] This is a very important point for the study of Greek political prisoners. As I have already said, the government denied the existence of political prisoners in the Greek Civil War. It was the prisoners who claimed recognition as political prisoners (in contradistinction to criminal prisoners), formed that identity, and established political prisoners as a category. In fact, the category of political prisoner was a result of the identity politics of the subject.

Now, there is a contradiction between what we theorize as identity and the identity that the subjects claim or, to put it differently, the politics of the subject in the construction of its identity. The concept of identity as a construction always in process and not fixed is juxtaposed with the identities claimed by the subjects. The identity that political prisoners present is that of a unified, homogeneous, continuous, coherent, and singular subject. Last but not least, although individuals identify themselves with the collective subject, they may be dislocated so as to undermine that very same identity, to be "within" and "without" with respect to an identity (which, as we shall see, was the case of those who recanted their political beliefs). The concept of identity, as useful as it may be for the analysis of certain social processes, remains highly normative and exclusionary. How may the other, the constitutive outside for the construction of an identity, be reincorporated into the study of the subject as the constitutive inside?

The concept of subjectivity can offer some solutions to the shortcomings of the concept of identity. Subjectivity is not another word for identity; on the contrary, it highlights the normative and exclusionary aspects of identity. Gilles Deleuze's definition of the concept of subjectivity, although he was referring to the relation to oneself rather than a category of analysis, is insightful:

> The struggle for a modern subjectivity passes through a resistance to the two present forms of subjection, the one consisting of individualizing ourselves on the basis of constraints of power, the other of attracting each individual to a known and recognized identity, fixed once and for all. The struggle for subjectivity presents itself, therefore, as the right to difference, variation and metamorphosis.[32]

I think that Deleuze's conceptualization of subjectivity, even negatively (as resistance), illumines the main questions that this concept addresses. Instead of seeing dichotomy between society and individual as determinism versus free will, subjectivity explores the intensity of the articulation between these two. It is construed as a process rather than an internal and human essence. Finally, it reconstitutes the subject as a potential agent of change and differentiation. In this last part of the introduction I shall further elaborate these points and relate them to the present study.

As I have already argued, the subject is constituted by different and antagonistic discourses, practices, and positions. In other words, the subject is made and at the same time makes itself. Subjectivity as a methodological tool describes and analyzes this process of the making of the (individual and collective) subject. The subject is made by the discourses and practices of various agents (such as, in the case of political prisoners, the prison administration, the Communist Party, the prisoners' collectivity, the individual prisoners), and this process produces different subject-positions with respect to the collective subject. From this viewpoint the subject is neither fixed nor unique. Political prisoners are one and a multiple subject at the same time: one, because they share a past in the resistance during the occupation and the experience of prosecution and imprisonment (at this point the differences between prisons, camps, and exile are relevant), and multiple because imprisonment generates different attitudes, experiences, and understandings according to the individual's past and the specific situation in prison. Men and women of different age, education, class, and cultural background make up a subject that transforms them through different enactments (position in the prisoners' hierarchy, dissidents expelled from the political prisoners' collectivity, and so on). The subject is enacted in the dynamics of intersection of "complex, contradictory and unfinished processes."[33] Instead of the dichotomies and binary oppositions upon which an identity is constructed by a homogeneous subject (in the present study it might have been political prisoners versus prison administration), the analysis put forward stresses that subjectivity, that is, becoming and being a subject, is produced through multiple contradictions and conflicts—hence the emphasis on differentiations among the political prisoners.[34]

The emphasis on diversity within the subject aims also at the illumination of the relation between the individual and the collective subject. The articulation between the individual and the collective can be viewed neither as deductive (the collective subject or the general conditions produce the individual) nor as contrastive (the collective subject suppresses the individual). This articulation is based on tensions. The collectivity, as a form of intersubjectivity, simultaneously sustains and constricts the individual prisoners, and the relation is under explicit or implicit negotiation and contest. Subjectivity as a category of analysis brings to the fore the different and varying positions of the individual with respect to the collective agent, and reconstitutes it as responsible and capable of action within the given historical restrictions, "to be the subject of one's own history."[35]

Thus, subjectivity does not refer to any human essence, but is grounded in the experience of the subject. Though I shall return to the discussion of political prisoners' experience at the very end of this study, here suffice it to say that the notion of experience points out the need to historicize subjectivity. In the case of the Greek political prisoners in the second half of the 1940s, we will not find any explosions of subjectivity of other eras or subjects. Identities were less fluid, individuals much more disciplined, and differences easily oppressed. One may say that the traumatic experience of internment and the deep polarization of the Civil War somehow made subjectivity more rigid. Subjectivity does not thrive in any historical context, and many aspects of its experience remain silenced, repressed, disguised, or denied. We must wait for memory, the elaboration and reconstruction of past experience, to give us some clues to the subjectivity of the past through the present one.

Notes

1. The most influential contributions were the pioneering study of Georg Rusche and Otto Kirchheimer, *Punishment and Social Structure* (New York, 1939) and David J. Rothman, *The Discovery of the Asylum. Social Order and Disorder in the New Republic* (Boston, 1971), Michel Foucault, *Discipline and Punish: The Birth of the Prison* (London, 1991, originally published in 1975); Michael Ignatieff, *A Just Measure of Pain: The Penitentiary in the Industrial Revolution 1750-1850* (London, 1978); David J. Rothman, *Conscience and Convenience. The Asylum and its Alternatives in Progressive America* (Boston, 1980); Dario Melossi and Massimo Pavarini, *The Prison and the Factory: Origins of the Penitentiary System* (London, 1981); Michelle Perrot, ed., *L'impossible prison* (Paris, 1980); Robert Roth, *Pratiques pénitentiaires et theorie social. L' exemple de la prison de Genève, 1825-1862* (Geneva, 1981), Patricia O'Brien, *Correction ou châtiment. Histoire des Prisons en France au XIX siècle* (Paris, 1988); and Jacques Petit, ed., *La prison, le bagne et l' histoire* (Geneva, 1984).
2. See, for instance, the essays in Norval Morris and David J. Rothman, eds., *The Oxford History of Prison: The Practice of Punishment in Western Society* (New York and Oxford, 1995); Sebastian Scheerer, "Beyond Confinement? Notes on the History and Possible Future of Solitary Confinement in Germany," in *Institutions of Confinement: Hospitals, Asylums, and Prisons in Western Europe and North America, 1500-1950*, ed. Norbert Finzsch and Robert Jütte (Cambridge, 1996), 349-361.
3. Norbert Elias, who developed the "civilizing process" theory, did not write on prisons. Nevertheless, the influence of his theory in the study of prisons is considerable. See, Pieter Spierenburg, *The Spectacle of Suffering: Executions and the Evolution of Repression: From a Preindustrial Metropolis to the European Experience* (Cambridge, 1984); idem, "Four Centuries of Prison History: Punishment, Suffering, the Body, and Power", in *Institutions of Confinement*, 17-35; David Garland, *Punishment and Modern Society: A Study in Social Theory* (Oxford, 1990), 213-248.
4. The prison population in the United States was 380,000 in 1975, 740,000 ten years later, and 1.6 million in 1995. In 2000 was expected to reach the record of two million inmates, or one-fourth of the world prison population. See Loic Wacquant, "L'emprisonnement des 'classes dangereuses' aux États-Unis," *Le Monde Diplomatique* (July 1998): 20-21; *The New York Times*, 21 December 1999.
5. Pitirim A. Sorokin, *Man and Society in Calamity: The Effects of War, Revolution, Famine, Pestilence upon Human Mind, Behavior, Social Organization and Cultural Life* (1942; reprint, Westport, 1973), 106, 121.
6. Jan Gross, "War as Revolution," in *The Establishment of Communist Regimes in Eastern Europe, 1944-1949*, ed. Norman Naimark and Leonid Gibianski (Boulder, 1997), 17-40.
7. Giorgos Margaritis in his brilliant analysis argues that in the beginning of the Axis occupation the social strata and local elites in rural and semiurban areas gained power and autonomy vis-à-vis the shattered state authority, which it was present only in the big cities. These areas were the locomotive of the leftist Resistance in Greece. The governments (during the occupation as well as after the liberation) tried to bring these areas under their control and reestablish state authority either through violence or through the distribution of foreign aid. See Giorgos Margaritis, *Apo ti itta stin exegersi. Hellada: Anoixi 1941-Fthinoporo 1942* (Athens, 1993).
8. David Garland and Peter Young, "Towards a Social Analysis of Penality," in *The Power to Punish: Contemporary Penality and Social Analysis*, ed. David Garland and Peter Young (London, 1983), 1-36.

9. See, for instance, V. A. C. Gatrell, *The Hanging Tree: Execution and the English People 1770-1868* (Oxford, 1994), ch. 11.
10. For the mutation of cultural beliefs and practices in mountainous Greek populations during the occupation and the Civil War see the excellent study by Rikki van Boeschoten, *Anapoda chronia. Syllogiki Mnimi kai Istoria sto Ziaka Grevenon, 1900-1950* (Athens, 1997),144-153.
11. For the "no rules" scenario in the case of republican anticlericalism in the Spanish Civil War, see Bruce Lincoln, "Revolutionary Exhumations in Spain, July 1936", *Comparative Studies in Society and History* 27, (1985): 241-260; Julio de la Cueva, "Religious Persecution, Anticlerical Tradition and Revolution: On Atrocities Against the Clergy during the Spanish Civil War," *Journal of Contemporary History* 33, no. 3 (1998): 355-369.
12. Michelle Perrot, "Délinquance et système pénitentiaire en France au XIXe siècle", *Annales ESC* 30, no. 1 (1975): 67-91.
13. For a critical review of the revisionist historiography on prisons, see Stanley Cohen, *Visions of Social Control: Crime, Punishment and Classification* (London, 1985), 13-30; Michael Ignatieff, "State, Civil Society and Total Institutions: A Critique of Recent Histories of Punishment," in *Social Control and the State*, ed. S. Cohen and A. Scull (Oxford, 1985), 75-105.
14. Among the exceptions are Georges Rude, *Protest and Punishment: The Story of the Social and Political Protesters Transported to Australia 1788-1868* (Oxford, 1978); Jean-Claude Vimont, *La prison politique en France. Genèse d'un mode d'incarcération spécifique XVIIIe-XXe siècles* (Paris, 1993) (although the title is misleading since by and large he deals with the eighteenth and nineteenth centuries).
15. Two book-length studies that discuss political prisoners' experience as it is reflected in memoirs and autobiographical writings are Bernadette Morand, *Les écrits des prisonniers politiques* (Paris, 1976), and Barbara Harlow, *Barred: Women, Writing, and Political Detention* (Hanover and London, 1992).
16. Michel Foucault in "Table ronde du 20 Mai 1978," in *L' impossible prison*, 40-56.
17. But after that observation, on the same page, he also posed a rhetorical question. "Old 'anatomies' are abandoned. But have we really entered the age of non-corporal punishment?" Foucault, *Discipline and Punish*, 101.
18. Ibid., 27.
19. Ibid., 170.
20. For a critical review of feminist critiques on Foucault, see Jana Sawicki, "Feminism, Foucault and 'Subjects' of Power and Freedom," in *The Later Foucault*, ed. Jeremy Moss (London, 1998), 93-107.
21. Michel Foucault, "The Subject and Power," in *Michel Foucault: Beyond Structuralism and Hermeneutics*, ed. Hubert L. Dreyfus and Paul Rabinow (Brighton, 1982), 208-226.
22. From a different viewpoint, Foucault's analysis is unsatisfactory for the reemergence of corporal punishment as well; the body in the age of prison can be the locus of punishment, as in the case of Civil War in Greece or the military dictatorships in Latin America. See Marcelo Suárez-Orozco, "A Grammar of Terror: Psychocultural Responses to State Terrorism in Dirty War and Post-Dirty War Argentina," in *The Paths to Domination, Resistance and Terror*, ed. Carolyn Nordstrom and JoAnn Martin (Berkeley, 1992), 219-259.
23. Stuart Hall, "Introduction: Who Needs 'Identity'?" in *Questions of Cultural Identity*, ed. Stuart Hall and Paul du Gay (London, 1996), 1-17
24. Elaine Scarry used the concept of "unmaking" in her study of torture. See Elaine Scarry, *The Body in Pain: The Making and Unmaking of the World* (New York, 1985).

25. For a similar point in the case of the study of working-class formation, see William H. Sewell, Jr., "How Classes are Made: Critical Reflections on E. P. Thompson's Theory of Working-class Formation," in *E. P. Thompson. Critical Perspectives*, ed. Harvey J. Kaye and Keith McClellan (Cambridge, 1990), 50-77.
26. Roger Chartier, "The Chimera of the Origin: Archaeology, Cultural History and the French Revolution," in *Foucault and the Writing of History*, ed. Jan Goldstein (Oxford and Cambridge, 1994), 167-186.
27. Sewell, "How Classes are Made," 58.
28. Hall, "Introduction," 2, 4.
29. Craig Calhoun, "Social Theory and the Politics of Identity," in *Social Theory and the Politics of Identity*, ed. Craig Calhoun (Oxford and Cambridge, 1994), 9-36.
30. Judith Butler, *Gender Trouble. Feminism and the Subversion of Identity* (New York and London, 1990), 147. Instead, she argues that the subversive repetitions of these constructions (the "parody") open up the possibility of undermining them.
31. Calhoun, "Social Theory and the Politics of Identity," 20-26.
32. Gilles Deleuze, *Michel Foucault* (London, 1988), 105-106.
33. Jane Flax, "Multiples: On the Contemporary Politics of Subjectivity", *Human Studies* 16, (1993): 33-49.
34. "Theorizing Subjectivity," in *Changing the Subject. Psychology, Social Regulation and Subjectivity*, J. Henriques, W. Hollway, C. Urwin, C. Venn, and V. Walkerdine (London and New York, 1984), 203-226.
35. Luisa Passerini, "Lacerations in the Memory: Women in the Italian Underground Organizations", in *Social Movements and Violence: Participation in Underground Organizations*, ed. Bert Klandermans and Donatella della Porta, International Social Movement Research, vol. 4 (Greenwich and London, 1992), 161-212.

Part One

FROM POLITICAL REPRESSION TO POLITICAL EXCLUSION

Chapter 1

The Phenomenon of Political Prisoners

Political prisoners in Europe are a phenomenon of the twentieth century. This is not to say that there were no political prisoners in earlier centuries. In France, for instance, 449 persons were incarcerated for political reasons in the Bastille prison under the reign of Louis XIV, 100 during the regency of Fleury, 346 under the personal rule of Louis XV, and 45 during the reign of Louis XVI.[1] These small numbers of political prisoners, however, do not mean that there was leniency towards political crime. On the contrary, the punishment was extremely severe. In the absolutist state, political order was identified with the person of the monarch. Since all political power derived from the monarch, any political offense constituted a crime against his person (*lèse-majesté*) and as such was punished by death, quite often a horrible one.

The French Revolution ushered in an era where the state, rather than the monarch, became increasingly the object of protection. The person of the monarch was replaced by the abstract entity of the state, and political crime was conceived as crime against the state. In this new definition an interesting distinction developed: on the one hand, there were crimes against the existence of the state (external security), and on the other, crimes against the government and political institutions (internal security). This distinction was important because in separating the internal from the external security of the state, political change was dissociated from the existence of the state. The overthrow of the regime was sharply distinguished from attacks on the state's external security.[2] In other words, the existence of the state was not bound to the established order or political institutions; the latter might change without affecting the existence of the state. In this case, according to liberal thinkers, if political institutions could change, the questions were to what extent, by whom, and how. Be that as it may, in the course of the nineteenth century the change of constitutional order came to be regarded as legitimate, to the extent that legal means were used.

Notes for this section begin on page 31.

Revolutions and uprisings were met with outward and violent repression. Following the suppression of the revolution of 1848 in Paris, 3,000 people were killed and 12,000 arrested; most of them were released but 4,300 were deported to Algeria.[3] The uprising against the coup of Louis Napoleon on 2 December 1851 resulted in a new wave of terror and 26,884 arrests. A third of the arrestees was convicted and sentenced to transportation to Algeria and Guinea. The suppression of the Commune of 1871 was even more violent. At least 17,000 communards were killed during the *Semaine Sanglante* and 36,000 were arrested; of the 10,000 convicted, almost half were sentenced to deportation (mainly to New Caledonia).[4]

The extralegal repression and use of terror in the suppression of revolutions, however, coexisted with legal repression of political offenses and provisions for their punishment. In this area, liberal ideas informed a lenient approach towards political offenses, especially after the suppression of the 1848 revolutions. This trend towards leniency in the legislation of many Western European countries took the form of lighter sentences for political offenses and preferential treatment for political prisoners. The general tendency towards liberalization, however, was conditioned by the domestic political and social challenges the regimes met. In France the regime was reluctant to proceed to the liberalization of legislation due to the radicalism of the urban strata produced by the revolutions. In England, Italy and Germany, leniency toward political offenses was reflected in the elimination of the death penalty for most political offenses, including treason and sedition, lenient treatment of attempts to commit a political crime, and light sentences for lesser political offenses.[5] Gradually, political prisoners came to enjoy different, preferential treatment compared to that of common criminals. In the form of *Festungshaft* in Germany, *détention* in France (especially after the Decree of 1890), or the "first division" in England (under the Act of 1865), political prisoners were separated from the common criminals, were not forced to work, and were allowed to wear their own clothing, have books and newspapers, have more visits, and so on.[6] This preferential treatment was based on the idea that political prisoners were motivated by noble ideas and not the selfish intentions of common criminals; their acts were not against the state or society in general, but against those institutions that hindered the progress and welfare of the society.[7]

Throughout the nineteenth century, harsh and violent repression alternated with legal liberal reforms, or, in other words, legal liberal reforms came after and as a result of the repression of revolutions. However, it would be a mistake to picture developments up to the outbreak of the First World War as a linear process towards an ever-more liberal and tolerant state. The emergence of a strong socialist party in Germany led to an unsuccessful attempt to repress it and check its advance with an antisocialist law in 1878. New forms of violent political activism, like anarchism, gave birth to strict new laws like in France in 1894. In the face of militant Irish nationalism English liberalism was seriously tested, as the repeated suspensions of habeas corpus reveal. Nonetheless, it would be equally mistaken not to acknowledge that state policies after the First World War represented a decisive break with the prevailing liberal spirit of the nineteenth century.

The decisive break with the liberal traditions of the nineteenth century may be traced in three ways: through the emergence of new formulations of the crime against the state, through increasing numbers of political prisoners, and through their status. From the end of the First World War until the end of the 1950s, violent persecution of political opponents, outlawing of political parties, and mass imprisonment would become part of the history of many European countries and of the experience of society. The mass scale of political prosecution is related to changes in the political and social subject. Sporadic rebellions, secret societies of conspirators, and barricades were replaced by well-organized and disciplined political parties and trade unions, with their own press and institutions, that could mobilize thousands of people in strikes, demonstrations, and elections. In the era of mass politics, political repression gained different proportions and significance. To explain the phenomenon of political prisoners in twentieth-century Europe we should first consider the impact of war upon the state, and second, the dynamics of revolution and counterrevolution and their decisive importance in shaping state policies.

After almost a century of relative peace on the continent, in 1914 modern states faced international wars for the first time. The Great War, despite the catastrophe it produced, did not lead nationalism, one of the main causes of the war, to wither away. Disputes over new borders, the presence of minorities, the lack of liberal democratic traditions in many European countries, and economic depression crippled the optimism of liberal statesmen. What was needed was not necessarily a liberal state but rather a strong state that could protect and forward the interests of the nation. At the same time, in several cases social discontent was channeled into movements that questioned the existing social and political order. From this viewpoint, the Bolshevik revolution ushered in an era that Arno Mayer has called "international Civil War."[8] The threat of revolution gave birth to counterrevolutionary movements and legitimized, in the eyes of the insecure ruling classes and state bureaucracy, interwar authoritarianism. Thus, I suggest that the phenomenon of political prisoners should be situated in the dynamics and interplay between war, revolution-counterrevolution, and nationalism-communism, and the policies they produced. The fundamental principle that informed these policies was that the state should protect the sociopolitical order. The security of the state was no longer dissociated from the political and social order; on the contrary, the aggrandizement of the state, its increasing intervention in interwar societies, made the protection of the state the prime concern of ruling elites and state bureaucracies. The political opponent, as enemy of the established order, became the enemy of the state.

In the following chapters I shall address the question of political prisoners in twentieth-century Europe. I shall begin with political prisoners in the interwar authoritarian regimes, and then turn to the examination of the phenomenon in the Soviet Union and the postwar people's republics. The question of political prisoners may shed a new light on the study of authoritarianism in twentieth century Europe. If in the nineteenth and early twentieth century there had been a tendency toward the inclusion of larger social strata in the political life of liberal states (the gradual lifting of suffrage restrictions is the best example of this point), from the 1920s on a countertendency developed: the exclusion of a regime's political opponents. Thus, political repression and exclusion provide a vantagepoint for the discussion of state policies in authoritarian regimes and their implications for the nation-state.

Political Prisoners in the Interwar Authoritarian Regimes

The Bolshevik revolution changed the political "map" of Europe. Not only had the socialist revolution triumphed in one of the Great Powers, but soon (between 1918 and 1920) parties that agreed with the program of the Russian Bolsheviks were established throughout Europe. Moreover, the revolution was not contained in Russia, but spilled over into Finland, Hungary, and Germany. Although the revolutionary tide was over by the beginning of the 1920s, antibolshevism was incorporated into nationalist rhetoric and became the rallying point for established conservative forces and emergent counter-revolutionary movements. In consequence, communist parties were banned in a number of European countries as soon as dictatorships or authoritarian regimes took over: in Hungary in 1919, in Italy in 1926, in Bulgaria in 1923 (and again in 1934), in Romania in 1924, in Finland in 1925 (and again in 1930), in Poland in 1926, in Yugoslavia in 1921, in Lithuania in 1927, in Spain in 1923 (and again in 1939), in Estonia in 1930, in Germany and Austria in 1933, and in Greece in 1936. These regimes introduced new policies against their political opponents, namely, mass imprisonment, new techniques of punishment, and stricter legislation with regard to political crime.

Under these regimes the number of political prisoners increased rapidly, marking a difference from the previous decades. In Finland, after the end of the 1918 Civil War, 70,000 to 80,000 "reds" were imprisoned, of whom some 10,000 died in prison. In Portugal, under Salazar's dictatorship, 18,714 persons were convicted for political reasons between 1932 and 1948.[9] In Hungary, the suppression of Bela Kun's Soviet Republic was followed by a reign of "white terror" in 1919-1920. The purpose, according to an order of the Minister of the Interior, was "to ensure that communist rule, which radically shook the foundations of the Hungarian nation (…) should never again come to life." Five thousand people were killed and 70,000 citizens were put into internment camps run by the army.[10] In Fascist Italy, some 16,000 were interned for political reasons between 1926 and 1943, and 160,000 came under police surveillance.[11] In Nazi Germany, within the months following the Reichstag fire, thousands of people arrestees were under "protective custody" (*Schutzhaft*), that is, in police detention awaiting trial. Twenty-five thousand persons were taken into protective custody by the police in Prussia in March and April 1933 alone. On 31 July 1933, according to the Reich Ministry of Interior, 26,789 persons were in protective custody.[12] In an attempt to "legalize" repression, most of them were tried and convicted. It is difficult to assess the number of political prisoners in prison due to the nature of classification of criminal statistics. One study, however, estimated that out of a total prison population of 170,000 in 1936, 50,000 were imprisoned for political reasons.[13] Over roughly the same period, the end of the Spanish Civil War was accompanied by mass executions (about 150,000 were killed in summary executions) and prisons were flooded with political prisoners. In 1940 the total prison population was 213,640, of which about 200,000 were political prisoners. Their numbers dropped drastically in the following years: they numbered 25,000 in the mid-1940s, and 7,000-8,000 at the beginning of the 1950s.[14]

Political prisoners during that era lost their special status and privileges. Except imprisonment political prisoners faced other forms of internment, such as house arrest, police surveillance and banishment. In Hungary, according to a decree of 1920, a person under police surveillance "could be forbidden to speak with people other than his ordinary entourage."[15] In Italy, the most frequent penalty for political offenses was banishment (*confino di polizia*) for one to five years as dangerous to the public security. The *confinati* were transported to the islands of Ustica, Lipari, Ponza, Ventotene, Sardinia, or to small villages in the south. Other, lighter forms of punishment were the *diffida* (persons were warned against involvement in antifascist politics) and the *ammonizione* (the accused had to present himself or herself weekly to the police station and was not allowed to leave his or her permanent residence).[16] The most significant measures, however, were those introduced in Germany and Spain. In Germany the large number of arrests and persons under "protective custody" led to the establishment of concentration camps, starting with Dachau in March 1933. The wholesale repression led to the opening of other "wild" concentration camps in Oranienburg, Papenburg, Esterwegen, Sonnenburg, and Sachsenburg, among others. From the end of 1933 onwards, the regime tried to achieve a certain "legality" by normalizing political repression. The number of prisoners in protective custody was reduced and most of the "wild" concentration camps were shut down. The number of prisoners in protective custody reached its lowest total in the winter of 1936-1937, about 7,500 persons. At the same time new categories of prisoners were interned in concentration camps: habitual criminals, "antisocial elements", and Jews. The number of political prisoners in concentration camps would rise again in 1939, when the outbreak of war led to new arrests of would-be political opponents. Moreover, between 1937 and 1938 forced labor was introduced in the concentration camps. For Nazi officials, forced labor was a form of retribution for the damage criminals had done to the national community. The introduction of forced labor also coincided with the four-year plans and the demand for the mobilization of every able-bodied person; SS-owned enterprises for the production of building materials were established in and near concentration camps.[17] In the same vein, in Franco's Spain in new types of imprisonment like the *destacamentos* and the *colonias penitenciarias militarizadas* (the latter run by the army) political prisoners were required to work mostly in public works. The idea behind forced labor was that work brought redemption. The political prisoners had damaged the country, and in order to be granted "Spain's mercy" they had to "redeem" themselves through labor.[18]

In the realm of law there were two parallel developments under the interwar authoritarian regimes: the compartmentalization of political justice and the introduction of special laws with regard to political crimes. In the administration of justice, political cases were transferred from the jurisdiction of ordinary courts to special bodies closely controlled by the regime. Such bodies were military tribunals (in Spain), administrative committees (in Italy), or special high courts, like the *Tribunale speciale per la difesa dello Stato* in Italy (which between 1927 and 1943 in 720 audiences sentenced 4,596 persons) or the *Volksgerichtshof* in Germany, which was established in 1934 and had jurisdiction over cases of treason and high treason. The *Volksgerichtshof* is the best example of the change in the conceptualization of the political crime: political crime was no longer simply a crime against the state but also a crime against the nation.

A common characteristic of legislation for the repression of political opposition in the interwar era was that it penalized not acts but ideas and intentions, and it depicted revolution as foreign and inimical to the nation, an international threat that jeopardized the state and the country alike. The interrelation between internal and external threat is demonstrated in a 1921 law in the Kingdom of Serbs, Croats and Slovenes. The law punished "any relation with any person or organization abroad with the view to obtain assistance for the preparation of revolution in the country or for the violent change of the current political order of the State" with death or twenty years of forced labor.[19] Hungary's Law VIII of 1924 made even more clear who the enemies of the state were; the political crime it punished was "the aim to overthrow and destroy the legal order of the State and Society ... especially a movement or organization that tends to impose the dictatorship of a social class."[20] A few years later, in 1926, the *Legge per la difesa dello Stato* was introduced in Italy and constituted the framework for the prosecution of Mussolini's political opponents. It promulgated the suppression of "antinational" parties and journals, criminalized political activities and introduced a series of penalties (deprivation of citizenship, confiscation of property, and so on). The law (as it was revised and incorporated in the Penal Code of 1931) provided that, "those who develop or have manifested their intention to develop, a rebellious activity aimed to violently overthrow the established political, economic and social constituents of the State, to oppose or to hinder the action of State forces, likewise any activity that causes damage to the national interests" were to be punished. In Spain, the law that enabled the prosecution of Franco's political opponents was the *Ley de repression de la masoneria y el comunismo* of March 1940. It punished "any propaganda in favor of the principles or alleged benefits of Freemasonry or communism, or spreading dangerous ideas against the Catholic religion, the country and its basic institutions or against social harmony."[21]

The country in which the political crime was framed *par excellence* as a crime against the nation was Nazi Germany. There the prosecution of political opponents was based mainly on the Reichstag Fire Decree of 28 February 1933. This decree in the face of "communist violent acts endangering the state" abolished fundamental constitutional rights and introduced the death penalty for high treason (*Hochverrat*). That same night, another decree was issued on "disloyalty to the German People and treasonable activities." It punished treason (*Landesverrat*) with death and punished severely, among other offenses, the discussion or communication of "true or untrue" state secrets and the making, distribution, or storage of treasonous printed material.[22] During the wave of mass terror in 1933-1934 political opponents were to a large extent prosecuted on charges of treason or crimes against the *Volk*. In 1933, out of 9,529 individuals sentenced for political offenses, 1,698 were convicted of high treason and the rest of crimes against "the people." Between January and September 1934 there were 408 mass trials for high treason with 2,699 convicted in the area of Düsseldorf and Cologne, and 395 cases with 2,675 convictions in the Ruhr area. Between 1937 and 1944 the *Volksgerichthof* sentenced some 13,000 people, of whom 5,191 were put to death (most of them during the war).[23] Telling of the new conceptualization of political crime as "antinational" crime was the deliberation of the Hanseatic Court of Appeals: "Every activity on behalf of the German Communist Party serves to prepare the violent overthrow of the government and the constitution of Germany. In consequence, every activity on behalf of the German Communist Party ... is to be considered as preparation for high treason."[24]

As Otto Kirchheimer argued on the development of legislation in Western Europe from the interwar era through the 1950s, in "reducing external and internal security needs to a common denominator, they [the laws] seek to protect the political order from any intellectual, propagandist, and especially organizing activity directed ultimately toward revolution."[25] This new conceptualization of the political crime as a crime against the state and the nation was accompanied by new state policies that were designed to protect the political order. First was the purge from the state apparatus of all "disloyal" civil servants. Second, was the establishment of special courts, directly controlled by the government, or administrative committees that had jurisdiction over political crimes. Third, was the organization of a powerful and brutal political police force (like the OVRA in Italy or the Gestapo in Germany), which was entrusted with the legal and extralegal repression of political opposition. Finally, political prisoners were stripped of all their rights and privileges. The privileged status of political prisoners was practically nullified, and new and strict measures of punishment (like the death sentence, concentration camps, and forced labor) were employed. Most of these policies, as we shall see, were followed in the Greek Civil War.

The extreme nationalism of the counterrevolution in the interwar years was aimed at protecting of the established order through the strengthening of the state and the elimination of political opposition. Nationalism identified the protection of the state with that of the nation; a political crime was deemed a crime against the nation-state. The growing significance of the security of the state, the interrelation of internal and external security, and political exclusion marked a radical departure from the liberal ideas and policies of the late nineteenth century. The tendency to include larger strata of the society in the political life was reversed, and restrictions or prohibitions that affected citizenship were introduced. Thus, political repression under the interwar authoritarian regimes signified a broader change: the rebuilding of the nation-state along the lines of unprecedented political exclusion.

Political Prisoners under Socialism

In 1922 a new Cirminal Code was introduced in the USSR. . It was distinctive because it dealt with three new types of crime: counterrevolutionary crimes, economic crimes, and crimes by officials.[26] Counterrevolutionary crimes were specified in articles 58.1-58.14. According to article 58.1: "Any action shall be deemed to be counterrevolutionary if it is directed towards the overthrow, undermining or weakening of the authority of the Workers' and Peasants' Soviets and the Workers' and Peasants' Governments of the USSR, ... or towards the undermining or weakening of the external security of the USSR and the fundamental economic, political and national conquests of the proletarian revolution." The remaining sections of article 58 punished other counterrevolutionary crimes such as assistance in carrying on hostile activities (58.4), espionage (58.6), undermining industry, trade, currency, or the system of credit (58.7), propaganda (58.10), participation in counterrevolutionary organizations (58.11), non denunciation of counterrevolutionary activities (58.12), and economic sabotage (58.14). One has to notice the blurred distinction between economic and political crimes: an economic crime intended to weaken the state economy or authority was considered counter-revolutionary. Most of the counter-revolutionary crimes were punished with the death penalty.[27]

Political prisoners had been interned in special camps as early as 1921, mainly at the camps of the Solovetski Islands on the White Sea. There were 4,000 prisoners in 1923 and 7,000 in 1925. Living conditions were harsh, and prisoners were divided into three categories: criminals, counterrevolutionaries (sympathizers of the prerevolutionary regime, White Army officers, etc.), and political prisoners (social democrats, social revolutionaries, anarchists, etc.). Political prisoners enjoyed privileged status: they were not forced to work, they retained their personal belongings, they were allowed to organize a communal life, men and women were not segregated, they received food packages from the Red Cross, among other advantages.[28] From 1927 the number of the total prison population started increasing dramatically and living conditions, after the introduction of forced labor, deteriorated. For political prisoners, however, the turning point was the Great Purges.

A wave of terror had begun already in 1934, after Kirov's assassination, although it gained momentum only in 1937-1938. As in the years of collectivization, political cases came under the jurisdiction not of courts but of special *troiki*, which were established in each province in 1937 and consisted of the NKVD chief, the procurator, and the party secretary of the region. In the framework of a campaign of vigilance against "people's enemies," the Great Terror was unfolded in two interrelated processes. The first was against targeted groups and individuals, that is, former party members and powerful party officials, potential challengers of Stalin. The second process, which consisted of mass arrests, was initiated after a Politburo order on 31 July 1937 that gave permission to shoot or imprison "former kulaks, members of anti-Soviet parties, White Guards, gendarmes and officials of tsarist Russia, bandits, returned émigrés, participants in anti-Soviet organizations, churchmen and sectarians [and] recidivist criminals."[29] The prison population of "counterrevolutionaries" from rose 104,826 in 1937, to 185,324 in 1938, and then to 454,432 in 1939. From 1939 until the death of Stalin in 1953 the annual prison population of "counterrevolutionaries" remained between 400,000 and 500,000 (with the exception of the years 1943-1946). In addition, 681,692 persons sentenced for "counterrevolutionary and state crimes" were shot between 1937 and 1938 —86.7 percent of all persons executed for political crimes between 1930 and 1953.[30] It was a wholesale operation against any potential enemy within or without the party, token of weakness rather than omnipotence of Stalin's regime. The Great Terror of the campaign against counterrevolutionaries was part of a series of campaigns either against ill-defined crimes (like the "socially dangerous and harmful elements" in 1934-1936, or "hooligan behavior" in 1939-1940) or for the strictest punishment of common crimes (like theft of public property in the years of collectivization and after World War II). I shall return to this point after the discussion of political justice in the postwar people's republics.

The problem of political prisoners in the people's republics of Eastern and Central Europe is more complicated because it is interrelated with a triple process that took place in almost the same brief period of time: the purge of Nazi collaborators (especially in Hungary, Romania, and Bulgaria, allies of Nazi Germany in World War II), the establishment of communist governments, and the impact of revolutionary social change in countries where communist parties and ideology had no mass following.

After the war, the first priority was the purging of Nazi collaborators from state apparatus, institutions, army, police, political parties, and other organizations. The purge, in contrast to Western European countries was thorough. In Hungary, 189 war criminals were executed, 60,000 people were investigated and tried, and 27,000 people were convicted of collaboration. In Bulgaria, 2,138 persons were executed, 3,500 were imprisoned, and 60,000 people were dismissed from their positions. In Czechoslovakia, 20,000 people were tried by 1946 —only one-third of them were Czechs and the rest were Slovaks.[31] In the Soviet-controlled German territory, 150,000 Germans were interned in special camps between 1945 and 1950; of them at least 43,000 died.[32]

The purge in Central and Eastern European countries, however, should be placed within a larger framework. Communist parties were striving to maximize their power within the postwar government coalitions through a loyal state apparatus. Starting in 1947 and 1948, when the communist parties and their allies gained control over the government, they set out to undertake the socialist transformation (collectivization and industrialization) of those countries. The process of assuming power and at the same time transforming society makes a strict distinction between political repression and enforcement of societal discipline both difficult and unfruitful. Both political prosecution and societal discipline were necessary and sufficient conditions for the establishment of people's republics within a few years.

This is not to say that there was no political prosecution. On the contrary, the political prosecutions had two phases. The first, massive phase of prosecution was against real or alleged Nazi collaborators and the anticommunist armed resistance movement. The second phase, after communist parties assumed power in 1947 and 1948, was the prosecution of political opponents and the purge of the communist parties themselves —a process reminiscent of the Great Purges of the 1930's.[33] In Poland as early as 1944 and 1945, political prosecution was focused mainly on former members of the Home Army. Military courts had jurisdiction over political crimes, and severe sentences were handed down for "particularly dangerous crimes during the reconstruction of the Polish state." From 1946 to 1953, 65,000 persons were convicted by military courts, and the number of political prisoners rose from 26,400 in

1948 to 35,200 in the mid-1950s.[34] In Czechoslovakia, according to communist party sources, 11,026 persons were in prison in 1950 for alleged crimes against the state, and in 1951 alone 2,997 people were arrested individually and 3,112 in groups by State Security. Moreover, between 1948 and 1952 the State Court passed 233 death sentences, of which 178 were carried out.[35] In Hungary a wholesale persecution commenced in the early 1950s and nearly 30,000 people were sentenced for political reasons.[36]

Following the legal pattern of the Soviet Union, political crimes in Eastern and Central European countries were incorporated in the penal code in a special chapter, usually entitled "Offenses against the People's Republic." The crime against the state *par excellence* was the aim to overthrow the state and constitutional order of the people's republic. Despite the differences in penal codes among the people's republics, there were certain similarities. The first was that although the penal codes dealt with economic crimes in special sections, it often was the case that economic crimes were associated with the internal security of the state and thus were prescribed as political offenses. In the Bulgarian, Romanian, and Yugoslav penal codes for instance, undermining the national economy (usually through the crimes of sabotage and wrecking) was an offense against the state.[37] The second similarity was that penalties for political offenses were not only heavier but also included forced labor.

The Czechoslovak Penal Code is illustrative of the changes that took place in postwar Central Europe. Political prisoners in the prewar democratic Czechoslovakia were incarcerated in a special prison (*státní*) and enjoyed privileges like exemption from work, having their own clothing, books, and writing materials, and physical exercise. In postwar Czechoslovakia, the sentence for eight serious political offenses was confinement for twenty-five years or death, although these penalties were prescribed for only two common offenses. Also, the Criminal Code for Courts of 1950 provided that: "Any person who, by his offense, has shown hostility to the people's democratic regime and has failed, while serving his sentence, to show an improvement such as to justify the hope that his future behavior will be satisfactory and befitting a good worker, may be committed to a forced labor camp for not less than three months and not more than two years after completing his full sentence of temporary deprivation of liberty."[38]

Discussion of the role of forced labor in the socialist criminal policy and economy lies beyond the scope of this book. Nevertheless, some remarks on forced labor with regard to political imprisonment are necessary because they may shed light on the relation between political prosecution and socialist transformation in these countries. Prisoners' forced labor in the Soviet Union became a common phenomenon after 1928. It was related to the increase of the prison population due to the resistance to collectivization and the social disruption it created, and to the big economic projects of the Soviet government that required cheap mass labor (the White Sea – Black Sea Canal, the gold mines of the Kolyma region, the Moscow River – Volga River Canal, etc.).[39] In the same vein, forced labor in the postwar people's republics was incorporated in economic planning to increase industrial production in the uranium mining district of Aue in East Germany, the hydroelectric plant on the river Bistritza in Romania, and the coal mines of Bulgaria and Poland. Since the penalty of imprisonment for political offenses usually included labor as a means of reeducation, a large number of persons sentenced to forced labor had been convicted for political reasons. In any event, forced labor became a form of punishment for both political and common crimes, which were brought together under such sweeping provisions as the People's Militia Act of 1948 in Bulgaria which enabled the People's Militia "to arrest and send to labor and education communities ... persons guilty of fascist activities and activities directed against the people, [and] persons who constitute a threat to public order and the security of the State," as well as blackmailers, pimps, beggars, and "persons guilty of scandalous conduct."[40]

As I have already argued, there was a prevalent trend in twentieth-century European legislation of identifying the state with the established social and economic order, and thus prescribing the overthrow of the established order as the definition of crime against the state. However, there is an important difference between the interwar authoritarian regimes and the communist regimes. The former, under the influence of nationalism, also identified the state with the nation, turning their political opponents into enemies of the nation and traitors, and defining political crime as crime against the nation. In people's republics, on the other hand, political opponents were portrayed as adversaries of the "construction of socialism," the social and economic transformation of the country. For this reason political offenses were associated with crimes against the economy. In other words, in "crimes against the people's republic" the distinction between political and economic offenses was blurred because such crimes were designated to penalize any activity that might hinder the socialist —that is, the political and economic— transformation. The socialist transformation, undertaken against the will of the populace, required strict political and societal discipline. Disciplining was also incorporated in the reconstruction of the state economy. The extended use of forced labor as a form of punishment was both a means and an end: a means to instill discipline in the "construction of socialism" and an end in itself, the mobilization of a cheap labor force to reconstruct the state economy. Forced labor as a measure of punishment is emblematic of the fusion of politics and the economy in the state policies of people's republics. The political crime in interwar authoritarian regimes was a crime against the state-nation, whereas under socialism it was a crime against the state-economy.

Notes

1. Vimont, *La prison politique en France*, 14-5
2. Pierre Papadatos, *Le délit politique: Contribution á l'étude des crimes contre l'État* (Geneva, 1954), 36-9; Otto Kirchheimer, *Political Justice: The Use of Legal Procedure for Political Ends* (Princeton, 1961), 32-3.
3. Robert J. Goldstein, *Political Repression in 19th Century Europe* (Totowa, 1983), 190; Alain Faure, "A la recherche des réfugiés et des prisonniers politiques," in *Répression et prison politique en France et en Europe au XIXe siècle*, ed. Société d'Histoire de la Révolution de 1848 et des Révolutions du XIVe siècle (Paris, 1990), 9-18.
4. Goldstein, *Political Repression*, 249-50; Faure, "A la recherche," 15; Vimont, *La prison politique*, 438-42.
5. Barton L. Ingraham, *Political Crime in Europe: A Comparative Study of France, Germany, and England* (Berkeley, 1979), 154-65, 170-84, 187-93; Papadatos, *Le délit politique*, 50-5.
6. Ingraham, *Political Crime*, 125-26, 138, 188-89, 210-11; Godstein, Political Repression, 85-8; Vimont, *La prison politique*, 457-58.
7. Dirk Blasius, *Geschichte der politischen Kriminalität in Deutschland 1800-1980* (Frankfurt a. M., 1983), 12-4.
8. Arno J. Mayer, *Dynamics of Revolution and Counter-Revolution in Europe, 1870-1956* (New York, 1971).
9. John Hodgson, *Communism in Finland* (Princeton, 1967), 88-9; *Presos politicos no regime fascista*, vol. 4, 1946-1948 (Lisbon, 1981), 415-26.
10. Jörg Hoensch, *A History of Modern Hungary 1867-1986* (London, 1988), 98.
11. Charles Delzell, *Mussolini's Enemies: The Italian Anti-Fascist Resistance* (Princeton, 1961), 38-41; Salvatore Carbone and Laura Grimaldi, eds., *Il Popolo al Confino. La Persecuzione Fascista in Sicilia* (Rome, 1989), 7.
12. Helmut Krausnick and Martin Broszat, *Anatomy of the SS State* (London, 1982), 150, 154, 188-89; Erich Kosthorst and Bernd Walter, *Konzentrations-und Strafgefangenenlager im Emsland 1933-1945. Zum Verhältnis von NS-Regime und Justiz* (Düsseldorf, 1985), 28-9.
13. Eberhard Kolb, "Die Machinerei des Terrors", in *Nationalsozialistische Diktatur 1933-1945. Eine Bilanz*, ed. Karl Dietrich Bracher, Manfred Funke and Hans-Adolf Jacobsen (Düsseldorf, 1983), 270-84.
14. Conxita Mir Curcó, "Violencia política, coacción legal y oposición interior," *Ayer* 33 (1999): 115-45; Angel Suárez, *Libro Blanco sobre las Cárceles Franquistas 1939-1976* (n.p., 1976), 63-6.
15. Ferenc Pölöskei, *Hungary after Two Revolutions (1919-1922)* (Budapest, 1980), 50-1.
16. Adriano Dal Pont, *I lager di Mussolini. L'altra faccia del confino nei documenti della polizia fascista* (Milano, 1975), 39-52; *Enciclopedia dell' Antifascismo e della Resistenza* (Milano, 1968), vol. 1, 655-57, and (1989) vol. 6, 137-41.
17. Krausnick and Broszat, *Anatomy*, 165-81, 190-204; Kosthorst and Walter, *Konzentrations-und Strafgefangenenlager*, 216-23.
18. United Nations and International Labour Office, *Report of the ad hoc Committee on Forced Labor* (Geneva, 1953), 347-72; Michael Richards, *A Time of Silence: Civil War and the Culture of Repression in Franco's Spain, 1936-1945* (Cambridge, 1998), 74-88.
19. Jean Robert, *Le communisme devant la loi pénale* (Besançon, 1930), 121-22.
20. Ibid., 120.
21. Suárez, *Libro Blanco*, 48.
22. Walter Wagner, *Der Volksgerightshof im nationalsozialistischen Staat* (Stuttgart, 1974), 50-8

23. Blasius, *Geschichte der politischen Kriminalität*, 121; Ingo Müller, *Hitler's Justice. The Courts of the Third Reich* (Cambridge, Mass., 1994), 140-52; H.W. Koch, *In the Name of the Volk: Political Justice in Hitler's Germany* (London, 1989), 38-50, 126-36.
24. Müller, *Hitler's Justice*, 57-58.
25. Kirchheimer, *Political Justice*, 41.
26. Peter H. Solomon, Jr., *Soviet Criminal Justice under Stalin* (Cambridge, 1996), 27-34.
27. Vladimir Gsovski and Kazimierz Grzybowski, eds., *Government, Law and Courts in the Soviet Union and Eastern Europe* (New York, 1959), vol. 2, 946-49.
28. David J. Dallin and Boris I. Nicolaevsky, *Forced Labor in Soviet Russia* (New Haven, 1947), 168-85; Michael Jakobson, *Origins of the Gulag: The Soviet Prison Camp System 1917-1934* (Lexington, 1993), 111-18.
29. Cited in Gábor T. Rittersporn, "Extra-Judicial Repression and the Courts. Their Relationship in the 1930s,",in *Reforming Justice in Russia, 1864-1996: Power, Culture and the Limits of Legal Order*, ed. Peter H. Solomon, Jr. (Armonk, 1997), 207-27; Solomon, *Soviet Criminal Justice*, ch. 7.
30. J. Arch Getty, Gábor T. Rittersporn and Viktor N. Zemskov, "Victims of the Soviet Penal System in the Pre-War Years: A First Approach on the Basis of Archival Evidence," *The American Historical Review*, 98, no. 4 (1993): 1017-49.
31. François Fejtö, *Histoire des democraties populaires* (Paris, 1952), vol. 1, 123; Ivan T. Berend, *Central and Eastern Europe, 1944-1993: Detour from the Periphery to the Periphery* (Cambridge, 1996), 4.
32. Alexander von Plato, "Zur Geschichte des sowjetischen Speziallagersystems in Deutschland", in *Sowjetische Speziallager in Deutschland 1945 bis 1950: Studien und Berichte*, ed. Alexander von Plato (Berlin, 1998), vol. I, 19-75; Norman N. Naimark, *The Russians in Germany. A History of the Soviet Zone of Occupation, 1945-1949* (Cambridge, Mass., 1995), 376-78. In 1945, some 117,500 persons were interned in the U.S. zone, 90,000 in the British zone and 21,500 in the French zone; however, half of the US zone internees would be released in 1946. See, Lutz Niethammer, "Alliierte Internierungslager in Deutschland nach 1945: Vergleich und offene Fragen," in von Plato, ed., *Sowjetische Speziallager*, 97-116.
33. The best known of these purges against communist cadres were the show group trials against Gomulka in Poland in 1948-1949, Coxe in Albania in 1949, Kostov in Bulgaria in 1949, Rajk in Hungary in 1949, Slansky in Czechoslovakia in 1952, and Patrascanu in Romania in 1954.
34. John Micgiel, "'Bandits and Reactionaries': The Suppression of the Opposition in Poland, 1944-1946," in Naimark and Gibianski, eds., *The Establishment of Communist Regimes*, 93-110; Krystyna Kersten, *The Establishment of Communist Rule in Poland, 1943-1948* (Berkeley, 1991), especially ch. 8.
35. Jirí Pelicán, ed., *The Czechoslovak Political Trials, 1950-1954* (London, 1971), 56.
36. Berend, *Central and Eastern Europe*, 72.
37. V. Gsovski and K. Grzybowski, eds., *Government, Law and Courts*, 987-90, 1089-93, 1113-15.
38. Ibid., 1009-16.
39. Dallin and Nicolaevsky, *Forced Labor*, 191-216; Jakobson, *Origins of the Gulag*, 119-38.
40. United Nations and International Labor Office, *Report of the ad hoc Committee*,198-213, 258-74, 300-16, 334-46.

Chapter 2

Legacies

The First Signs of Political Exclusion

The first attempts at systematic political repression and prosecution in Greece occurred during the period of the "National Schism," a conflict arising from a disagreement between the government of the Liberal Party of Eleftherios Venizelos, who supported the participation of Greece in the First World War on the side of the Entente, and King Constantine, who opted for the neutrality of Greece. This disagreement generated a conflict between republicans and royalists that went beyond the issue of Greece's participation in the Great War to dominate the political life of the country in the interwar era, deeply dividing Greek society into two adversarial camps with different political cultures, aspirations, and economic and societal projects.

In the context of the civil strife generated in 1915 and 1916 by the "National Schism", the 1917 Liberal government purged state mechanisms (the army, the gendarmerie, and the judicature in particular) of royalists and employed an old law against brigandage to prosecute royalists and other opponents of the Liberals' foreign policy.[1] The 1871 law on the suppression of banditry, an endemic problem in Greece during the nineteenth century, gave administrative or military authorities the power to banish the relatives of bandits.[2] In 1913 a further law stipulating the penalty of banishment for individuals suspected of the disturbance of public security enabled the banishment of the first socialists and trade unionists.[3] The law for the suppression of banditry, together with its completions and amendments and the penalty of banishment, would be used extensively not only throughout the interwar era but after the Second World War as well. It provided for establishing in every prefecture (*nomos*) a Public Security Committee, consisting of the prefect, the chief of the gendarmerie and the public prosecutor. The committee could banish anyone suspected of breaching "the public order, peace and security of the country" for one year. The laws for "administrative banish-

Notes for this section begin on page 48.

ment," as it was officially called (because the individuals were sentenced by an administrative committee rather than a court) would be used in the following years by the republicans against the royalists (1917-1920, 1922-1923) and vice versa (1920-1922).[4] Even though administrative banishment as a measure of political persecution was embedded in the context of the National Schism, by the mid-1920s it was already being used against a new target group: socialists and trade unionists. Although administrative banishment may be considered the first legal measure of political repression, the turning point was the *Idionymo* Law of 1929. It was a critical moment, first because it reflected a shift in the old political conflicts, and second because it was the first law that penalized communist activities and ideas as such. A brief discussion of the changes in Greek society in the first years of the interwar era is necessary in order to understand changes in political repression.

The interwar era is marked by the end of the expansion of the Greek state, a project conceptualized as the *Megali Idea* (Great Idea). This was the incorporation by the Greek state of the territories inhabited by Greek-speaking Orthodox populations, and was a common objective for royalists and republicans alike. The expedition to Asia Minor, the defeat of the Greek army, and the 1,200,000 refugees who fled to Greece from Asia Minor in 1922 put an end to the *Megali Idea*. The issue was no longer territorial expansion but rather the internal development and modernization of the country. Internal problems were many, mainly the rehabilitation of refugees, agrarian reform for the landless peasants, and the economic, especially industrial, development. The state took an active part in this process of modernization by providing a framework for social reform and financing development through foreign assistance.[5]

On the one hand, there was an element of continuity between the pre- and post-1922 periods: the perpetuation of the conflict between the royalist and republican blocs. The National Schism with the civil strife of 1915-1916 and the defeat of Greek expedition to Asia Minor (and the relevant question of the responsibility for what in the Greek literature is called the "Asia Minor Catastrophe") had divided the country so deeply that the conflict continued to dominate the political life in the interwar years. On the other hand, the end of the *Megali Idea* would mark the end of the broad social and economic alliances that had been grounded in Greek irredentism. As George Mavrogordatos has pointed out, both blocs were cross-class alliances under bourgeois leadership, but Venizelism drew its support mainly from the lower social strata. The republican bloc was in power until the beginning of the 1930s, and the domestic, especially its economic, policy revealed the fragility of the Venizelist cross-class alliance: the enterpreunial strata became more conservative, and the lower strata more radical. The shift in the old political conflicts came in the late 1920s with the emergence of a new force that stood alongside the anti-Venizelist and Venizelist blocs but challenged the latter in particular: the Left.[6]

In 1918 the Workers' General Confederation of Greece and the Socialist Labor Party of Greece were established—the latter to be transformed in 1924 into the Communist Party of Greece (KKE). The overall influence of the Communist Party was not significant, due to the slow industrialization of the country (which remained an agrarian one), the small number of unionized workers, the party's doctrinaire working class advocacy, which hindered its appeal to peasants and refugees, and its internecine rivalries.[7] Nevertheless, in the late 1920s it was a potential threat to the regime: the Communist Party could give shape to and take advantage of the social unrest. More workers (especially tobacco workers) were joining unions, and most important, for the first time there was a political party questioning not the constitutional form of the regime (monarchy or republic) but the very foundations of the regime itself. The "specter of communism," while not a sufficient threat to unite the bourgeois parties (the rivalry between republicans and royalists would not cease in the interwar era), did constitute a common enemy; its suppression raised no opposition. Last but not least, the Bolshevik revolution had changed the political context internationally. The ruling classes' obsessive fear that working-class struggles might lead to socialist revolution spurred an excessive anticommunism, which was reflected in the severity of the relevant legislation.

The *Idionymo* Law (*idionymo* stands for "special crime") of 1929 was passed by the government of the Liberal Party, who most strongly felt the challenge of the Left. According to this law, "whoever aims at the implementation of ideas whose manifest purpose is the overthrow of the established social order by violent means or the detachment of part from the whole of the country, or proselytizes in favor of these ideas" could be imprisoned for six months and exiled for one month to two years. The same law also applied to all those who by "taking advantage of strikes or lockouts, were creating disturbances and riots." Authors who advocated these ideas or the publication of materials endorsing the aforementioned ideas were punishable. Rallies and unions for the propagation of these ideas were prohibited, and civil servants and officers suspected of such sympathies were to be dismissed.[8] In the following years 95 percent of the citizens convicted for crimes "against the security of the country" would be convicted under the *Idionymo* Law—2,850 people out of 2,945 between 1929 and 1937.[9] Moreover, in September 1925 a new unit was founded in the police, the Special Security Service (*Ypiresia Eidikis Asfaleias*), with the purpose of keeping a close eye on the "foreign propaganda" and communism.[10]

Political exiles were sent to the islands of the Aegean sea: Folegandros, Anafi, Kimolos, Naxos, Paros, Gavdos, etc. Even though the islands received the majority of the prosecuted individuals, a place close to the Greek-Albanian frontier became the most dreaded for the leftists in the 1920s. On the mountains of Epirus, close to Kalpaki, a disciplinary platoon was established in 1924. In the beginning disobedient soldiers were sent there, and later communist soldiers as well. The platoon was under the command of the Second Lieutenant Christos Papachristou, and the camp was run on the principles of violence and hard labor. Beatings when the new soldiers arrived in the camp and while they worked, hard labor in road construction, woodcutting, and the transport of coal, surprise attacks at night by the guards, censorship of correspondence, wretched living conditions, nationalist songs, suicide attempts by detained soldiers: these tribulations give the flavor of life in that disciplinary platoon. "Violence is unorganized," noted a correspondent of the communist daily *Rizospastis* who visited the camp. He was right; it was just the beginning of what two decades later would become more systematic, elaborated, and organized at the camps on the island of Makronisos.[11]

There was no form of *custodia honesta* in Greece.[12] Political prisoners did not enjoy any privileged status and were not exempted from labor. The only reference that the law made regarding political prisoners was that they should be interned "in a special prison or in a special department of a prison."[13] Moreover, political prisoners convicted after the *Idionymo* Law who wished to be released after serving one-fourth of their sentence had to fulfill one further requirement: they had to state that they had "repented" and they would not be involved in any activity "whose manifest purpose is the overthrow of the established social order by violent means or the detachment of part from the whole of the country."[14] After a few years, this kind of statement would be well known as a "declaration of repentance".

Although the history of prisons in Greece has not yet been written, it is a history of modernizing ideas and ambitious reforms that corresponded neither to the existing societal conditions nor to the capacity of the state. Some of these mostly imported ideas and reforms remained on paper, while others were materialized partly and with poor results. The 1836 law that organized Greek prisons was in pace with the contemporary corrective ideas, but most of the prisons were old fortresses and rented buildings that had had diverse previous uses.[15] Greece acquired its first proper prisons through the annexation of the Ionian islands from the British in 1862 and the donations of wealthy individuals towards the end of the century. In 1885 there were twenty-four prisons with 5,487 prisoners. In the decades before the outbreak of the Second World War the number of prisons was almost tripled (sixty-eight prisons in 1940) while the prison population was barely doubled (9,800 in 1937).[16] After a century of legislative reforms, from the 1920s on a serious effort was made to solve the practical problems of prisons and prisoners. Still, living conditions in prisons remained appalling. A lawyer in the 1930s found that only the Averof prison was worthy of being called a prison; as for the rest, he continued, "their characterization as graves for living people is not an exaggeration."[17] The judge of a court of appeals in Kyparissia, found the prison in that town to be a typical example of a Greek prison: windows were broken or missing, tiles were missing from the roof of the building and rain leaked through, the wooden floor was broken or rotten, and there was hardly any physical light in the dormitories.[18]

One of the long-standing criticisms concerned segregation among the different categories of prisoners, especially because most prisons in Greece did not have cells but dormitories. Long-term convicts lived together with small-time crooks and drug addicts. Stylianos Glykofrydis was an ardent advocate of the idea of special prisons, including one for communist prisoners. He had first-hand experience of prisons, having served as prison director and general inspector of prisons. In a book published in 1936 he argued that the major danger coming from communist prisoners was that they "corrupt the soul and the mind of the inmates" with their "Bolshevik propaganda." He suggested that communist prisoners should be interned in a separate department of a prison, that the judicial process should be swift, that their visitation rights be restricted, and that their contact with common prisoners be avoided. For him the solution to the problem would be the establishment of a special prison for communists, where prisoners would live under a "special strict regime" and be isolated from each other. Stylianos Glykofrydis did not hide his ideological sympathies. Discontent with the "rotten bourgeois regime," he called on the Greek government to combat communism "imitating, even though in a milder way, Hitler, who undoubtedly saved Germany, and through Germany the whole of Europe, from the sore of Communism."[19]

The threat from communism in Greece, however, was largely exaggerated. Although the power of the KKE was rising, it remained relatively small.[20] In the elections of 1933 the KKE received the 4.64 percent of the vote; two years later in the elections of 1936, the "All People's Front," which was supported mainly by the KKE, received 5.76 percent, and elected fifteen members of Parliament.[21] In the meantime, the 1933 elections were a victory for the anti-Venizelist bloc and the transfer of power marked a new period of tension. The turning point was the abortive Venizelist coup of March 1935. After that the anti-Venizelist bloc tried to consolidate its power by all means. This meant the purge of the armed forces, the widescale dismissal of public servants, wholesale repression against all republicans, and at the end the restoration of the monarchy by the Kondylis dictatorship in 1935 (the monarchy had been abolished in 1924). In the same year the Communist Party abandoned the self-isolating policy that regarded all the republican parties as "social-fascists" or "agrarian-fascists," and following the new line of the Communist International, launched a "popular front" policy. After the elections of 1936 the communist policy of the "popular front" provided the Liberals with a new but troublesome ally against an ever more reactionary anti-Venizelism. The Liberal Party needed the support of the Communists to form a government, and for that reason the Liberals and Communists reached an agreement to support a Liberal government in February 1936. The Liberal Party, caught in an intractable dilemma between cooperation with the anti-Venizelist bloc and acceptance of the monarchy on the one hand, and the formation of a republican bloc with the Left on the other, accepted the King's appointing as prime minister General Ioannis Metaxas, whose party had polled almost 4 percent in the previous elections.

Does all this justify General Ioannis Metaxas' proclaiming dictatorship on 4 August 1936 "on the eve of a subversive rebellious movement," one day before the trade unions' general strike? Certainly not; the growing power of the Communist Party and the ever more violent social and class struggles were the excuse but not the reasons for the dictatorship. Metaxas' dictatorship was an answer to the political stalemate of the 1930s. On the political level, the two major political blocs (Venizelists and anti-Venizelists), mired in controversy for over twenty years, had reached a point where neither could impose itself as a hegemonic power. Moreover, their political strategies, based on the National Schism and the economic liberalism of the 1920s, were outdated because social and economic change had undermined their very foundations. The outcome of increasing political instability was reflected in the rise and fall of governments (between 1926 and 1936 nine governments took office, including the most stable one, that of Venizelos from 1928 to 1932), the intervention of the army in politics (two dictatorships and five pronunciamentos), and the internal splitting of the blocs into rival fractions.[22] On the institutional level, there was a tendency for increasingly authoritarian solutions. The strengthening of executive power, the diminishing role of Parliament, and the readiness of the political establishment to accept non-constitutional governments provided the framework for authoritarian solutions.[23]

On the social level, the emergence of the labor movement alarmed the bourgeois parties. It may be argued that the strength of the trade unions, both numerical and political, was not great enough to excuse the excessive repressive measures of the state. However, both the labor movement and the Communist Party represented potential and serious threats to the political establishment, which perceived the danger as imminent. Anticommunism was incorporated into bourgeois policies and discourse and became a legitimate excuse for authoritarian policies.[24] For these reasons the bourgeois parties, although they did not welcome the dictatorship, did not try to overthrow it (in addition the dictator enjoyed the support of King George). Ioannis Metaxas' dictatorship was an answer but not a solution to the political deadlock. The political situation in Greece was "frozen" for the four years of the dictatorship, and when the country was liberated after the war and the foreign occupation, the political situation had radically changed.[25]

The Dictatorship of Ioannis Metaxas

Metaxas, in his first address on 4 August 1936, defined the principles of his dictatorship: it was to be antiparliamentarian and anticommunist. Though Metaxas' accession to power may be analyzed in the framework of the emergence of fascist regimes throughout Europe in the 1920s and 1930s, it cannot be considered one of them. While the role of the police became crucial for the maintenance of the regime and many officials of the dictatorship did not hide their ideological and political affiliations with Fascist Italy, and in spite of the fact that initiatives were taken to organize society according to the corporatist model, Metaxas' dictatorship remained an authoritarian regime and did not become a fascist one.[26] One of the most basic common characteristics of the fascist regimes in Europe was the existence of mass fascist movements; no such movement occurred in Greece before or during the dictatorship, despite the considerable efforts of the dictator.[27] The dictatorship did not become fascist not even after 1938 when Ioannis Metaxas secured and strengthened his position after the prosecution of the leaders of the bourgeois parties[28] and the failure of the antidictatorial rising on the island of Crete in July 1938.[29] The lack of the independent political and social basis that a fascist movement could have furnished made him dependent on traditional alliances (the King and Great Britain) to remain in power.

In Metaxas' project the connecting link between antiparliamentarianism and anticommunism was nationalism—not an aggressive and expansionist nationalism, but rather a nationalism embodied in the form of a strong state. His antiparliamentarianism lay in achieving the national unity of social classes and political parties around a state that was beyond and above politics, because, to use Carl Schmittt's formulation, the state was the political unity of the people. Metaxas was aware on the one hand of the new role that the state had to play in planned economic development and the regulation of social conflicts after the economic world crisis, and on the other of people's disillusion with the dominant political parties. His answer to the latter was to replace the old conflict between Venizelists and anti-Venizelists with a new dividing line between nationalism and communism.

In the *Neon Kratos* (New State) that Ioannis Metaxas envisioned, there was no place for communism. On 18 September 1936, a few weeks after the dictatorship was proclaimed, Emergency Law 117 "on measures for the fight against communism and the consequences resulting thereof" was issued. Following the spirit of the *Idionymo* Law, it provided that anyone "who in writing or orally or with any other means whatsoever, directly or indirectly, aims at the diffusion, development or implementation of theories, ideas or social, economic and religious systems, tending to overthrow the existing social system of the country" would be sentenced to three months in jail and from six months to two years in exile. A case was considered "aggravating" if the aforementioned offense was committed by the press or in workplaces, or if the offender was a civil servant. A new feature in the prosecution of political ideas was that the law provided that the owners of books opposed to the spirit of the law had to deliver them to the police authorities; otherwise they could be sentenced to three months to one year in jail or exile.[30]

Emergency Law 117 was complemented by the Emergency Law 1075 "of security measures of the social regime and citizens' protection," issued on 11 February 1938. The Emergency Law 1075 repeated the basic articles of Emergency Law 117 but was more detailed and introduced three important measures. The first measure was the "declarations of repentance." As in the law of 1933, persons convicted under this law could be released, after serving one-third of their term, if they stated in writing or orally that they had repented and would not be involved in offenses covered by this law in the future. In this book, the issue of declarations of repentance will be discussed on many different occasions because it became one of the most critical issues for political detainees. The second measure was the establishment of "concentration camps" (*Stratopeda Sygkentroseos*) for banished individuals, where they were organized in a "disciplined life" and were obliged to work. The third measure was the "loyalty certificate." Anyone who wished to become a civil servant had to submit "a certificate from the Secretary of Public Security concerning his social convictions."[31]

Before discussing political internment during the Metaxas dictatorship two issues related to the legislation should be pointed out. These three measures made up the groundwork for the prosecution of leftists and trade unionists not only during the dictatorship but also in the postwar era. From this point of view one may claim that Metaxas was in fact a forerunner; the declarations of repentance, loyalty certificates, and internment camps for communists constituted the elements of the interwar legacy that would be used extensively in the postwar era for the exclusion and rehabilitation of leftists. Moreover, the interwar legislation was characterized by the prosecution and punishment of ideas rather than deeds. It penalized communism as a political ideology and prosecuted individuals for their political views; what was punished was the motive, not the act. It is no coincidence that in these two laws there was no connection between the political ideology and specific crime, such as sabotage or carrying arms. The laws did not punish a crime, but constructed a crime that had to be punished.

The number of people prosecuted under the Metaxas dictatorship cannot be estimated, although it is believed to be large. It is said that 45,000 individuals signed declarations of repentance during the four years of the dictatorship, a number by far exceeding the 15,000-17,000 membership of the KKE at that time.[32] The repressive measures of the dictatorship were directed not only against leftists, but also against anyone who might oppose the regime. The indiscriminate mass arrests and deportations troubled even the

British ambassador, who was "disagreeably impressed ... by [the] growth of objectionable police methods as exemplified by arrest and imprisonment without trial of large numbers of harmless persons known to hold Liberal views."[33] The repressive measures were accompanied by the growth of the police and intelligence services within the state mechanism.[34]

The Communist Party was actually dissolved during the dictatorship and its secretary general, Nikos Zachariadis, was arrested and imprisoned. The fact that the very same day dictatorship was proclaimed, the front page of the communist daily *Rizospastis* warned of the danger of a coup d'etat, did not mean that it was organizationally prepared for this. It seems, however, that despite the repressive and harsh measures against the communists, the party mechanism somehow maintained some operations until a wave of mass arrests in the spring of 1938. After that the underground mechanism was dissolved, and a general confusion was added to the mass arrests and imprisonment of communists. The few members who escaped arrest decided in 1939 to continue underground party activities under the name "Old Central Committee," while a few months later, in 1940, the secretary of Public Security, with the participation of former communists, set up another leading center under the name "Provisional Administration," which published its own *Rizospastis*. The confusion—among the rank and file as well as the jailed leadership—over which of the two was the original one was so widespread that in the end, the phony leadership was recognized by the imprisoned leading cadres as the authentic one. With the majority of its members in prison and the rest confused and without a mechanism, the Communist Party of Greece was almost nonexistent on the eve of the Second World War.[35]

The islands of Folegandros, Anafi, Gavdos, Agios Efstratios, Kimolos, Sikinos, Sifnos, and Amorgos, and the prisons of Akronafplia, Aegina, Pylos, and Corfu hosted most of the political detainees. The vast majority were not sentenced by courts, but were banished (i.e., exiled or imprisoned) by decrees of public security committees. The number of the political detainees can hardly be estimated. One scholar suggests that between 1929 and 1937 3,000 individuals convicted under the *Idionymo* Law were banished, and a further 1,000 to 5,000 under different laws during the Metaxas dictatorship.[36] According to another scholar there were 2,000 political detainees in Greece just before the outbreak of war in 1940.[37]

Instead of reviewing the overall situation of political detainees in prisons and on islands, I will focus on the Akronafplia prison for three reasons. First, it is exemplary from the point of view of political detainees' organization, an example that was also followed in the postwar era. Second, political detainees' morale and discipline in the Akronafplia prison became legendary in the leftist popular memory and political tradition, and it is interesting to discuss why that happened. Third, because the fate of the Akronafplia prisoners during the

Second World War and the occupation can be regarded as typical for the rest of the political prisoners and exiles as well.[38]

The Akronafplia prison, previously been a military camp, was changed and renamed to "Akronafplia Communist Prison" by a decree of the secretary of Public Security on 3 February 1937.[39] The same month, many of the political detainees exiled to Aegean islands were transferred to the Akronafplia prison. At its peak between 600 and 650 men were incarcerated there. The director was the captain of gendarmerie Vretteas. The political prisoners organized themselves in "cohabitation groups" (*omades symviosis*), one in each of the four large dormitories, and they elected a "bureau of the group" (*grafeio omadas*), which arranged the prisoners' everyday life. This bureau assigned detainees to the several "duty-parties" (cooks, bakers, shoemakers, tailors, blacksmiths, cleaners, etc.), was responsible for the finances of the group (each detainee had to give 50 percent of the checks and part of the foodstuffs he received to the group), and organized educational and recreational activities. The illiterate had reading and writing lessons, and the rest were taught subjects as mathematics, history, foreign languages, and geography; there was also vocational training taught by craftsmen. The most important aspects of that self-organization of everyday life were that it gave them the opportunity to improve their living conditions (they built an oven where they baked bread and cooked food, made cisterns to store water, etc.), and lessened the tension or regulated the conflicts arising among the political detainees.

The political detainees at the Akronafplia prison became legendary not only for their well-organized life but also for their discipline. Any form of organization implies a certain degree of discipline, but the Akronafplia case went far beyond that. Akronafplia owes its legendary status to the small number of declarations of repentance signed by detainees in contrast to, for example, the case of the political detainees in the Corfu prison. Despite the fact that the leading cadres of the KKE (the secretary general included) had been incarcerated in the Corfu prison and spent two or three years in solitary confinement under far worse living conditions than at the Akronafplia prison, their case did not become equally memorable in the leftist political tradition because many of them signed declarations of repentance. The prisoners at the Akronafplia prison were remembered not only because a number of the political detainees were already or subsequently became leading cadres of the Communist Party after the liberation of the country in 1944, but primarily because they set the example of party discipline inside prisons.[40] In the beginning a number of political detainees signed declarations of repentance, due to strong pressure from the administration and the atmosphere of terror after the murder of a political detainee, Pavlos Stavridis, on 30 August 1937. However, as the party mechanism grew more organized, party discipline was restored. The "party committee" (*kommatiki epitropi*) was a shadow power in the Akronafplia prison. Its members were not elected but appointed (usually according to their position in the party hierarchy outside prisons) and their membership remained secret from the rest of the detainees. They suggested who should be elected from the cohabitation groups in the bureau, and supervised detainees' life in the Akronafplia prison. "Listen, watch and be silent" was the rule, as a former Akronafplia prisoner wrote to point out that "the individuality of the comrade had disappeared."[41] Those who did not conform to the party line were subjected to a series of measures: critical comment, isolation, expulsion from the party, even sacking from the dormitories, as was the case of two dissidents in 1939. Vigilance against "enemies," strict discipline, submission to the leadership, and forbearing to criticize the monolithic party became the virtues of the communist political prisoner at the Akronafplia prison.[42]

The third reason for focusing on Akronafplia is related to the fate of the Akronafplia prisoners in the war and the occupation that followed. After the German invasion and the occupation of the country in the spring of 1941, the political detainees were not released by the government but, on the contrary, handed over to the Italian and German occupation forces. The Akronafplia prison was shut down in 1943 and many political detainees were transferred to other camps in Katouna, Vonitsa, Larisa, and Trikala, and to the small island of Lazaretto, near Corfu. Lazaretto was under Italian occupation, and for that reason detainees there were released upon the collapse of the fascist regime in Italy in September 1943. However, many political prisoners and exiles had a different fate. During the harsh winter of 1941/42 political exiles were left without food supplies, and as a consequence eighteen political exiles on the island of Anafi and thirty-three on the island of Agios Efstratios (Ai-Stratis) died of starvation.[43] In addition, a large number of political prisoners were executed during the occupation. Out of the 677 political prisoners executed by the Germans and the Italians, 299 were former prisoners at the Akronafplia prison.

The fact that the political prisoners of Metaxas' regime were handed over to the occupation forces and many of them were later executed should not go unnoticed. It indicates that the collaborationist government of General Tsolakoglou and the Axis forces had a common enemy, namely, the communists. And in turn, both the collaborationist government and the Axis forces became the targets of the communist-led resistance. In occupied Greece, as in Yugoslavia, Italy, and to a lesser extent, France, resistance was intertwined with civil war. Moreover, executions of political prisoners were not carried out at random. On 27 April 1944 guerrillas ambushed and killed General Krentz and three officers, and wounded several soldiers. The response was swift. On 30 April 1944 the German Military Commander of Greece, General Speidel, ordered the execution of communist prisoners. The next day, 1 May 1944, two hundred political prisoners were transferred from the Chaidari camp and executed.[44] Executions in reprisal for the activities of the resistance were just one form of the violence that was generated during the occupation. I shall further discuss the combination of resistance with civil war and the spread of violence during the occupation not only because they are important aspects of the years between 1941 and 1944, but also because they are interrelated with developments in postwar Greece.

Occupation and Resistance

The four years between the outbreak of the Greek-Italian War in October 1940 and the liberation of the country from triple occupation (by German, Italian, and Bulgarian forces) had profoundly changed the country. Greece was devastated after four years of war, foreign occupation, and economic havoc. From 1940 to 1944, 500,000 people died (more than 7 per cent of the population), and the economic effects of the war, as the chief historian of the United Nations Relief and Rehabilitation Administration acknowledged, were "little short of disastrous":[45] 34 percent of the total national wealth was destroyed; 409,000 houses were completely destroyed, leaving 1.2 million people homeless, and 1,770 villages were burnt down.[46] At the same time, the emergence of the resistance during the occupation had changed the social and political landscape. At the moment of liberation the EAM claimed that it had between one and one and a half million people, which means that one out of seven Greeks had some form of affiliation with leftist resistance organizations. The rapid and expansive growth of communist-led resistance organizations, such as the *Ethniko Apeleftherotiko Metopo* (National Liberation Front), the *Ethnikos Laikos Apeleftherotikos Stratos* (National People's Liberation Army), the *Eniaia Panelladiki Organosi Neon* (United Panhellenic Organization of Youth), and the *Ethniki Allileggyi* (National Solidarity), among others was surprising, if one takes into account the situation of the KKE before the war, but not incomprehensible.

The EAM organizations represented a revolutionary drive that rapidly radicalized wartime society. The resistance radicalized large sections of the population that had been neglected, suppressed, and deprived of their voice, like peasants, women, youth, and ethnic minorities. It mobilized thousands of people in a huge network of grassroots organizations that covered every aspect of life in occupied Greece, from relief to guerilla warfare. Moreover, the resistance revolutionized institutions. Towards the end of the occupation the resistance movement was a protostate organization. The collaborationist government and state apparatus were discredited in the eyes of the population due to the collaboration with the occupation forces, and their power was minimized or in many areas even eliminated after the attacks of the resistance. As the official state withered away, the institutions of the resistance took over. The left-wing resistance had its army in the mountains, was responsible for law enforcement in liberated territories, drafted laws, collected taxes, organized the administration of justice ("people's courts") and the local authorities ("people's self-administration"). The resistance also held elections (in which women voted for the first time) in the liberated areas of Greece in the spring of 1944 and had a government, the Provisional Committee of National Liberation, independent of the government-in-exile.[47] But despite its newfound power, the political agenda of the resistance remained rather moderate and vague: the aim was national liberation and what was called *laokratia*, people's rule.

In contrast to Italy or France, where republican and liberal parties and politicians were actively involved in the resistance, the left-wing resistance organizations in Greece grew in a political vacuum, in the absence of the political establishment. King George in London, on the one hand, and the government-in-exile and political elites in Cairo on the other, showed little if any interest in organizing the resistance in occupied Greece. Their disputes over the distribution of power in the government and the fate of monarchy were balanced by their shared enmity towards the EAM and the challenge to the established order it represented. The political establishment and the government-in-exile sought to bring the resistance under their control, and in that they had the full support of the British, who were afraid of a communist takeover in the event of the Germans' withdrawal.[48] Two agreements paved the way in the direction desired by the political establishment and the British. In May 1944 in Lebanon, the EAM consented to take part in the exiled government under the premiership of the liberal Anglophile George Papandreou, holding six ministries of minor importance, and to put the guerilla forces under the control of the exiled government. Later that year, in September 1944, a few weeks before the withdrawal of the Germans, EAM representatives agreed acquiesce to the arrival of British troops, to place the ELAS forces under the command of British General Ronald Scobie, and to keep ELAS troops out of the metropolitan area.

In occupied Greece army officers had formed several small and local nationalist organizations. These organizations faced a precarious situation with the growth and expansion of the EAM-ELAS. Some of their members joined the ELAS, but most of them became fervent anticommunists. Caught between the ELAS and the Germans, most of the members of nationalist groups opted for the latter, not out of philo-Nazism but rather out of anticommunism. Some of these groups remained active as anticommunist bands thanks to the protection of the Germans or joined the Security Battalions.[49] Of the noncommunist resistance organizations only two, the Ethnikos Dimokratikos Ellinikos Syndesmos (*National Republican Greek League*) and the Ethniki kai Koinoniki Apeleftherosi (*National and Social Liberation*), gained some following. These two organizations were formed by army officers, and although they were strong in some areas (central and western Greece) they never managed to expand nationwide. Moreover, they were guerilla organizations and did not develop any political program, and were heavily dependent on British parachute drops of money and arms. As the ELAS grew stronger and expanded, tensions between the ELAS and the rival noncommunist resistance organizations also grew over the control of territories and access to the British parachute drops. The ELAS suspected the EDES and EKKA of acting in the interest of the British and scheming to restore monarchy in Greece, while the EDES, EKKA, and British feared that expansion of the ELAS would result in communist domination over Greece. As early as February 1943, the clashes between the left-wing and right-wing resistance organizations became more violent. Despite temporary agreements and attempts to coordinate resistance activities against the Germans in the summer of 1943, the conflicts resumed in October 1943. As a result, the EDES was restricted into a specific region (Epirus) and reached an agreement with the Germans to avoid any resistance activity—the EDES was not involved in any clashes with Germans until June 1944.[50] The fate of the other non-communist resistance organization was worse. It was dissolved in April 1944, when 350 members of the EKKA were attacked and many of them killed by 4,500 ELAS men.[51] The government-in-exile would capitalize on this event, accusing the EAM of waging not a war of liberation but rather a civil war.

The nationwide polarization was not restricted to the conflict between left-wing and right-wing resistance organizations, but also arose between the resistance and collaborators. As the ELAS' attacks on the Germans became more frequent and violent, after the surrender of Italy the Germans were under the pressure to reinforce their troops in Greece. The solution was the Security Battalions, Greek armed units that cooperated with the Germans in counterinsurgent campaigns. The initiative to create the Security Battalions was not taken by the Germans, but instead by the collaborationist government of Ioannis Rallis. The Security Battalions were masterminded by the former dictator General Pangalos, whose initial idea was to form an army of republican anticommunists. Rallis, however, recruited fanatical royalists and pressured army officers to join them. In Macedonia, nine such units were formed, totaling 6,000 men; in the rest of Greece the occupation forces created nine *Evzone* battalions (5,724 army officers and soldiers) and four gendarmerie battalions (3,370 army and gendarmerie officers and men).[52]

In the same vein, the collaborationist government of Ioannis Rallis and the Minister of the Interior Anastasios Tavoularis, himself a former member of the EDES, transformed a large part of the gendarmerie into an anticommunist task force by recruiting, according to a gendarmerie officer, "the scum of society, criminals, people of the underworld in general, as long as they were anti-Communists."[53] The gendarmerie (especially the anticommunist death squad, the Special Branch, headed by Alexandros Lambou) and Security Battalions were energetically involved in the roundups in Athens in 1944, in which hundreds of civilians were arrested and many of them executed on the spot.[54]

Violence was an integral part of the policies of the three occupying forces. It was organized and served specific ends. The Bulgarian atrocities in the region of Drama in late September and early October 1941, in which 4,000-5,000 Greeks were killed, aimed the removal of the Greek population from Eastern Macedonia and the subsequent "Bulgarization" of the region. The extermination of Greek Jews was part of the Final Solution. Between March and May 1943 the Jewish population of Salonica, where the vast majority of Greek Jews lived, was deported to Auschwitz. Very few survived. Out of 70,000 Jews who lived in Greece before the occupation, 59,000 were killed. Finally, there were German and Italian reprisals for the resistance. In 1943 and 1944 entire villages were burnt down and their inhabitants, especially the male population, were shot on the spot. Some of the sites of that bloody campaign were Kalavryta (between 8 and 13 December 1943; 800-1,000 people were killed), Distomo (10 May 1944; 300 inhabitants killed), and Kommeno (16 August 1943, 317 people killed). Prisoners bore their share in the reprisals. Some of them had been in prison since the Metaxas dictatorship (like the 200 political prisoners from the Chaidari camp who were executed on 1 May 1944), but most had been arrested in roundups. Ten prisoners were transferred from the Chaidari camp for execution on 13 May 1944, another hundred on 18 May, another fifty were hanged on 21 July, and another fifty were shot on 9 August. This list of executions is far from complete; according some authors, 1,800 prisoners from the Chaidari camp were killed within a year (September 1943-1944).[55]

The violence that spread during the occupation was not without consequences. Violent practices like executions, reprisals, taking hostages, roundups, and the public exhibition of corpses became part of the everyday experience. Those practices were sustained by agents and structures of violence like terrorist bands, death squads, and concentration camps. Within this context, and as the resistance became intertwined with the civil war between the EAM/ELAS and right-wing organizations and collaborators, a deep division was generated within Greek society. When the country was liberated, the resistance was over. But what about the civil war? As long as the communist-led EAM dominated the country, it was a certainty that its power would not go unchallenged.

Notes

1. William Edgar, "Oi ekkathariseis tou 1917. I simasia tous gia to metarrythmistiko programma tou Venizelou," in *Meletimata gyro apo ton Venizelo kai tin epochi tou*, ed. Thanos Veremis and Odysseas Dimitrakopoulos (Athens, 1980), 519-550.
2. For the problem of banditry in Greece, see John Koliopoulos, *Brigands with a Cause. Brigandage and Irredentism in Modern Greece 1821-1912* (Oxford, 1987).
3. Law 121, 31 December 1913, article 2. In 1914, Avraam Benaroya and Samuel Gionas would be the first socialists to be exiled to the island of Naxos. See Nikos Alivizatos *Oi politikoi thesmoi se krisi, 1922-1974. Opseis tis ellinikis empeirias* (Athens, 1995), 342.
4. Alivizatos, *Oi politikoi thesmoi*, 340-350; K. S. Vasileiou, *I dioikitiki ektopisi stin Ellada* (London, 1974), 16-26.
5. For a discussion of state policies towards the labor movement, see, among others, Georgios Leontaritis, "To elliniko ergatiko kinima kai to astiko kratos 1910-1920," in Veremis and Dimitrakopoulos, *Meletimata gyro apo ton Venizelo*, 49-84; Antonis Liakos, *Ergasia kai politiki stin Ellada tou mesopolemou. O rolos tou Diethnous Grafeiou Ergasias* (Athens, 1993).
6. George Mavrogordatos, *Stillborn Republic: Social Coalitions and Party Strategies in Greece, 1922-1936* (Berkeley, 1983), 323-337.
7. Gunnar Herring, *Die politischen Parteien in Griechenland 1821-1916* (Munich, 1992), vol. 2, 983-1001.
8. Law 4229, *Government Gazette* 245, 25 July 1929.
9. Roussos Koundouros, *I asfaleia tou kathestotos* (Athens, 1978), 93-103. To estimate the number of political detainees from 1929 to 1936 one must also add those who were exiled under the law for the suppression of banditry. This is very difficult since there are no official data for the decrees of the public security committees.
10. The head of the Special Security Service was Georgios Fessopoulos, who became an anticommunist theoretician, see his books *O kommounismos en ti praxei* (Athens, 1927), and *I exelixis tou kommounismou en Rossia kai i proodos autou en Elladi* (Athens, 1929). See also Alexandros Dagkas, *O hafies. To kratos kata tou kommounismou. Syllogi pliroforion apo tis ypiresies Asfaleias Thessalonikis, 1927* (Athens, 1995), 35-39.
11. See *Rizospastis*, 22 January to 14 February 1929. See also Petros Pikros, *Kalpaki -Fylakes-Xeronisia* (Athens, 1978), 221-274.
12. Dimitrios Karanikas, *Sofronistiki* (Salonika, 1948), vol. I, 343-347.
13. Royal Decree, *Government Gazette* 194, 17 July 1923, article 37.
14. Law 5764, *Government Gazette* 269, 18 September 1933, article 3.
15. After the establishment of the Greek state the Akronafplia prison, once a medieval fortress, became first a military hospital and later a military camp. Averof prison was first a penitentiary for juveniles (1896) and then, after 1916, a prison. Aegina prison was first an orphanage built in 1830, then successively it was used as a training school for officers, a place of quarantine, a mental hospital, and an accommodation for refugees before becoming a prison in 1880. Itzedin prison, a fortress built after the Cretan revolt against Ottoman rule (1866-1869), was transformed into a prison after 1898. Pylos prison was previously a fortress built by the Ottomans in 1573. Eptapyrgio prison was a medieval fortress that had been restored and improved by the Venetians (1423-1430) and the Ottomans (1431). Chatzikosta prison in Athens, before becoming a prison in 1943, had been an orphanage since its construction in 1855. Despite their diversity of age and use, one cannot but think of Michel Foucault and see that even before they became prisons, the architecture of these buildings facilitated the surveillance of individuals.

16. Karanikas, *Sofronistiki*, 254-266, Dimitrios Kamvysis, *I Sofronistiki metaheirisis ton egklimation* (Athens, 1949), 139-141.
17. Aristeidis Prokos, *Symvoli eis tin organosin tou sofronistikou systimatos en Elladi* (Athens, 1936), 89.
18. I. P. Petrounakos, *Ai fylakai kai i dikaiosyni mas* (Athens, 1936), 7-9.
19. Stylianos Glykofrydis, *Fylakai* (Athens, 1936), 79-86.
20. The KKE had 1,500 members in 1930 and 17,500 members in 1936, according to Angelos Elefantis, or 15,000 according to Charis Vlavianos: see Angelos Elefantis, *I epaggelia tis adynatis epanastasis* (Athens, 1979), 289; Charis Vlavianos, "The Metaxas' Dictatorship: The Greek Communist Party under Siege," in *Aspects of Greece 1936-1940. The Metaxas' Dictatorship,* ed. Robin Higham and Thanos Veremis (Athens, 1993), 193-225. See also Herring, *Die politischen Parteien*, vol. 2, 1039-1045.
21. In the elections of 5 March 1933 the United Front received 51,656 votes; in those for the Constituent Assembly of 9 June 1935, from which the Liberal Party abstained, the United Front garnered 98,669 votes, and in the elections of 26 January 1936 the All People's Front received 73,411 votes.
22. Elefantis, *I epaggelia*, 159-172; Christos Chatziiosif, "I venizelogenis antipolitefsi sto Venizelo kai i politiki anasyntaxi tou astismou sto mesopolemo," in *Venizelismos kai astikos eksyhronismos,* ed. George Mavrogordatos and Christos Chatziiosif (Herakleio, 1992), 439-458.
23. Alivizatos, *Oi politikoi thesmoi*, 84.
24. Lito Apostolakou, "'Greek' Workers or Communist 'Others': The Contending Identities of Organized Labour in Greece, c. 1914-36," *Journal of Contemporary History*, 32, no. 3 (1997): 409-423.
25. George Mavrogordatos, "The 1940s between Past and Future", in *Greece at the Crossroads. The Civil War and its Legacy,* ed. John O. Iatrides and Linda Wrigley (University Park, 1995), 31-47.
26. The Fourth of August regime did not enjoy any considerable political support from the European fascist regimes. The case of relations with Italian Fascism is a case in point. Though Fascist Italy and Metaxas' regime shared an ideological affiliation, reflected in societal institutions, their political divergence did not allow the establishment of close relationships between them. By political divergence I mean the attachment of Greece to British interests and the issue of Italian rule in the Dodecanese islands. See, Romain Rainero, "Le coup d'état de Metaxas et ses echos dans l' Italie fasciste," *Revue d'Histoire Moderne et Contemporaine* 36, (1989): 438-449.
27. For the character and the ideology of the dictatorship, see John Koliopoulos, *Greece and the British Connection, 1935-1941* (Oxford, 1977), 51-58; Constantine Sarandis, "The Ideology and Character of the Metaxas Regime," in Higham and Veremis, eds., *Aspects of Greece*, 147-178; Giorgos Kokkinos, *I fasizousa ideologia stin Ellada. I periptosi tou periodikou "Neon Kratos", 1937-1941* (Athens, n. d.); Panagiotis Noutsos, "Synistoses tis ideologias tis 4is Augoustou," in *Ellada 1936-1944. Dictatoria-Katochi-Antistasi,* ed. Hagen Fleischer and Nikos Svoronos (Athens, 1990), 59-69; Jon Kofas, *Authoritarianism in Greece. The Metaxas' Regime* (Boulder, 1983), 52-64.
28. In January 1938 an antidictatorial pamphlet signed by Themistocles Sofoulis, George Kafantaris, Ioannis Theotokis, and George Papandreou was distributed in Athens. It was the only public attempt of the political establishment to question the authority of the regime. It is noteworthy that although the pamphlet was very critically worded (the regime is characterized as "tyrannical" and "terrorist"), it did not call for mass action to overthrow the dictatorship but chracterized itself as "a protest out of an obligation to the history." Nevertheless, in the following months many liberal politicians were arrested and

banished (one of them, former minister Andreas Michalakopoulos, was banished to Paros, where he died in February 1938). See Spyros Linardatos, *4i Augoustou* (Athens, 1988), 295-302.

29. The antidictatorial uprising occurred in Chania on 29 July 1938, but it was so poorly organized (its leaders had counted on a nationwide uprising) that it lasted for only one day. The movement was over before the navy, sent by the dictator, even reached the island.
30. Emergency Law 117, *Government Gazette* 402, 18 September 1936, article 1, pars. 1 and 4, article 10.
31. Emergency Law 1075, *Government Gazette* 45, 11 February 1938, article 5, par. 1; article 8 par. 2; article 11, par. 1. See, Alivizatos, *Oi politikoi thesmoi*, 417-422.
32. D. George Kousoulas, *Revolution and Defeat: The Story of the Greek Communist Party*, (London, 1965), 140. This number refers to persons arrested but not necessarily imprisoned or exiled. Jon Kofas maintains that "there were 45,000 communists in prisons and concentration camps," a very high figure by any standards. See, Kofas, *Authoritarianism in Greece*, 136.
33. FO 371/22362 R8047, Athens to FO, 6 October 1938.
34. Undersecretary of Public Security Konstantinos Maniadakis, the size of the gendarmerie increased by 20 percent, the anticommunist unit of the intelligence service increased from less than fifteen to eighty men, and the Special Security reached a strength of 445 officers and NCOs, 30 political agents, and 1,200 privates, whereas before the dictatorship it had been only 190 strong. See, David H. Close, "I astynomia sto kathestos tis 4is Augoustou," in Fleischer and Svoronos, eds., *Ellada 1936-1944*, 77-91.
35. Elefantis, *I epaggelia*, 261-267.
36. Koundouros, *I asfaleia*, 119-120.
37. Elefantis, *I epaggelia*, 257.
38. For the life of political prisoners at the Akronafplia prison, see the memoirs of Pavlos Nefeloudis, *Stis piges tis kakodaimonias* (Athens, 1974); Antonis Flountzis, *Akronafplia kai Akronafpliotes, 1937-1943* (Athens, 1979); Giannis Manousakas, *To chroniko enos agona. Akronafplia 1939-1943* (Athens, 1986); Gerasimos Antonatos, *Akronafplia* (Athens, 1965); Vasilis Bartzotas, *Ki astrapse fos i Akronafplia* (Athens, 1977); Vasilis Giannogonas, *Akronafplia*, (Athens, 1963).
39. When Akronafplia prison opened its gates it carried the signboard "Akronafplia Communist Prison." This signboard changed after detainees' protests to "Akronafplia Concentration Camp of Communists," because they argued that they were not prisoners but exiles, see Flountzis, *Akronafplia*, 73.
40. At the seventh congress of the Communist Party (October 1945), thirty-three former political detainees who had served terms at Akronafplia prison were appointed to leading posts, some in the Central Committee of the party. Bartzotas, *Ki astrapse fos*, 210.
41. Giannogonas, *Akronafplia*, 47.
42. In one of the talks organized by the political detainees, the speaker said of the "internal" enemies: "With the same hate, the same intransigence, the same fanaticism our group faced all the enemies. In all the cases the monolithicity of the group, the strict vigilance, and our labor for the enlightenment on their role in the movement and here [in the prison], rendered them incapable of doing us any harm." Zisis Zografos, "The five years of Akronafplia, 16 February 1942", in, *Akronafplia – Dialexeis* (Athens, 1945), 17.
43. Giorgis Zarkos, *Omada symviosis politikon exoriston Anafis* (Athens, 1946); Kostas Bosis, *Ai-Stratis. I machi tis peinas ton politikon exoriston sta 1941* (Athens, 1947).
44. Antonis Flountzis, *Chaidari. Kastro kai vomos tis Ethnikis Antistasis* (Athens, 1976), 379-393.

45. George Woodbridge, *UNRRA: The History of the United Nations Relief and Rehabilitation Administration* (New York, 1950), vol. 2, 95.
46. Konstantinos Kalligas, "Oi thysies kai oi apoleies tou Ellinismou kata ton B' Pagkosmio Polemo," proceedings of the conference *I Ellada tou '40* (Athens, 19-20 April 1991); Jon Kofas, *Intervention and Underdevelopment. Greece during the Civil War* (University Park, 1989), 8-9. Constantine Tsoucalas compared the degree of destruction Greece had suffered with that in Yugoslavia, Poland, and Russia. Constantine Tsoucalas, *The Greek Tragedy* (London, 1969), 91-92.
47. Georgoulas Beikos, *I laiki exousia stin Eleftheri Ellada* (Athens, 1979); Thanasis Tsouparopoulos, *Oi laokratikoi thesmoi tis Ethnikis Antistasis* (Athens, 1989); Dimitrios Zepos, *Laiki dikaiosyni eis ta eleftheras periohas tis ypo katohin Ellados*, (Athens, 1945; republished Athens, 1986).
48. John A. Petropoulos, "The Traditional Political Parties of Greece during the Axis Occupation," in *Greece in the 1940s. A Nation in Crisis*, ed. John O. Iatrides (Hanover and London, 1981), 27-36.
49. Hagen Fleischer, *Stemma kai svastika. I Ellada tis katochis kai tis antistasis* (Athens, 1995), vol. 2, pp. 95-149.
50. Ibid., 249-259; idem, "Contacts between German Occupation Authorities and the Major Greek Resistance Organizations. Sound Tactics or Collaboration", in Iatrides, ed., *Greece in the 1940s*, 48-60; Ole Smith "'The First Round'—Civil War during the Occupation", in *The Greek Civil War: Studies of Polarization*, ed. David H. Close (London and New York, 1993), 58-71.
51. David H. Close, *The Origins of the Greek Civil War* (London, 1995), 113.
52. John L. Hondros, "I M. Vretania kai ta ellinika Tagmata Asfaleias," in Fleischer and Svoronos, eds., *Ellada 1936-1944*, 262-276.
53. Konstantinos Antoniou, *Istoria Ellinikis Vasilikis Chorofylakis 1833-1965* (Athens, 1965), vol. 3, 1891-1892.
54. Mark Mazower very vividly describes one of the first roundups that took place in Athens in the spring of 1944 and the undeclared Civil War in Athens before the liberation. See Mark Mazower, *Inside Hitler's Greece: The Experience of Occupation, 1941-1944*, (New Haven, 1993), 340-351
55. For the massacre at Kommeno, see Mazower, ibid., 190-200. For the German attrocities, Fleischer, *Stemma kai Svastika*, vol. 1, 90-101, vol. 2, 292-348, Flountzis, *Chaidari*, 413-422, 463-469, 593; Dimitrios Magkriotis, *Thysiai tis Ellados kai egklimata Katochis 1941-1944* (Athens, 1949), 106-113, 233-239.

Chapter 3

The Civil War
A Case of "Nation-State Rebuilding"

The return of the government-in-exile on 18 October 1944 did not appease the country. The government did not reestablish its legitimacy or its power. The real power over all Greece outside Athens lay in the hands of the EAM organizations. Giannis Kordatos, a prominent Marxist historian of the time, soundly described the situation as a "cosmogony" in which "the established political and social values are pushed aside and the new ones are arising."[1] The most important feature of the cosmogony in 1944 was that a return to prewar institutions and practices was impossible; people could no longer be ruled as they had been in the 1920s and 1930s.[2] The political and social landscape in Greece, had changed radically between 1940 and 1944, due not only to the absence of the old political establishment during the occupation that deprived it of any legitimacy, but mainly to the fact that the political vacuum was filled by an unprecedented societal mobilization. Wartime radicalism (rather than communism) propelled the *en masse* entry for the first time in Greece of a wide cross-section of social strata into the political arena with the purpose of social and political reform.[3]

The real issue for the political establishment was the transfer of power from the EAM-controlled regions to the government of Athens. In the negotiations between the EAM and the government, that transfer of power took the shape of the demobilization of the guerilla forces and the formation of a national army. In an atmosphere of precariousness, tension, and distrust of one another's future intentions, the negotiations led to a deadlock. The six EAM ministers resigned from the government, further aggravating the crisis, and the EAM called for a demonstration on 3 December 1944.[4] When large crowds started to assemble that day in Constitution Square in the very center of Athens, suddenly and without any provocation policemen fired on the unarmed demonstrators. Several people (probably sixteen) were killed and hun-

---

Notes for this section begin on page 68.

dreds were wounded. The next day a protest demonstration was organized by the EAM. Three young women were at the head of the demonstration carried a placard reading: "When the people are in danger from tyranny they choose either chains or arms." Being under pressure and constructing a dilemma out of a far more complicated situation, the KKE opted for the latter. It was the beginning of what was later called *Dekemvriana* (the December events).

For one month, the city of Athens became a battlefield for a number of the EAM/ELAS units (on the instructions of the KKE, the bulk of the ELAS guerilla forces stayed in their positions and did not fight in Athens), and the police, those "purged" from communist army units, the National Guard, extreme rightist bands, and the ever increasing British troops (up to 75,000 men). On 6 January 1945, after thirty-three days of fighting in the streets of Athens and Piraeus, the EAM/ELAS forces were withdrawn. The losses were heavy. Seven thousand people were dead. Twelve thousand leftists were arrested by the British and the government, out of whom 8,000 were transferred to camps in the Middle East; and 15,000 people were arrested as hostages by the ELAS and taken to camps outside Athens.[5]

The Varkiza agreement was signed on 12 February 1945 between the EAM and the government. Though the agreement *prima facie* was designed to provide the framework for political life after the December events (the government was bound to reconstitute civil liberties, purge the civil service of collaborators and Metaxas' cadres, etc.), the only clause of the agreement that was even partially fulfilled was the demobilization of ELAS forces, the issue over which the late November crisis had originally occurred leading to the *Dekemvriana*. However, another article was also destined to be critical. Article 3 provided amnesty for crimes committed during the December events, except "common-law crimes, which were not absolutely necessary to the achievement of the political crime concerned."[6] The disarmament of the guerillas and article 3 of the Varkiza agreement would render thousands of resistance members defenseless against the "white terror" of armed rightist and royalist bands, and would make possible the prosecution and internment of thousands accused of crimes "not absolutely necessary." Though a large number of arms had been hidden under instructions from the party, the KKE had opted at that time for a legal course of action.

In the next pages I will examine the reorganization of the state vis-á-vis the challenge from the Left in postwar Greece. What is striking in the reorganization is the strong sense of continuity between the prewar, wartime, and postwar eras concerning state policies and state apparatus. The state in Greece after the war was reorganized as an anticommunist state that drew heavily on the policies and personnel of previous eras (primarily the collaborationist governments during the occupation and the Metaxas dictatorship). I shall begin the investigation of the continuity of the state with the period extending from the Varkiza agreement until June 1946. This period may be considered the first phase of political persecution, the "white terror" phase, because it was characterized by right-wing terrorism as an "endeavour of the lower echelons of power"[7] rather than by the introduction of special measures by the state. Then I will move to the second phase (1946-1950) which is directly related to the Civil War. This was the "institutionalized" phase, in the sense that political persecution took on characteristics of political exclusion. Political exclusion, an outcome of close cooperation between the political, military, and judicial authorities, was crystallized by the introduction of special legislation. Finally, I will focus on the status of political prisoners during the Greek Civil War. Greek legislation avoided any distinction between common and political crimes and prisoners, and thus rendered political prisoners an elusive subject.

1945-1946: The "White Terror"

For several months after the liberation the situation remained chaotic, especially in the provinces. The population relied heavily upon supplies distributed by the United Nations Relief and Rehabilitation Administration (UNRRA) to cover their primary needs.[8] Communication systems were destroyed, the devaluation of the currency and inflation gave speculators and black marketeers the opportunity to flourish, and the reconstruction of the country would continue to exist only on paper for the period under examination. In the dilemma of reconstruction or stabilization, the government opted for the latter because "what stabilization really entailed was the reconstitution of government authority."[9]

The reconstitution of government authority, in a country already divided by civil war during the occupation and the *Dekemvriana*, did not bring security and peace; on the contrary, in many instances, it heightened tension. The reconstitution of the government required weakening the influence of the resistance organizations, to put an end to what was derogatorily called "EAM rule" (*Eamokratia*). The government, in order to restore its authority, had to rely on a loyal state apparatus capable of containing the resistance organizations. The government sought to bring the state mechanism under its firm control by excluding members of the resistance, and to diminish the influence of the resistance by terrorizing its members. The results of this policy were pointed out in a statement that former prime ministers Emmanuel Tsouderos and Nikolaos Plastiras, together with liberal and republican politicians such as Konstantinos Mylonas, Georgios Kafandaris, and Themistocles Sofoulis, issued on 5 June 1945:

> [T]he terror initiated by the extreme right in the whole country after the December events is amplified every day. ... The terrorist organizations of the extreme right, which were partly armed by the Germans and collaborated with them in

many different ways, have not been disarmed or prosecuted, but cooperate with the security forces in order to strangle completely all democratic thought.[10]

The National Guard, sent all over the country by the government to restore law and order, became a force of vengeance and of the prosecution of leftists. Premises of newspapers and offices of leftist organizations were destroyed, leading cadres of the EAM/ELAS were prosecuted, women were pilloried, army officers who had joined the ELAS were put on the retired list, and even metropolitan bishops were deposed.[11] The following incident, reported by a U.S. officer, is telling. In Agrinio, on 7 April 1945, a National Guard patrol entered the premises of the EAM newspaper *Phoni tou Laou* (People's Voice) and arrested five men for illegal assembly. "In apologising," the U.S. officer wrote, "for the arbitrary action of his men, the Commander of the Battalion (which is locally recruited and generally speaking, excluded all left-wing sympathisers from its rank) explained that they could not contain themselves when they saw a Communist."[12]

The case of the National Guard men who "could not contain themselves when they saw a communist" bespeaks the role of the security forces in the postwar era. The National Guard consisted of men who had either been conscripts in the *Dekemvriana* fighting against the ELAS or regular army conscripts—in the latter case those suspected of leftist views were rejected on various grounds. In May 1945, the National Guard had 60,000 men, but a number of National Guard men were relocated to the gendarmerie as it gradually took over responsibility for the maintenance of order in the provinces. The manpower of the security forces was rapidly increased: within a year of the Varkiza agreement the gendarmerie had increased from 16,200 to 23,000, and the police from 4,500 to 6,500.[13] The reorganization of the security forces was undertaken by British officers (the British Police and Prisons Mission) in July 1945. The head of the mission, which remained in Greece until 1951, was Sir Charles Wickham, founder and former head of the Royal Ulster Constabulary. The reorganization did not affect the political orientation of the staff. "The Gendarmerie is at present being exclusively recruited from persons professing Anti-Communist political beliefs," observed the British Legal Mission, which visited Greece in November and December 1945.[14]

In contrast to France, Belgium, or the Netherlands where—at least in the first two years after the liberation—governments prosecuted and punished wartime collaborators, in Greece there was no real purge of the state apparatus.[15] Although a number of enactments concerning the prosecution and punishment of collaborators were passed by the government of the republican premier Nikolaos Plastiras in the first months of 1945, in fact very few collaborators were tried and condemned. In the first major trial of collaborators in Athens in 1945, three were sentenced to death (they were not executed), and two collaborationist prime ministers were sentenced to life. Paradoxically leading politicians who were called as witnesses for prosecution, turned out in the court room to be witnesses for the defense of the collaborators. For most of the collaborationist government ministers who were condemned to death, the death sentences were not carried out and the prisoners were granted amnesty in 1948.[16] The overall record of the government in the punishment of collaborators was very poor and the process of bringing collaborators to trial extremely slow. Within two years (1945 and 1946) about a thousand persons were tried for crimes of collaboration in northern Greece and only half of them were found guilty.[17] In June 1945, although there were 18,000 individual charges against collaborators, only 1,100 were in jail awaiting trial; eleven had been sentenced to death, six to life imprisonment and two had been executed. A year later, in June 1946, there was not much progress: the courts had reviewed the cases of 3,500 persons, but only 7 percent of them were designated for prosecution.[18] On 12 December 1946, the collaborators' trials stopped by order of the Special Magistrate. No more than twenty-five collaborators and four war criminals were executed after the liberation; only 1,275 collaborators were still in prison in 1951.[19]

The case of Security Battalionists is equally interesting. A large number of Security Battalionists were imprisoned after the liberation in October 1944, but only for a short while. At the time of the December events 12,000 Security Battalionists were enrolled in the National Guard and remained in service after the ceasefire. Another 228 officers who had served with the Security Battalions were reinstated in the national army. But out of the 103 senior army officers who had joined the ELAS, only five returned to service, whereas the rest were relegated to List B, the list of the retired officers.[20]

Most of the rightist and royalist bands had begun their activities during the occupation as anticommunist bands fighting against the EAM/ELAS, often in cooperation with the occupation forces, and by 1944 such bands had become one of the main targets of the EAM/ELAS. In the *Dekemvriana* they had the opportunity to prove their loyalty to the government which was fighting against the EAM/ELAS units in Athens, and to escape prosecution for their crimes and collaboration during the war.[21] In the months following the Varkiza agreement they became part of the state mechanism in the persecution of leftists and terrorized the countryside, a situation the state tolerated. Within one year of the Varkiza agreement, according to EAM sources, the results of the "white terror," were: 1,192 people killed, 159 women raped, 6,413 people injured, and 551 offices and printing shops raided.[22]

It would be a mistake to consider the activities of these bands as simply a consequence of the general postwar disorder. They were forces of vengeance on the violent left-wing campaign of the last months of the occupation. Moreover, the rightist and royalist bands substituted for a state apparatus: not yet sufficiently organized to impose a "law and order" form of persecution, the state had to rely on the extreme right elements for the suppression of the

Left—the immunity from prosecution enjoyed by those elements supports this view.[23] Even the chief of the British Police and Prisons Mission to Greece himself observed, confessing at the same time the failure of the mission to organize an efficient, non-biased police force, that there were "too many cases in which the Gendarmerie has actively or passively assisted these Right bands and murderers."[24] The rightist and royalist bands, in an informal alliance with the police, the National Guard, army officers, political organizations, and individuals subjected to the EAM violence during the occupation, became part of the repressive mechanism of a state under reconstruction and constituted the hard core of the forces that unleashed the "white terror".[25]

Thousands of individuals were prosecuted and imprisoned in 1945, mainly for crimes committed during the *Dekemvriana* that were "not absolutely necessary to the achievement of the political crime concerned." In 1945, 80,000 warrants were issued, 50,000 persons were arrested and, according to an official report dated the 1 October 1945, 16,700 were in jail. Out of the detainees, 2,896 were collaborators, 7,077 common criminals, and 6,027 persons detained for offenses connected with the *Dekemvriana*.[26] While the number of the overall prison population seems to be correct, the number of the political detainees is certainly small.[27] Also, it is important to remember that the prewar prison population was about 9,000 prisoners, almost all of them convicted of common crimes.[28] Perhaps a total of 10,000 leftist political prisoners in 1945 is more accurate.

A closer examination of some aspects of imprisonment will help to understand its character. On 17 September 1945 there were 16,600 prisoners and on 6 October there were 17,735; meanwhile, 5,535 had been released and another 6,670 had been imprisoned.[29] This high fluctuation is indicative of the large number of people unjustly prosecuted and imprisoned and is telling of the role of imprisonment during that period. Imprisonment was a means to terrorize leftists rather than a measure of punishment for a crime, a measure of prosecution rather than a measure of punishment.

We can draw the same conclusion from another set of statistics: of the 6,027 political detainees, 5,896 were awaiting trial and only 131 had been convicted, whereas 231 collaborators and 2,086 common law criminals had been convicted.[30] Even though the courts could not cope with the ever increasing number of cases, it seems that in the case of political detainees the process was especially slow. During the whole period under examination, a large number of individuals had been in jail for a considerable period of time without having been convicted. This gave the government the opportunity to jail a large number of "suspects." The long period of detention—up to six months—while awaiting trial confirms that imprisonment served as a form of prosecution in a period of mass arrests. The political orientation of the imprisoned spoke also of the political orientation of those who tried them—an orientation that was evident in the trials of collaborators. "Justice cannot work," the former minister of Justice Georgios Mavros said. "Ninety percent of the judges belong to the extreme Right." [31]

The campaign of mass imprisonment, however, raised strong criticism, both domestic and international, especially as general elections approached.[32] In a move of reconciliation, the government passed Emergency Law 753 in December 1945. That law provided that persons "morally responsible" for homicide and not covered by the amnesty were provisionally released. The same law provided that the period of awaiting trial should not exceed one hundred days.[33] As a result, 7,471 prisoners of all categories were released by April 1946 and the total number of prisoners decreased in the first months of 1946.[34] Nevertheless, a large number of political prisoners remained in jail, and many of those sentenced to death were executed in the following years.

Although most of the laws concerning political offenses passed by the caretaker governments before the elections of March 1946 were aimed at the appeasement of the country, what in fact happened was that they facilitated the repression of the Left. Laws that punished offenses like the possession of arms and armed resistance to authority, production or dissemination of critical publications concerning the army, or demonstrations that might have caused disquiet, were designed to ease the tension in a country deeply divided by the strife of the preceding years. There was even a law passed to guarantee the unobstructed circulation of the leftist press.[35] Nonetheless, given that the state apparatus was staffed by fervent anticommunists, partial implementation of the law and the ensuing prosecution of leftists could not be avoided. Laws appear to have been explicitly directed against the Left were Law 453, which reenacted the Law of 1871 for the suppression of banditry, and Emergency Law 890 which effectively reintroduced the *Idionymo* Law.[36]

The law for the decongestion of prisons, the British pressure to release political detainees, the protests of several politicians against the "white terror," the government's attempts to suppress right-wing excesses in the beginning of 1946, and the widespread fear among republican politicians that the growing power of rightist bands might end in a coup d'etat in cooperation with the army, demonstrate the differences in the various actors' policies toward the EAM.[37] The very fact of the violent, mass persecution of members of the resistance a few months after the end of the Second World War was an embarrassment. However, as the postwar crisis escalated in Greece and the Cold War advanced, the differences would be minimized and the policy vis-á-vis the Left would be crystallized.

1946-1949: Institutionalized Exclusion

In the general elections held on 31 March 1946, the KKE and other, minor parties abstained on the grounds of the white terror and the bias of the government holding the elections. It seems that before the elections, at its Second Plenum in February 1946, the KKE had decided to combine both political and military means.[38] In the last months of 1945 the first leftist armed groups were formed, mainly in northern Greece. They were comprised of leftists who took to the hills as a result of the "white terror" and, following the slogan of the Communist Party for "mass popular self-defense," organized retaliation attacks against right-wing bands and gendarmes. The Communist Party neither encouraged nor condemned those armed groups, so it seems that they were considered an additional means of putting the government under pressure. At the same time the Communist Party was under pressure. The party members in the countryside, as Giorgos Margaritis shows, could not see any future in political legality because the "white terror" had deprived them of any political means (local organizations, newspapers, and rallies) and the systematic economic discrimination had driven them to destitution—the armed struggle, after the very recent experience of the resistance, seemed a viable solution.[39] The bloody attack of one of these groups on the Litochoro gendarmerie station on 31 March 1946, the very date of the elections, is generally held as the beginning of the Civil War.

In the elections of March 1946, given the abstention of the Left and the "white terror," the royalist parties polled an overwhelming majority—65 percent of the valid votes and 67 percent in the seats of the parliament. It is estimated that the deliberate abstention and thus the "votes" of the Left were 25 percent. In the plebiscite for the reconstitution of the monarchy (in which the parties of the Left participated) on 1 September 1946, under conditions of coercion and intimidation, 68 percent voted for the return of King George.[40] The king who had consented to the Metaxas dictatorship and the abolishment of democracy had been reconstituted. The restoration of the prewar political order was complete.

One of the things that changed in postwar Greece was the foreign power that would guarantee the continuity of the regime. After the war Great Britain faced enormous economic difficulties and could not meet the increasing financial and military needs of the Greek government. The British and the Greek governments urged the United States government to take over.[41] The speech Harry Truman gave before the United States Congress on 12 March 1947, known as the Truman Doctrine, marked the new phase of heavy United States involvement in Greek affairs. He pointed out the general worldwide struggle between two ways of life (one based on freedom, while the other "relie[d] upon terror and oppression"), but also the particularity of the Greek case. "If Greece," Harry Truman declared, "should fall under the control of an armed minority, the effect upon its neighbor, Turkey, would be immediate and serious. Confusion and disorder might well spread throughout the Middle East."[42] For the Truman administration, the Greek Civil War was an alarming sign of Soviet aggression. Greece (together with Turkey, the only noncommunist countries in the Balkans) became an integral part of the newly formed United States global strategy for the containment of communism.

It was the first time that the United States, as an emerging world power after the Second World War, had to face and suppress a communist revolution in an allied country. The establishment of communist regimes in Central and Eastern Europe and the Chinese revolution were alarming signs of a communist-inspired world revolution that called for immediate action. However, the United States was presenting itself as the champion of democracy a few years after the collapse of totalitarian and fascist regimes; it therefore could not support an authoritarian regime. The repressive measures against resistance members stimulated world opinion not only against the Greek government but also against the United States foreign policy that supported the Greek government.[43] The regime in Greece could not become an authoritarian one; the democratic facade had to be preserved. This explains the fact that the KKE and EAM were not outlawed until December 1947. More concerned about international and domestic criticism than the respect of civil liberties, U. S. policymakers in the Civil War were tracing the boundaries between authoritarianism and democracy, and Greece soon became to be regarded as a case of nation-state rebuilding.[44]

The United States was determined that there should be no reconciliation with the Democratic Army of Greece (the guerillas). There should be no room for political compromise with the belligerents, and the only solution should be a military one, namely the defeat of the Democratic Army of Greece on the battlefield. The policy of nonreconciliation was fully endorsed by the right wing and army officers in Greece, but the United States's goal was the unity of the political establishment vis-á-vis the communists. That was attained by the formation of a coalition government under the premiership of Themistocles Sofoulis in September 1947, which put an end in the old feud between Populists and Liberals. In the meantime, economic and, mainly, military aid was pouring into Greece. Together with military personnel and advisors (the United States Army Group Greece and, later, the Joint United States Military Advisory and Planning Group), enormous resources were allocated to Greece: between 1947 and 1949 about $345.5 million in military grant funds was channeled to Greece. Thanks to military aid, army manpower also skyrocketed. From 98,200 men in December 1946, the army swelled to 130,000 after one year, reaching 147,000 in 1948.[45] Moreover, the army was backed by another 100,000 men, half of whom belonged to the National Defense Corps (into which the rightist terrorist bands had been amalgamated)[46] and the rest to the gendarmerie, the air force, and the navy. No comparison can be made with the Democratic Army of Greece, which at its peak had 26,000 men and women.

Although skirmishes or, in some cases, bitter fights between leftist armed groups and gendarmes or the army had started in the spring of 1946, only in the fall of 1947 did they become a full-scale civil war. The government, backed by the British and the U.S., from the beginning had adopted a policy of nonreconciliation with the guerillas. The appointment of fervent anticommunists to critical ministries deepened the polarization. Napoleon Zervas, for instance, leader of the EDES (the main rival of the EAM) during the occupation, was minister of Public Order from January to August 1947. Zervas' policy towards the Left was adamant: "We will answer terrorism with terrorism ten times as strong, disaster with disaster ten times as strong, and slaughter ten times greater."[47] During his tenure he had many opportunities to implement his policy. In July 1947, between 9,000 and 14,000 citizens were arrested and deported to islands on the grounds of a fictitious plot for insurrection in the cities.[48] After all this, a small wonder that the new Sofoulis cabinet's September 1947 offer of amnesty to guerillas who would lay down their arms fell on deaf ears.

The polarization that finally resulted in full-scale civil war and the government's resolute avoidance of any political solution were mirrored in the introduction of increasingly strict legislation. Two and a half months after the elections, on 18 June 1946, Tsaldaris' cabinet passed Resolution 3, "on extraordinary measures concerning the public order and security." According to Resolution 3, anyone who "aimed to detach part of the whole of the country or assisted plans of the aforementioned aim, conspired or incited rebellion or came to an understanding with foreigners or organized armed groups or participated in such treasonous leagues" was sentenced to death. The death sentence was also passed against those who organized groups with a view to assail the authorities by the use of force, as well as those involved in individual and collective armed attacks against the authorities. In addition, anyone who was preparing to commit these crimes or was propagating ideas that encouraged them could be sentenced to life imprisonment. The same resolution heavily penalized participation in illegal rallies and strikes in public corporations without prior notice to the employer, among other offenses.[49]

The novelty that accompanied Resolution 3, introduced by the government two days later, was the establishment of special courts-martial in the whole of central and northern Greece (Macedonia, Thrace, Thessaly, and Epirus). They were responsible for judging all cases concerning breaches of Resolution 3. Gradually, special courts-martial would be set up all over the country.[50]

Special courts-martial became notorious for their severity and their willingness to pass the heaviest of sentences. Some evidence of this severity is provided by the archives of the Ministry of Justice, where there is a large number of reports on decrees (total 11,545) of special courts-martial from 1946 to 1949. Out of 7,771 convicted persons, 1,185 (15 percent) were sentenced up to one year of imprisonment, 1,956 (25 percent) were sentenced to one to ten years, 1,290 (17 percent) from ten to twenty years, 1,309 (17 percent) to life, and 2,031 (26 percent) to death, which means one out four convicted individuals was sentenced to death.[51] Though it is certain that the vast majority of political prisoners condemned to death were convicted by special courts-martial and the rest by civil courts, precise figures are lacking. Neither it is easy to estimate the total number of death sentences. British sources claim that in 1950 there were 4,500 political prisoners in jail sentenced to death (1,700–2,000 by civil courts and 2,500–3,000 by special courts-martial).[52] According to the Ministry of War, from 1946 to 1949 out of a total of 36,920 persons court-martialed, 4,849 were sentenced to death.[53] However, for obvious reasons the last figure is too low; a total number of at least 8,000 death sentences from 1946 to 1949 is perhaps closer to the reality.[54]

Between June 1946 and December 1947 a series of laws were passed that, among other things, provided for the dismissal of civil servants who supported the guerillas and the banishment of the relatives of army officers who left the army to join the guerillas. The circulation of newspapers and reviews that supported the guerillas was banned, and Greeks living abroad who "acted antinationally" were stripped of their Greek nationality. Moreover, in December 1947 a law was passed prohibiting any strike in the public or private sector (due to the uproar it stirred, the law would be repealed in March 1948).[55]

The formation of the Provisional Democratic Government on 24 December 1947 would be the decisive rupture between the KKE and the government, and would provide the government with the opportunity to enact a very severe legislative framework. Of these laws, two deserve special attention. The first, is Emergency Law 516 of 1948, which introduced "loyalty certificates." Anyone who wished to apply for a job or already worked in the public sector was examined by a "loyalty board" for his or her political beliefs and was required to sign a declaration of his or her loyalty. All those who were "animated by antinational opinions or propagate[d] by any means whatsoever for the Communist Party" were labeled "disloyal" and were fired.[56] Although loyalty certificates had been introduced earlier by the Metaxas dictatorship, the postwar loyalty law was strikingly similar to its U.S. counterpart, the Loyalty Program of the Truman administration. Executive Order 9835 of 22 March 1947, known as the Loyalty Order, was the beginning of the purge from the federal civil service of any "disloyal" employees. The concept of "disloyalty" was not clarified but could include those who were members or had any "sympathetic association" with "totalitarian, Fascist, Communist or subversive" organizations. Loyalty Boards were established to carry out the screening of federal employees. Moreover, the Taft-Hartley Act of 1947 required trade union officials to sign loyalty oaths, that is, affidavits renouncing communism.[57]

The second law, which characterized the era and would mark the political life of Greece for the following decades, was Emergency Law 509, "on security measures of the State, the constitution, the social regime and protection of citizens' liberties." It was passed on 27 December 1947, three days after the formation of the guerillas' Provisional Democratic Government. The law banned the KKE, the EAM, and any other party that was involved in the "treasonous insurrection against the integrity of the Country". The same law punished anyone "aiming at the implementation of ideas that overtly intend to overthrow by violent means the Constitution, the existing social system or to detach a part from the whole of the country" with heavy penalties, even the death sentence. It also prohibited rallies of such persons and the propagation of "communist principles," and provided for the dismissal of civil servants and the cashiering of officers, and stipulated that responsibility for the trial of the above-mentioned offences lay with the special courts-martial.[58] To Karl Rankin, chargé d'affaires at the U.S. Embassy in Athens, it was evident that "there should be a long period of peace, relative economic stability, and education [*sic*] before Communism is again permitted legal existence in Greece."[59] In fact a very long period elapsed: it was not until 1974, when the Communist Party became legal again. Greece became the first country of the postwar "Free world" in which the Communist Party was outlawed, but not the only one; in the 1950s the Communist parties of the United States and West Germany were also banned.[60]

Within this legislative and political context the number of political prisoners reached its climax. In September 1947, according to a report of the Communist Party, 19,620 political prisoners were in jail and 36,948 in exile, including 12,000 soldiers and officers in the Makronisos camps. In May 1948, according to British sources, 21,853 people were in prisons (66 percent of whom were classified as left-wing), 10,365 in exile, and 15,242 at the Makronisos camps. By the end of the Civil War, in September 1949, according to the Greek government there were 18,000 political prisoners and 31,400 persons (civilians and soldiers) at Makronisos and other camps; almost one year later, in August 1950, there were 18,816 political prisoners, 3,406 exiles, and 4,641 soldiers and officers detained at the camps on the island of Makronisos.[61]

At any given moment from 1947 to 1949, between 40,000 and 50,000 individuals were interned in prisons and camps. It is not possible to estimate the total number of persons who spent a term in prison or exile for political reasons, but it is by far larger than the number of political prisoners under the two dictatorships, that of Metaxas and that of the colonels' junta (1967-1974).[62] In general, the measures that the government took against the leftists went well beyond political repression, which, according to one definition, refers to government acts of discrimination against persons or organizations because of their perceived political beliefs.[63] In the Civil War, however, political repression culminated in political exclusion. Political exclusion means that individuals were deprived of their civil rights because of their political beliefs, and political organizations were banned from any participation in the political life on the basis of their professed ideas. During the Greek Civil War, leftists, and even their relatives, were deported or imprisoned, were fired from their jobs, had their property confiscated, or were deprived of their Greek nationality. The Communist Party and a number of leftist organizations were outlawed, and their press was banned. What is even more interesting is that at the time, the political exclusion was disguised and was never presented as such. The concerted enterprise of military, police, and judicial authorities against leftist individuals and organizations was framed as a campaign in defense of the nation.

The Elusive Subject

If today we use the term political prisoners to refer to individuals who have been incarcerated for political reasons, this does not necessarily mean that these individuals were seen and described in the same way by their contemporaries. In other words, categories are historically conditioned and should never be taken for granted. Framing and categorizing seldom go undisputed and unchallenged. Who names what and whom is of paramount importance in the construction of categories and the analysis of subjects. The category of political prisoners will be under scrutiny in this chapter. I will argue that political prisoners in the Civil War years constituted an elusive subject because they were never recognized as such by the government and the law. Rather, they were prisoners who referred to themselves and sought to be recognized as political prisoners.

My starting point will be the legislation because it provides insight into the legal status of political prisoners. The political prisoners in Greece between 1945 and 1950 may be placed in four different categories. In the first category were the political exiles, individuals who were banished, mostly to islands, following decrees of the public security committees (although some were banished following decrees of courts), and who were under the jurisdiction of the Ministry of Public Order. The second category included political prisoners convicted of common crimes during the occupation and the *Dekemvriana*, were sentenced by civil courts and were under the jurisdiction of the Ministry of Justice. In the third category were individuals who were convicted of offenses against the state, as they were defined by the emergency laws passed in 1946 and afterwards, and sentenced by special courts-martial (the judicial section of the Ministry of War presided over these trials). Finally, the fourth category—the most obscure from a legal point of view—comprised soldiers and army officers interned for reindoctrination at the camps on the island of Makronisos, and were under the jurisdiction of the Army and the Ministry of War.[64]

None of the prisoners in the categories above was ever recognized by the government as a political prisoner. In fact, during the Civil War the government repeatedly declared that there were no political prisoners in Greece. To use the words of the Michael Ailianos, Minister for Press and Information: "The Greek Government denies, once again, that there have been any executions for political crimes. It also emphatically denies that there any individuals of the above category detained in prisons."[65] And since these crimes were not political but common crimes, the government declined to intervene on the prisoners' behalf because to "interfere with the Judicial Authority by suspending or canceling decisions … would amount to assuming dictatorial powers."[66]

The government took advantage of the fact that there was a gap in the law with regard to political crime and the treatment of political prisoners. Greek penal law did not define political crime. It did distinguish between a simple political crime and a complex one (the combination of a political and a common crime). For simple political crimes there were certain special provisions: the possibility of granting amnesty, the interruption of detention, and the abolition of the death penalty; (however, no such provisions were made for complex crimes).[67] At any rate, since there was no definition of political crime, it was left to the courts to decide whether a crime was political or not. The differences in the ways Greek jurisprudence dealt with political crime reflect not only the general legal difficulties of defining what a political crime is, but also, as one scholar has argued, the submission of the legislature to the executive.[68] However, the question remains: what was the crime that most political prisoners were charged with?

The vast majority of political prisoners were convicted for violating emergency laws, Resolution 3 and Law 509 in particular. The crime that Law 509 punished—namely, the implementation of ideas that aim at overthrowing the regime or detaching part from the whole of the country—had its origin in the interwar years. From this point of view, the continuity in Greek legislation is striking. The law of 1929 as well as the laws of 1936 and 1938 under Metaxas' dictatorship punished exactly the same crime. Offenders were those who *aimed* at the implementation of ideas inimical to the status quo. The legislation punished ideas and intentions rather than acts. However, the remark Otto Kirchheimer made on postwar anticommunist legislation will help me to illuminate the second feature I plan to discuss.[69] The correlation of external and internal security as it was formulated in Greek laws from 1929 to 1947, specified as political crime any attempt to "overthrow the existing social system" *or* to "detach part of the whole of the country." The latter was related to the thesis of the KKE in 1924 for an autonomous Macedonian state in the framework of a Balkan confederation; despite the fact that this thesis had been changed by 1935 (to equal rights for the minorities living in Greece), legislation in the Civil War continued to identify the revolution with separatist aims.

Equally interesting is how this crime was framed. The Greek Penal Code had a special section on high treason. The crimes that article 123 of the Penal

Code deemed high treason punishable by death included, among others, changing the existing regime with the use of violent means (par. 2) and the detachment of part from the whole of the country (par. 4). Finally, according to article 125 of the Penal Code, instigation to civil war and the formation of armed bands were deemed crimes of high treason.[70] In the same vein, Resolution 3 punished with death those who "conspired or incited rebellion or came to an understanding with foreigners or organized armed groups" with a view to detach a part from the whole of Greek territory.

The idea of high treason overshadowed any political motivation. The image that the legislation constructed of the communist and the political prisoner was that of both the adversary of the existing social order, and a menace to the territorial integrity of the country. In the dominant discourse communists were not political opponents but enemies of the country who, in alliance with neighboring socialist countries, plotted against the territorial integrity of Greece. The political crime was transformed into a crime against the nation, and, therefore, the division was no longer between the Left and the Right, but between the "traitors" or "EAM-Bulgarians" and the *ethnikofrones* (national-minded). Just as *ethnikofrosyni* (national conviction) became the principal element of the post-Civil War dominant ideology, communists were depicted as completely alien to the nation.[71] Thus, it is not surprising that in the 1950s many of the KKE cadres who secretly entered Greece through the "iron curtain" and were arrested, were convicted of espionage under Emergency Law 375.

In the way that the government never recognized that there was a Civil War and commonly referred to it as a "bandit war," in the same way it did not recognize its prisoners as political prisoners. For the government, all persons in jail were common prisoners, bandits, and murderers. It was the prisoners themselves who claimed their status as political prisoners, or rather as political detainees. In the Greek language, the term "political prisoner" does not exist, and the term "political convict" (*politikos katadikos*) gave way to "political detainee" (*politikos kratoumenos*), which is used as an equivalent of political prisoner. The term political detainee is probably a remnant of the interwar years, when the majority of political prisoners were imprisoned following decrees of public security committees, not of courts. Although there was not any form of *custodia honesta* in Greece, and there was no actual difference between the penalties of detention and imprisonment, the penalty of detention was designated for criminals who did not have base motives.[72] However, given the vagueness that the term "detention" denotes—it could arrest, confinement while awaiting trial, or sentence without a trial (in the case of exiles)—it was prioritized as a generic term by the prisoners because it equated convicted and non-convicted individuals alike as victims of a politically motivated and unjust persecution.

In their memoranda and appeals from prisons, political prisoners describe themselves as political exiles, political detainees, people's fighters, imprisoned fighters, or National Resistance fighters. They underline that they were persecuted because they were members of the resistance, and because "their only crime was their love for Freedom and Independence."[73] The participation of the political prisoners in the resistance, and their achievements or suffering during the occupation, are common currency among Greek political prisoners. In other words, prisoners' identity as "National Resistance fighters" is prerequisite for their recognition as political prisoners. A resistance fighter during the occupation, unjustly persecuted and imprisoned after the liberation: such is the profile political prisoners put forward for themselves.

The concept of the injustice of their persecution and imprisonment is particularly important because it was related to their current status as prisoners and their demand for release. From this viewpoint, political prisoners' biographical notes published at the time in newspapers and books are revealing. These notes give a full account of political prisoners' life stories up to 1944, but almost nothing about their activities after the liberation—whether, for instance, they had joined the Democratic Army or not. If they were charged with a murder committed during the occupation, it was always the murder of a collaborator or a Security Battalionist.[74] Nevertheless, a great number of prisoners were persecuted and imprisoned for crimes after the liberation. If a story is not one of obviously unjust persecution (and undoubtedly there were thousands of those), then again silence is interposed. This silence safeguards the profile of the political prisoners from potential negative connotations and incrimination from their active participation in the Civil War.

For the Civil War prisoners, their recognition as political prisoners was important not just for their identity alone. It could also lead to a substantial improvement of their living conditions in prisons and camps. Prisoners and exiles lived under a strict regime; for any violation of prison rules they could be court-martialed, and their rights (visits, correspondence, etc.) arbitrary suspended or curtailed. Political prisoners could enjoy certain privileges, although these were not sanctioned and were extended in the discretion of the administration. Among such privileges were that political prisoners' correspondence with their families should not be censored, they should not be obliged to work, they should freely circulate in the yard, and that they should be allowed to read books and newspapers.[75]

Of the sanctioned privileges, the most important were two: the abolition of death penalty for political crimes and the eligibility for amnesty. And in fact, political prisoners' campaigns after the end of the Civil War and the cessation of executions focused on the demand for general amnesty. The government, of course, turned a deaf ear. Apart from political considerations, granting amnesty would mean that the government recognized them as political prisoners. Instead, the government offered them the opportunity to have their cases reviewed—and indeed, death and long-term prison sentences decreed by special courts-martial were considerably reduced after review. But the question of general amnesty and the unconditional release of political prisoners was connected with one other critical issue: political prisoners who wanted to mitigate their position before the review court or political exiles who wanted to be released they had to sign declarations of repentance. For political prisoners, declarations of repentance were the token that "the government punished not the offenders of any specific law but its political opponents."[76] Declarations of repentance, as we shall see in the next chapter, mirrored more than the underpinnings of politically motivated (in)justice. They encapsulated the conflict of loyalties and multiple exclusions generated by Civil War.

Notes

1. Giannis Kordatos, *Ta simerina provlimata tou ellinikou laou* (Athens, 1945), viii.
2. John O. Iatrides, "Greece at the crossroads, 1944-1950," in Iatrides and Wrigley, eds., *Greece at the crossroads*, 1-30.
3. Mazower, *Inside Hitler's Greece*, 314-315.
4. George Alexander, "The Demobilization Crisis of November 1944," in Iatrides, ed., *Greece in the 1940s*, 156-166.
5. FO 371/48247 R1193, Athens to FO, 16 January 1945. See also, John O. Iatrides, *Revolt in Athens: The Greek Communist "Second Round," 1944-1945* (Princeton, 1972); Lars Baerentzen and David H. Close, "The British Defeat of EAM, 1944-1945," in Close, ed., *The Greek Civil War, 1943-1950*, 72-96.
6. For an English translation of the Varkiza agreement, see Heinz Richter, *British Intervention in Greece: From Varkiza to Civil War* (London, 1986), 561-564. The Varkiza agreement was ratified by Emergency Law 119, "granting amnesty to political offenses," *Government Gazette* 31, 14 February 1945.
7. Thanasis Sfikas, *The British Labour Government and the Greek Civil War: The Imperialism of Non-Intervention* (Staffordshire, 1994), 48.
8. Greece was declared eligible for the receipt of UNRRA assistance in September 1944. However, due to the *Dekemvriana* the UNRRA delayed its operations in the country until January 1945. In the meantime the program and the delivery of supplies was under the jurisdiction of the British Commander of Land Forces in Greece, and consequently the UNRRA supplies were a means to exert pressure on the government and the resistance organizations. Discussion of the full responsibility of the UNRRA over the relief supplies started after the signing of the Varkiza agreement and it was decided that the UNRRA would assume complete responsibility on 1 April 1945. An agreement between the UNRRA and the Greek government was signed on 1 March 1945. The agreement stipulated that the Greek government not the UNRRA but was responsible for the distribution

of supplies, which then became a weapon of discrimination against members of resistance organizations. UNRRA aid covered the fields of food distribution, agricultural rehabilitation, clothing, footwear, and medical supplies, as well as welfare and health programs. The mission activities declined after the spring of 1946 and it was officially closed on 30 June 1947. For the UNRRA Mission in Greece, see Woodbridge, *UNRRA*, vol. 2, 94-137. For a discussion on the negative impact of UNRRA aid on the reconstruction of the country: Kofas, *Intervention and Underdevelopment*, 13-37.

9. Stavros Thomadakis, "Stabilization, Development and Government Economic Authority in the 1940s," in Iatrides and Wrigley, eds., *Greece at the Crossroads*, 173-226.
10. *Eleftheri Ellada*, 8 June 1945.
11. See Politikos Synaspismos ton Kommaton tou EAM, *Lefki Vivlos. Paravaseis tis Varkizas (Flevaris-Iounis 1945)* (Athens, 1945). See also Richter, *British Intervention*, 125-176.
12. NARA 868.00/4-3045, Athens to State Department, 30 April 1945.
13. David H. Close, "The Reconstruction of a Right-Wing State," in idem, ed., *The Greek Civil War*, 156-189.
14. *Report of the British Legal Mission to Greece* (London, 1946), 26. For the role of Charles Wickham and the British Police and Prisons Mission, see Mark Mazower, "Policing the Anti-Communist State in Greece, 1922-1974," in *The Policing of Politics in the Twentieth Century*, ed. Mark Mazower (Providence and Oxford, 1997), 129-150.
15. In 1947 there were 26,000 collaborators in prison in Belgium, 24,298 in France and 33,819 in the Netherlands. Three years later, in 1950, there were 6,115, 6,715 and 3,000 respectively. See Luc Huyse, "La reintagrazione dei collaborazionisti in Belgio, Francia e nei Paesi Bassi," *Passato e Presente* 16, no. 44 (1998): 113-126.
16. Nikos Karkanis, *Oi dosilogoi tis katohis* (Athens, 1983), 75; Richter, *The British Intervention*, 138-144. For political justice in post-war Greece, Gabriella Etmektsoglou, "Collaborators and Partisans on Trial: Political Justice in Post-War Greece, 1944-1949," in *Keine "Abrechnung": NS-Verbrechen, Justiz und Gesellschaft in Europa nach 1945*, eds. C. Kuretsidis-Haider and W. Garscha, (Leipzig and Vienna, 1998), 231-256; Mark Mazower, "Three Forms of Political Justice: Greece 1944-1945," in *After the War was over. Reconstructing the Family, Nation, and State in Greece, 1943-1960*, ed. Mark Mazower (Princeton, 2000), 24-41.
17. Eleni Haidia, "Dikes dosilogon Makedonias. Mia proti proseggisi," in, Institute for Balkan Studies, ed., *Macedonia and Thrace, 1941-1944: Occupation, Resistance, Liberation*, (Salonica, 1998), 169-178.
18. Procopis Papastratis, "The Purge of the Greek Civil Service on the Eve of the Civil War," in *Studies in the History of the Greek Civil War, 1945-1949*, eds. Lars Baerentzen, John O. Iatrides, Ole Smith, (Copenhagen, 1987), 41-53. See also, *I komodia tis dikis ton dosilogon*, (Athens, 1945).
19. Eleni Haidia, "The Punishment of Collaborators in Northern Greece, 1945-1946," in Mazower, ed., *After the War*, 42-61; Close in idem, ed., *The Greek Civil War*, 164.
20. Close, *The Origins*, 152; Close in idem, ed., *The Greek Civil War*, 165; Politikos Synaspismos ton Kommaton tou EAM, *Lefki Vivlos*, 27.
21. Not paradoxically, a few years later many of these bands and organizations were recognized by the state as the national resistance organizations. A royal decree on 18 March 1950 named the following among others as "national resistance organizations," (besides the EDES and EKKA), the royalist terrorist organization "X," the terrorist band of Tsaus Anton, and the extreme nationalist and royalist newspaper *Ellinikon Aima* (Greek Blood). See, *Government Gazette* 83, 18 March 1950.
22. *Rizospastis*, 12 February 1946

23. At the end of October 1945, warrants had been issued for the arrest of 117 individuals from rightist bands, but only 67 had been arrested. FO 371/48283 R18317, Athens to FO, 27 October 1945.
24. FO 371/58757 R8293, Athens to FO, Letter of Sir Charles Wickham to the minister of Public Order, 24 April 1946.
25. See Close, *The Origins*, 156.
26. *Report of the British Legal Mission to Greece*, 11, 15.
27. Several ELAS guerillas were accused of collaborating with the occupation forces on the grounds that the victims of certain alleged murders were Greek guerillas in rival resistance organizations. In this sense they assisted the enemy and their offense came under Law 6 "concerning the imposition of penal sanctions on enemy collaborators."
28. In 1939 there were 9,500 prisoners in Greece. See *Sofronistikai pliroforiai* 4, no 1 (1939): 75.
29. *Report of the British Legal Mission to Greece*, 18.
30. Ibid.,15
31. Norman Dodds, Stanley Tiffany, and Leslie Solley, *Tyranny and Terror: The Betrayal of Greece* (New York, 1946), 12.
32. For British pressures on granting amnesty, see FO 371/48282 R16631, Athens to FO, 29 September 1945; FO 371/48282 R16980 Athens to FO, 5 October 1945; FO 371/48282 R17081 Athens to FO, 7 October 1945. These telegrams from the British Ambassador Sir Reginald Leeper to the Foreign Office, seen from a different perspective, are telling of Greek-British relations and British intervention in Greece. The second telegram reads: "I spoke to the Regent this morning on the lines of your telegram under reference. I told him that I had given Admiral Voulgaris [the premier] until Saturday for his final reply about the release of prisoners and asked him to see his Prime Minister this evening. He is doing so. ... *They also know that without adapting themselves to British wishes Greece is lost*" (my emphasis).
33. Emergency Law 753, *Government Gazette* 311, 21 December 1945.
34. The prison population in Greece was 17,000 prisoners on 1 January 1946, 15,500 on 1 February, and 14,500 on 1 March. FO 371/58780 R5162, Athens to FO, 1 April 1946, NARA 868.00/5-2346, Athens to Secretary of State, 23 May 1946.
35. Emergency Law 265, *Government Gazette* 86, 31 March 1945, articles 1 and 2.
36. Alivizatos, *Oi politikoi thesmoi*, 496-499. Emergency Law 453 reenacted the Law of 1871 against banditry with the penalty of administrative banishment and also allowed heavy penalties (even the death sentence) for the organization of armed groups. It is interesting that the law did not clarify the political orientation of the armed group as Resolution 3 did (see below), and perhaps for that reason nobody was sentenced to death under that law during the Civil War. Nonetheless, because it reintroduced "administrative banishment" it remained in force for the next eighteen years. See, *Government Gazette*, 180, 10 July 1945, and also Koundouros, *I asfaleia*, 131.
37. George Alexander, *The Prelude to Truman Doctrine. British Policy in Greece, 1944-1947*, (Oxford, 1982), 118-119, 143-144, 189-190.
38. The topic of the decisions of the Second Plenum in February 1946 remains even today one of the most controversial in the study of the Greek Civil War. See, Heinz Richter, "The Second Plenum of the Central Committee of the KKE and the Decision for Civil War: A Reappraisal," and Ole Smith, "Self-Defence and Communist Policy," in Baerentzen, Iatrides, Smith, eds., *Studies in the History*, 159-178, 179-187; Ole Smith, "Communist Perception, Strategy and Tactics, 1945-1949," in Iatrides and Wrigley, eds., *Greece at the Crossroads*, 90-121; Charis Vlavianos, *Greece 1941-49: From Resistance to Civil War*, (Basingstroke, 1992), 171-188.

39. Giorgos Margaritis argues that the combination of political and military means reflected the bifurcation of the social basis of the Communist Party. The cities, Athens in particular, did not suffer from the "white terror" and were the main recipients of the foreign aid and that oriented the party members towards the political legality and struggles for fair distribution of the foreign aid. The party members in the countryside facing the "white terror" and destitution (they were cut off from the UNRRA supplies) were left with very few choices other than taking up the arms. For Margaritis, "in the Greek Civil War only the half of the KKE, the half of the Left was involved, while the other half remained distanced." Giorgos Margaritis, *Istoria tou ellinikou Emfyliou Polemou, 1946-1949* (Athens, 2001), vol. 1, 152, 205-212.
40. Elias Nikolakopoulos, *Kommata kai vouleftikes ekloges stin Ellada, 1946-1964* (Athens, 1985), 120-155; George Mavrogordatos, "The 1946 Election and Plebiscite: Prelude to Civil War," in, Iatrides, ed., *Greece in the 1940s*, 181-194. It is noteworthy that voting in Greece is obligatory, so the voting booklet became a token of one's political views and facilitated the tracking down of leftists who had abstained from the elections. For the electoral rigging, see Politikos Synaspismos ton Kommaton tou EAM, *Mavri Vivlos. To eklogiko praxikopima tis 31 Marti 1946* (Athens, 1946).
41. Lawrence Wittner, *American Intervention in Greece, 1943-1949* (New York, 1982), 64-69; Howard Jones, *"A New Kind of War": America's Global Strategy and the Truman Doctrine in Greece* (New York and Oxford, 1989), 30-35.
42. Cited in Jones, *"A New Kind of War,"* 240.
43. Van Coufoudakis, "The United States, the United Nations and the Greek Question, 1946-1952," in Iatrides, ed., *Greece in the 1940s*, 275-297; Wittner, *American Intervention*, 145-148, 155-158.
44. In a 1952 essay entitled "The Reconstruction of Greece: An American Experiment inAdministration," J. P. Maynard, former member of the American Aid Mission to Greece (AMAG), asserted that the Greek experience was important because of "lessons for the administrators of a future 'Greece,' Korea, or any other war-plagued nation that might need, in a hurry, to be saved from Communism." Cited in Jones, *"A New Kind of War,"* 233-234.
45. Close, *The Origins*, 200, 216; Jones, *"A New Kind of War,"* 106; Wittner, *American Intervention*, 233; Michael Mark Amen, *American Foreign Policy in Greece 1944/1949. Economic, Military and Institutional Aspects* (Frankfurt a. M., 1978), 166, 173.
46. In October 1946 the government decided upon the formation of paramilitary units. These were called MAY (*Monades Asfaleias Ypaithrou*, Country Security Units) and MAD (*Monades Asfaleias Dimosyntiritoi*, Municipal Security Units) and incorporated the rightist bands. In September 1947, they were changed into *Tagmata Ethnofrouras* (the National Defense Corps) and operated in close connection with the army. In November 1947 there were forty such battalions and in June 1948 there were ninety-eight. See, Dimitrios Zafeiropoulos, *O antisymmoriakos agon 1945-1949* (Athens, 1956), 83-84, 101-104.
47. Frank Smothers, William Hardy McNeill, and Elizabeth Darbishire McNeill, *Report on the Greeks: Findings of a Twentieth Century Fund Team which Surveyed Conditions in Greece in 1947*, (New York, 1948), 32.
48. NARA 868.00/7-1047, Athens to Secretary of State, 10 July 1947; Wittner, *American Intervention*, 138-139.
49. Resolution 3, *Government Gazette* 197, 18 June 1946, articles 1-8.
50. Konstantinos Oikonomopoulos, *Ektakta stratodikeia kai nomothesia aforosa tin dimosian taxin kai asfaleian* (Athens, 1951), 5-8.
51. Archives of the Ministry of Justice, Anafores apofaseon ektakton stratodikeion (Register of decrees of special courts-martial). These reports were sent from the "local" special

courts-martial (there is a small number from "divisional" courts-martial as well, which are not included in my sample) to the Ministry of Justice/Department of Criminal Affairs. They mainly cover north and central Greece (and occasionally Chania, Mytilene, and Theva), but they are not complete as they lack reports from major cities (like Athens and Salonica). One has to notice that in this sample the overwhelming majority of the persons who stood trial were men: 10,019, or 87 percent of the total.

52. FO 371/87668 RG10113/5, Athens to FO, 9 February 1950
53. NARA 868.00/11-949, Athens to Secretary of State, 9 November 1949.
54. If 4,500 prisoners had been sentenced to death by 1950 and during the Civil War at least 3,411 political prisoners were executed, then at least 7,911 political prisoners were sentenced to death. For the executions, see chapter 7.
55. Resolution 9, *Government Gazette* 51, 28 August 1946; Law 98, *Government Gazette* 284, 17 September 1946; Resolution 31, *Government Gazette* 221, 17 October 1947; Resolution 32, *Government Gazette* 224, 22 October 1947; Resolution 37, *Government Gazette* 267, 7 December 1947; Resolution 39, *Government Gazette* 268, 7 December 1947. Wittner, *American Intervention*, 208-210.
56. Emergency Law 516, *Government Gazette* 6, 8 January 1948, articles 1 par. 1; 2 par. 1; 4 pars. 1 and 3. For a discussion on the notion of "loyalty" and the relation between "loyalty" and law, as it was defined in Civil War legislation, see Giannis Drosos, *Dokimio ellinikis syntagmatikis theorias* (Athens, 1996), 373-389. A sample of the questionnaire they had to fill in to obtain a loyalty certificate was published in the press. Among the questions were the following: whether they were members of resistance organizations, whether they propagated directly or indirectly in favor of those organizations, and whether they condemned the communism. See *To Vima*, 5 May 1948.
57. Minas Samatas, "Greek McCarthyism: A Comparative Assessment of Greek Post-Civil War Repressive Anticommunism and the U.S. Truman-McCarthy Era," *Journal of the Hellenic Diaspora* 13, nos. 3-4 (1986): 5-76; Alivizatos, *Oi politikoi thesmoi*, 479-487; David Caute, *The Great Fear: The Anticommunist Purge under Truman and Eisenhower* (London, 1978), 349-359; M. J. Heale, *American Anticommunism: Combating the Enemy Within 1830-1970*, (Baltimore, 1990), 138.
58. Emergency Law 509, *Government Gazette* 293, 27 December 1947. See Alivizatos, *Oi politikoi thesmoi*, 511-523.
59. NARA 868.00/5-1548, Athens to Secretary of State, 15 May 1948.
60. The Communist Party of the United States was outlawed in 1954 and the German Communist Party in 1956. Both the German Communist Party and, prior to it, the neo-Nazi Socialist Reich Party in 1952, had been outlawed pursuant the same article 21 of the Basic Law (*Grundgesetz*) of the Federal Republic of Germany, which is interesting because it punished ideas and intentions, not acts. Article 21 read, "Parties which, according to their *aims* and the *behavior* of their members, *seek* to impair or abolish the free and democratic order or to jeopardize the existence of the Federal Republic of Germany, shall be unconstitutional" (my emphasis). Cited in Ingraham, *Political Crime*, 268-269.
61. ASKI, box 425 F25/5/105; FO 371/72317 R8119, British Police and Prisons Mission report, 30 June 1948; NARA 868.00/6-248, Athens to Department of State, The Greek "concentration" camp at Makronisos, 2 June, 1948; NARA 868.00/9-649, Athens to Department of State, Translation of Pipinelis' memorandum on amnesty, 6 September 1949, FO 371/87668 RG10113/28, Athens to FO, Figures of political prisoners in Greece, 1 September 1950.
62. For the Metaxas' dictatorship see above, chapter 2. During the colonels' dictatorship about 10,000 people were banished and 1,700 were sentenced to various prison terms

for political reasons. See Koundouros, *I Asfaleia*, 23-27, Alivizatos, *Oi politikoi thesmoi*, 605-606.
63. Robert J. Goldstein, "Political Repression in Modern American History (1870-present): A Selected Bibliography," *Labor History* 32, no. 4 (1991): 526-550.
64. See below, chapter 5.
65. FO 371/72354 R6123, Athens to FO, copy of the minister's statement to the foreign press correspondents, 14 May 1948.
66. FO 371/72355 R10822, Athens to FO, copy of the minister's letter to Mr. Vincent Tewson, General Secretary, Trade Union Congress, 11 September 1948.
67. Konstantinos Kostis, *Ermineia tou en Elladi ishyontos Poinikou Nomou*, (Athens, 1928), vol. 2, 15, 21-26. For a discussion of the different theories on political crime and Greek jurisprudence, Andreas Loverdos, *Gia tin tromokratia kai to politiko egklima*, (Athens, 1987), chapters 6 and 7.
68. Loverdos, *Gia tin tromokratia*, 189-191.
69. Kirchheimer, *Political Justice*, 41.
70. Kostis, *Ermineia*, 26-28, 43.
71. Constantine Tsoucalas, "The Ideological Impact of the Civil War," in Iatrides, ed., *Greece in the 1940s*, 319-341.
72. Karanikas, *Sofronistiki*, 344.
73. Memorandum of Greek women detained at the Averof prison, in *Ta thymata tou monarchofasismou kataggeloun*, (n.p., 1951), 77.
74. See the biographical notes of fifty-six political prisoners who were executed, in *Matomeni Vivlos* (n.p., 1949), 113-123.
75. Georgios A. Katopodis, *Fylaki. Esoteriki leitourgia, sofronistiki metaheirisis*, (Athens, 1947), 110-111.
76. Memorandum of political exiles at Ai Stratis, in *Ta thymata*, 63.

Chapter 4

Emblems of the Civil War
Declarations of Repentance

> The undersigned Eftychia K. … I state that during the December rebellion I was misguided into the EAM organization by deceptive words without knowing of its antinational activities and its treasonous and destructive actions against my Motherland. I renounce the organization as the enemy of my Motherland, by whose side I stand. Moreover, I pledge the quick extermination of the bandits.[1]

This declaration of repentance (*dilosi metanoias*) was one of hundreds published in newspapers during the Civil War. After arrests, at trials, and during imprisonment, the authorities repeatedly asked detainees to recant their political views and to sign a declaration of repentance. It was almost the *sine qua non* for the release of a political prisoner. Declarations of repentance were tokens of political exclusion: those who did not sign one were excluded. More to the point, for the authorities the renunciation of leftist ideas through conversion was a way to construct a passive consensus in support of the regime, to deconstruct the individual, and to liquidate political prisoners' community. For the political prisoners, the declaration of repentance was experienced as self-negation associated with their condemnation by the Communist Party. Declarations of repentance occupy an emblematic position in the study of the Greek Civil War: then, they represented the only alternative to the political exclusion undergone by political detainees, and now they provide us with the opportunity to scrutinize the articulation between, on the one hand, the declaration of repentance as a technology of conversion and, on the other, its implications for subjectivity.

Declarations of repentance —that is, the renunciation of the political beliefs under prohibition—and their consequences for political prisoners (release from exile or a lighter sentence, for instance) demonstrated that political ideas rather than acts were under persecution and revealed an often neglected side of political exclusion. Political exclusion was in force, and could

Notes for this section begin on page 87.

even become absolute, as long as the detainees were and remained political opponents. But conversion or "repentance" testified that the prisoner was no longer a political opponent; consequently, a gradual inclusion or lifting of exclusion was possible. It was an essential part of the political exclusion strategy that a number of the politically excluded would be reintegrated, provided that they had converted. The differentiated status in prisons and the release of repenters (*dilosies*) demonstrated to the rest of the prisoners that exclusion need not be permanent and in fact was dependent on the prisoner's decision to "repent" of his or her past and be integrated into society.

In the following pages I will first discuss the system of declarations of repentance and its role in political exclusion to argue that the authorities' aims were the liquidation of the opposition (inside and outside prisons) and the deconstruction of political detainees' subjectivity. Then I will examine the views of the Communist Party of Greece, to argue that the condemnation of those who signed declarations of repentance led to a new exclusion, this time the exclusion of the repenters from both the party and the political prisoners' collectivity. At the end, I will discuss the regime's stratagem of publishing of declarations of repentance so as to map the topos of the Left in the public arena.

The Misguided

The system of declarations of repentance was introduced in 1933. Persons convicted under the law of 1929 could be released, after serving one-fourth of their sentence, if they stated that they had repented.[2] Declarations of repentance, however, are associated with Ioannis Metaxas, because they were widely used during his dictatorship. The dictator himself boasted that forty-five thousand individuals had signed such declarations, a figure that should not be taken at face value. The reasons for the introduction of declarations of repentance were clarified by undersecretary of Public Security, Konstantinos Maniadakis:

> The acceptance of declarations in which the Communists denounce their principles has become one of the most important means of combating Communism. ... The acceptance of such declarations aims not so much at the prosecution of the organized Communists, as it does at the smashing of the party's internal cohesion. The declarations of repentance have spread so much confusion among the party members that suspicion and mutual distrust prevail.[3]

From the outset of the introduction of declarations of repentance, the major political objective of the initiative was clear: the weakening of the Communist Party ("smashing of the party's internal cohesion") by discrediting its members as *dilosies*. The authorities' purpose did not change in the postwar era, since these declarations had proved very efficient under Metaxas' dictatorship. One of the reasons for the dissolution of the Communist Party under Metaxas' regime was that a great number of members had been rendered politically inactive after signing declarations of repentance.

The process of declarations of repentance was systematized in the postwar era. A recent study gives a detailed account of the formal procedure of a declaration of repentance.[4] Once a prisoner signed, the director of the prison communicated it to the public prosecutor of appeal. The public prosecutor sent the declaration to the Ministry of Justice, and to the church and the municipal authorities of the prisoner's residence, for it to become public knowledge. Sometimes it was also sent to the local military authorities and the press. The declaration of repentance was followed by a memorandum, a lengthy text, in which the prisoner renounced his or her ideas, which was again sent to those mentioned above. At the same time the public prosecutor was in contact with the prison administration concerning the process of prisoners' repentance. In order to prove that his or her repentance was sincere, the prisoner was required also to help the judicial or police authorities in the prosecution of other individuals by providing any relevant information. The diversity of legal, political, and social institutions interested in the declarations indicated the importance attached to them, the various uses of them, and the close cooperation within the state apparatus on this issue during the Civil War.

In most cases, the recantation of political views was just the beginning of a whole process. The detainees had to state in their declarations, all their collaborators nominally inside and outside the Party, with full details of the identity and residence. The next step was to demonstrate their repentance by deeds (i.e., by public declaration, by lectures, speeches and publications to the press, or by voluntary enlistment in the armed forces).[5] Thus, declarations of repentance were related to the strategy of political exclusion in three different ways. First they demonstrated that conversion was the only alternative to political exclusion. Second, repenters were utilized as police informers and incorporated into the prosecution mechanism. Third, by presenting them as "the misguided who had seen the truth," incorporated them into the propaganda mechanisms of the government.

As the word "repentance" denoted, the regime was ready to "forgive." To forgive what, and why? A declaration of repentance may be considered the counterpart of the religious confession. The individual recognized and confessed his sin and asked for forgiveness. It is well known that in Christian theology, confession refers to a sin committed and the intention to commit a sin alike. For the latter, the notion of intention was the kernel of the confession because it denoted the decision to commit a sin, the interiorization of the responsibility for it.[6]

In the case of recantation of political views in the Civil War, the forgiveness of the intention to commit a sin was founded on the notion of fallacy, which invalidated intention as a conscious decision to commit a sin. The repenters were forgiven because they had not known what they were actually doing, they had not consciously wished to commit the sin (or crime) concerned, and they had been misled by the leadership. By the same token, a separation was being manufactured between the "treasonous" leadership and the "misguided" members. The latter, if they repented, could be pardoned. As Panteleimon, metropolitan bishop of Chios, put it, they were "stray children," who, like the whore in Jerusalem who repented and was then eulogized by Jesus Christ, could be saved.[7] A parallel was drawn between the communists —*miasma* to use a common insult of that time—and the "morally disgusting" whore of the New Testament, who nonetheless could be saved. Thus, internment was a punishment for a sin committed without intention, and declarations of repentance were a chance for the detainees to repent for their unintentional sin and thus be pardoned. It is not surprising that these religious connotations caused a renowned anthropologist to describe the whole procedure of the declaration of repentance as "latter-day secular inquisition."[8]

The religious connotations revealed the major influence of the Greek Orthodox Church in the shaping of nationalist ideology, and spoke for the role of the Church in the Civil War. The Orthodox Church had neither the power nor the influence that the Catholic Church wielded in the Spanish Civil War, yet, like in Spain, it decisively sided with the political establishment. Panteleimon, for instance, had taken the place of Ioakeim in the diocese of Chios; the latter had been prosecuted as an EAM sympathizer. After the liberation, the Church, like any other single institution, was purged of clergymen involved in the resistance: the metropolitan bishops of Kozani Ioakeim, of Heleia Spyridon, of Chalkis Gregorios, among others, were prosecuted or deposed. Chairman of the Holy Synod on 15 March 1945 was the metropolitan bishop of Giannina Spyridon, who in the face of the German invasion had recommended capitulation and drawn up a list of persons suitable for ministerial posts in a collaborationist government.[9] Moreover, clergymen played an important role in the rehabilitation of political prisoners. The Ministry of Justice acknowledged the prisoners' "need for moral cleansing through religious and moral instruction," and for that reason ordered the prison administration to make sure that priests or religion teachers gave lectures once or twice a week.[10]

On the other hand, the religious discourse justified administration's rehabilitative practices. It justified corporal punishment —the body, as the locus of sin, had to suffer so that the soul might be cured. For Father Stylianos Prokopios, who very often preached at the Makronisos camps, the body was destined to suffer in this life, so what was important for the inmates was to save their souls. He compared the Makronisos camps to Siloam's Font, where "thousands of young Greeks were baptized in the gutters of National and Christian values."[11] Also, this discourse, which held a certain "treasonous" leadership separate from the "ignorant" and ready-to-repent masses justified the harsh treatment of the unrepentant, and aimed at turning the inmates against their leaders. Finally, it inculcated individualism: with a declaration of repentance a detainee could save only himself and no one else. The religious connotations of sin and repentance (and *mutatis mutandis* the medical, and hence "scientific," discourse on communism as a disease that might be cured)[12] fell squarely with the promise of inclusion in the national community. Conversion was the only prospect that inmates should envision. No wonder that the church at the Third Battalion at the Makronisos camps was dedicated to Saint Paul, the archetype of conversion.

For the detainees themselves, things were simpler. A declaration of repentance gave them a chance to stop being tortured, to be released if they were in exile, to have a death sentence commuted to life imprisonment, or even to rescue themselves from execution. The importance of declarations of repentance for the future of the political detainee did not wane even after the end of the Civil War. As late as 1951, "the most important factor in the eyes of judges was whether or not the prisoner had made a statement denouncing the KKE," and with regard to the political exiles, "in order to be released, the exile must denounce the KKE in writing and must also submit a detailed account of his crimes and why he is repenting."[13]

For the political detainees the signing of a declaration of repentance was not an easy decision. On the contrary, it was a very painful one because the system of declarations of repentance involved the self-negation of the political detainee. In their statements, repenters presented themselves as misguided, ignorant, and deluded by the leaders and the slogans of the Communist Party —but now, since the truth about its anti-Greek role had been revealed, they were denouncing and renouncing it. The penitentiary and internment, in the case of declarations of repentance, were mechanisms of the production of truth/fault, to use Foucault's terms. The fallacy was the past; the truth was the present. However, inasmuch as past experience is constituent of an individual's identity, renunciation of the past as fallacy distorted self-identity. Declarations of repentance were experienced by the political detainees as self-negation, self-betrayal; they renounced their comrades, their fellow inmates, and themselves.

At the camps on the island of Makronisos declarations of repentance were part of a process of endless and violent degradation. The detained soldiers who under a reign of terror and violence signed such declarations also had to prove their repentance by their deeds. At the Makronisos camps it was not enough to give anticommunist lectures to their colleagues, to send letters to newspapers and the local authorities of their hometowns, and to write articles for the newspapers of the camps. In the end, they had to become tormentors of the unrepentant, to supervise, insult, and beat them. Many *dilosies* became part of the rehabilitative mechanism and surpassed the regular personnel in cruelty. For the administration this was a way to secure that the repentant soldiers had been rehabilitated, or, to put it in other terms, to show that the repenters did not represent a situation in between the authorities and the detainees. Under conditions of violence, terror, and propaganda, the vast majority of the interned soldiers and civilians signed declarations of repentance. In January 1950, according to the director of the Makronisos camps, out of 16,768 interned soldiers and civilians only 1,494 had not signed declarations of repentance.[14]

Declarations of repentance were the outcome not of free will but of torture and terrorization. Such declarations were important to the authorities because they dissolved prisoners' collectivity, deconstructed prisoners' subjectivity, and incorporated the repenters into state mechanisms of propaganda and prosecution. The political prisoner experienced the signing of such declarations as self-negation. It was a violent deconstruction of one's subjectivity, "our humiliation, dishonor and our moral suicide," to use political exiles' own words.[15] The experience of signing a declaration of repentance as self-negation was also fostered by the views of the Communist Party.

The Renegades

The views of the Communist Party on this issue had been clear since the prewar era. Declarations of repentance were condemned, *dilosies* were expelled from the party, and in the case of political prisoners, no longer belonged to their community and were transferred to separate cells. However, during the occupation the party adopted a less strict line. Many *dilosies* started forming resistance groups, while others helped in the reconstruction of the underground party mechanism. The party could not but recognize the situation and accepted the participation in resistance organizations, and even in the party, of "the great majority of dilosies … who regretted bitterly and wish to render their services to the struggle under the party leadership."[16] This was a necessary step because a large number of party members were in jail and the dissolved party mechanism could not be reorganized by the few free and loyal party members. The participation of *dilosies* in resistance organizations revealed the complexity of the problem: the signing of a declaration of repentance did not mean that they belonged politically or ideologically to the opposite camp; rather they were mostly people who signed out of fear, pain, or despair.

After liberation, party discipline had to be restored. The Twelfth Plenum of the party, in June 1945, decided to reexamine the cases of those who had signed declarations of repentance under Metaxas' dictatorship and become party members during the resistance. In October 1945, the seventh congress of the party, characterized declarations of repentance as "apostasy and treason," and decided that "*dilosies* would not be admitted again to the KKE."[17] Party members who had been *dilosies* were suspended, and future *dilosies* were *ipso facto* expelled from the party. The screening of the *dilosies* of Metaxas' era finished in 1947, and the party organizations took over the responsibility of reinstating those "who with their deeds and sacrifices proved that they have again the right and the honor to become members of the KKE." In September 1947, the Third Plenum also discussed again the issue of the *dilosies* after the liberation, but the decision was kept secret.[18] It seems that the reason for the nonpublication of the decision was that a less strict line —perhaps even admission—was adopted after a careful examination of each case in the lower posts of the organizations.[19]

To understand the views of the Communist Party, it is necessary to take a closer look at the two sides of the problem. One was the liquidation of the party mechanism under the Metaxas regime, which constituted the background of these decisions on the issue of declarations. The other was party discipline, or to put it in broader terms, the relation between the individual and the party.

The Communist Party was actually dissolved on the eve of the war, as we have already seen. Under the dictatorship the party went underground, and consequently the secrecy and loyalty of party members were of vital importance to the existence of the party mechanism. The security services needed inside information to smash the party mechanism, and arrested members often provided that information. Moreover, the fact that leading cadres repentance, (like the former deputy Stelios Sklavainas) signed declarations of, while others collaborated closely with the security services (as in the cases of Manoleas and Tyrimos, who formed the phony party leadership known as the "Provisional Administration") spread confusion, distrust, and disappointment among the party rank-and-file.

During the Civil War, many *dilosies* became fervent anticommunists (for example, Makis Dogkas who became the editor of *Scapaneus*, the newspaper published by the army on Makronisos) and helped the police to break up the underground party mechanism. Many tried to mitigate their position by collaborating with the authorities, especially after arrests, while in custody awaiting trial and heavy sentences. After the murderous attack on a Royal Hellenic Air Force bus on 30 April 1947 in Salonica, the police traced and arrested Andreas Papageorgiou as the leader of the group ("self-defense unit") that organized the attack. The subsequent investigation led to the arrest of other suspects, who when, they saw Papageorgiou in custody and under psychological pressure, became informers to the police against any communist they knew. The result was a mass trial, not of the specific group but of sixty-seven persons involved in underground work, by special court-martial on charges of several murders. At the trial, many of the defendants repudiated the Communist Party, showing, as a newspaper reported, "an admirable competition in revealing and confessing." Finally, fifty-two of the accused were sentenced to death.[20] A similar case is that of Stratis Moutsogiannis, who on 1 May 1948 assassinated Minister of Justice Christos Ladas, on the instructions of the party, and was arrested on the spot. Reprisals for the assassination resulted in the execution of one hundred and nine political prisoners within seven days; Moutsogiannis himself escaped execution because he revealed the underground mechanism in Athens.

Laws sanctioned the benefits of collaboration with the authorities. Resolution 29 granted amnesty to surrendered guerilas, and Emergency Law 809 pardoned their offenses if they gave information or any kind of help in the suppression of the guerillas. In addition, Resolution 53 provided for the release of detainees from the Makronisos camps upon decision of the general director.[21] Because a declaration of repentance might be the first step toward closer collaboration between the detainee and the police, the Communist Party soundly considered that such declarations jeopardized its unity and existence.

However, I will not discuss the case of those who collaborated with the authorities and became informers, but of those who only recanted their political beliefs (which almost always included public renunciation in various ways as well) during their arrest, trial, or imprisonment. This distinction corresponds to a certain extent to the one the political prisoners adopted. Only the prisoners who signed a declaration of repentance inside the prison were expelled immediately from the prisoners' collectivity. The cases of those who renounced the party while they were in custody, on trial, or at the Makronisos camps, were individually examined, and often these detainees were accepted into the political prisoners' collectivity, though only in the lower echelons of the informal hierarchy.[22]

Seen from a different point of view, the strict line on the issue of declarations reflected the party's demands of its members: full commitment and absolute dedication. To a large extent the "new type of man" that the party promoted was constructed upon the issue of declarations of repentance, as is evident in a front-page article by the editor of the communist daily *Rizospastis*, Kostas Karagiorgis:

> And the "declarations" are *ten times more* sinful than then [under Metaxas' dictatorship]. Now it is an all or nothing struggle! We are living in a tragic and epic period, when the modern Greek drama is culminating and heading towards its catharsis. The faint-hearted do not have a place near us and will never find a place among us ... There will be no one *unworthy* who will not be able to uphold his views like a *bastion*.[23]

The condemnation of declarations is so clear that it does not need further comment. More interesting is that a distinction was drawn between the brave and the faint-hearted, the worthy and the unworthy. The judgments were moral rather than political. The language of religion was co-opted: declarations, for instance, were not a political mistake but a sin. *Dilosies* were not less politically conscious but faint-hearted. Behind these strong oppositions and dichotomies, the "new type of man" as a way of disciplining human differences was being constructed. The "new type of man" was distinguished by the "conscious, steely discipline" to the party, "courage and honesty, dedication and belief in the party."[24] The party cadres were "engineers of the soul," (to use a famous saying from the communist jargon of the era), who produced disciplined and loyal members. Party discipline became the virtue *par excellence* of the communist.

The power mechanism of party discipline was the answer to the question of the relation between the individual and the collectivity, between subjectivity and the collective subject. The manufacturing of the profile of the communist as a "new type of man," whose main virtues were party discipline and dedication to the cause, was inscribed in the strategy of circumscribing the heterogeneity of the subject and regulating the tension between subjectivity and the subject. On the one hand, party discipline constructed and granted an identity, that of the communist. On the other, it prioritized the collectivity over the individual, requiring the subordination of the individual. The tension of the relation between the individual and the collectivity was transferred into the domain of party authority. Thus, the exclusion was of those who broke party discipline, who questioned the legitimacy of the party as a power mechanism.

Political prisoners did not sign declarations of repentance on political or ideological grounds but on personal grounds. Many times, in cases of torture or terrorization, it was not even a rational decision but an instinctual reaction of self-preservation. Even if they had signed declarations out of fear, pain, or despair, from the party viewpoint signers had prioritized the individual over the collective. Party discipline as a precondition for the existence and unity of the party required political prisoners' conformity and submission to party authority.

However, the situation was complex because many *dilosies* felt attached to the party and their comrades. Even if they had signed declarations of repentance, they later proved that they had not repented at all. Especially after 1949, when the executions had stopped, many *dilosies* withdrew their declarations. Some sent letters to newspapers stating that they had signed a declaration after being severely tortured and now retracted their declaration, while others tried to cross the divide between the repentant and unrepentant inside prisons. At the Akronafplia prison, for instance, 373 prisoners classified as "repentant" were segregated from the 330 "unrepentant." On 16 June 1950, twenty-four repenters pushed the guard "away from the open door of the Communist dormitory and entered. The Director has stated that there are thirty-six more repenters who wish to be transferred to the Left Wing dormitories and who wish to withdraw their declaration of loyalty."[25] Classified and categorized by the authorities and the bureau of the prisoner's collective, but not by themselves, political prisoners transgressed the boundaries and showed the fragility of the dividing lines that separated them.

Though today one is tempted to maintain that *dilosies* represented a place between the authorities and the prisoners' collectivity, during the Civil War there was no such place. The polarization and the conflict of the Civil War demanded that the political camps in conflict expand and secure the domain under control by eliminating anything that might stand between them.

The Public Topos

Why were declarations of repentance published in newspapers? True, it was not only declarations of repentance that were published in newspapers. One may find all kinds of similar statements denying any affiliation to the Communist Party or resistance organizations. To put it in broader terms, why did all kinds of renunciation of the Left find their way into the press? And if we consider the press as a public arena, what was the topos of the Left in that public arena? I will answer the first question by arguing that the publication of declarations of repentance was the moment of evidence and truth. To answer the second question I shall examine the publication of declarations of repentance together with journalistic reports on the violent deaths of guerillas to argue that political exclusion in the Civil War defined the position of the leftist political opposition in the public arena as a nonexistent one. The alternative public topoi for the Left were either incorporation in the state mechanisms (declarations of repentance) or, strictly speaking, nonexistence (death or refuge).

The pages of the newspapers in the Civil War mirrored a highly politicized era where individual political views were a public issue. All sorts of declarations and statements found their way to the press. A father renounced his whole family (his wife, two sons, and one daughter), because it "got out of its destination and it turned against the interests of my country"; meanwhile, there were plenty of letters from individuals who stated "I have never been a communist or member of similar organizations such as EAM, EPON, etc., which collaborate with the Bulgarians and Slavs for the subjugation of my country."[26] After the end of the Civil War, declarations of repentance were withdrawn by many individuals their, like Georgia Koutsonikou, who sent a letter to a newspaper "to be published and make it well known that I retract a declaration they took by violent means."[27] Perhaps even more interesting are declarations of repentance from right-wing individuals published in leftist newspapers in the first years after the liberation, like that of Ioannis Stavropoulos, who discovered the "antipopular" role of the EDES and therefore recanted it, promising to fight for "people's interests."[28] The moment of publication is the moment of evidence. In the case of declarations of repentance, it is also the moment of the revelation of truth, a truth that contrasted past and present and canceled prior views and acts. Publication transformed something into a fact, positive and irreversible. Unlike religious confession, which remained private and secret, political confession required the public as a witness in order to be valid.

A recent study on public recantations in Iran points out their two underlying preconceptions. One is that the external enemy is plotting against the country in collaboration with forces from within the country. This kind of conspiracy theory laid the groundwork for the staging of the Moscow trials in the 1930s and the fabrication of defendants' confessions. Similarly, the declarations of repentance explicitly made the connection between the KKE and the Slav threat from the north. The other preconception is that the audience ignores what precedes public recantations, which seem to have a voluntary character and are associated "with truth, guilt, and redemption and moral conscience —not with torture, coercion, violence and unbridled power."[29] Lambros Kokkas, who served as a soldier on the island of Makronisos, gave a public talk in Igoumenitsa under the title "How I fared on Makronisos," in which he expressed remorse for his past involvement with communism and pride in his newfound commitment to his nation:

> Unfortunately, during the years of triple occupation, misfortune and poverty drove me the wrong way and I was led astray into the hell of communism, for I believed that in this way I might be saved. ... But the Motherland, as she saw my bad past, sent me to the Third Sappers' Battalion, to that National University. ... I am proud, for I've found the way of God and Motherland at this great National University called Makronisos, and I advise every stray Greek to open his eyes and return to the way that leads him to the glory and the grandeur of the Motherland.[30]

The nationalist clichés were more powerful when they were uttered by former opponents who now affirmed the tenets of governmental propaganda. By depicting the Makronisos camps not as a place of torture and terrorization but as a place where the misguided were helped to see the truth and regain their moral integrity, Kokkas made his recantation look voluntary and therefore credible.

These speeches and letters were no longer the voice of the opposition but the voice of the regime. They represented the choice of gradual incorporation into the regime. As for the leftist opposition, there was no place for it in the public arena. Since 1946 all public rallies or meetings of leftist organizations had been prohibited and, since 1947 all leftist newspapers and organizations had been outlawed (except the small Socialist Party SK-ELD and its newspaper *Machi*). All publishing activities of the Communist Party went underground; meanwhile, part of the mechanism was reestablished abroad, in Yugoslavia (notably, as the guerilla radio station "Free Greece").

The topos that the Left occupied in the public arena was that of literal nonexistence, of death. Numerous in the press of that era were the pictures of guerillas' corpses and severed heads, along with detailed reports on executions. The following is an extract from a newspaper report on the execution of four youths, members of the so-called "Chassia band," which had killed a man of the MAY, the auxiliary paramilitary units:

> The salvo of the eighteen rifles is horrifying, the flash of the bullets of the firing squad like lightning almost invisible to the naked eye; there is a white wave of smoke that follows it almost immediately. Nemesis has shot her arrows callously, without mercy, exemplarily. The four convicts lie on the ground amidst a cloud of dust caused by the bullets that pierced their chests and hit the mound behind them. Diamantis is crouched down on Kondylis' body. ... An officer runs and with his revolver gives the coup de grace to each one of them. ... Diamantis is not dead yet. There is a certain weak moan. With the first coup de grâce his body started. The second is right on the head. He is still alive! Nemesis seems to wish to execute him as many times as the court martial sentenced him to death. At last, with the third shot, he is quiet.[31]

Such detailed journalistic reports mark the reemergence of public executions. Even if in the aforementioned case the public was only indirectly present, in many cases it was actually present. The exposition of guerillas' severed heads in town squares became very frequent during the Civil War, and photos of them were often published. On 10 November 1947, the front page of the British newspaper *The Daily Mirror* featured two big photos of the severed heads of two guerillas paraded by armed men through the city of Trikala city, under headline "What are we British doing here?" This front page caused a stir in Britain, and a series of minutes were exchanged between the British Embassy in Athens, the Greek government, and the Foreign Office. According to the head of the British Police and Prisons Mission in Larisa, "Prices were fixed on the heads of these bandits, and following the *usual custom* their heads were removed to be produced when the reward was claimed. ... There is no evidence at all of *any atrocity* having been committed ... there is no *disfigurement* in any of the heads shown." The officer concluded his report by saying that "the whole matter has been grossly exaggerated."[32] The British Embassy held the same view, i.e., that the exhibition of severed heads "is a regular custom in this country which cannot be judged by western European standards."[33] In its attempt to support the Greek government, the embassy brought to the fore an older order of the minister of Public Order, Napoleon Zervas, according to which "adequate photography of the corpse" should replace the practice of "expos[ing] to view the heads, obviously in order to have their identity ascertained."[34]

The practice of decapitating guerillas and exposing their heads in public was not a "usual custom." Decapitation and public display of the heads had been introduced as a form of demonstrating state authority over brigands.

During the nineteenth century many such incidents occurred, there were fewer in the twentieth century, since brigandage had been stamped out in the 1920s.[35] It seems that this practice was reintroduced in the Civil War, although there were isolated incidents during the resistance as well. Moreover, the issue was not the identification of the dead (not even for the soldier or the gendarme who would get the reward). Everyone recognized the two severed heads hanging on a lamppost in the central square of Trikala in June 1945: one belonged to Aris Velouchiotis, one of the legendary three leaders of the ELAS, and the other to his comrade Tzavelas. This act symbolized the ultimate and humiliating punishment of the defeated enemy. The unburied corpse and the exhibited head manifested that the way someone died could be and was a form of punishment. The unburied corpse was a negation of all funeral rituals, and the decapitated corpse was the deletion of the most distinct individual characteristics of a human being. Moreover, because the practice in earlier times was employed against brigands, it associated guerillas with criminals. The British colonial discourse (claiming noninterference in the "barbarous natives'" affairs while at the same time actively backing the Greek government) could not disguise a practice that, to use Nietzsche's words, was punishment as a festival, in the form of violating and mocking the totally defeated enemy.[36]

The reemergence of punishment by death as a public spectacle in the Civil War contradicts Foucault's argument that the birth of the prison signifies the abandonment of punishment as a public spectacle and as a penalty to the body of the convict.[37] In the Civil War, death as a form of punishment is no longer enclosed inside the penitentiary, is no more disguised but overt and direct in order to regain its deterrent and symbolic power. The citizens are the public in this exhibition of power and violence, confirming that state violence becomes highly visible when sovereignty is questioned.[38] The public display of violent death strengthens terrorization by adding cruelty to violence, and semiotically represents the drive of the state to regain the monopoly of violence (a monopoly challenged in the Civil War).

The front-page picture of the corpse of an "inhuman monster", guerilla captain Diamantis, on a piece of wood among soldiers and officers, and the publication of declarations of repentance in the inner pages are interrelated because they represent the two possible topoi for the communists.[39] Whereas the first is the exhibition of the dead body as a form of punishment, the latter is the exhibition of the living truth in the form of confession. Death as punishment and repentance as redemption, the defeat of the dead body and the triumph of the living truth, were not just emblems of violence but also represented *in extremis* the two possible options for the communists: either collaboration with the authorities and incorporation into the regime, or death.

Notes

1. *Acropolis*, 24 December 1947
2. Law 5764, *Government Gazette* 269, 18 September 1933, article 3.
3. Konstantinos Maniadakis' archives, cited in Kousoulas, *Revolution and Defeat*, 132.
4. Dionysis Moschopoulos, "Politikoi kratoumenoi stis fylakes tis Kerkyras, 1947-1949", in *Geia sas adelfia.... Fylakes Kerkyras 1947-1949 - Martyries*, ed. Somateio Lazareto (Athens, 1996), 19-66.
5. NARA 868.00/4-848, Athens to Secretary of State, 8 April 1948. In this telegram there is a copy of an order of the Ministry of Public Order on the "elements and nature of the statements to be signed by the Communists," dated 21 August 1947.
6. Alois Hahn, "Contribution à la sociologie de la confession et autres formes institutionalisées d' aveu: Autothematisation et processus de civilisation," *Actes de la recherche en sciences sociales*, 62-63 (1986): 54-68. Moreover, and this is a hypothesis, one can relate two parallel phenomena that occurred in Europe in the thirteenth century: sacramental confession becoming obligatory, and confession becoming the "queen of proofs" in judicial procedure, which could incorporate torture. It seems that for both ecclesiastical and secular interests, confession became a salient method for the investigation of the individual in the troubled times of new forms of religious dissent. On the relation between confession and torture, see Edward Peters, *Torture* (Philadelphia, 1996), 40-54.
7. Panteleimon, metropolitan bishop of Chios, *O kommounismos* (Athens, 1950), 141-143.
8. Michael Herzfeld, *Portrait of a Greek Imagination: An Ethnographic Biography of Andreas Nenedakis* (Chicago, 1997), 118.
9. *Lefki Vivlos*, 39, 53-54; Richter, *British Intervention*, 141, 160
10. Ypourgeion Dikaiosynis, *Egkyklioi kai ypourgikai apofaseis 1945-1953* (Athens, 1954), 41-43.
11. Lefteris Raftopoulos, *To mikos tis nyhtas. Makronisos '48-'50* (Athens, 1995), 163.
12. Stratis Myrivilis, a famous writer of the time, refered to communism as the "ideological heroin." See his article, "I simaia tis anthropias," *Scapaneus* 4 (25 March 1948): 5
13. NARA 781.001/6-2251, Athens to Department of State, Current status of imprisoned and exiled communists, 22 June 1951.
14. FO 371 RG 87647/1016/6, BMM to Greece, Report on Makronisos, 20 January 1950, Appendix C.
15. *Ta thymata tou monarchofasismou*, 64.
16. Cited in Elefantis, *I epaggelia*, 259-260.
17. Seventh congress, Resolution on declarations, 6 October 1945, in KKE, *Episima Keimena* (Athens, 1987), vol. 6, 127.
18. Third Plenum of the Central Committee of KKE - Resolution on the *dilosies* of the Metaxas' era and the first occupation, published in *Rizospastis* on 8 October 1947, ibid., 248. For the non publication of the decision on the *dilosies* of the Civil War, see *I trichroni epopoiia tou Dimokratikou Stratou Ellados 1946-1949* (Athens, 1998), 259-260.
19. There are several reasons to assume this. The Communist Party had decided to launch a full-scale civil war, and the Democratic Army was in desperate need of new guerillas. In addition, many former *dilosies*, soldiers of the national army, defected to the guerillas. Finally, in prisons, only those who signed declarations of repentance *inside* the prison were expelled from the political prisoners' collectivity, whereas the cases of the rest were closely examined.
20. FO 371/67076 R8968, Salonica to Athens, 1 July 1947; FO 371/67076 R9158, Salonica to Athens, 4 July 1947; FO 371/67078 R13031, Salonica to Athens, 18 September 1947. See also *Kathimerini* from 3 September to 16 September 1947.

21. Resolution 29, *Government Gazette* 197, 14 September 1947, articles 1 and 2; Emergency Law 809, *Government Gazette* 255, 29 September 1948, article 1; Resolution 53, *Government Gazette*, 262, 14 October 1949, article 17, par. 2.
22. See chapter 11.
23. *Rizospastis*, 27 July 1947, original emphasis.
24. Zisis Zografos, "To KKE kai oi 'dilosies,'" *Kommounistiki Epitheorisi*, 41 (September 1945): 19-22.
25. FO 371/87772 R1642, British Police Mission Headquarters, Monthly report (June 1950), 19 July 1950.
26. *Macedonia*, 22 July 1951; *Acropolis*, 20 July 1947.
27. Letter of Georgia Koutsonikou from Makronisos on 28 May 1950, published in *Dimokratikos Typos*, 18 June 1950.
28. *Rizospastis*, 9 July 1946. Declarations of repentance from right-wing individuals published in left-wing newspapers are few. This specific one is interesting because it was sent from the Averof prison, where the sender had been imprisoned for wounding a left-wing bill-poster. It seems that prisons at least until early 1946 were a political "laboratory," and the influence of the Communist party mechanism was not solely confined to leftist prisoners. Another interesting example of this kind of repentance was that of a former torturer. In 1964, Captain Eleftherios Miliadis sent a letter to one of his victims, Panos Kallidonis, who was then writing a book on the Makronisos camps. In that letter Captain Miliadis confessed that he "fell into error." He had been misled by his chief and the political and intellectual elites and had come to believe that he was punishing criminals and serving the national interests. The case of Captain Miliadis, however, is unique. None of the torturers has ever publicly apologized or been brought to trial. The letter was published in Panos Kallidonis, *Makronisos. O Golgothas tis Dimokratias* (Athens, n.d.) and is also cited in, Raftopoulos, *To mikos tis nyhtas*, 211.
29. Ervand Abrahamian, *Tortured Confessions: Prisons and Public Recantations in Modern Iran* (Berkeley, 1999), 8.
30. Lambros Kokkas, "Pos perasa stin Makroniso," *Skapaneus*, 11 (28 November 1948): 20, republication of a speech that originally appeared in the newspaper *Foni tis Thesprotias*, 12 September 1948.
31. *Acropolis*, 30 October 1947.
32. FO 371/67011 R16181, British Police and Prisons Mission, Thessaly High Command to Athens, 22 November 1947 (my emphasis). In the same report, apart from the two pictures already published in the *Daily Mirror*, a third one is enclosed showing eight severed heads of guerilas.
33. FO 371/67011 R15110, Athens to FO, 12 November 1947. The reply of the Foreign Office is equally interesting, exhorting the British Embassy to exert pressure to the Greek government to issue immediately instructions to cease the decapitation of guerilas, not on humanistic grounds but because if these practices "continue to receive publicity in this country, strong pressure may be exercised on us to withdraw military and police missions." FO 371/67011 R15208, FO to Athens, 14 November 1947.
34. FO 371/67011 R15227, Athens to FO, 15 November 1947, Order issued by Napoleon Zervas to Gendarmerie on the 13 May 1947.
35. Mazower, "Policing the Anti-Communist State," 134-137.
36. Friedrich Nietzsche, *On the Genealogy of Morality*, trans. Carol Diethe (Cambridge, 1995), 58.
37. Foucault, *Discipline and Punish*, 8-16.
38. Gatrell, *The Hanging Tree*, 15.
39. *Embros*, 23 June 1949.

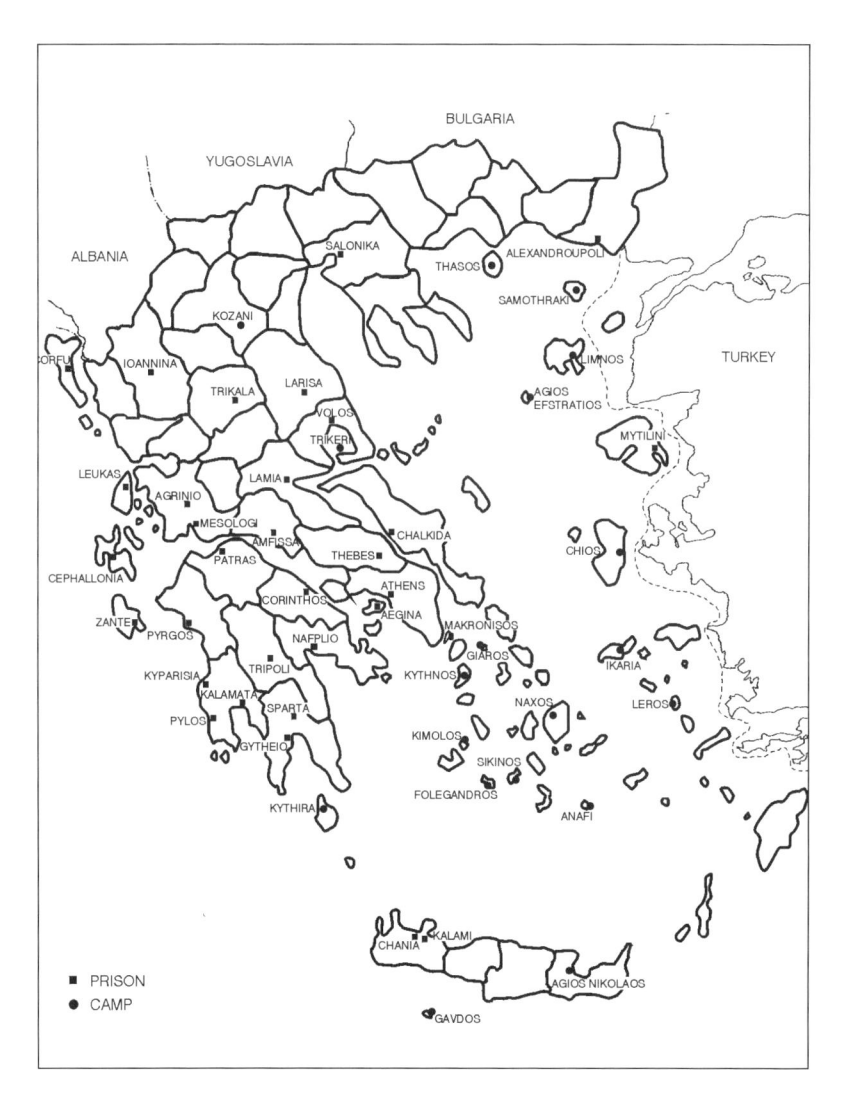

Main prisons and camps during the Greek Civil War, 1945–1950.

Political detainees during transport.
Source: Contemporary Social History Archives.

Father Stylianos Kornaros, conducting a ceremony for the foundation of St. Anthony's Church, First Battalion, Makronisos Island.
Source: Nikos Margaris, private collection.

Camps on Makronisos Island.
Source: Nikos Margaris, private collection.

The prison yard, as it stands abandoned today, Aegina Prison.
Source: Takis Benas's family

Distribution of aid, Agios Efstratios.
Source: Contemporary Social History Archives.

Political prisoners, Giaros, 1948.
Source: Giorgos Christodoulakis, private collection.

Execution of political prisoners.
Source: Contemporary Social History Archives

The heads of three murdered leftists in the central square, Lefkas 1945.
Source: Contemporary Social History Archives

Easter Sunday observance, Itzedin Prison, 1953.
Source: Panagiotis Aronis, private collection

Detained soldiers, Makronisos Island.
Source: Nikos Marzaris, private collection.

Part Two

THE BODY AND THE PSYCHE IN PAIN

Chapter 5

A Confined Life

The situation in prisons throughout Europe after the end of the Second World War was deplorable. Prisons are overcrowded, without sufficient funding, and hygiene conditions were appalling. Prisoners were barely fed, clothed, and medically examined. Italy saw an unprecedented wave of uprisings and riots in prisons throughout the country from 1945 to 1946. The demands were "more and better food, better living conditions, quicker trials and less brutality."[1] Most of the prisoners belonged to a new category: they were Fascists, Nazis, or their collaborators. In Belgium in 1945, out of 45,696 prisoners only 6, 438 were common criminals, the rest being convicted or detained collaborators; in 1947 there were 26,000 collaborators in prison. Such prisoners were required to work, to repair the damage they had done to their country by collaborating with the Germans. In 1947, 15,397 imprisoned collaborators were put to work, mostly in mines—their prison labor yielded seven hundred thousand tons of coal that year.[2] In Sachsenhausen, in the Soviet occupation zone in Germany, the daily ration consisted of one and three-fourths liters of thin soup and 450 grams of bread; small wonder that ten to twenty inmates died every day, mostly of tuberculosis.[3]

The picture of Greek prisons was not very different: extremely overcrowded, brutal guards, little and bad food, damp cells, endemic tuberculosis, hard labor, and frequent protests. What was different, however, were the prisoners. In contrast to the other liberated countries, Greek prisons were packed not with collaborators but with resisters. And as the Civil War developed, more and more former members of resistance organizations would be incarcerated in camps and prisons. The wretched living conditions in prisons demonstrated that the state, paralyzed due to the occupation, was completely unprepared and incompetent to solve the problem of a skyrocketing prison population. It lacked the resources, the trained personnel, and the infrastructure to meet the pressing needs of prisons and prisoners alike. It also lacked the political will to improve living conditions. The political prisoners' situa-

Notes for this section begin on page 111.

tion inside prisons was also related to political conflict outside prisons. Loose or rigorous discipline, more freedom or more restrictions, tolerable or wretched living conditions, were connected with the state of affairs outside prisons. The more acute the threat to the regime, the more the situation behind walls deteriorated.

Exile

Agios Efstratios (Ai Stratis), Ikaria, Folegandros, Leros, Kimolos, Sikinos, Anafi, Gavdos, Kythira, Alonisos, Limnos, Samothraki, Zakynthos: these were but some of the islands used for exile or administrative banishment, as it was officially called. This type of internment is in fact the oldest way in which governments have dealt with their political opponents. During the interwar era many liberal and conservative politicians were banished, although the vast majority were trade unionists and members of left-wing political parties and groups. Islands in the Aegean Sea, such as Anafi, Agios Efstratios, Gavdos, Kimolos, and Naxos, as well as mainland villages were used for this purpose.[4]

The UNRRA reports that in November 1946 there were 3,869 exiles on forty-seven small islands. A few months later their numbers rose to 5,809. The summer of 1947 saw a dramatic rise in the number of political prisoners as a result of mass arrests and deportations in July 1947—the Communist Party in September 1947 put the number of exiles at 24,000, a figure that seems to be inflated. Many exiles were released after a few months, and one year later, in September 1948, 12,878 persons were in exile. Starting at the end of 1948, the majority of the exiles were transported to the Makronisos camps. In September 1949, according to Greek officials, 15,000 persons were in exile, of whom 12,000 were at the Makronisos camps. Exiles stayed on Makronisos until the camps were closed down in August 1950; men were then transported to Agios Efstratios and Ikaria, and women to Trikeri. One year later, in September 1951, according to British sources, there were 2,807 men on Agios Efstratios and 544 women on Trikeri island.[5]

Exiles, as we have already seen, were mostly banished by decrees of public security committees, not of civil courts. Sometimes even such decrees were not necessary. In mass arrests, the suspects were first arrested without any warrant or decree of any authority and banished, and then the individual cases were examined by the public security committees. For the government, it was enough that "their past records create serious presumptions of their participation in or fostering of the rebellion."[6] Moreover, though in the beginning the heaviest sentence that a public security committee could pass was twelve months, later this was prolonged. A legislative decree of 1948 gave public security committees the right to prolong banishment for more than twenty-four months. The sentence of an exile could be prolonged without any specific justification other than the political exile's "obstinate persistence and assiduity in the communist antinational ideology." In this way, exile could become a sentence of indefinite term.[7]

Political exiles' living conditions were heavily dependent on the resources of the island, the self-organization of the political exiles, and the relations between the exiles and the island's inhabitants. Islands had no infrastructure whatsoever for hosting political exiles. There were no accommodation, kitchens, or health facilities. Even though they managed to find ways to organize their lives, the problems were so intractable that UNRRA officials described the situation in several camps as "deplorable."[8] Water and food supplies constituted the exiles' greatest problem on these barren islands. Cisterns for rainwater, which were insufficient even for the native population, or tanks of dirty water, did not solve the problem; rather, they were sources of diseases. As for food supplies, the exiles were dependent on the government and relief organizations, which were also the sole suppliers of camping gear, clothing, medicines, food for babies and soap.[9]

Anafi is a small rocky island in the Cyclades, where 750 people lived in 1946. Within two months, August and September 1946, 405 exiles were deported there. Most of them were farmers, sentenced from three to twelve months in exile, for "being dangerous to public security." Every available house—even the school of the island—was used to accommodate the men and the forty-five women exiles, who together with their six children lived in separate houses. Perhaps they considered themselves lucky to be living under a roof—in many cases, exiles lived in tents, as late as in 1951 on Agios Efstratios. In these overcrowded houses they had to make their own beds of bamboo, and the one blanket that each had was not enough for the winter. They could not carry many things with them, nor were they allowed to do so, and since they had been arrested in summer, they did not have winter clothes. Even if the housing problem was somehow solved, their lot was not substantially improved. The cisterns were either empty or contained dirty water, so the exiles had to carry water from a spring, twenty minutes away from the village. The scrub of the island was used as fuel, but forty men and two hours of walking were needed to carry the quantity necessary for cooking. Cooking was done communally in an old bakery, but the main concern was the eventual shortage of food supplies. The food supplies arrived by a caïque every two weeks, and the exiles had to pay for them in advance; the five hundred drachmas daily allowance that some of them (the "indigent and fit to work") received was insufficient and usually delayed. Luckily, there was a clinic and a hospital room with eight beds, though there were very few drugs.[10]

As the number of political exiles reached its climax the next year, following the mass arrests in July 1947, the living conditions of the political exiles worsened. On Agios Efstratios in August 1947 out of 4,000 exiles, 3,500 lacked any form of shelter, a large number suffered from chronic diseases, and the combination of the acute shortage of water and of lack of sanitary facilities made a British officer wonder how an epidemic had not yet started.[11]

The political exiles were organized in what they called *Omada Symviosis Politikon Exoriston* (OSPE, Political Exiles' Cohabitation Group), or simply "collectives" or "communes." The self-organization of the political exiles did not derive from political considerations or imperatives alone but was a means for organizing their lives under unfavorable conditions. A committee was elected to organize exiles' life: arrange classes, collect money, set up a canteen, assign duties and jobs, even publish their own underground newspapers, like the "We are not slaves" on Folegandros, and the "Unconquered voice" on Sikinos. Everything was organized on a communal basis, which improved their living conditions. Working parties of tailors, shoemakers, barbers, bakers, and cooks were organized to take care of the exiles' well-being.[12] The pattern for the organization of everyday life came from the interwar years. In the 1930s, during the Metaxas dictatorship, up to 750 people were exiled on Anafi. Exiles' committees controlled every aspect of communal life and everything was organized on a communal basis. Food parcels that exiles received were shared with their roommates, after half was given to the collective; people were assigned duties on a rotating system; the collective bought grain in bulk, cleaned it, and took it to a windmill for grinding; the exiles even pooled funds to buy cigarettes.[13]

Good relations with the islanders were very important. Both exiles and islanders shared the same problems (like shortage of water, fuel, and food supplies, or lack of medical assistance), and exiles' life was based on the cooperation of the islanders. The political exiles had to rent houses, fields to cultivate them, and animals for transportation, and often they had to labor for the islanders. Generally speaking, exiles had good relations with the islands' inhabitants, and a UNRRA official observed that "in all cases the islanders and exiles had cooperated completely in sharing what food was available." In addition, in many cases political exiles managed to revitalize these otherwise impoverished and neglected islands. On Kythnos they repaired damages to the island's small powerhouse, which had been out of order for two years. On Folegandros the islanders flocked to see the theatrical performances the exiles staged. On Easter in 1947, choirs of exiles chanted in the churches of the island of Ikaria, and the inhabitants exchanged gifts and sweets with the exiles.

Life in exile seems to have been better and more free than life in prisons. Initially, the sole obligation of the political exiles was to report to the gendarmerie station; the gendarmes censored their correspondence and informed them about letters, money orders, and parcels received. Starting in 1947, however, state policy towards them changed. Stricter rules were imposed, and the exiles' camps were changed into "camps of disciplined living." According to Emergency Law 511, which was passed a few days after the proclamation of the guerillas' Provisional Government in December 1947

> The Police authorities (...) may: a. oblige them to present themselves before the authorities at definite temporal intervals, b. impose curfew at definite night hours, c. prohibit them from moving further away than a specific distance from their place of exile, d. oblige them to declare every change of address, e. carry out house searches at any time of the day or night, f. prohibit them from assembling, g. prohibit them from founding any kind of society, club, or meeting-place, h. prohibit them from the publishing and the circulation of printed material or papers that may be considered harmful to the public order, i. prohibit them from practicing a craft, if it is judged that it is not entirely for bread-winning objectives, j. determine the maximum amount of money that all those banished are entitled to have.[14]

In the framework of these changes, the authorities decided in August to "restore order" to the camps of Ikaria, Limnos, and Agios Efstratios, where the bulk of political exiles were concentrated. A visitor could no longer see the organized classes and feasts, or listen to the exiles' choir singing the "International."[15] Posters were removed from their clubs, the schools, canteens, and theaters were closed down, lectures and songs were prohibited, the artisans' companies were banned, contacts between exiles and islanders were restricted to a few hours every day, and a curfew was imposed after nine o'clock in the evening.[16]

Far from being dispatched for a "few months, with living expenses paid by the Government, to one of the sunny, though lonely, Aegean islands,"[17] the political exiles were left to their own devices all these years. As late as 1950, when all the male exiles were concentrated on Agios Efstratios and the females on Trikeri, living conditions were still deplorable. On Agios Efstratios there was no road or port. The 2,756 exiled men were lived in tents, "which were anything but weatherproof", and there was only one doctor and two nurses with very minimal medical facilities, despite the fact that 450 exiles were suspected of having tuberculosis.[18]

Under such living conditions their lives became heavily dependent on the weather. Tents were not the best of shelters against the high winds so common on Greek islands, or sudden storms. Many times storms and the floods on Agios Efstratios left nothing but destroyed tents, mud, and wretched people looking for clothes, blankets, and personal belongings at the shore. Even though they were singing "I am not afraid of Ai-Stratis / It is just another part of Greece / Even if our black hair turned white / The harsh winter doesn't scare us," they knew what the harsh winter meant: not only hardship and illness, but also less frequent ships to these remote islands. Dependent as they were on the caïques and ships, which carried water, food stocks, parcels, and correspondence, and, in the case of sick exiles, transported patients to hospitals, the deportees' lives were dependent on the rough sea. As supplies ran out, the exiles were possessed by the fear of dying of starvation.[19]

The numerous appeals of the political exiles to various organizations stressed the fact that they were in a state of need. They were in need of medical checkups as well as treatment for cardiopathy, rheumatism, tuberculosis, and gastritis, which were the most usual serious diseases among the exiles. They were in need of the most elementary goods, such as those that the Greek Red Cross had noted: parcels to exiles could contain one or two blankets, a suit, underwear, a pair of shoes and socks, and no more than four kilos of food. They were in need of money to purchase these elementary goods. In a bitter outburst one exile wrote in a letter: "You've sent thirty thousand drachmas, so what's the worth? What can I buy with this money? A mattress that I don't have or a blanket?"[20]

Above all, their main demand was their release, because when they had served the sentence of their banishment, it could be renewed for another one year. In the beginning their petitions were for the release of the old, the sick, and the female political exiles. Although Premier Konstantinos Tsaldaris maintained that "men of over sixty can be just as dangerous, if not more so, than their younger co-disciples," occasionally, due to the pressure of public opinion, within the country or abroad, the Greek government released, certain categories of political exiles, such as mothers, old people, children under sixteen, or those who were seriously ill. After the end of the Civil War their demand was "general amnesty", unconditional release. The exiles knew that they could be released almost immediately, but only on one condition: the signing of a declaration of repentance.

Prisons

Already, during the events of December 1944, twelve thousand leftists had been arrested and imprisoned. Eight thousand of them were interned in British camps in the Middle East, and later were transferred back to Greece. After the Varkiza agreement the "white terror" kept up the flow of leftists to jail. At least half of the 18,639 persons held in prisons in early November 1945 were imprisoned for political reasons. In the spring of 1946, after a number of prisoners the release by the law for the decongestion of prisons, 8,514 political prisoners were to be found in jail all over Greece, according to the resistance organization *Ethniki Allilegyi*. After that, the political prisoners' population constantly increased. In January 1947, there were 11,244 political prisoners. In September 1947, according to a report by the Communist party, 19,620 political detainees were in prison. One year later, in September 1948, the British Police and Prisons Mission reported that there were 24,208 prisoners, of whom 68 percent were classified as left-wing prisoners. As the last battles of the Civil War were fought, the government unofficially stated that in September 1949 there were 18,000 political prisoners (of whom 3,000 were women) in Greece. One year later, the number of political prisoners had not decreased at all—on the contrary, according to the British Police and Prisons Mission, in September 1950 there were 19,424 left-wing prisoners.[21]

As the number of political detainees increased, the living conditions in prisons became more and more deplorable. If one takes into account that the prison population in the prewar era was less than the half of that in the postwar era, and that sixteen prisons were ruined and fifteen were seriously damaged during the occupation and in the months immediately after the liberation, a more coherent picture of the problem emerges. Any kind of building that could provide a minimum of security and surveillance—houses, schools, abandoned warehouses and factories, military camps—was transformed into a prison.[22]

UNRRA staff visited several prisons between 1945 and 1946. Their reports give a firsthand account of the pathetic situation they encountered. The problems they spotted were many and serious: Greek prisons were overcrowded; they had no sick-bays or infirmary accommodations; the sanitation was bad due to lack of water, soap, and disinfectant; the food and clothing problem remained unsolved. the Eptapyrgio prison (Salonica), in a space intended to accommodate 175 prisoners, three times that number were interned. It became so overcrowded in 1947 that the prisoners protested against the transportation of additional prisoners. In the Tripolis prison, there was no doctor or sickbay for the 269 prisoners, and lice were prevalent. It is difficult to imagine how 260 women and children could manage to live in an attic room measuring ten by twenty meters in the Alexandroupolis police station, even if 130 of them were children under twelve years, and 13 babies under one year old. It goes without saying that this lack of space created additional hygiene problems. In the Trikala prison, 120 political detainees were interned in one dormitory. There were no beds, so the detainees slept on mattresses on the floor; there was no toilet, so instead they used chamber pots. The living conditions of the 347 inmates at the Italian school in Patras were worse than deplorable. The prisoners and their clothes were filthy because there was running water for only one hour per day and they had no soap; rats and scabies were widespread. Nevertheless, there was one exception: the building on Zelioti St. in Athens, where prisoners enjoyed such amenities as wireless sets and electric heaters, was destined for convicted collaborators and members of the quisling governments.[23]

The government was not prepared for such a large number of political prisoners, so the overcrowded prisons were not an outcome of deliberate action but an intractable problem for the authorities. Greek prisons were the antipode of the panoptic prison model, where each prisoner was kept in isolation from the other prisoners. The prisoners' main problem was not their isolation, but their overcrowded dormitories. As living space decreased, the facilities of the prison became more and more inadequate, and given the other difficulties, the tension among the prisoners was heightened. The results of Emergency Law 753 of 21 December 1945, for the decongestion of prisons, were inadequate. A number of prisoners were indeed released, but at the same time other people were arrested. By April 1946, 7,471 prisoners had been released, and 3,500 new arrests and incarcerations had been reported. For many people, the "decongestion law" was nothing more than a short break of freedom. For the many more political prisoners who remained in jail, it did not signal an improvement in their lot. Half of the prisoners on the island of Cephalonia were released under the "decongestion law," but the 155 who remained in the Argostoli prison had to live in rat-infested conditions, without bathrooms. As thousands of new people were imprisoned during the Civil War, the government decided in 1947 to transport thousands of prisoners from the mainland to the camps on the island of Giaros. [24]

In January 1946, the Ministry of Justice issued a circular that gives a picture of the prisoners' nutrition. According to the circular, each week the following meals had to be prepared: four meals consisting of pulses, three of greens or vegetables, two of potatoes, three of pasta, one of fish, and one of olives. However, the prison reality was quite different. At the Themistocleous St. women's prison the menu consisted of canned food (sardines, meat, and pulses), and fat. The fish and potatoes that were mentioned in both the circular and the meal plan of the Zakynthos prison were actually served only once or twice over a period of months. Although it might be reasonable to assume that prisoners' nutrition improved in the following years, it seems that this did not happen. In 1952, the Ministry of Justice noted that in defiance of its orders, many prisons fed prisoners with whatever they had stocked. The prisoners in the Itzedin prison were still complaining as late as 1950 that their food consisted of "split peas, beans, greens and potatoes, all of them rotten." Moreover, in their memoirs prisoners generally recall the small quantity and poor quality of their food (especially in the cases of the sick and children, who did not receive an extra portion) the badly cooked food, and the repetition of the same menu—indeed, many prisoners write of diseases caused by bad nutrition. Their nutrition could be improved only by food parcels delivered by relatives, or by individual purchasing. For the prisoners, visits and food were the most important things, which sometimes created bizarre situations. Despite the extreme overcrowding at the Volos prison, designed for 100 prisoners but housing 458 in 1949, the prisoners were not very keen on transfers: they preferred to be incarcerated in their local prisons, even under bad conditions, since this at least allowed them visits and food from friends and relatives.[25]

Thus, the improvement of living conditions was left to the prisoners, their families, and relief organizations. The political prisoners organized themselves in *omades symviosis* (cohabitation groups), which, in the beginning, were unofficially recognized by the authorities. They had a say in the composition of the menus, met and spoke with missions from relief organizations, and organized the preparation of meals. After 1946, however, prisoners' committees were prohibited. Prisoners' committees did not cease to exist as a form of prisoners' self-organization, but went underground in the context of a stricter regime.[26]

At this point we can see the difference between prewar and postwar prison conditions. Under the Metaxas regime prisoners enjoyed relative freedom inside the prisons, with the exception of the Corfu prison, where the leading cadres of the Communist Party were held in solitary confinement. The living conditions of the political detainees were bad, but they had the opportunity to organize their life inside the prison and improve their situation. In the Akronafplia prison the inmates built an oven to bake bread, renovated the kitchens, and made cisterns to collect and store water. In the Pylos prison, after many protests, they succeeded in building an oven, and making trips to the city to purchase food supplies, to level the rocks of the yard, to have books, and to clean a few old pitchers to use as storage tanks for water. They also took advantage of the loose discipline of the prison administration, and of the organization of the prisoners' collectivity, to develop other activities like reading lessons for the illiterate, lectures, feasts, an orchestra and dances. However, these activities often became an issue between the prisoners and the governor because they were informal; the administration occasionally prohibited some of them in order to undermine the prisoners' morale. Books were taken away, newspapers were banned, lessons were interrupted to make it clear that the detainees enjoyed their privileges only at the discretion of the authorities.[27]

In the years when the Civil War was at its climax (1947-1949), political detainees found themselves in a state of almost total heteronomy. The situation in prisons deteriorated, not just because the practices of violence (in the form of the execution of political prisoners) and coercion were systematically employed, but mainly because the rigorous discipline did not permit the detainees to improve their lives. From this viewpoint, living conditions—particularly key concerns such as food, hygiene, and labor—were transformed into measures of punishment within the context of rigorous discipline and rehabilitation. New prohibitions and restrictions made political prisoners' life less bearable. Political detainees from the Averof prison enumerated the new strictures that the administration imposed: newspapers, periodicals, and books, the possession of money, electric lighting in cells, the organization of any recreation, and classes for the illiterate were prohibited.[28] It was prisoners' subjectivity, expressed in labor, lessons, feasts, and all other activities that forged bonds of solidarity, that became the object and the objective of discipline.

Camps

Historically, camps of mass internment have been related to wars. They first appeared during the Boer War, at the turn of the twentieth century, and thereafter they recurred in close connection to the wars of the twentieth century (camps for prisoners of wars, for war refugees, for suspects of treason or subversion during war, and so on). However, a differentiation between two types of internment had already occurred in the First World War: detention camps and indoctrination camps. The first operated as places for the detention of actual or potential enemies and victims of war, whereas the second, which were fully incorporated into the political, social, and ideological mechanisms of states waging a war, had as their objective the conversion of the detainees. A prevalent feature of the latter was that detention was combined with indoctrination. Examples of indoctrination camps include the Bolshevik camps for prisoners of war during the First World War I, or the British camps for German prisoners of war in the Second World War.[29]

Whereas the indoctrination camps mentioned above were intended for the internment of non-nationals, in the Greek camps it was Greek citizens who were detained. Indoctrination camps in Greece appeared during the Civil War as an attempt by the regime to solve the problem of the increasing surplus population of political prisoners (the "suspect" soldiers who joined the army, and those civilians convicted of political offenses or suspect for their political views) and, primarily, to rehabilitate political prisoners under extreme conditions.[30] Violence in any form constituted the primal characteristic; violence in the form of insult, physical harassment, fatigue duty, arbitrary punishment, and hard labor was the stuff of everyday life in the camps. It is not irrelevant that a great number of the political detainees of that era served a term of their sentence in these camps. The authorities believed that the extreme conditions that prevailed in these camps would make political detainees convert. The main camps were situated on the islands of Makronisos, Giaros (Gioura), Trikeri, and Chios, the last two for female detainees.

Makronisos

Despite the fact that the Makronisos camps had been opened since 1947, typically the "Makronisos Reformative Organization" was founded by Resolution 73 of 14 October 1949, "on measures for national rehabilitation." Resolution 73, like several other laws passed during the Civil War, as scholars have noticed, revealed the peculiarity of the emergency laws: they legalized political persecution retroactively.[31] The objective of the camps was, according to the legislation, "the rehabilitation through the enlightenment and education" of the detainees.[32] The camp, the administration, and the staff were subordinate to the General Staff of the Army. The reason for the delayed ratification of the rehabilitative experiment at the Makronisos camps seems to be that the government, which until then had presented them as ordinary camps for soldiers, envisioned the Makronisos camps as a permanent penitentiary solution, not only for soldiers but also for civilians. The fact that the army managed a penitentiary, which the government saw as a model, reflected the increasing power and influence of the army in Greek society.

Makronisos is a completely barren and, to this day, uninhabited island; "stones and flies are two basic features of the nature" of the island.[33] Eighteen square kilometers in size, it lies very close to the Attica region—about five kilometers off Lavrion on the east Attica coast. The island had previously served as the site of camps for Turkish prisoners of the Balkan wars (1912-1913) and for Greek refugees from Minor Asia after 1922. At the beginning of the Civil War, the detainees were soldiers and officers. Apparently the Makronisos camps resembled any other military camp where soldiers were trained and did their military service. The inmates were not classified as prisoners, since they had committed no offense whatsoever, but they shared something in common: they were suspected of holding leftist beliefs. Screening, based on information from the police intelligence and the Intelligence Bureau of the Army, concerned their communist "tendencies" and activities "throughout the period of occupation up to their enrollment."[34] In the summer of 1946, the suspected were divided into three battalions and concentrated in camps (the first was on Crete, the second in Larisa and later in Attica, and the third in Salonica). As of May 1947 soldiers and officers were transferred to Makronisos. There the soldiers were again divided into three battalions, this time according to their degree of "national conviction" (*ethnikofrosyni*). The first battalion was made up of those who had not recant their political beliefs, the second of those "who had renounced Communism and were well along the road to becoming 're-indoctrinated' patriots," and the third of those "who had completed the course and were almost ready for release to the regular armed services." Later, however, these distinctions were dropped, because apparently all the detained soldiers had been rehabilitated.[35]

A U.S. official referred to Makronisos as an "indoctrination camp."[36] The peculiarity of the Makronisos camps was that they combined the organization of an ordinary military camp with the purpose of an indoctrination camp. Soldiers were not trained to carry arms (unless they had been rehabilitated), but they were "enlightened" under conditions of extreme violence and terror. Hard labor, strict discipline, torture, and anticommunist propaganda were the main features of the camps.

A few days after their arrival on Makronisos, the soldiers were called to the offices for interrogation, which often followed a questionnaire that included such questions as: "Did you belong to the EPON, EAM, EA, etc. from … to … in what place, by your own will or not, and who suggested that you should enlist?" and "What is your opinion of bandits?" If they were not willing to answer and sign a declaration of repentance, the military police took over. The questions were then shorter, such as "Are you Bulgarian or Greek?" and torments intensified the ordeal of the interrogations. Those who signed declarations of repentance were not released but still had to undergo the rehabilitation process; in addition, they had to prove that they had repented. In the following paragraphs I shall examine the means, the content, and the results of the soldiers' rehabilitation.

Rehabilitation started in the third battalion, the "blue battalion," as it was called, in reference to the colors of the Greek flag, in this way denoting the soldiers' conversion to the nation. For one year, the third battalion under the command of Captain Giannis Skaloumbakas, became the field of experiments in soldiers' rehabilitation. Hard labor under all weather conditions, malnutrition, surprise attacks in the night by the military police, unceasing interrogations, and torture were the means employed by the command; after a short while, 70 percent of the battalion soldiers had signed declarations of repentance.[37] The everyday order of the camps combined hard labor with torture. Soldiers not only had to carry out their usual duties, but they also had to build the camps' roads, offices, kitchens, furnaces, theaters, church, radio station, etc., and to decorate the camp with, among other things, with arches, slogans formed from stones on the hillside, and an imitation of the Parthenon.[38] Gradually, and not without resistance, the other two battalions would become like the third. To convert the first battalion, the battalion of the "unrepentants," sheer violence was employed. With two murderous attacks on 28 February and 1 March 1948, the administration eliminated the last nucleus of resistance on the island.[39] The road to the conversion of all the detained soldiers was then open.

The content of the rehabilitation, as it was exemplified in the various forms of propaganda in the battalions, combined fierce anticommunism and nationalism. Communism was identified with the expansive aspirations of neighboring countries (the "Slavs"), and nationalism with the defense of the country. The soldiers had to attend lectures given by repentant soldiers, priests, and ministers on topics like "Our Race and the Slav attack", "The Marxist Error," "Greece, Outpost of Liberty," or "What I Saw in Russia."[40] Each battalion published its own journal, to which soldiers were required to contribute articles praising the achievements at Makronisos.[41] At the same time, conversion was also based on the supposed misguidance of the detainees, their depraved past and discovery of a new self on Makronisos. They lived in camps plastered with slogans such as "To err is human," and "Greece is an ideal, she therefore cannot die." They had to march singing "Even if criminals betrayed us / and contaminated our souls / now once more / our life belongs to Mother Greece." They had to work under the sound of loudspeakers broadcasting nationalist songs, like "Modest Makronisos, the embrace of the pioneers / a fatherland of heroes with great glory / a fatherland great and well-known, not one of slaves / the menace and the grave of the barbarian

Slavs." All this was incorporated within the framework of the disciplined routine of military life, which included uniforms, crew cuts, roll calls, marching, standing formations, and so on.

Rehabilitation had an outcome as well: the converted soldier. For *Scapaneus*, the magazine published by the third battalion, the soldier "who was lost in the communist mud found himself in the third battalion. He cured his sick soul, taking the red poison out. He detoxicated himself, and made himself ready to receive tonic national injections. The cure had come to an end".[42] The end was that the repentant soldiers had to turn against the unrepentant soldiers, literally speaking—or, to use the General Director's words, "to point out to their colleagues with incontestable arguments and facts beyond doubt, their gross mistake and the consequences resulting thereof."[43] Their "arguments" consisted of beat unrepentant soldiers, insulting them, and being their guards and tormentors; the "fact" was that they were no longer colleagues. The military authorities' aim was to destroy any bonds of solidarity among the soldiers, to establish an irreversible dividing line between repentant and unrepentant by rendering the former perpetrators.

> There was no middle ground. ... They would see their "unrepentant" colleagues, they would shout "Death," and then, armed, with a club become tormentors ... They always had to be in a nationalist frenzy, with reformative fury, with the club in their hands. If they showed mercy, they were considered to be "suspects." If they got tired, "hypocrites."[44]

Thus, rehabilitation was not just a discourse or a process but must have an outcome as well, one that was exposed and celebrated. The repenter was the embodiment of rehabilitation. He had to be visible and audible in order to clarify the differentiation between the repentant and the unrepentant. Giorgos S., an ELAS member and law student, was described by a fellow inmate as a "politically well-formed cadre." For three months he was threatened; after spending ten nights at the offices of the camp he began to give talks on topics like "The collaboration of the Bulgarian and separatist organizations with ELAS," and he was given an office job at the camp.[45] The other outcome of rehabilitation was that after Makronisos many soldiers served in the national army in the war against the Democratic Army. The first reformed soldiers were sent to the front as early as November 1947. One of the army's most praised battalions in the Civil War was the 596 Battalion, formed exclusively of Makronisos soldiers. The military claimed that about fourteen thousand soldiers and a thousand officers were at various times sent to fighting units after Makronisos. If these figures are not inflated, they represent a considerable proportion of army manpower, which in the spring of 1948 numbered 130,000 men.[46]

The Greek General Staff claimed that twenty-five thousand soldiers and officers had been reformed by October 1949.[47] The apparent success of the

Makronisos camps in the rehabilitation of leftist soldiers made the government to decide the transfer of political exiles, a number of political prisoners, and civilians after preventive arrests to the island. New camps were established, and hundreds of meters of barbed wire fences were erected, as thousands of new people arrived on the island. The west side of the island was covered with camps. The first political exiles and detainees arrived in November 1948. Civilians, victims of preventive arrests after the national army operations against the guerillas in the Peloponnese, were added in the winter of 1948/1949. The renaming of the detained soldiers' battalions from "Sappers' Battalions" to "Special Battalions" in the spring of 1949 coincided with the end of the first phase of the Makronisos camps. The majority of the soldiers were rehabilitated and the focus shifted to civilians: now the reformed soldiers had to rehabilitate the detained civilians. From March 1949 onwards, the majority of political exiles were gradually transferred from other islands to Makronisos and interned in the two camps for civilians, the *Eidika Scholeia Anamorfoseos Idioton* (Special Rehabilitation Schools for Civilians), which were attached to the first and second "Special Battalions." In January 1950, the female exiles were transferred to a separate camp on Makronisos, the *Eidiko Scholeio Anamorfoseos Gynaikon* (Special Rehabilitation School for Women). According to the Undersecretary of Foreign Affairs Panagiotis Pipinelis, in September 1949, 10,000 male political exiles, 9,000 civilians victims of preventive arrests by the army, and 7,500 soldiers and officers were detained at the Makronisos camps.[48]

Civilians and exiles received the same treatment as the soldiers had before them. Vardis Vardinogiannis' testimony is typical of what happened when newcomers arrived in the camps:

> From the hill twenty soldiers come around, armed with batons. They attack us furiously. They strike us anywhere with the batons and their feet. They step on us and they "dance." They drag some men by their hair and throw them fully clothed into the sea. No one stands in the same position for more than a few seconds. There is no way to protect yourself ... Beside me lies a youngster unconscious with his head on the ground. His shirt is torn and doesn't have a coat. His nose and mouth are constantly bleeding. ... Not far from me they had a comrade of mine, a sailor. They took his heavy clothes off him, they threw him into the sea and afterwards they beat him till he fell unconscious onto the paving stones.[49]

Makronisos became synonymous with violence and torture. Government propaganda tried to present Makronisos as an ordinary camp, as a "school" or a "National University" for young, misguided communists. Visits by the king and queen, ministers, and foreign officials gave them the opportunity to praise the rehabilitation project. The army organized a photo exhibition in Athens, in April 1949, to inform the audience of the work being done on Makronisos. Ceremonies in which the king delivered arms to reformed soldiers, who then marched in the streets of Athens, gained a lot of publicity.[50] The government had to justify the operation of these camps and answer to accusations leveled both at home and abroad. Only a few years had passed since the revelation of the horrors of the Nazi concentration camps, and moreover, Greece was the only Western European country that ran camps where members of resistance organizations rather than collaborators, were interned.

Despite the government's efforts, the reality of the Makronisos camps could not always be disguised. Some visitors gave accounts in their official reports that were closer to the camps' reality and atmosphere. Lieutenant Colonel Strangeways, of the British Military Mission to Greece staff, visited the Makronisos camps in January 1950, and his report was quite revealing. His general remarks were that "the scheme is *not* conducted in a manner which is a credit to the Western Powers," and that there was "a state of affairs which is contrary to the British and American conception of humanity and justice." What made this British officer, who had witnessed the release of prisoners from the Nazi concentration camps, so critical of the Makronisos camps? The discussion with General Director Brigadier Georgios Bairaktaris, "who launched into a long and rather pointless propaganda speech during which he drew a pistol to stress his point?" His driver who begged him to tell nobody that the car had broken down several times, "as if we did he would be beaten?" The sight of a boy who "had been wearing his shirt for a month and did not know when he was going to wash it," since in most cases detainees had only one shirt and no fresh water. Or was it, the loudspeakers and the men's faces when they were "listening to the exhortation of an ex-communist who has seen the light?" Perhaps it was all of this that led him to write that the atmosphere "was lethargic and very reminiscent of similar German camps in 1945."[51]

But the Makronisos camps were a product of the extraordinary circumstances of the Civil War and of the need of the army to secure the loyalty of its soldiers. After it ended, the camps became less and less necessary, and criticism of the whole scheme in the press mounted. Moreover, the elections of 1950 brought to power a more liberal government, which promised reconciliation not revenge. The appointment of Major General Papagiannopoulos as new director at Makronisos camps reflected these changes. In an order in June 1950 he prohibited political insults, removed the barbed wire, condemned discriminatory treatment of soldiers on the basis of their political beliefs, and prohibited visits by officials. Finally, in August 1950 the Makronisos Reformative Organization closed down. By that time 2,815 male exiles had been transferred to Agios Efstratios and 532 female exiles to Trikeri; 4,641 soldiers, 26 officers, and 1,601 political prisoners remained on the island. Makronisos would continue for a few more years to be used as training center for suspect soldiers, but nothing was reminiscent of the Civil War years except the theatres, arches, and buildings that had been constructed by the detained soldiers.[52]

The women's camps

Female political detainees were first interned on the island Chios and then on Trikeri. Their status was closer to that of the exiles: they had not been convicted by courts but by the public security committees. It seems that eventually all the women exiles, who since their sentencing had been in exile with men, were transported to Chios in 1948. On 8 March 1948, the first female detainees arrived on Chios and were housed in military barracks near the city of Chios.[53] In June 1948, 910 women were interned together with their forty-four children; half a year later there were 1,316 women and fifty-two children. In the beginning the detainees enjoyed some freedom, even organized a feast for the national holiday on the 25th of March. But after July 1948 the situation changed. One hundred and ninety-nine women were classified as "dangerous" and transferred to a different building, whereas the rest were divided into "Bulgarians" (women who were relatives of guerillas) and "Russians" (women classified as communists). Living conditions worsened and the overall scheme combined the characteristics of prison and exile.

The women exiles faced the problems of life in prisons: rooms were overcrowded (thirty to fifty women in each room), sanitary facilities were inadequate, the quality of food was poor, many detainees with health problems were not transferred to the hospital, and strict restrictions were imposed: exercise outside the buildings was allowed only for three hours every day, and any organized recreational activity such as songs, theater, or dance was forbidden. Nevertheless, the women had a say in the running of the camp, and life was organized on a communal basis: for example, they carried out the purchase, distribution, and cooking of food and ran the canteen. Also, due to the absence of doctors, deportees were in charge of medical inspection. Needless to say, these privileges could be retracted without any particular reason—for instance they were prohibited from purchasing goods from the city. Even if discipline was not as rigorous as in other camps, life was no less depressing; furthermore, the gendarmes knew how to remind them who had the power: mothers were separated from their daughters, when one or the other was considered as "dangerous," or from their children, in order for the latter to be taken to orphanages. The day that twenty-one children were transferred to an orphanage, a detainee recalls, "almost none of us ate, and when the night came we lay on our mattresses silent and crushed."[54]

In March 1949, the female detainees were transferred from Chios to Trikeri. Trikeri is a very small, almost uninhabited island in the Gulf of Pagasitikos, where male detainees had been first deported in 1947 before being transferred to Makronisos. The first women had arrived on the island in 1948. Women from all over Greece would be added to the female detainees from the Chios camp, as a consequence of the army's preventive arrests of guerillas' relatives. At its peak in the summer of 1949, 4,500 women and children were interned in the island's camp.

At first, female detainees were settled in the damp cells of the island's monastery, but later, as hundreds of new arrivals swelled their ranks, most of them lived in tents around the monastery. In the beginning the camp was under the jurisdiction of the army. The guards were soldiers, many of them "repenters" from the Makronisos camps, and the scheme was organized according to military discipline (roll calls, division of detainees to platoons, etc.); later the gendarmerie took over. What differentiated the Trikeri camp from the one on Chios, was that from every perspective, detainees' lives became worse.[55]

No water supply existed in the camp. The detainees had to walk outside the camp to get water from wells, which was not always drinkable. There were no toilets; the detainees were forced to use open fields for that purpose. They washed themselves, their clothes, and the dishes in the sea. Although there were many children in the camp with their mothers (more than two hundred children during the summer of 1949), no special care was provided; moreover, the female detainees had to do all the camp's maintenance work. Besides cleaning and cooking, they had to unload and carry the supplies brought by the caïques. Sacks and barrels, iron and bricks, bread and firewood, had to be carried by hand from the port to the camp. The rehabilitated female body had "blisters and corns on the hands, especially the girls coming from the cities, the body was hunched up and lost its freshness, the wrinkles deepened and the faces got rugged."[56]

In November 1949, the Trikeri camp was incorporated into the Makronisos Reformative Organization scheme and so again came under the jurisdiction of the army. Once more the women endured soldiers, military officers, roll calls, lectures, threats, and new pressures for "declarations," a kind of preparation for the worst that was yet to come. The worst was the transfer to the Makronisos camps—the women knew from rumors that the situation was horrible there. Their turn came in January 1950, when almost 1,200 women and children boarded the tank landing ship *Acheloos* on its way to Makronisos. As an officer had recommended a few months before their transportation, "all the necessary personnel and equipment for 'indoctrination' can be found there."[57]

The slogan "We want arms" in huge letters formed on the hills, thousands of men's eyes looking at them, loudspeakers calling the women to ask for the pardon of the motherland, and a barbed wire-fenced camp called the *Eidiko Scholeio Anamorfoseos Gynaikon* (ESAG, Special Rehabilitation School for Women): these were the female detainees' first impressions of Makronisos. The "Bulgarians," and "whores" had to sign declarations of repentance, and were coerced by any means: taking children away from their mothers; exposing women to the stories of "repentant" soldiers, who described the torments they themselves had suffered while others threatened them; beatings; rumors that spread fear and despair; solitary confinement for the "instructors;" surprise attacks by military policemen during the night, interrogations lasting for hours. A few days later the officers' objective had been achieved: the ESAG was divided into "repentant" and "unrepentant" companies segregated by barbed wire.[58] For six months the women endured the same hardships as all the other inmates on the island. The captors' task, the declaration of repentance, was the same, and the means to accomplish it were similar: military discipline, fatigue duty, malnutrition, indoctrination, and the usual threat that "whether you want to or not—even if it's on a stretcher—you will sign." In July 1950, when the Makronisos Reformative Organization was dissolved, more than five hundred unrepentant detainees would be transferred back to the Trikeri camp.[59]

The particularity of women's detention lay in the type of indoctrination. "Greek women, sign to return to your homes" was the usual exhortation of the (male) officers. The female detainees were always inscribed within the domain of family relations; the appeal was to daughters, mothers, or wives, as representatives of Greek women. Being in exile or in detention implied that they were alienated from their nation and away from their homes and households, where by definition they belonged. Due to their alienation from the nation, they had lost their proper destiny; consequently, the return to the "motherland" would open the way to return to "their men." Above all, and as the concept of family implied, women were perceived mainly as mothers. The juxtaposition between "Bulgarians" and "whores" on the one hand, and "Greeks" and "mothers" on the other, denied the first the right to be mothers—their children were taken away from them because the women could not raise them properly, "nationally." The discourse of the reform stressed the concept of motherhood and family, precisely because the radicalism and societal mobilization of the 1940s had changed the socialization of women. During the occupation and afterwards, women, *en masse* and for the first time in their lives, had experienced a world which was not restricted to the family ties, and had participated in a movement that not only created new societal ties (in youth organizations, protests, relief organizations, guerilla units, etc.) but promised their liberation as well.[60] Or, to cite a women's song of the resistance: "We are fighting to get rid / of the triple slavery / conqueror, boss and man."[61] The nationalist discourse on communism as adversary to the family was founded on the exclusion of women from the social and political sphere, and their confinement to the family and the household. Women had to return to their homes, in the strict sense of the phrase.

Giaros

Giaros (or Gioura) is a small, rocky island in the Cyclades among Syros, Kea, and Tinos. The first detainees there were suspect soldiers, who arrived on the island at the beginning of 1947 and were later transferred to Makronisos. As prisons on the mainland became more and more overcrowded with political prisoners, the government took the step of transferring the surplus population of political prisoners to this uninhabited island. The first 1,650 political detainees arrived from the Salonica and Kalamata in July 1947. Within the next few months, thousands of prisoners arrived on the island from the Aegina, Averof, Akronafplia, Cephalonia, Lamia, Patras, and Salonica prisons, among others.[62] It is difficult to estimate the number of detainees on Giaros, since they were only part of the overall prison population. However, it was reported that in November 1947 there were 6,000 political prisoners interned on the island, in August 1948 there were 8,600, and in June 1951 more than 5,000 political prisoners were still on Giaros.[63]

The directors of the camps were, successively, Ioannis Papadimitropoulos, Georgios Glastras, and Emmanuel Bouzakis.[64] Since there were no prison buildings on the island, the detainees were placed in five bays of the island. They lived in tents and worked separately in each bay; no contact among prisoners of different bays was allowed. Each of the five bays had its own camp fenced with barbed wire. The first bay, where the majority of the detainees were interned, was the largest and the site the camp administration as well. In the camps of the other three bays, different categories of detainees were interned separately (the criminal prisoners together with the repenters, the intellectuals, and the sick). The fifth bay was used for solitary confinement for one year.[65] Communication among the prisoners of the bays was only permitted several months after the end of the Civil War, in the spring of 1950.

The life of the Giaros prisoners was characterized by wretched living conditions, hard labor, and violence. Many times the inmates ran out of supplies because the supply ship could not approach the island due to bad weather. Since there was no drinkable water on the island, water had also to be transported by boat. The living conditions were so bad that it was felt that the guards should get a bonus in their salary and, "owing to the isolated position of the island and the unpleasant conditions for staff, nobody should be required to serve there for more than six months." This, of course, did not apply to the prisoners.[66]

Under the command of Glastras, and later Bouzakis, sheer terror reigned on the island. From the very first moment that the prisoners arrived on the island, they were made to understand that Giaros was not ordinary prison. When, 280 prisoners arrived on Giaros in September 1949,

> As soon as they went ashore, Glastras' cry 'Kill the Bulgarians' was the signal for the guards' attack. They beat them furiously and indiscriminately on the heads and all over the body with batons and whips. Valuable personal things were stolen and all their foodstuffs and clothing were thrown into the sea. They were obliged to spend the whole day out, exposed under the sun and without water.[67]

Torment was incorporated into prisoners' everyday life in the form of hard labor. The motivation for hard labor was not primarily economic (although neither the profits from the exploitation of a cheap labor force should be ignored, nor the profiteering), but punitive. At the Giaros camps the prisoners worked to build their own prison on the island. After various attempts to locate the prison in the right place, by the end of 1948 the construction began, only to be completed two years later. The political detainees were not only forced to build a prison for themselves, but it was one that was so badly designed that it would be very difficult to live in. According to testimonies of political prisoners who worked on the construction, the buildings were made of concrete only, with no kind of insulation in the roof; each dormitory was designed to house 250-300 prisoners; the bunks were three-tiered and only fifty centimeters in width; the windows were small and high.[68]

Camp labor was not confined to Giaros alone; as has already been mentioned, on Makronisos the detainees worked on the construction of roads, offices, theatres, churches, and so on. What characterized the labor in the camps were the shifting boundaries between labor, forced labor, and punishment. Within this range labor had an ambiguous and unspecified status. In an attempt to trace these boundaries, it can be further clarified that unfavorable labor conditions and the purpose of the labor were what transformed labor into punishment. Political prisoners worked under the sun or rain without any kind of protection, no breaks were allowed, few tools or technical facilities were provided, working hours could be prolonged arbitrarily, and, of course, there was no payment—an extra piece of bread and some cigarettes were given to them.

> On 20 May 1948, one hundred and fifty detainees of the fifth bay unload 3,000 sacks with cement during the night, whilst the guards beat them. The same day one hundred detainees of the fifth bay carry sacks full of sand and lime to the pillbox on the highest hill. On the way up they are chased and beaten by the tormentors Filippou and Stratos, and the superintendents Aiginitis and Leousis. They carry them for twenty kilometers without a break. At eleven o'clock in the morning when they return to their bay, the guards Akrivos and Tsatalas force them to carry sacks full of cement for the whole day from the beach to the generators buildings without food or water under ceaseless thrashing. They return to their bay late at night.[69]

Under such conditions labor became a form of punishment, even more so given the nature and the purpose of the labor. Labor was either purposeless or enclosed in the self-referential prison framework. Purposeless or meaningless, work was reduced to the repetition of the same movement, which produced nothing. Carrying heavy stones from one point to another and then back again for a whole working day, or spending a day catching flies, as was the case at the Makronisos camps, can be theorized as unproductive in one sense, but in another, it is the production of nothing.[70] The production of nothing deconstructs a worldview where everything has a purpose and can be rationally explained. Labor, on the other, enclosed in the self-referential prison framework, it was a kind of work substantially directed against the prisoners themselves because it reproduced and justified the conditions of their imprisonment. It was a corporal as well as a psychic ordeal for the political prisoners to construct their own prison on Giaros or for the detained soldiers to build the radio station on Makronisos that propagated and facilitated their rehabilitation. The body and the psyche had to suffer for something that was apparently labor, but was essentially a form of punishment.[71]

An objection may be raised to the argument that a purposeless activity cannot be categorized as labor but as punishment. But it should be noted that first, this kind of activity was called labor by the authorities and it did not differ from any other work (a group of detainees could be assigned to construction on one day and to carry stones from one place to another the next day) except for the fact that it was meaningless. "They obliged us," the Giaros detainees write, "to carry stones from a long distance and throw them into the sea. When someone complained (...) they threatened us saying 'Get it right, you won't stop, not even for a second, until you make a road [sic] to connect Giaros with Syros island.'"[72] It was as hard as any other manual labor in the camp and it was realized under the same working conditions. It was punishment disguised as labor. Second, it is true that it represents a border case, in the sense that it reveals the shifting boundaries between labor and punishment. But that is exactly the point: the distinction between labor, forced labor, and punishment did not actually exist, since within the camp nothing was defined and everything could be transformed into something else. An activity that started as labor and finished as a fatigue duty, labor at night or on holidays, a prisoner alone doing the work of three men, or working for hours without food or water: such scenarios illustrate how labor could be transformed into, and experienced as, punishment.

Notes

1. John Foot, "The Tale of San Vittore: Prisons, Politics, Crime and Fascism in Milan, 1943-1946," *Modern Italy* 3, no. 1 (1998): 25-48.
2. Luc Huyse and Steven Dhondt, *La répression des collaborations 1942-1952. Un passé toujours pr(sent* (Brussels, 1993), 138, 141.
3. Naimark, *The Russians in Germany,* 377-378.
4. For figures on exiles during the Interwar period, see chapter 2.
5. UNRRA PAG 4/3.0.12.2.0, Box 6, File W/17 (0) General, Political exiles by place of exile, 1 November 1946; Ethniki Allileggyi Elladas, *Sta xeronisia tis Elladas* (Athens, 1947), 54; ASKI box 423 F25/5/105; FO 371/72317 R12838, BPPM, Monthly report

(September 1948), 30 October 1948; NARA 868.00/9-649, Athens to Department of State, Translation of Pipinelis' memorandum on amnesty, 6 September 1949; FO 371/87772 R1642, BPM, Monthly report (September 1950), 20 October 1950.
6. FO 371/67018 R4155, Letter from political deportees on the island of Ikaria, 28 March 1947; FO 371/72355 R10822, Letter by Minister for Press and Information Mr. Michael Ailianos to Mr. Vincent Tewson, General Secretary, Trade Union Congress, 11 September 1948.
7. ASKI box 421 F25/3/53, Decree of Public Security Committee of Drama, 1 August 1953. See also Alivizatos, *Oi politikoi thesmoi*, 463-464; Vasileiou, *I dioikitiki ektopisi*, 32-41.
8. NARA 868.00/11-546, Athens to Secretary of State, 5 November 1946.
9. FO 371/58941 R14576, Appeal of National Solidarity to International Red Cross, 2 September 1946.
10. UNRRA PAG 4/3.0.12.2.3, Box 7, File 08-20, Exiles and deportees. Report on state of political exiles, island of Anafi, 31 October 1946, and the attached Memorandum of political exiles of Anafi, 22 October 1946.
11. Wittner, *American Intervention*, 142.
12. NARA 881.561/3-2751, Athens to Department of State. Report on conditions prevailing at Agios Efstratios, 27 March 1951; Moysis Michail Bourlas, *Ellinas, Evraios kai aristeros* (Skopelos, 2000), 91-99.
13. Margaret E. Kenna, "Making a World: Political Exiles in 1930s Greece", *Cambridge papers on Modern Greek* 2 (1994): 21-45; idem, "The Social Organization of Exile: The Everyday Life of Political Exiles in the Cyclades in the 1930s," *Journal of Modern Greek Studies* 9 (1991): 63-81; Bert Birtles, *Exiles in the Aegean* (London, 1938), 107-139.
14. Emergency Law 511, *Government Gazette* 299, 31 December 1947, article 1, par. 1.
15. NARA 868.00/11-2746, Memorandum of conversation on political exiles in Cyclades islands, 20 November 1946; *Rizospastis*, Letter of Stefanos Sarafis from Ikaria, 22 November 1946.
16. *The Manchester Guardian*, 27 August 1947; *Eleftheri Ellada*, 20 August 1947; Notification no. 6/5/2 of the Gendarmerie major on Agios Efstratios, N. Kaltsedakis, *Rizospastis*, 26 August 1947; Notification of the Gendarmerie commander to exiles' concentration camp on Northern Ikaria, *Rizospastis*, 4 July 1947.
17. Kousoulas, *Revolution and Defeat*, 17.
18. NARA 881.561/3-2751, Report on conditions at Agios Efstratios.
19. Tasos Tsouknidas, "Oi plimmyres ston Ai-Strati," in ed. Vardis Vardinogiannis and Panagiotis Aronis, *Oi misoi sta sidera*, 216-223. The fear of dying of hunger, though it seems unreasonable, was founded on the past experience of the death of exiles on Anafi and Aghios Efstratios under the German occupation during the winter of 1941-42. See above, chapter 2.
20. FO 371/58941 R14576 Appeal of the EA to the International Red Cross, 2 September 1946; ASKI box 423 F25/5/17, Report of political exiles on Agios Efstratios, November 1952; ASKI box 423 F25/5/16, Letter of an exile from Agios Efstratios, 26 January 1953; ASKI box 423 F25/5/21 Memorandum of political exiles of Agios Efstratios to the International Red Cross, 21 April 1953; *Eleftheri Ellada*, 2 August 1947; ASKI box 422 F25/4/13, Letter of an exile from Agios Efstratios, 26 November 1950.
21. FO 371/48247 R1193, Athens to FO, 16 January 1945; *Report of the British Legal Mission*, 15, 18; MGA/LDG, Info X, Statistics of the political prisoners throughout Greece, *Ethniki Allilegyi*, Athens, 8 May 1946; *Sta xeronisia*, 48-49; ASKI box 423 F25/5/105; FO 371/72317 R12838, BPPM, Monthly report (September 1948), 30 October 1948; NARA 868.00/9-649, Translation of Pipinelis' memorandum on amnesty, 6 September 1949; FO 371/87772 R 1642, BPM, Monthly report (September 1950), 20 October 1950.
22. *Report of the British Legal Mission*, 18, 23.

23. UNRRA PAG 4/3.0.12.2.0, Box 6, File W/17 (0) General, Report on prison conditions in Greece (General conclusions, 30 October 1945; UNRRA PAG 4/3.0.12.2.0, Box 6, File W/17 (1), Visit to Criminal Prisons of Eptapyrgion, 26 January 1946; UNRRA PAG 4/3.0.12.2.3, Box 12, File Individual Prisons, Report on the Trikala prison, 30 August 1945, and, in the same box, Visit to Tripolis prison, 15 April 1945; NARA 868.131/9-2446, Athens to Department of State. Observations of UNRRA Medical Officer concerning prison conditions in northern Greece, 24 September 1946; Nikos Gouriotis, "Stis fylakes Trikalon," and Nikos Michailidis, "Fylakes Eptapyrgiou," in Vardinogiannis and Aronis, eds., *Oi misoi sta sidera*, 54-57, 88-95; UNRRA PAG 4/3.0.12.2.3, Box 12, File Individual prisons, Visit to the prison at the Italian school, 30 April 1946; *Report of the British Legal Mission*, 24.
24. See Dale E. Smith, "Crowding and Confinement," in *The Pains of Imprisonment*, ed. Robert Johnson and Hans Toch (Beverly Hills, 1982), 45-62; NARA 868.131/5-2346, Release of prisoners under the Law for the decongestion of prisons, 23 May 1946; UNRRA PAG 4/3.0.12.2.3, Box 12, File Individual prisons, Visit to the Argostolion prison, 9 June 1946.
25. Ypourgeion Dikaiosynis, *Egkyklioi*, 169-170, 214-215; UNRRA PAG 4/3.0.12.2.0, Box 6, File W/17 (1) Prison reports, Themistocleous women's prison, 10 December 1945; UNNRA PAG 4/3.0.12.2.3, Box 12, File Individual prisons, About the present position of living of the prisoners in the prison of Zakynthos, 19 November 1945; *Dimokratikos Typos*, 23 April 1950; FO 371/78497 R11292, BPPM, Visit to Volos prison, 8 November 1949.
26. See chapters 9 and 11.
27. Flountzis, *Akronafplia*, 90-93, 160-161.
28. MGA/LDG, Info IV, National Solidarity press bulletin no. 3, 5 November 1946.
29. David Cesarani, "Camps de mort, camps de concentration et camps d' internement dans la mémoire collective britannique," *Vingtième siècle* 54 (1997):13-33; Arnold Krammer, "Soviet Propaganda among German and Austro-Hungarian Prisoners of War in Russia, 1917-1921," in *Essays on World War I: Origins and Prisoners of War,* ed. Samuel R. Williamson and Peter Pastor (New York, 1983), 239-64; Matthew Barry Sullivan, *Thresholds of Peace: Four Hundred Thousand German Prisoners and the People of Britain 1944-1948* (London, 1979).
30. Sometimes security reasons obliged the transfer of political prisoners, if prisons were in areas of considerable guerilla activity. For these reasons, for instance, after the attack of guerilla units on the Gytheion prison and the subsequent escape of twenty-three political prisoners in February 1948, the political prisoners at Kyparissia, Kalamata, and Pylos were evacuated to Makronisos. See FO 371/72317 R5447, BPPM, Monthly report (March 1948), 26 April 1948.
31. Nikos Alivizatos, "The 'Emergency Regime' and Civil Liberties," in Iatrides and Wrigley, eds., *Greece at the Crossroads*, 220-228.
32. Resolution 73, *Government Gazette* 262, 14 October 1949, article 2.
33. Andreas Fragkias, *Loimos* (Athens, 1972), 47. In this book Andreas Fragkias, an eminent novelist who was interned at the Makronisos camps, gives one of the best accounts of the brutality that prevailed.
34. FO 371/87647 RG1016/18, Athens to FO, General Director's report on Makronisos Reformative Organisation, 24 January 1950.
35. NARA 868.00/6-248, Athens to Department of State, The Greek "concentration" camp at Makronisos, 2 June 1948. See also Nikos Margaris, *Istoria tis Makronisou* (Athens, 1966), vol. 1, 492-493; Chrysostomos Mavridis, "Proto Tagma Skapaneon – Makronisi 1947-48," in Vardinogiannis and Aronis, eds., *Oi misoi sta sidera*, 153-161; *Acropolis*, 1 October 1947

36. NARA, 868.00/6-248, The Greek "concentration" camp.
37. ASKI box 421 F25/3/123; Margaris, *Istoria tis Makronisou*, vol. 1, 176-364.
38. For some visitors those kitschy immitations were art; however, the following conversation tells us not of the bad taste of the visitors but of the administration's cynicism. Robert Miner, Second Secretary of the U.S. Embassy in Athens, after his visit to Makronisos in August 1949, wrote: "Some of the decorations, such as scale models of the Parthenon and some of the paintings in the church, are very well done. When I remarked on the apparent wealth of artistic talent on Makronisos, Colonel Bairaktaris said, only half humorously, that all the young intellectuals in Greece had passed through this camp". NARA 868.00/8-1949, Athens to Department of State, Memorandum concerning visit to the island of Makronisos, 19 August 1949.
39. See below, chapter 8.
40. C. P. Rodocanachi, *A Great Work of Civil Readaptation in Greece* (Athens, 1949), 10-11. See also Stratis Bournazos, "O anamorfotikos logos ton nikiton sti Makroniso," *Dokimes* 6 (1997): 101-134.
41. *Anamorfosis* (Rehabilitation) was published by the first battalion, *Foni tis Patridos* (Voice of the Motherland) by the second battalion, and *Scapaneus* (Sapper) by the third battalion. The third battalion also published a magazine with the same name that was distributed nationwide. The references in this book are from the magazine *Scapaneus*.
42. *Scapaneus* 1 (1947): 11-12.
43. FO 371/87647 RG1016/18, General Director's report on Makronisos Reformative Organisation.
44. Margaris, *Istoria tis Makronisou*, vol. 1, 184.
45. ASKI box 421 F25/3/132
46. FO 371 RG 87647 RG1016/18, General Director's report on Makronisos Reformative Organisation.
47. FO 371/87647 RG1016/8, Athens to FO, Numbers at Makronisos. Figures given by Greek General Staff, 1 February 1950. Of those 25,000 men, 15,000 went on from Makronisos to serve in the Greek National Army, 4,500 were released and sent home, and 5,500 remained on Makronisos.
48. NARA 868.00/9-649, Translation of Pipinelis' memorandum on amnesty. See also Antonis Flountzis, *Sto kolastirio tis Makronisou* (Athens, 1984), 41-79, 120-189; Margaris, *Istoria tis Makronisou*, vol. 2, 407ff.
49. Vardis Vardinogiannis, *Makronisos, Oktovris 1948 - Mais 1949* (Athens, 1983), 16.
50. See, for instance *To Vima* and *Acropolis*, 22 June 1948
51. FO 371/87647 RG1016/6, Athens to FO. British Military Mission to Greece. Report on Makronisos, 20 January 1950.
52. Organismos Anamorfotirion Makronisou, *Imerisia Diatagi 10 Iouniou 1950*. I would like to thank Panagiotis Mendrakos, a former detainee at Makronisos, for providing me with a copy of the order. For a brief overview of the history of the Makronisos Reformative Organization, see Tasos Sakellaropoulos, "Idrysi, Diarthrosi kai Leitourgia tou Organismou Anamorfotirion Makronisou," in proceedings of conference, *Istoriko Topio kai Istoriki Mnimi. To Paradeigma tis Makronisou*, (Athens, 2000), 147-157.
53. Athina Konstantopoulou, in *Stratopeda Gynaikon*, ed. Victoria Theodorou (Athens, 1976), 39-41.
54. NARA 868.00/6-2548, Greek detention camp for women on the island of Chios, 25 June 1948; MGA/LDG, Info II, Letter from women exiles on the island of Chios, 15 December 1948; FO 371/78369 R1617, BPPM, Visit to women's detention camp, Chios, 22 January 1949; FO 371/78369 R696, FO to Mrs. E.M. Braddock, M.P., 25 February 1949; Athina Konstantopoulou and Stasa Kefalidou testimonies in Theodorou, ed., *Stratopeda Gynaikon*, 35-123.

55. Victoria Theodorou, in idem, ed., 123-223; Nitsa Gavriilidou, *O pateras mou Kostas Gavriilidis* (Athens, 1988), 179-182.
56. Victoria Theodorou in idem, ed., *Stratopeda Gynaikon*, 156-157.
57. FO 371/78369 R11235, British consulate's report on the women's concentration camp on Trikeri island, 17 October 1949.
58. Gavriilidou, *O pateras mou*, 191-203.
59. Afroditi Mavroeidi-Pantelescou in Theodorou, ed., *Stratopeda Gynaikon*, 327-403; MGA/LDG, Info II, Appeal of Mme. Rosa Imvrioti to Premier Plastiras, June 1950. The female detainees were interned on the island of Trikeri until September 1953 and, then, they were transported to the island of Ikaria.
60. For the participation of women in the resistance and afterwards, see Tasoula Vervenioti, *I gynaika tis Antistasis. I eisodos ton gynaikon stin politiki* (Athens, 1994), and Janet Hart, *New Voices in the Nation: Women and the Greek Resistance, 1941-1964*, (Ithaca, 1996).
61. Cited in Fani Manolkidou-Vetta, *Tha se leme Ismini* (Athens, 1997), 34.
62. To a large extent information about political prisoners on Giaros is based on the 1951 detainees' memorandum to Dimitrios Papaspyrou, Minister of Justice of the Plastiras' government, hereafter cited as *Gioura detainees' memorandum*. This lengthy memorandum was photographically reproduced and published by Gnosi, (Athens, 1984).
63. FO 371/72317 R600, BPPM, Monthly report (November 1947), 14 January 1948; FO 371/72317 R11732, BPPM, Monthly report (August 1948), 30 September 1948; NARA 781.001/6-2251, Current status of imprisoned and exiled communists, 22 June 1951.
64. According to the political prisoners Georgios Glastras had been an officer at the infamous "Pavlos Melas" camp in Salonica during the German occupation. Emmanuel Bouzakis was former director of the juvenile prison in Kifissia (a suburb of Athens). In 1950, in a series of articles in the newspapers *Dimokratikos* and *Dimokratikos Typos*, Bouzakis was accused, of allowing during his administration many incidents of torture and sexual abuse of interned minors. See, *Dimokratikos Typos* 20 and 26 August 1950; *Dimokratikos*, 12 September and 11 November 1950.
65. *Youra. Livre de sang no. 2*, (n.p., n.d.), 106-108.
66. "Epidoma Giarou", *Sofronistiki Epitheorisis* 2, nos. 5-6 (1949): 55-56; FO 371/72317 R5447, BPPM, Monthly report (March 1948), 26 April 1948; FO 371/87772 R1642, BPPM, Monthly report (July 1950), 22 August 1950.
67. *Gioura detainees' memorandum*, 155
68. *Gioura detainees' memorandum*, 121-125; *Yura. Livre de sang no. 2*, 234-236; *Yiura. Ile de la mort* (n.p., n.d.), 11-12, *Dimokratikos Typos*, 12 August 1951.
69. *Gioura detainees' memorandum*, 161.
70. Andreas Fragkias described the humiliating experience of catching flies: "He passed bowed through the others. He was afraid that they might also claim his fly. This particular insect became the purpose of his life, he shouldn't lose sight of it. The single purpose of all the past years had been to arrest this fly that noon. Maybe he was born for that purpose. Moreover, he thought that if the fly got away he would die at once. How otherwise could such a lot of sweat of agony be explained?" In Fragkias, *Loimos*, 81-82. For the same humiliating activity, see Louis de Villefosse, "Makronissos, laboratoire politique," *Les Temps Modernes* 51 (January 1950): 1287-1299.
71. The idea that labor in prison should entail an element of corporal punishment can be traced back to the birth of the prison. Benjamin Constant, a liberal intellectual of the nineteenth century, argued that if prison labor was moderate it would not be differentiated from labor in the free community, then the free workers could conceive their labor as punishment. Cited in Roth, *Pratiques p(nitentiaires*, 265-267.
72. *Gioura detainees' memorandum*, 86.

Chapter 6

The Domain of Deprivation

Anastasia Kouderi, after her detention at Makronisos camp, was transferred back to the island of Trikeri as an "unrepentant." There she did not face beatings, solitary confinement, and thirst, as she had on Makronisos. On Trikeri, she wrote to her brother, ""they use other means. The only way to put pressure on us is to tear up our correspondence, to stop delivering our checks, to stop delivering our mail."[1]

Internment was not only the experience of damp cells and tasteless food; it was the separation from friends, families, and relatives as well. The penitentiary as a total institution can be theorized as the domain of deprivation.[2] No matter what activities prisoners organized inside prisons, they could not overcome certain restrictions that prison as an institution imposed. In this chapter, and within the broader framework of deprivations or restrictions on relations with the free community, visits, correspondence, and intimate relations will be discussed. The visits, correspondence, and intimate relations of political prisoners have something in common: they are emotionally charged and they belong to what is generally conceived as private life. The conditioning of emotions and the fragility of the line that separates private and public life will help me to illustrate the ambiguity of the concept of "privacy" in the social reality of prison, and that individual prisoners' emotions are an arena where the administration and the prisoners' community intervene and contend.

The unmaking and remaking of the psychic world of the prisoner lies at the center of that contest. Unmaking is a process of maximizing a person's powerlessness and deconstructing his or her subjectivity by instilling despair, fear, and shame. Remaking, which is undertaken by the prisoners' collectivity, is a process of boosting a prisoner's morale and confirming a collective identity by instilling a sense of pride and self-control over emotions. The conditioning of emotions requires that private life, where emotions thrive, become public, become knowable. From this point of view, visits, correspondence, and intimate relations, highly emotional as they are for political pris-

---

Notes for this section begin on page 127.

oners, are cases of intersection between the private and the public, the individual and the collective.

Presence

Officially, the number of visits varied according to the sentence: prisoners sentenced to death, life, or ten to twenty years could have two visits per month; those sentenced from five to ten years, three visits per month; and those sentenced for up to five years, one visit every week. Visits were allowed twice a week and each visit could not last more than half an hour.[3] However, the number of visits a political prisoner could have and the prisons' visiting hours varied greatly.[4] Actually, the frequency of these visits was under the governor's control. More than a prisoners' entitlement, visitation was a privilege subject to the authorities' decision on when and to whom it should be awarded. One of the most frequent measures of punishment was the cessation of visits and the withholding of correspondence and parcels. In camps like Makronisos and Giaros, visits were almost impossible. Besides the restrictions, one should take into account that on many occasions, the distance of a prison from the prisoner's hometown and the consequent travel expenses posed additional problems for visitors.

Visits represent a special experience for both the political prisoners and their visitors. The imprisonment of a family member was already a heavy shock; the stigma of prison could not be easily removed, even when someone was in jail for political reasons. The first shock gave way to a second when it came time to enter the prison gate and visit someone. For years, such visitors had seen prisons from the outside, believing that the prison walls protected them from the "evil" within—thus, entering the prison gate to visit a beloved person required confrontation with, and revision of, their own preconceptions. The visitors had to wait in front of the prison for the gates to open, to deliver their identity cards to the guards, to undergo a bag and body search (often a humiliating experience),[5] and then to wait until their turn to go to the visiting room. It was not uncommon for visitors to be insulted by the guards or summoned, after the visit, for interrogation.[6]

On the other hand, for the prisoners this was the big day, the long-awaited moment. They groomed themselves, put on clean clothes, and waited for their names to be called. When, finally, the two worlds met each other, they were separated by wire netting. In groups of ten, under the supervision of guards, amidst the voices and the eyes of other prisoners and visitors, and within the space of a few minutes (there is never enough time on such occasions), the two worlds tried to come closer. News about family or personal issues, news from lawyers about the prospects of a trial, and information about the political situation reached the side behind the wire netting.

When these long-awaited meetings finally did occur, they were a source of both joy and frustration for the prisoners. The powerlessness of the prisoners pervaded the visits; things took on different dimensions and emotions were heightened. Prisoners expected their visitors to come more often, to bring news, to take care of their families and businesses, to bring food and clothes, and so on, while they were in jail and could do almost nothing. At the same time, the presence of the other was a reminder of what the prisoners were missing. They realized that all their activities in prison, and the visits alike, could not but be poor substitutes for real life. The joy of a visit afterwards became a source of sorrow, until the next visit. Good and bad news, emotions, demands, and plans were filtered through the feeling of dependence on their visitors and the memory of their free lives.

Visits create their own temporality in prison life. One prisoner, writing to his wife, described Sundays and Mondays as "sad, wearisome, annoying, and unbearable."[7] And this because visiting days were Tuesdays, Thursdays and Saturdays, and the lapse of two days without visiting gave different dimensions to Sundays and Mondays. The experience of time in prison is marked by the absence or the presence of the free other. Moreover, the routine of prison, where every day is the same, where nothing happens, distorts the sense of time; only events like transfers or holidays mark the passage of time. Visits, exceptional as they are, reconstitute the subjective experience of time. Visits interrupt the repetition of nothing in prison life, as exemplified in an excerpt from a diary Georgoulas Beikos kept while he was at the Lamia prison in 1948.

> 23/6 My father-in-law left [he had come to visit Beikos]. Nothing else.
>
> 24/6 Visit. My cousin Aliki came. She brought my clothes. Nothing else.
>
> 25/6 Nothing. The lawyer came. We want to lodge an appeal. I haven't heard anything yet about my *in absentia* sentence.
>
> 26/6 Visit. Marianthi came. She brought a picture of me and Mario [his wife] from 1945. Nothing else.
>
> 27/6 [illegible] Sunday. Nothing else. It was cold. [illegible]
>
> 28/6 Nothing. I signed the appeal for the misdemeanor of 24/4/48. I reported to the director and he told me that I will return to the Averof prison. I wrote a letter to Al. Palamioti in America and to my lawyer [name illegible].
>
> 29/6 I had a letter from Antonis. He is fine. Aliki visited me. Nothing else. My lawyer came and we talked about the trial. The weather is good. It was not very cold.[8]

The initial shock of seeing a beloved person behind the wire netting quickly gives way to observation of the changes the passage of time has brought upon the other. "Our families are tortured like we are," a prisoner wrote after meeting her sister and noticing that "her eyes are examining me, observing me."[9] The prisoners and their families experience the calamity of the civil war, but from different positions, which creates a distance. The prisoner and the visitor are aware that some things are hidden, not told to each other—sometimes on purpose, because a prisoner does not want to worry the visitor; sometimes because the prisoner believes that no matter how hard one tries, it is impossible to convey to the other the experience of internment: the free person cannot understand what it means to be in jail. What separates them in the visiting room is not the wire netting but the experience of imprisonment, which remains incomprehensible to the free citizen. Visits are not occasions on which the distance between inside and outside is removed. On the contrary, the participants realize their different positions, what it means to be outside or inside.

The number of visits depended not only on the regulations but also on the distance of the prison from a prisoner's hometown. Lucky were those who were imprisoned in their hometowns. Visits went together with news, clean clothes, and homemade food, very important things in prison. Even when the news was discussed or the food shared, an invisible distinction divided those who had frequent visits and those who had none. Apart from distance, sometimes also the stigma of having a relative in prison or allegiance to opposite political views made people reluctant to visit a political prisoner. Gradually in the collective life of prison, the out-of-towners were partially integrated into a new network of acquaintances is made where—a network quite useful when they were released and decided to live in that town.[10]

Most importantly visits were subject to the authority of prison administration. Often, the authorities gave permission for visits on the condition that the visitor would persuade the political detainee to sign the declaration of repentance. These visits were the most painful, because they distanced the prisoner from his loved ones even more. For instance, one prisoner saw his father crying because he had declined his father's suggestion to sign a declaration. The same prisoner, Giorgos Giannopoulos, later dissuaded his girlfriend from visiting him at the Makronisos camps. Only relatives were allowed to visit prisoners, but it was not only that. "The reason why," he wrote to her, "thousands of reasons: all kinds of humiliations and indignities."[11]

Visits always took place under the supervision of guards. According to a circular from the Ministry of Justice, "the visit must always take place in the presence of a prison guard, who follows the conversation and supervises to prevent the delivery of hazardous objects to the prisoners."[12] This gave the guards the opportunity to intervene, advising the prisoners to think about their own and their families' situation. Visits were not moments of privacy, but instances in which the private lives of political prisoners came under public scrutiny. The sign "Speak quietly," which even today hangs in the visiting room of the abandoned Aegina prison, reminded prisoners and their visitors that there were rules of conduct for both. Feelings of solitude, shame, desire, and nostalgia due to exclusion from civil society and the deconstruction of private life were sometimes sharpened during visits, and sometimes repressed. But visits were small intervals in the long period of incarceration. Most of the times, prisoners had to cope not with the presence but the absence of the other.

Absence

The frequency of correspondence was regulated much as visits were. Those imprisoned for life, or sentenced to death or ten to twenty years, could send and receive two letters per month; those sentenced from five to ten years could send and receive three letters per month; and those convicted for up to five years, one letter every week.[13] Additional restrictions were that prisoners could not send letters addressed to state or other authorities or to the press, that their correspondence should concern only family matters, and that correspondence between prisoners was not allowed.[14] The letters from and to the prisoners were collected and then censored (phrases or words considered objectionable were obliterated) by the authorities. Collection or delivery could be arranged on an individual basis or assigned to a prisoner. Letters from the prisoners were written on official stationery that was distributed for this purpose.[15]

Correspondence was itself an exceptional event. How many political prisoners had corresponded before in their lives? Probably very few, and those very few times, considering the high level of illiteracy and the low development of communications. This is all the more so when we think of the occasions on which people from the lower social strata did correspond, war and migration being the most usual reasons. Imprisonment and exile, therefore, created new conditions and new needs for thousands of people. Correspondence was one of the new needs, since often it was the only way to communicate with the free community.

Correspondence substituted for all other means of information and communication. Networks of information needed to be reconstructed; for that purpose, in many cases, there were two senders the same letter, or one sender who sent the letter to two recipients—the first recipient was supposed to forward the letter to the second. For the same purpose, senders tried to give or request information about other people, at least whether they were still alive, and sometimes wrote the news of a death. Thus letters, though were a private matter, had an interpersonal purpose, the reconstitution of a network that had been destroyed due to civil war.

On a sheet of paper, political prisoners had to compress feelings, demands, needs, and anxieties—the desperate need to be in touch with one's family, partner, or friends. The distance sharpened the feelings, and the letters are full of emotional outbursts.

> My darling, Maria. Hi! You will rub your eyes in disbelief. And if you don't count me among the living, you won't believe your own eyes. (…) It's a year now since I heard anything from you or from Pavlos. Since March 1949 from you and since August 1949 from Pavlos. I try to guess what has happened. Many prisoners have received letters, and I am worried about you. They wrote that Pavlos was killed in May 1950, near to Karditsa. I've prepared myself for this as well. But my joy will be great on learning that you are all right. And joy here is unusual. And we can expect it only from you; the joy of one person becomes joy for all of us, a real party. When they wrote about Pavlos, everybody was sad. On August 15th, we celebrated your name day, as much as we could. The same happened last year on death row; we celebrated you with songs and dances.[16]

In this note, smuggled out of Corfu prison by a prisoner, the most contradictory feelings of pain and happiness, grief and celebration, are interlaced within a few lines: joy that the letter would bring joy to the recipient, anxiety while waiting for a letter that had not yet arrived, grief for an unconfirmed death. A note can be as contradictory as life in prison, like singing and dancing on death row. And these emotions were not strictly personal; they were shared by the prisoners' collectivity. The prisoners' collectivity celebrated a happy event with the prisoner and supported him when bad news arrived.

Some occasions heighten these feelings further. In one of the few love letters available, Koula Ntakou, a female prisoner at the Averof prison, writes to her husband, a political refugee in Romania:

> Aristeidis, my treasure, I got your letter of 17 December, and you ask me why I worry. Yes, you don't understand my worry; it's not that my health is not good, it is very good. What makes me collapse is that I'm away from you, and there is nothing but worry left. (…) On 20 December I sent you another letter, but they returned it to me twice because I've written too many, so I made a third one of two pages. (…) Oh, my sweetheart, when will the prison bars break, so we can meet each other again? This question bothers me a lot. Aristeidis, be patient to get over this critical situation and be sure that one day we shall meet each other again. Oh, my love, how did I leave you and find myself in prison. You write me to study in order to elevate my cultural level. I think that we have enough of education here in prison. I wish you knew the sorrow and the sighs that I have been through these days, my tears make a river in my eyes, because, since I was born, I haven't lived a happy day; all my life has been full of sorrow and bitterness. Why, my love, to be so unhappy? It is my destiny to live my life in sorrow. Finally I kiss you with pain in my lips. Your beloved wife Koula Ntakou. Goodbye, till we meet again.[17]

Her love and her sense of loneliness and worry are salient in this letter. The distance and their different positions (she, a prisoner in Greece; he, a refugee abroad) create a communication gap (*you don't understand my worry*) that she tries to bridge by assuring him of her love and her unhappiness about the separation. Their separation as a consequence of the political involvement makes her question that involvement implicitly in the form of doubting her previous decisions (*how did I leave you and find myself in prison*). Pain overrides all other concerns, as is alluded in the way she mentions the classes in the prison. In her world of unhappiness and sorrow there is only one concern: her husband. These emotions are heightened by the fact that her letter has been returned because it was too long, which means that she had to rewrite it and undergo the same process of reenacting painful emotions, this time in order to compress them even more. On top of that, she sends her letter on 1 January, the first day of a new year and a day for family occasions, which makes her even more sad and lonely. For her, prison is void of political connotations and becomes the latest episode in the unhappy life of a woman from the lower social classes.[18]

Prisoners find themselves in the position of being the demanding ones. They ask for money, clothes, medicine, information about family issues (especially the health of family members) and photos. "Send me a picture of you," prisoners write in their letters, or occasionally they manage to send pictures of themselves from prison or exile. Photographs are tokens that political prisoners are alive and well. Signs of the ordeal of prison are absent in these pictures: prisoners wear their best clothes, the men are shaved, and the locations are carefully chosen not to remind prison or camp. They are constantly afraid of being forgotten, and they need to remember. A picture is the imaginary presence of the other. For friends and relatives, a picture of the prisoner is an awkward reminder and presence of a captive in a world where "life goes on." For the prisoner, a picture of a beloved person is a desired presence, a remembrance of free life and a future orientation whilst in the prison world, where nothing happens and which therefore cannot be but a break, a transitory world, a liminal place.

In relation to correspondence, two issues may be raised: the censored letter and the distribution of letters. Both are linked to the separation of the private and public spheres. The censored letter reflected a censored society and carried the imprint of the personal experience of censorship. The imprint of the censored society was already visible on the envelope, where the post office stamped messages like "Love religion and heroic Greece—Respect her laws" or "Do not forget that you were born Greek." Under the state of censorship, the private sphere was literally transformed into a public one, just as the private lives of citizens was under police surveillance. Moreover, the prisoners when they wrote letters had to "confine themselves to family issues" (a phrase printed on the official writing paper distributed to the prisoners) in order to avoid censorship by the authorities. The private (family issues) was intended to become public as the censor read the letter, but the public (the political situation, the course of the civil war, or prisoners' living conditions) was to remain secret; marking a reversal of the established separation between private life and the public sphere in terms of state interference and public knowledge. Thus, the prisoner was to "confine himself" (the irony of the rhetoric schema is obvious), to censor himself before the authorities stamped "Checked" on the letter. The prisoner had to learn to be self-restrained before the authorities intervened, which "reenact[ed] the drama of the powerlessness of [the] writer."[19] Since private life was penetrable by the power of the authorities, self-restraint became the quintessence of individuals' everyday conduct—the ideal Foucauldian disciplinary society.

The distribution of letters, and the reading that followed, posed the same problem of private/public, but from a different point of view. Correspondence was an exceptional event in the life of the prison, and the infrequency of delivery strengthened this impression. As all the letters were delivered to the prisoners on the same day, the personal letter was transformed into a public event inside the prison, a matter for the prisoners' community. The letter that arrived was discussed, shared with the fellow inmates. Many times it became public in the strict sense, in the case of illiterate prisoners who needed the help of the literate to write or read a letter. Jean Hebrard argued for the collective character of the popular sociability of correspondence, and political prisoners' correspondence is a case in point.[20] This was true not only for the illiterate but more generally, because the intersection of the need to reconstitute a social network and the simultaneous need for privacy and secrecy blurred any distinction between private and public.

The distinction between the private and public spheres may be seen in the light of the relation between the individual and the collectivity. On the one hand, it should be pointed out that the political prisoners' community was based not only on the fact of their imprisonment but also on their common past. Societal and political ties created during the resistance and afterwards constituted the background of such a community. This common background permitted the detainees to share feelings and news, so that a detained mother would write to her son that "It was not just me that was happy but all the women who are here, and in particular those who knew you outside the prison."[21] Just as life in prison was shared by the prisoners, so the personal issues were part of the community's life.

On the other hand, privacy was undermined both by the authorities' censorship and the control of the collectivity. The latter refers to the fact that political prisoners' letters were read and censored first by members of the party mechanism and then by the authorities. Just as a part of the goods delivered in parcels was to be shared with fellow inmates, and a share of the postal order was to be given to the treasury of the collectivity, private issues and the small secrets of one's correspondence became public as well. Private becomes public in order to support the coherence of the community, and at the same time the private is conceived as a potential adversary of the community (bad news, for instance, could make someone to seek his or her release and sign a declaration of repentance). Privacy presupposes the secrecy of personal life, which is opposed to the exercise of power by the party mechanism. Prerequisite for the exercise of power is the knowledge of the individual. In order to maintain and exercise its power, the leadership of the collectivity renders the private life of the political detainees a field of its knowledge.

"Send us your body in a picture"

The deprivation of heterosexual intercourse is common to all total institutions. The birth of prison comes along with the classification and separation of prisoners, also with regard to sex: the first modern cellular prison at Ghent, begun in 1773, had separate sections for criminals, petty offenders, women, and juveniles.[22] The punishment, once more, focuses on the prisoner's body through the negation of the satisfaction of sexual desire. Separate prisons and camps for male and female detainees, or separate cell blocks; in all cases, except in exile and only for some time, as we shall see, men and women political prisoners of the Greek Civil War lived apart.

The prisoner is deprived both of the sexual relationship and of the object of sexual desire. Inasmuch as the prison is a world apart, consisting exclusively of either women or men, the prisoner's self-image and identity are at stake, and "since a significant half of his audience is denied him, the inmate's self image is in danger of becoming half complete, fractured, a monochrome without the hues of reality."[23] Or, as a female political prisoner bluntly put it, "we ran the risk of forgetting our sex."[24] A photo of the other can be a substitute for his or her presence. Female prisoners wrote in verse: "You are abroad we are abroad / in a foreign province, send us your body in a picture."[25] Distance is coupled with separation. The women in the Averof prison who wrote this poem consider themselves to be in a "foreign province," an unfamiliar place. The picture of the beloved mitigates the pain of separation and may also help in reconstituting familiarity with the world. But what is more striking is the collective expression of these feelings. Intimate relations that are normally at the core of one's own private life are shared among prisoners and take on the form of a collective appeal marked by the use of "we" and "us." In the same vein, the beloved person becomes idealized and abstract—he is not a specific person. The absent loved ones are all the female prisoners' partners; nevertheless, they have one body, because what the women are missing is only their partners but also the male presence in their segregated world. The "I" is intertwined with the "we," denoting the shared painful experience of prison life; the line between the private and the public is blurred, and the "we" can be an almost automatic expansion of the "I."[26]

The substitution, repression, or transference of sexual desire, can be detected in the love songs that prisoners sang, the love poems they wrote, the dances and the feasts they organized, or their writings. Dimitris Glinos, a prominent leftist intellectual, wrote from the Akronafplia prison: "[When I enter the dormitory] it is like entering in a room that is heated by the beloved woman's breath."[27] In the segregated male and female world of political prisoners, we may assume that there is to some extent a homoerotic atmosphere, but no satisfaction; or at least, silence is interposed on this topic. Homosexual intercourse was not only prohibited by the rules but was also something unthinkable for the communists and their ethos. In the literature of political prisoners' memoirs there is only one mention, to my knowledge, of a homosexual political prisoner, which I think is interesting because it is full of stereotypes. The political prisoner who expressed his homosexuality was incarcerated at the Corfu prison. In his defence before the prisoners' leadership he told his story. In his youth, he had been a victim of a priest's pederasty, but in the resistance he broke with his past. "It was my mistake", he said in his defense, "my old self woke up after four years. I won't do it again. Yes, I am homosexual, but I'll try to stop it." Nevertheless, the leadership decided upon his expulsion from the political prisoners' wing; when he did not consent, they kicked him out. His case remained a secret in the prison.[28]

For certain periods of time (before 1947 and after 1954) men and women lived together in exile on the same islands. In these cases the women and men lived separately, and the political exiles' sexual life was supervised by the collectivity and the leadership. Personal relations between persons of the opposite sex, and the problems that might arise, were considered by the exiles' collectivity to be a potential threat to its coherence. The bureau of the collectivity kept an eye on the exiles' private lives and something like a code of "good conduct" ruled their comportment. According to a female exile's testimony, as soon as she arrived on the island of Agios Efstratios, the bureau of collectivity informed her about the restrictions on her relations with men: among other things, it was forbidden to hold a man's hand except in greeting, to go to a man's room while he was alone, to walk on the street only with one man, for a man to enter the women's dormitories.[29] The same code also ruled sexual relations between exiles and islanders. Inasmuch as the exiles were heavily dependent on good relations with the native population, anything that could damage these relations or the image of the political exiles in general, was prohibited. Since the issues of personal life were considered issues of public interest, they were treated the same way: the "bureau" discussed the case and decided the penalty.[30]

The policing of political prisoners' sexuality was organized by the "bureau." On the island of Giaros, the "bureau" assigned to certain prisoners the duty of supervising the prisoners' tents at night to look out for "misconduct." Given the absence of any kind of permitted sexual satisfaction, the object of sexual desire was prohibited too. In the 1950s, when the reading of certain newspapers was allowed in prisons, the bureau first read the newspaper to censor not only the political articles that might undermine political prisoners' morale, but also "reprehensible" pictures that might go against their morality. Pictures of women in "provocative" skirts, for instance, were covered with other, irrelevant pictures.[31] The policing of political detainees' sexuality sought to imbue them with the properties of self-restraint and self-control. Communists should learn to conquer their passions and tame their drives. They should learn to be cool: "the golden mean, serenity and restraint,"[32] are for the "engineers of the human soul," the properties of the communist. The need to fulfill their wishes and desires may have driven them to step closer to their release and their families, but away from the prisoners' collectivity. The process of imbuing the prisoners with self-restraint in the presence of the opposite sex, which by definition was very limited and controlled (visits), was portrayed as a source of distraction and danger. In the end, self-restraint for the prisoners meant placing themselves beyond sexual desire and ignoring, or pretending to do so, the presence of the opposite sex. In his letters from prison, one prisoner mentioned a window at the Averof prison from which prisoners watched women and couples passing by in the street. He described that street as "dangerous," acknowledging that every time he looked from that window, he needed some time afterwards to restore his equilibrium. "How many times," fellow prisoners would say to someone looking out from that window, "have I told you that it's not good to sit here and watch that, the street? Come on, let's go to the cell."[33]

The policing of sexuality cultivated an ethos based on the paradigm of asceticism, austerity of morals, and the conjugal virtue of monogamy. To better understand this aspect one must take into consideration the anticommunist propaganda and discourse. According to anticommunist and nationalist propaganda, communism was an adversary of the three pillars of the Greek nation: motherland, religion and family. Communism was the enemy of the family; it stood for "common ownership of women," for the "abolition [sic] of women's virginity."[34] One of the arguments against the Democratic Army was that guerilla men were seducing young women and introducing them into "free love." A typical example of this is found in a propaganda brochure publicizing testimonies of repentant communists: "The Political Commissariat (…) had a whole bunch of lovers, whom he had promoted to officers (…) With one of them, the most favorite, he had ambitions to have a child, although he was married and had a child in Athens."[35] The anticommunist propaganda was incorporated into a discourse that considered female communists to be either misguided (if they denounced communism) or of loose morals, and communism to be an adversary of the family.

Equally interesting is that the Communist Party discourse on sexuality focused on women's sexuality in particular. Women were regarded as the dangerous sex. What were the virtues of the female communist, according to politburo member Chrysa Chatzivasileiou? They are, as she wrote in a brochure published in 1947, "impeccable morals, a sober appearance, modest doings, civilized behavior in her private and social life," and, finally, her "courageous performance in the struggle for the liberation of the Greek woman."[36] "Morals" and "appearance" were ranked first in the profile of the female communist, showing that the patterns of control over women's sexuality in the domestic field were transferred to the public and political field. The entrance of women into politics made politics an additional field of control of women's sexuality.

Political prisoners and exiles had to demonstrate that they supported the institution of the family and the established ideas on gender in a society as traditional as Greece was in the 1940s. The policing of sexuality in exile was a way to remove the stigma of communism being the enemy of the family, and to restore the image of communists as householders and the upholders of austere morals. The institution of family could not and should not be questioned, but supported.

Notes

1. ASKI, box 422 F25/4/19, Letter of Anastasia Kouderi from the Trikeri women's camp, 20 December 1950.
2. Gresham Sykes, *The Society of Captives* (Princeton, 1958), 63-78. Gresham Sykes, in this authoritative study, categorized these deprivations into the deprivation of liberty, of goods and services, of heterosexual relationships, of autonomy, and of security. He studied the case of maximum security prisons in the United States and for this reason his analysis cannot be fully applied to political prisoners. For instance, the deprivation of security concerned criminal relations among prisoners (i.e., offenses by other prisoners), a feature that seldom appears among political prisoners.
3. Royal Decree, On Prisons' Internal Regulation, *Government Gazette* 194, 17 July 1923, article 21.
4. At the Averof women's prison the visiting hours were three days a week for three hours each time, whereas at the Aegina prison in 1946 they were two days a week for two hours. Aegina Prison Archives, Correspondence of Ministry of Justice, 1945-1946, box 34, From the ministry to the director of Aegina prisons, 15258, 27 February 1946. After the end of the Civil War, in 1953, the visits that prisoners could have were doubled. See, Aegina Prison Archives, Book of orders of the day, Aegina Penitentiary, Order of the day of the penitentiary on 24 July 1953.
5. Betty Ambatielou, after her visit to her husband Nikos Ambatielos in prison while he was awaiting trial, described her experience as follows: "We showed our food at the table and moved on. We were searched by an old hag of about sixty, who screamed the most lewd jokes at the women as she ran her hands over them. She had a thin, shrill voice. The

women felt ashamed when she ran her hands round their hips and between their legs." In Anthony Simmons, *They Shall Not Die. The Trial of Greek Freedom* (London, n.d.), 8.
6. *Eleftheri Ellada*, Letter from Thebes prison, 15 January 1947.
7. Thodoros Ydraios, *Grammata apo ti fylaki* (Athens, 1984), 22.
8. I would like to thank Dimitra Lambropoulou, who gave me a copy of Georgoulas Beikos' diary. The diary, as well as letters and other writings, is part of his personal archive.
9. Gavriilidou, *O pateras mou*, 207.
10. Maria Sideri, *Dekatessera chronia* (Athens, 1981),133-4.
11. Giorgos Giannopoulos, *Makronisos. Martyries enos foititi 1947-1950* (Athens, 2001), 11-12, 30.
12. Ypourgeion Dikaiosynis, *Egkyklioi kai ypourgikai apofaseis*, 37
13. Royal Decree, On Prisons' Internal Regulation, article 22.
14. Aegina Prison Archives, Circular from the Ministry of Justice to the Directors of State Prisons, 41833/28, 14 May 1946; Ypourgeion Dikaiosynis, *Egkyklioi kai ypourgikai apofaseis*, 77-78, 106-107, 153.
15. It is worth noting that aat the top of the writing paper distributed by the administration one read: "The dispatch of coffee and cigarettes is forbidden. Be brief. Confine yourselves to *family issues*." (Original emphasis.)
16. ASKI, box 422 F25/4/7, Note of Babis Georgoulas from Corfu prison, 15 September 1950.
17. ASKI, box 422 F25/4/22, Letter of Koula Ntakou from Averof prison, 1 January 1951.
18. For Greek political prisoners' love letters, see also the interesting remarks in Dimitra Lambropoulou, *Grafontas apo ti fylaki. Opseis tis ypokeimenikotitas ton politikon kratoumenon 1947-1960* (Athens, 1999), 105-113.
19. Jann Matlock, "Doubling Out of the Crazy House: Gender, Autobiography, and the Insane Asylum System in Nineteenth-Century France," *Representations* 34 (1991): 170.
20. Jean Hebrard, "La lettre représentée. Les pratiques épistolaires populaires dans les récits de vie ouvriers et paysans", in *La correspondance. Les usages de la lettre au XIXe siècle*, ed. Roger Chartier (Paris, 1991), 279-365.
21. ASKI, box 422 F25/4/6, Letter of Panagiota Tsitoura, Athens, 30 August 1950. One has to notice that the word "you" is in the plural; the fusion of the individual (the son she is referring to) and the collective (his fellows) is indicative of the way that the two were inextricably related.
22. Leslie Fairweather, "The Evolution of Prison", in *Prison Architecture*, United Nations Social Defence Research Institute (London, 1975), 16.
23. Sykes, *The Society of Captives*, 72.
24. Pagona Stefanou, *Ton afanon* (Athens, 1997), 80.
25. ASKI, box 422 F25/4/8, Letter from Averof prison, 16 September 1950.
26. Lambropoulou, *Grafontas apo ti fylaki*, 125.
27. Letter of Dimitris Glinos from Akronafplia prison, 14 September 1937, cited in, *Sti mnimi Dimitri A. Glinou* (Athens, 1946), 180-181.
28. Stamatis Skourtis, *Aftoi pou dropiasan to thanato* (Athens, 1996), 301-306.
29. Anonymous testimony in Vardinogiannis and Aronis, eds., *Oi misoi sta sidera*, 514-515; also, Maria Karra, *Emeis oi ap' exo. PEOPEF: 1948-1954. Mia mikri epopoiia* (Athens, 1995), 212.
30. Kenna, "The Social Organization of Exile," 63-81.
31. Vardis Vardinogiannis, "Ta 'kyria arthra'," in Vardinogiannis and Aronis, eds., *Oi misoi sta sidera*, 529-531.
32. Nikos Zachariadis, *O kommounistis, laikos agonistis melos tou KKE* (Athens, 1946), 17.
33. Ydraios, *Grammata apo ti fylaki*, 59.

34. D. G. Panagiotopoulos, *O vourkos tou kommounismou* (Salonica, 1947), 53; Georgios Themelis, *O erythros fasismos* (Patras, 1947), 48.
35. Anastasios Kotzias testimony, in the brochure *Epistrofi stin Ellada* (n. p., 1949), 28.
36. Chrysa Chatzivasileiou, *To KKE kai to gynaikeio zitima* (Athens, 1947), 30.

Chapter 7

Probing the Limits of the Other

Torture and solitary confinement represent two different but extreme situations for prisoners. In the case of torture, they are alone with their tormentors, during interrogations in particular. This is the domain of extreme physical pain: beatings, elaborate torture techniques, malnutrition, exhaustion—anything that can be used to bring the inmates to the edge of their physical and psychic endurance. Solitary confinement, on the other hand, tests the limits of physical as well as psychic endurance, but in a different way. The inmate is completely alone, spending days and nights in a dark cell with a minimum of food and water and without any communication whatsoever.

These two extreme situations have some things in common. The inmate is alone, without fellow inmates. This sense of loneliness and powerlessness is heightened by the fact that the inmate is brought, defenseless, under the domain of the custodians' power. The body and the psyche no longer belong to the inmate; they become objects of the custodians. Torture and solitary confinement gradually deconstruct the prisoner's world in a systematic attempt to turn it upside down. Anything that is regarded as an essential need, as human, as normal, is questioned or negated.

In the Greek Civil War, solitary confinement was not necessarily used as a measure of punishment. Nor was torture always a means to extort information from the inmate. At this point, as Edward Peters argues, lies the difference between torture in earlier times and torture in the twentieth century. From the thirteenth to the eighteenth century, torture was part of the legal procedure within the framework of confession, that is a means to obtain the victim's confession. The use of torture in the twentieth century was aimed not at the victim's information but at the person of the victim.[1] During the Greek Civil War torture was systematically employed not to obtain the prisoners' confessions of alleged crimes, rather to make them sign declarations of repentance. The authorities' aim was to deconstruct prisoners' subjectivity and dissolve their collectivity. From this viewpoint, torture can be ana-

---

Notes for this section begin on page 142.

lyzed as technique to unmake the prisoner's world through corporal pain and psychic violence.

Within the same framework of unmaking the political prisoner's world, solitary confinement serves a specific purpose. In this chapter, solitary confinement will be discussed both in the strict sense, that is, one person serving a prison term in solitary confinement, and also in a broader sense, that of segregating a prisoner or a group of prisoners from the others for a limited period of time. In both cases, I will argue, solitary confinement is a technique of imposing individualism with the object of breaking up political prisoners' collectivity. Removing prisoners, creating different categories of prisoners, and granting privileges or imposing restrictions are different aspects of the same strategy: attacking and dissolving political prisoners' collectivity.

Torture

The pain that a body feels cannot be literally described. Only the use of metaphor or simile provides the means for the tortured to speak or write about the pain suffered. A political detainee, describing his experience of being heavily tortured at a police station in Patras in May 1945, writes: "[T]hey beat me furiously on the soles of my feet until I lost my light, I lost the world."[2] The tormented person is incapable to describe the pain because, Elaine Scarry tells us, pain destroys language. Pain can not be verbalized because "physical pain—unlike any other state of consciousness—has no referential content. It is not *of* or *for* anything. It is precisely because it takes no object that it, more than any other phenomenon, resists objectification in language."[3] Expression of pain is limited to non-verbal forms, namely the groan, the scream, the cry.

New prisoners were encouraged and advised by the older ones to shout, not to weep.[4] Weeping was a sign of collapse, maybe because tears are not simply an emotional expression but are mediated by thought, the thought of the political prisoner's defeat and its consequences.[5] The purpose of the shout was to communicate the pain. Expression rather than internalization made the pain more bearable. It was the message, directed at the torturers, that their aim of inflicting pain had been achieved, and was sometimes also a good device for the prisoner to alleviate the duration and brutality of the torture. However, what was communicated was the sheer fact of pain and not the experience of it; the tormented person was always alone in his or her pain.

"I lost the world," wrote a former prisoner to describe how he felt being tortured: this phrase grasps the essence of torture. Torture is the violent deconstruction of a prisoner's subjectivity, the unmaking of prisoner's world. Torture will be discussed in the following section as a technique that combines different but interlinked phases. These can be analyzed as three processes: the process of performance, related to the place and the time of the torture; the process of corporal violence, related to techniques of causing corporal pain; and the process of psychological violence, related to techniques of inflicting psychic pain. The distinction between psychic and corporal torture, though necessary, is to a certain extent artificial. Emotions like fear and hopelessness may actually increase the victim's perception of pain, and therefore lower one's ability to endure pain.[6]

The Process of Performance

Any site can be transformed into a place for torture, if it meets the requirements of a certain isolation. The authorities know that the place must satisfy two necessary conditions. First, no well-disposed eyewitness should be present. Second, those who should know what is happening must in some way— that is, by some means under the authorities' control—be made aware of it. Away from or impenetrable to the public but close to other inmates, a controlled diffusion of fear is the authorities' aim. A prison cell, a tent in a camp, the basement of a police station may provide the necessary setting. Many times the place itself arouses fear. Panagiotis Vidalis did not need to be told by a lieutenant, "We will shoot you in the same place that the Germans shot others during the occupation", since he found himself in the Chaidari camp, which during the occupation had been a concentration camp where, he knew, several people had been executed.[7] Perhaps something more can be added to the setting, something that is linked to the process of corporal torture. In a place for torture, anything can be turned into a tool or a medium for this purpose. A chair, a table, or even a fig tree, like the one at the Giaros camp, may be used by the torturers to tie up the prisoners. The sea becomes a place to drown them; the cloth of a tent, a cover to blind them when they are being attacked, and so forth.

Torture usually takes place during interrogations, which means after the arrest and before the trial—except for the camps on Makronisos and Giaros, where torments constituted an everyday reality. Torture has its timetable. Most torture takes place during the night, not for safety measures but rather to startle the inmate. The inmate must be in a state of constant fear and the torturer must manipulate it. At night, the torturer can take advantage of the sleeping inmate's exhaustion and relaxation, and exhaust the victim further through sleep deprivation. At the Makronisos camps, the prisoners slept in shifts in an attempt to protect themselves from these surprise night attacks.[8] Torture could last for many hours or even days. Each phase of the torture finished whenever the prisoner was completely exhausted or unconscious. Sometimes a doctor examined the sufferer to pronounce whether the torture might be continued. In the hours between bouts of torture, the prisoners would recover and, the tormentors hoped, rethink their conduct. In this process the prisoners were by turns the objects and the witnesses, the actual and the imaginary victims: actual when they were being tormented, imaginary when they were listening to the shouts or seeing the wounds and blood of their fellow inmates.

Party members had also their instructions on what to do in case of interrogation. They were advised to deny any affiliation with the Communist Party, to deny any accusation, to refuse to sign any confession whatsoever, to help and encourage other inmates, to be careful not to jeopardize the underground party mechanism through their contacts with friends and relatives, and not to be talkative with fellow inmates because an undercover police agent might be among them.[9] The emphasis of these instructions was on safeguarding the party mechanism rather than the individual detainee.

The Process of Corporal Torment

Torture is a study and a technique in the bodily geography of pain. The body was broken into pieces that each produced its own pain effect: nails pulled out or pins inserted under the nails, the joints of the legs beaten with a hammer, genitals twisted, breasts burned with cigarettes. The body was no longer the prisoner's body—it was a material, a body of knowledge for the torturer. It was not the prisoner's body anymore because it would become a new one, the tormented body: unrecognizable with blood and wounds, swollen and sweaty, changed as it carried the signs of the pain experienced, broken parts and scars. A prisoner described the horror of the Makronisos camps as follows

> Continuous beatings with canes, iron rods, batons till the victims fell unconscious. Thirst for many days (there are occasions when the victims suffered from delusions and drank their own urine). Hunger for many days to the point of exhaustion. In the summer, naked in the sun and walking on glowing corrugated metal, and in the winter, naked and up, having buckets of water thrown on our bodies. Other times they were thrown into the sea, and then left with their wet clothes to dry on them while they carried their wet luggage. Systematic beating on the joints, twisting of the genitals, sleeplessness for days and nights. (…) Throwing into the sea and pushing the victim with a piece of wood so that he would stay in the water, until he would fall unconscious.[10]

New methods were adopted and others were abandoned, variations on methods appeared, new devices were added to improve the efficacy of the torture. Even if we identify certain torture methods as characteristic of that era, it is also important to keep in mind that since there were no strict orders for tortures, they varied according to the torturer's personality, temperament, and vices. Torture is a domain of extreme arbitrariness and violence that has only one limit, the physical extermination of the political prisoner; its technique is based on the infliction of the most severe pain for the longest duration. Although there are cases of political prisoners who died during interrogation or torture, generally speaking the authorities' aim was to bring the inmates to the end of their endurance, both physically and psychologically. The long-term consequences of torture also have to be taken into consideration. In their memoirs, many political prisoners mention their own or their fellow inmates' nightmares of being tortured, as well as cases of mental aberration in prisoners or disabilities caused by torture.

Under the Metaxas regime, the most brutal tortures were coercing the prisoner to drink castor oil or to sit naked on a column of ice. These methods could not be exercised intensively because after a few times, the inmates had to be hospitalized for dysentery and pneumonia. The bastinado is a method whose period of use exceeds the era under examination (it was to be the dominant method of torture also during the Colonels' dictatorship in Greece between 1967 and 1974). Victims were laid on the floor with their feet pulled through the back of a chair, or they were laid on a bed with their feet jutting out from the bed; then they were beaten on the naked sole with a baton (sometimes the victims were allowed to wear their shoes because in this way the stroke of the baton covered the whole sole). One detainee described a method called *litarisma,* or "penicillin." The hands and feet were bound firmly with thin rope or thick string, hands behind the back, and tied like this she had to stand for hours: "the blood circulation stops, the heart beats fast, the ears ring, the head 'beats' loudly as well. You lose your senses, you fall …"[11] Another female detainee recalls that her hands and knees were tied with wire to a pillar as she stood barefoot on the wet ground; then four tormentors beat her with thin cables and wire from the top down, all over the body.[12] On Makronisos political prisoners were tied in a sack together with a cat and thrown into the sea, so that the frightened cat would attack the prisoner; they were left for hours standing with their hands outstretched and the left foot stretched back (a position called "airplane"); they were thrown with their clothes and shoes on into the sea and then dragged out of the water with a rope. The torments that the minors in the juvenile prisons of Kifissia (a suburb of Athens) underwent in 1948 were beyond imagination. The tormentors beat the young boys with batons, wires, and socks full of concrete; they forced them to eat soap; they used a method the detainees called "balloon", whereby a guard punched an inmate along a corridor and then pushed him to the next guard; on the boys' chests, they sewed nametags with Slavic endings added to the names; they forced the exhausted inmates to give blood; many boys were raped.[13]

In the spring of 1949, several of those minors were transferred to the Makronisos camps. Undergoing a similar ordeal of humiliation and maltreatment, some of them swallowed their spoons.[14] This was both an act of despair and an attempt to achieve temporary removal from the camp by being admitted to the hospital, where they would be left in peace for some time. For them, their bodies became a medium and a locus for using a device that might have been fatal to achieve the goal of transfer.

The process of psychic violence

The authorities knew well that torture is a question to which no prisoner can give an a priori answer.[15] For that reason, psychic violence is crucial to the process. Psychic violence seeks to inflict and maximize fear, as well as anxiety and shame, and to break the mental and psychic resistance of the prisoner. When the political exiles at the Makronisos camps came under the jurisdiction of the army in the last months of 1949, they signed declarations of repentance without being heavily tortured corporally. The military police employed psychological violence to a large extent. First, they asked the political exiles in each group transferred to the military camp whether they would sign declarations of repentance; of those who refused, a small number were severely beaten in front of the others, who, terrified that they would be beaten in the same brutal way, signed declarations.[16]

Psychic violence requires the insecurity and degradation of the prisoners. It is a technique that combines psychic and corporal aspects. The preparation for torture focuses both on the diffusion of fear and anxiety over prisoners who know that they may be tormented, and the ill treatment of bodily needs. As one prisoner writes, the corporal torment took place at night but the psychological violence lasted the whole day. At the Chaidari camp in Athens, the same prisoner continues, the guards described the previous night's tortures to the prisoners and they forced them to sing rightist songs. Because the fear of torture resulted in frequent urination, the inmates urinated in the cells because they were not allowed to go to the latrine. Besides urinating in the same place where they slept, they were dirty and unshaven because they were not allowed to wash themselves.[17] The ill treatment of prisoners' bodily needs is the starting point of the degradation psychic violence presupposes. The normal, the usual, and the familiar become the exceptional, and vice versa. The unmaking of the prisoners' world entails the reversal of the established reality. That reversal renders them powerless, and therefore vulnerable. The degradation of the body is a necessary condition for the imposition of fear, shame and anxiety.

While the authorities aimed to spread an unspecified anxiety, it was concretized in the prisoners' imagination. For Giannis Politis, that specific fear was that he would confess and inform against his comrades. He was a builder, thirty-five years old when he was arrested in 1948. The Security Service believed that he knew the location of a hidden arsenal for guerillas. He refused to confess; after being heavily tortured, being afraid that he could not endure the pain, he tried to commit suicide. He was transferred to the hospital and refused medicine, fearing that he would be given some kind of serum that would make him confess involuntary. What he finally did, once he was transferred back to the police station to find that a new ordeal of torture was about to begin, was to bite off his own tongue—to make sure that he would not confess.[18] In Giannis Politis' case, the anxiety and insecurity that psychic violence created took the specific form of fear of confession. Losing control over his body, he had as a consequence to perceive it as something alien. He punished his body for its weakness, for its potential "betrayal." True, the punishment of the body was not his sole motivation: biting off his tongue was also a way to protect his comrades from an involuntary confession.

The authorities' intention was to maximize the prisoners' anxiety. Their anxiety was based on the unknown that torture entailed and the lack of knowledge about the tormentors' plans and intentions. And what made the prisoners' position worse was the waiting of the torture, the waiting for a situation that could cause more pain and danger.[19] In these moments of waiting and not knowing, anxiety could become fear. Though it is difficult to make general assumptions about prisoners' fears, since their fears are related to their unique past experience, two kinds of fear seem to reoccur, implicitly, in the prisoners' memoirs: the fear of one's sexuality and the fear of death.

One aspect of the psychological violence was that the inmates were often naked or partly naked during the torture. In this way they were exposed to and unprotected from their torturers. "To be beaten when you are standing and dressed, this is not torture. To be beaten by a dressed man while you are naked, this is the beginning of the torture."[20] Nudity signified shame and danger, a state of absolute insecurity and vulnerability. Male prisoners, exposed as they were to the eyes, the malicious jokes, and the hands, often armed with weapons for torture, of people belonging to the same sex, felt stripped of their dignity; their masculinity was under attack. Male prisoners during torture were afraid that they would be beaten in the genitals and were seized by the fear of impotence. Younger prisoners, the minors in particular, were afraid of sexual maltreatment or even rape.

For female prisoners, fears related to sexuality were more manifest because they were tortured by men. Female detainees naked, and tormented by the opposite sex, humiliated and insulted as "whores," were undergoing the same process having their world unmade through the enmity and the brutality of male tormentors. It was the same process, yet different because women in detention in general, and in torture in particular, can become sexual objects. In the eyes of the female detainees fear often took the form of sexual harassment or rape. Rape was the fear par excellence, the ultimate humiliation, and it was regarded as worse than death.[21] There were not only the hints that inspired the fear of rape, but also the constant fear that their tormented bodies might become the object of sexual desire. Maria Sideri recalls that when she was being beaten, she was trying to cover her bare legs. There was no place for her body in this world of violence; for women to protect themselves they have to cover their bodies, to mask their femininity, and to disguise or hide the female body's biological functioning. The same woman recalls how she felt when she was menstruating whilst in detention: "These brutes, they will see me. I was not thinking of the thrashing. The only thing that concerned me was that they should not see me."[22]

Sexual difference is important during torture, from the point of view of the social construction of masculinity and the polarizations masculine/feminine, active/passive.[23] The ability to endure pain is considered masculine; the male prisoners had to behave like men, whereas women who did not give in were *pallikaria* (brave men). For the tormentors the torture of men and women alike was a way to enhance their masculinity. But for the female detainees, the male torturers who tormented women were cowards, non-masculine.[24] In the torture chamber, the power to inflict pain is proof of masculinity for the perpetrators, and a victim's ability to endure pain and not make confessions is an expression of virility and proof of safeguarding one's integrity and honor. Femininity is either absent or has negative connotations: loss of integrity, passivity and submission.

The inmates must be brought to the end of their psychical endurance, must be desperate. Fury and pride must become fear and submission. The tormented must be brought to such a state that he will face his own death as something very close:

> They ordered the tormented to dig their own graves, and, since there was no shovel, to do it with their bare hands. Then, they gave us their permission to say our last prayer and our last wishes, while in front of our eyes they were preparing for the shooting. The guns were loaded and reloaded so that the sounds would be heard; some soldiers took position to shoot and some others covered our eyes with our underwear.[25]

The soldiers did not have orders to shoot, but that was something that was discovered later. Not knowing their intentions, for a few minutes the detainees faced their deaths. In a similar case one political prisoner broke down facing the firing squad and made "confessions," that led to the arrest and conviction of other individuals. [26] In the same vein, political detainees were used as "mine detectors": when there was a convoy of military vehicles all the detainees were put in the first one, so that if the convoy ran over a land mine they would be the ones killed.[27] All these practices aimed at maximizing a specific fear, the fear of one's death. It was not an ungrounded fear. Many guerillas, after their arrest by the army, were not put on trial but were killed after being interrogated. Political prisoners knew that during interrogation or torture, their death might just be a contingency. Not having any control over one's life or death and not knowing the authorities' intentions created an extreme state of powerlessness, and the tormentors manipulated the fear of death by making death not just a contingency but a probability.

If the limit of corporal pain is death, what is the limit of psychic pain? Insanity? What happened later in the life of a young female prisoner, who after been severely beaten, was forced to stand in a square in Kastoria holding the severed heads of her uncle and brother-in-law?[28] We know that after the ordeal of torture and terror, scores of detainees of the Makronisos camps were driven insane and hospitalized. Eleni Skarpeti was not insane, but for years she suffered from recurring nightmares that replayed what happened on 2 September 1948. At the age of twenty-two, she was arrested and court-martialed together with forty-five other people. On 28 August 1948, the special court-martial of Athens sentenced her and another six accused people to death for a violation of the Emergency Law 509 (they were alleged to have maintained an underground party organization in Athens). She was transferred first to the Averof women's prison, and three days later to the execution site. The place was full of blood from previous executions and, as she remembers, her white shoes turned a deep red, almost black. She and the other six convicted political prisoners waited for the firing squad to get ready. A few minutes before the execution, an officer appeared and asked her to come closer to him. He asked her to inform against an underground party contact. She refused, and the soldiers took her back to the group of the other six. Within a few seconds he called her again with the same request. She again refused, but while she was talking to the officer she heard some shouts, then the noise of guns, and finally the salvo of gunfire. She fainted, and in a state of shock was transferred back to the Averof women's prison. The officer had in his pocket a decree for the suspension of her execution, yet he said nothing and instead manipulated Eleni Skarpeti's predicament of facing her own imminent death. As we shall see below, her ordeal did not end on that morning of 2 September 1948 ... [29]

Torture is grounded in the powerlessness of the inmates and its manipulation. Inmates do not know whether, when, for how long, or how they are going to be tortured, whether they are going to stay in the same place or be transferred to another, whether the authorities have any evidence with which to prosecute them, and so forth. On top of this, everything that is part of the reality of everyday life is reversed to deconstruct what the inmate conceives as reality. The inmate's world slowly disintegrates: what is familiar becomes strange, the true turns out to be false, and what is useful might well be dangerous.

Solitary Confinement

Solitary confinement is part of the history of prisons, or, to put it differently, is the characteristic of the birth of prison.[30] First realized in the United States, known as the Auburn and Pennsylvania models, by the 1830s the practice had become world-famous. According to the Auburn model, prisoners were to sleep alone at night and work together in the workshops of the penitentiary during the day; any conversation among the prisoners was forbidden (the rule of silence). Under the Pennsylvania model, the prisoners were isolated in their cells for the whole period of their confinement. But for both models "the promise of institutionalization depended upon the isolation of the prisoner and the establishment of a disciplined routine."[31] Solitary confinement seemed to be a panacea, a combination that accomplished the ends of the penitentiary in accordance also with religious beliefs.[32] Isolation and individualization for the prisoner and occasioned contemplation: alone in his cell with the Bible (the sole book that was then permitted), the wrongdoer was supposed to think about his previous, depraved life and repent for his sins away from any kind of distraction or bad influence. Security and surveillance were the main tasks of the guards and the authorities; rigorous discipline and the rule of silence guaranteed law and order inside the penitentiary.

Neither of these systems was employed in Greece because prison buildings had had diverse uses before they became prisons. The exceptions were a handful of prisons, like the Averof prison and the prisons on the Ionian islands, inherited by the British that followed some of the principles of prison architecture. Rather than individual cells, Greek prisons had dormitories where a usually large number of prisoners lived together day and night. Of the sixty-three prisons in prewar Greece only ten had individual cells.[33] In this section, however, the discussion of the solitary confinement will focus on two cases. The first will be the Corfu prison under the Metaxas dictatorship, as the only case where solitary confinement, in the narrow sense, was systematically employed. The second will be the case of solitary confinement, as a temporary measure of punishment, and will be discussed within the larger context of segregation and individualization.

The prison on Corfu, built by the British in the nineteenth century, was used for the detention of communist cadres during Metaxas' dictatorship. The Corfu prison followed the system of close confinement. Vasilis Nefeloudis, who was imprisoned there, mentions the names of thirty-five political prisoners confined in the Corfu prison. It was a cellular radial prison; each cell was 5 meters high, 1.80 meters wide and 1.30 meters long. Each prisoner had the use of two abutments and two planks for a bed, a mattress, a blanket, a piece of soap, a pitcher and a chamber pot. The prisoners had to spend the whole day in their cells except for thirty minutes to wash themselves and their clothes, under the supervision of a guard. Correspondence was also restricted; the political detainees could send and receive one letter per month. Face-to-face communication among the prisoners was impossible, since they had to spend twenty-three and a half hours of their day alone in their cells and the half-hour allowed for washing was also spent alone. The confinement was so total, Nefeloudis writes, that he saw his fellow inmates only after two and a half years. The close confinement ended in November 1940, when the Italian air force bombarded Corfu and safety measures necessitated the opening of cells.[34]

Although the political detainees managed to communicate with each other through the walls using a sort of Morse code, the grave consequences for their mental health were undiminished. Solitary confinement as the ideal punishment was abandoned in Europe and United States, not only because it became uneconomical as the prison population was increased, but also because it was considered dangerous to the prisoners' mental health. Stylianos Glykofrydis, former general inspector of prisons, condemned the seclusive model as "inhuman," one that "drives the incarcerated to despair, and sometimes even to insanity."[35] The most important thing for a prisoner in solitary confinement was to manage to keep himself occupied and to use his brain. After his experiencing solitary confinement one prisoner wrote:

> Be careful during solitary confinement! It is the worst enemy. Our most precious weapon: don't let your mind slip in inertia. Constantly keep your mind on something, whatever. On thoughts, stories, accounts. Try always to do something. Organize your life. Love your cell. I love my cell. I find it interesting. I love my washbasin as well. I embroider. I cut shapes on the wall, I draw, I recall verses.[36]

Nevertheless, the number of things a prisoner could do was limited. Gymnastics and communication with the other prisoners in Morse code were the sole occupations. For some prisoners, torture was added to the solitary confinement. One prisoner, Christos Maltezos, secretary of the Communist Youth (OKNE), was tormented for weeks and driven insane; he died in November 1938. In December 1938, the administration moved one step further. The guards emptied the cells, leaving inside only the chamber pot. They took the prisoners' clothes, leaving them with only their underwear, and fed them on water only or water and bread for five days. Under such extreme conditions, designed to break down the leading cadres of the Communist Party, the boundaries between being and not-being became indiscernible or contradictory—the being, in the strict sense of survival, presupposed the political non-being, the declaration of repentance. Many, almost half of the political detainees in the Corfu prison, signed declarations of repentance during their confinement there.[37]

The other form of solitary confinement employed it temporarily, as a measure of punishment. Usually, punishment is related to a breach of law or a violation of duty, but within the domain of arbitrariness no such breach or violation was necessary for the imposition of punishment. Punishment had to be arbitrary, because otherwise the power to punish would be restricted by the rules and regulations.

The place of solitary confinement depended on the place of internment. If it was a camp, then the inmate was removed to a tent in a distant place exposed to unfavorable weather conditions. In the Giaros camp, solitary confinement took place in open-air enclosures fenced with barbed wire, where the prisoners had no protection from the sun or the rain.[38] If it was a prison, then the cell was a small, dark, damp place, often without any bed, so that the prisoner had to sleep on the floor. During confinement the prisoners were fed on bread and water, or they had food only every other day. What a can a human being do alone in a dark cell for days? Silence and loneliness can drive anyone crazy, and Chronis Missios, who became a political prisoner before even reaching the age of twenty years, knew that. At the Kassaveteia juvenile prison, where he spent forty days in solitary confinement, he kept himself busy fighting with and talking to the rats, and invented a new world—he was "traveling," and dreaming of the sea.[39]

In many cases, especially during the years 1948 and 1949, when the Civil War reached its climax, all forms of punishment and confinement were practiced without any reason in order to "break" political prisoners. In the internment camps of Makronisos and Giaros, various forms of confinement became the rule for the unrepentant. On Makronisos, these places were distant from the camps and were called *syrma* (wire) by the detainees, because they were fenced with barbed wire. Groups of around twenty prisoners were often sent there with a tent. They had to spend evenings and nights inside the tent without any light, the days being occupied by fatigue duties. The whole group was allotted one bucket of drinking water for their daily needs, they were not allowed to buy anything (like food or cigarettes) from the canteen of the camp, and quite often they were attacked and beaten by military policemen during the night.[40] Solitary confinement incorporated punishment into the everyday routine of prison life. Punishment, inscribed in techniques of disciplining the different (the unrepentant) that aimed "to eliminate certain habits, propensities, and morals and to inculcate others, thus made visible the difference between those who did or did not, could or could not, would or would not learn the lessons of the institution."[41]

Solitary confinement is related both to punishment and to classification. Different categories of detainees are separated from each other, new categories are invented, new dividing lines are drawn among them. Different places and treatment are prescribed for soldiers and the civilians, communists and their relatives, intellectuals and illiterate. On Ikaria the so-called leadership was segregated from the rest of the political prisoners and was confined in a school.[42] At the Giaros camps, the political prisoners were accommodated in different bays depending on whether they were educated, "leaders," etc. The Trikeri women's camp was divided into two camps. According to a British consul, who visited the camp on 16 October 1949, there were "[t]he 1,000 women in the 'top' Camp, most of whom have already signed declarations or are willing to do so (…) The 800 women in the 'bottom' camp, who are separated from the rest, present a very different picture. They are all dyed-in-the-wool communists, and for the most part well-educated and intelligent and extremely voluble (as I found to my cost!)"[43] The issue was, as he himself put it, whether or not they were "suitable subjects for conversion". Providing the framework (separation from the others) and speculating on the differences (the attributes of each category) were the means to determine who was "suitable for conversion".

These differences among prisoners did exist, but what is more important is that the authorities turned these differences into antagonistic features. Creating differences and manipulating them, dividing and segregating were means to liquidate the community of the political detainees and to impose individualization. In almost every prison and camp the administration segregated the leadership from the rank-and-file, the repentant from the unrepentant, and the intellectuals from the rest. These cases illustrate solitary confinement not in the literal sense, but in the broader sense of categorizing, segregating, and constructing boundaries, by differentiating the treatment of the one from the others, in such ways as allowing three hours of exercise for all the prisoners, except the "dangerous" ones, who had two hours, or providing a better food for the repentant than for the unrepentant.[44]

The reason for a separate examination of solitary confinement is that it represents a distinct function in the mechanism of the prison. Despite the fact that many prisoners were tormented during their close confinement, its particular feature is not physical pain, but segregation from the other inmates, the imposition of individualization, and the impact of the transformation from a "we" situation into an "I" and "they" juxtaposition. The rehabilitation process implies a form of individualization, at the end of which the prisoner must confront all the other prisoners as the cause of his punishment. A prisoners' community is unthinkable when the individual experiences antagonism between self and others. Thus, the imposition of individualization in this case can be thought of as the fragmentation of the already existing collectivity, as the mapping of the individual and the collectivity in adversarial positions, and the breach inside the being: the other-in-self and the self-in-other diametrically opposed.[45]

Notes

1. Peters, *Torture*, 40-73, 103-140, 164.
2. Andreas Baris, "Anamniseis," in Vardinogiannis and Aronis eds., *Oi misoi sta sidera*, 43.
3. Scarry, *The Body in Pain*, 5
4. Giannis Manousakas, *To chroniko enos agona. Akronafplia 1939-1943* (Athens, 1986), 37-38.
5. Jerome Neu, "A Tear Is an Intellectual Thing," *Representations* 19 (1987): 35-61.
6. Peters, *Torture*, 166.
7. ASKI, box 421 F25/3/13, Letter of Panagiotis Vidalis to *Rizospastis* and *Eleftheri Ellada*, 15 January 1947.
8. Vardinogiannis, *Makronisos*, 116, 120, 136.
9. *Vasikoi kanones epagrypnisis* (Athens, 1947), 13-15.
10. ASKI, box 421 F25/3/129, Letter from Makronisos.
11. Olympia Papadouka, *Gynaikeies Fylakes Averof* (Athens, 1981), 169-170.

12. Rosa Imvrioti, in Theodorou ed., *Stratopeda gynaikon*, 294-295.
13. *Dimokratikos Typos*, 20 August 1950. The letter of accusation was signed by twenty-five prisoners, at that time at Itzedin prison, who were interned as minors at the juvenile prison in Kifisia in 1948.
14. *Dimokratikos Typos*, Letter of Vasileios Fytsilis, 30 April 1950.
15. Morand, *Les écrits de prisonniers*, 105.
16. Interview with Spyros Andreadis on 2 April 1998. See also Antonis Flountzis, *Sto kolastirio tis Makronisou*, 122ff.
17. ASKI, box 421 F25/3/104, Anonymous note from the Chaidari camp.
18. For testimonies on Giannis Politis' case, see Takis Benas, *Tou Emfyliou* (Athens, 1996), 79-80; Vardinogiannis, *Makronisos*, 129-132; Margaris, *Istoria tis Makronisou*, vol. 2, 438-439; Ydraios, *Grammata apo ti fylaki*, 117-131.
19. F. Skouras, A. Hatzidimos, A. Kaloutsis, G. Papadimitriou, *Symvoli sti meleti tis psychopathologias tis peinas, tou fovou kai tou aghous* (1947, reprinted Athens, 1991), 148.
20. Ibid., 150.
21. According to the EAM, between February 1945 and October 1946 75 women were raped, see MGA/LDG, Info XVI, Rapport sur l' activité des Femmes de la Resistance depuis décembre 1945 jusqu' à octobre 1946, Le Bureau Féminine du Comité Central de l' EAM (one has to notice that this figure is much lower than the 159 rapes reported in *Rizospastis* on 12 February 1946; see above chapter 3). It is remarkable that in this list of victims of the "white terror," the number of raped women comes first, even before the much larger number (109) of women killed. It is relevant that a synonym of the word "raped" is "dishonored." Rape is considered as worse than death, because to die for a cause is honorable, and, on the contrary, to live a life after being "dishonored" is unbearable.
22. Sideri, *Dekatessera chronia* (Athens, 1981), 32, 50-51.
23. Jean Franco, "Gender, Death and Resistance: Facing the Ethical Vacuum," in *Fear at the Edge: State Terror and Resistance in Latin America,* ed. J. Corradi, P. Fagen and M. Garreton (Berkeley, 1992), 104-118.
24. Gavriilidou, *O pateras mou*, 204, 208. In Greek the word *anandros* (coward) means non-masculine. See also, Nikos Kotaridis, "Oute 'atimos' oute 'ntropiasmenos'. Antistasi kai emfylios sto idioma tis syggeneias kai tis axies tis androprepeias", *Dokimes* 6 (1997): 75-100.
25. ASKI, box 423 F25/5/88, Notice for the history of the Chaidari camp.
26. MGA/LDG, Info XI, Individual dossiers.
27. *Eleftheri Ellada*, 5 February 1947. Letter of the political detainee Konstantinos Kremmydas from the Katerini prison.
28. Papadouka, *Gynaikeies Fylakes Averof*, 158.
29. Nikos Antoniou and Eleni Skarpeti-Tsali, *Apofasi 225A/1948* (Athens, 1989), 73-160.
30. Rusche and Kirchheimer, *Punishment and Social Structure*, 127-137.
31. Rothman, *The Discovery of the Asylum*, 82.
32. There was a strong influence of the Quakers' beliefs on the invention of the solitary confinement and the underlying discourse on sin and self-contemplation: see Rusche and Kirchheimer, *Punishment and Social Structure*, 129; Roth, *Pratiques pénitentiaires*, 28-31.
33. Glykofrydis, *Fylakai,* 72; Prokos, *Symvoli*, 86.
34. Vasilis Nefeloudis, *Achtinaé* θ, Athens, 1974), 130, 138.
35. Glykofrydis, *Fylakai,* 65.
36. Cited in Skouras et al., *Psychopathologia*, 159.
37. Nefeloudis, *Achtina,* 157-161, 168-170; Flountzis, *Akronafplia,*182-183.
38. *Giura detainees' memorandum*, 87.
39. Chronis Missios, *... kala, esy skotothikes noris* (Athens, 1988), 108-113.

40. *Dimokratikos Typos*, 9 April 1950. Also, Ilias Staveris, "Mia nychta sti glarofolia," in Vardinogiannis and Aronis eds., *Oi misoi sta sidera*, 179-201; Vardinogiannis, *Makronisos*, 23-25, 36-40; Margaris, *Istoria tis Makronisou*, vol. 2, 575ff.; Flountzis, *Sto kolastirio*, 190ff.
41. Nikolas Rose, "Calculable Minds and Manageable Individuals", *History of the Human Sciences* 1, no. 2 (1988): 179-200.
42. *Manchester Guardian*, 27 August 1947.
43. FO 371/78369 R11235, Athens to FO, British consul's report on the women's concentration camp on Trikeri island, 17 October 1949. Actually, the women in the "top" camp had been detained after preventive arrests and relatives of guerillas. Those in the "bottom" camp those directly involved in the resistance and the Civil War.
44. FO 371/78369 R1617, Visit to women's detention camp, Chios, 22 January 1949, NARA 868.00/6-248, Athens to Department of State, The Greek "concentration" camp at Makronisos, 2 June 1948.
45. Edward E. Sampson, "The Deconstruction of the Self," in *Texts of Identity*, ed. John Sorter and Kenneth J. Gergen, (London, 1989), 1-19.

Chapter 8

"Everything Comes to an End"

A former political prisoner recalled in his memoirs a phrase written on the wall of a cell at the Athens Security Department: "Everything comes to an end."[1] Another arrested activist had written the message to encourage the tormented detainees to endure the tortures. However, the notion of the end is an ambiguous one, evoking not only the end of torture and imprisonment, but also the end of life, the death of the political detainee.

Dying in prison is seldom an accident, the political prisoners knew that. While in prison they might die from disease or a lethal attack by the guards; those condemned to death might face the firing squad. If these different forms of dying shared anything in common, from the point of view of political prisoners' experience, it was the fear of death, as it was spawned by the administration's action or inaction. Yet, it is difficult, even wrong, to attempt to homogenize people's experience of death. Instead it is more interesting to explore the various subject-positions in relation to death. The dead and the living ones, victim and hero, fear and pride, individual and collectivity are different subject-positions with respective experiences. In that relation between subject-position and experience, neither has a priority or determines the other. They are interlaced in, and constitute, the political prisoner's subjectivity. Moreover, these different positions and experiences are not juxtaposed but interwoven with one another. The same prisoner who sick or terrorized may present himself as a victim, might later, facing the firing squad, present himself as a hero who sacrifices his own life. But in neither case he is just a victim or a hero; rather, such frames are attempts to make sense of one's experience of dying.

Notes for this section begin on page 157.

Dying Slowly

The most common fatal diseases in prisons in the prewar era were tuberculosis and malaria. Between 1936 and 1939, in an average general prison population of 9,355 inmates, 2 percent of inmates were hospitalized for tuberculosis, 14 percent for malaria, and almost 23 percent for what was classified "other diseases." In the same period, 0.1 percent of the total prison population died.[2] For the political detainees of that era there are no official data; according to one former political prisoner, eighteen political detainees died in prisons and sanatoriums, the majority of tuberculosis.[3]

Data for the postwar period are even more fragmented and scarce. Nonetheless, an official list of the deceased at the Makronisos camp and a former prisoner's account of the deceased at Giaros camp are available. Between June 1949 and November 1951 at Makronisos camp forty-nine political detainees died;[4] the association of Makronisos political detainees' claims that another seventy political prisoners who were interned in Makronisos but buried elsewhere, ought to be added. Sixty-one political detainees were transferred from the Giaros camp and died in the hospital of the island of Syros.[5] In addition, ninety-five exiles died on Agios Efstratios in the postwar era.[6] The only official prison administration data available are from the Aegina prison, where 452 cases of an average of 755 prisoners were admitted to hospital in 1948. Two thirds of the cases were diagnosed as flu and colitis.[7] In 1946, the UNRRA mission estimated that the sickness rate was 4 percent for the prison population of the capital area.[8] However, since official data are not available, no detailed analysis of the death rate and the diseases themselves can be carried out; moreover, the number of political detainees who did not die and were released with more or less serious health problems cannot be even approximately estimated.

Most prisons in the first postwar years did not have any doctors, and prisoners were in desperate need of medicines and disinfectants. In the Trikala prison, an UNRRA official saw several sick prisoners suffering from malaria lying on the floors in the rooms. In the Patras prison tubercular prisoners slept on the floor in the same room with uninfected prisoners. At the Akronafplia prison, there was no doctor for the 374 prisoners, and two political prisoners had taken over their care.[9] Out of 5,800 political exiles at the beginning of 1947, seven to eight hundred were sick and 130 had tuberculosis and other contagious diseases. A few years later, in 1951, about 60 percent of the 2,800 political exiles had health problems. Most of them had different forms of tuberculosis, stomach ulcer, and rheumatism.[10]

The Amfissa sanatorium begun to operate as a hospital for political prisoners in 1949, having previously served as a military barracks. The conditions that the first tuberculars faced there were far from appropriate for a hospital. It was dirty, the windows were broken, and the kitchen was destroyed. Later, the tubercular political prisoners at the Amfissa sanatorium claimed that the building was totally inappropriate: there was neither heating nor showers, their diet was improper, and water was scarce. When they protested for their living conditions, the administration transferred a number of them back to prisons.[11] Nevertheless, the hospital was a more suitable place for a sick detainee to be than a tent or a cell. The medical care gave them a feeling of reapproaching civil society. A political prisoner wrote from the Sotiria hospital for prisoners, "You should know that I am at the free [*sic*] Sotiria for six months. And that for me this is something, to be away from irons and prisons. I hope that in this way I will be able to look after my health."[12]

The procedure for admitting prisoners to hospitals was rather lengthy and complicated, and did not depend only on a prisoner's state of health. The prison doctor certified to the prison director that the case needed hospitalization. The director sent the certification to the district attorney, who dispatched another doctor to examine the case. After the second evaluation, the district attorney made his decision. This procedure always took several weeks to be completed. Moreover, sometimes even if permission was granted, the transfer of the sick prisoner could be postponed if the gendarmerie was short of the necessary transport or if there was no vacant bed in the hospital.[13]

Doctors were not always on the prisoners' side. Many of them were identified with the penitentiary mechanism by establishing medical grounds that justified and prolonged the internment of prisoners and thereby led to the deterioration of their health. These doctors became part of the prison personnel and were identified with the guards and the torturers; the prisoners counted them among the custodians, like the doctor on Giaros whom a prisoner described as "dwarfish, an ape-man in his body and his soul … [he] comes to the first bay to examine us and the first thing he does is to be sarcastic (you suffer from celibacy, you suffer from love)."[14] In these cases, medicine and justice may be thought of as complementary aspects of the internment process. Panagiotis Timogiannakis, interned in the Argostoli prison on the island of Cephalonia, described that interrelation in a memorandum sent to the Minister of Justice. In the cases of nine prisoners (himself included) who requested release on the grounds of irreparable damage to their health, the district attorney of Argostoli appointed the same three doctors to pronounce whether there was indeed irreparable damage. All the requests were turned down. "It is beyond doubt," Panagiotis Timogiannakis commented in his memorandum, "that the district attorney found the negative opinion over so many severely ill prisoners very convenient."[15]

Political prisoners tried to solve their medical problems by themselves. The sick prisoners, tuberculars in particular, lived in a separate room. Those prisoners who were doctors tried to help their fellow inmates by asking for medicines and a proper diet for the sick from the prison administration, and took hygiene measures. Nevertheless, the fear of contamination and death hung over them. Tuberculosis, especially, was a collective nightmare. Anyone who coughed was suspected of having tuberculosis, which helps to explain why the numbers of tubercular prisoners are so exaggerated in the appeals. Another approach prisoners used was to stress how unfavorable their living conditions were and to ask for their transport or release. Generally speaking, the number of appeals from political prisoners regarding their state of health increased after the end of the Civil War. Political prisoners could no longer rely on political grounds for their release, but they did stand a chance of being freed on humanitarian ones. The introduction of leniency measures by the post-Civil War governments (the release of prisoners with irreparable damage to their health) also contributed to the rise in the number of appeals.

The general hypothesis that can be posited is that the living conditions in prisons were so bad and the medical care so poor, that they were the cause of death for many detainees. Imprisoned in dark, damp, badly ventilated dormitories, or concentrated in camps, where they lived in tents in all weather conditions and worked hard, many detainees, unable to withstand the additional burdens of poor diet, hygiene problems, and tortures, were driven to the hospitals or even to death. The British officer who visited the hospital at the Makronisos camps bitterly remarked that "a broken rib is an occupational disease."[16] The lack of sick-bays or infirmaries in many prisons (in several cases, sick prisoners lived in the same room as the rest of the prisoners), the rarity of diagnostic investigation, and the insufficient number of doctors and nurses, put the lives of sick prisoners in further danger. Long-term political prisoners always ended up with some health problems. "Don't be scared," a prisoner wrote in letter, "that I'm wearing glasses. Eh! after so many years in prison what else could have happened to my eyes, they are damaged." Indeed, the sixteen years he had already spent in prison were too many.[17]

Sickness among political prisoners, sometimes fatal, was an effect of the ordeal of prison life. A cold might have been the cause of pneumonia, sleeping on the ground of pleurisy, bad food or psychological stress of colitis, a poor diet of vitamin deficiency, dirty water of typhus or gastritis, and so on. The question of how many of the 160 political prisoners at the Aegina prison who were admitted to hospital for the flu, were in fact suffering from tuberculosis will remain unanswered. The political detainee knew only that he or she could easily be the next one to fall ill.

Unexpected Death

The 29th of February 1948 started like any other Sunday for the three thousand or so soldiers of the First Sappers' Battalion at the camps of Makronisos. The routine was, first a morning roll call and, later, a church service at the camp theater. But after the roll call that day, when the companies were heading to the theater, certain soldiers quarreled with the military police, possibly because the policemen had found a few soldiers who had been absent from the roll call and had started beating them. Within a few seconds, shots were fired from the building of the companies' command against the unarmed soldiers. Some nearby officers, who heard the shooting ran to the place and ordered a cease-fire. The shooting stopped, but five soldiers had been already killed whilst ten had been injured. The anger of the soldiers did not abate, not even when Commander Antonios Vasilopoulos arrived at the camp and promised to carry out an investigation. The soldiers placed the five corpses inside a tent and went on a hunger strike as a token of mourning and protest. The next morning, a group of between 200 and 250 armed soldiers from the Third Battalion arrived at the camp. Colonel Bairaktaris (the general director of the Makronisos camps) speaking from a patrol boat, urged the soldiers to hand over the "instructors" of the previous day's "mutiny" and to move the rest, "the misguided," to another location. The terrified soldiers did not move, preferring instead to stay inside their tents. Soldiers from the Third Battalion, armed with batons, dragged them out of the tents, and those who tried to run away found themselves being shot at, both from the boat and by the armed soldiers of the Third Battalion. The results of this second attack were far more murderous. The exact number of victims is uncertain because even official accounts reveal discrepancies: eleven or sixteen soldiers were killed and fifty-four were injured. The political detainees, on the other hand, claimed that more than two hundred soldiers were shot dead. The soldiers who survived the attack were quickly moved away and mustered for interrogation and "selection." Most of them, under the impact of the terror and threats of the officers, signed declarations of repentance. More than one hundred allegedly responsible for the mutiny were transferred to the military prisons of the island, while another seven hundred, who did not sign declarations, continued their ordeal at the Third Battalion (the "blue battalion"). The epilogue to the incidents of 29 February and 1 March 1948 at the First Sappers' Battalion was written two months later. That May 114 soldiers were court-martialed in Athens for "mutiny." Five of them were sentenced to death and five to life imprisonment.[18]

Why did the authorities choose that specific battalion? The First Sappers' Battalion was where the "unrepentants" were concentrated, the so-called "red battalion." The attack against this specific battalion served several purposes: to eliminate the last nucleus of disobedience on the island, to use the incident as an opportunity for more repressive measures, to impose fear over the soldiers as a whole, and to display limitless power over the detained soldiers' lives. The First Battalion was the last battalion of unrepentant soldiers at that time on the island. After the two-day attack, only a few hundred had not yet signed a declaration of repentance, and it became a common feeling that a phase in the history of the Makronisos camps, that is, the rehabilitation of soldiers, was over. It was the turn of the political detainees and exiles.

Captain Katsareas was one of the most notorious rightist band leaders in the Civil War. His field of operations was the region of Lakonia in the Peloponnese. His name became synonymous with terror and death, for both civilians and political detainees. G. Vareias, Commander of the gendarmerie on the island of Kythira, frequently mentioned Katsareas' name when he talked to political exiles. "Wherever you go", he told them, "you won't escape from Katsareas. Kythira is only two hours from the coast of Lakonia."[19] In one of his bloodiest endeavors in Vamvakou in October 1946, Katsareas ordered the killing of 37 leftists, most of them civilian hostages, in reprisal for the death of nine rightists in a battle with the guerillas.[20] On 21 March 1947 Katsareas was ambushed and killed by guerillas. The same day men from his band broke into the Gytheio prisons and the police station of the city, pulled out the thirty-two communist inmates, and executed them.[21] In a similar vein, on 13 April 1948 armed men broke into the prisons of Sparta and killed twenty-five political prisoners. This was also an act of retaliation; earlier that day a gendarmerie bus had driven over a mine on the road from Tripolis to Sparta.[22] Similar incidents had been reported at the prisons of Pylos, where an armed band had killed three political prisoners in April 1946, as well as of Tripolis, Kalamata and Akronafplia.[23] All these prisons shared something in common. They were located on the Peloponnese, a region where the right wing and royalists had traditionally been quite powerful, and where the right-wing bands had never ceased to be active since the occupation. In this stronghold of the right wing, political prisoners became a target and the object of retaliation; none could protect or protest for the political prisoners in these cities.

Even though political prisoners were not the only targets of terrorism in the Civil War, the cases discussed above illustrate that political prisoners were deprived of any security whatsoever. The deprivation of security seems to reverse the so-called purpose of the prison, namely that the offenders are put in jail in order to protect society from their offenses. The incidents mentioned above do not contradict this purpose; on the contrary, they reveal aspects that are often neglected. Internment is the necessary and sufficient condition to render a group of people insecure and vulnerable, to neutralize them by depriving them of any means to defend themselves. In other words, by whom and how could the prisoners have been protected? The Communist Party did not encourage the use of force against the guards. Unlike Italy, where the civil war of 1943-1945 was continued in prisons after the end of the Second World War, in Greece political prisoners did not smuggle arms inside prisons, organize mass escapes, or stage violent riots, perhaps because Greek prisons lacked the explosive combination of leftists, fascists, and bandits as inmates.[24] Prisons constituted one more arena of the Greek Civil War, but it was the most unfavorable one for the political opponents of the regime.

The murderous attacks against political prisoners, either by right-wing bands or by the authorities, were a demonstration of power in its most elementary and direct form, violent death. The retaliatory attacks by bands or furious nationalists in right-wing regions showed the cooperation between the state apparatus and extreme rightists on the local level, which dated back to the months of the "white terror." The Makronisos incidents—like the executions as we shall see in the next section—demonstrated to both political prisoners and society that the state had the power of life and death over its enemies.

Executions

Two villagers from Kilkis, Theocharis Sapranidis and Georgios Kalemis, who died in Salonica on 16 July 1946, were the first political prisoners executed in the Civil War. A week after the first execution, Eirini Gini, a member of the resistance, was executed. She was the first woman political prisoner in Greece to face the firing squad, but not the last. According to the British consulate in Salonica, whose opinion was not unique, "in most cases the female of the bandit species is more deadly than the male."[25] Executions stopped in October 1949, shortly after the last battles of the Civil War. It is difficult to estimate the number of people executed. The Ministry of Justice has archived a number of reports on the decrees of courts-martial for the years of the Civil War, but these should be considered indicative of the decrees, not of the executions, since only a proportion of those sentenced to death were actually executed.[26] In one of the very few official statements concerning the number of executions, the Minister for Press and Information maintained that 1,778 political prisoners had been executed by mid-1948;[27] these figures should not be taken at face value since the Greek government reduced them for obvious reasons. Several scholars claim that out of 7,500 death sentences, between 3,000 and 5,000 political prisoners were executed. In any case, the lower estimation corresponds to the figures given by the British officials, according to whom 3,033 political prisoners were executed following sentences by special courts martial, and 378 upon sentencing by civil courts.[28]

The political prisoners on death row fell into two general categories. The vast majority had been convicted by special courts-martial for breach of Emergency Laws, namely Resolution 3 of 1946, and Emergency Law 509 of 1947.[29] The second category was comprised of those political prisoners who had been convicted by civil courts for offenses (mostly homicide) during the foreign occupation and the December events. Those sentenced to death by special courts-martial in unanimous agreement or by a majority of four to one were to be executed within three or five days, while the execution of those convicted by a majority of three to two was usually suspended, to allow the convicts enough time to petition for mercy.[30]

Political prisoners on death row felt to be "hostages" of the government. To a large extent they were right, as their lives depended on the decisions of the government and the political situation. The majority of the 109 political prisoners who were executed between 1 May and 11 May 1948, in retaliation against the assassination of minister of Justice Christos Ladas, were convicted by civil courts for crimes during the occupation and had already been in prison for some years.[31] Executions of political prisoners became one of the major weapons in the hands of the government. The British consulate in Salonica, echoing the views of the Greek government on the issue of the frequency of death sentences passed by special courts martial, commented that "very dark forces are at work in this country, almost the only deterrent to which are the Special Courts Martial."[32]

Strong criticism, however, both domestic and abroad, was leveled against the government on the issue of executions. Cases of mass executions and women's executions became widely known through the campaigns of solidarity organizations, the activities of pressure groups and foreign press correspondents.[33] The Greek government often found itself in the uneasy position of having to defend the policy of executions, as did the British and the U.S. governments, which strongly supported the Greek government. The issue of executions was not humanitarian but political, given the publicity that executions gained in the foreign press. The regime did not want to be portrayed as a police state; therefore the government had to justify the executions of political prisoners. In order to do so, the government stigmatized the political prisoners on death row as criminals.[34] A few days after the mass executions of May 1948, the undersecretary for Press and Information Michael Ailianos made that point quite clear when he spoke of the "execution of criminals in Greece, who had been sentenced to death for crimes of the common penal law" and the "misinformation" of the foreign press.[35] The regime, in order to maintain a democratic facade, placed political prisoners beyond the political arena. The legitimization of the political prisoners' executions presupposed the negation of any political motivation from either side.

As of 1946, but especially in 1948 and 1949, executions became a constant anguish for political prisoners on death row, in particular for those convicted by civil courts, who (unlike those sentenced by extraordinary courts-martial) did not know whether or when they were going to be executed. In the Aegina, Averof, Corfu, Itzedin, Eptapyrgio, Akronafplia and Cephalonia prisons, among others, from which political prisoners quite often were transferred for executions, no one knew when or who would be the next to face the firing squad.[36] Every day and night the prisoners tried to guess from rumors, from the glances and hints of the guards, whether anyone and, if so, who was going to be transferred for execution. The following paragraphs will discuss the rituals of the condmned upon leaving their fellow inmates and the perception of death on the part of the political detainees.

The prisoners who were transferred for execution were taken from their cells during the night, so when the guards entered their wing, the sound of their footsteps and the doors put them on the alert. The only thing to discover was who would be taken. The political prisoners who were transferred always cried out a few words to their fellow inmates, like "Farewell brothers, it's my turn now. I promise to do my duty, dying with my head high. I hope that I'll be the last one. Long live the Greek people. Long live our Party."[37] These words were not just a farewell, but proof that they were not afraid to die and a gesture of encouragement to their fellow prisoners. A few minutes later their fellow prisoners would run to the windows of their cells to cry out, trying to break through the isolation of the penitentiary and make the citizens witness the fact that once again, political prisoners were being taken to the firing squad.

Then, the condemned inmates were transferred to a solitary confinement cell, referred to in the prison jargon as Golgotha, tying in to the topos of pain and martyrdom, where the innocent one suffers alone before his death. The connotations of the metaphor carry the weight of eschatological traditions (found in religion and political ideologies) and of the popular habits that tend to dramatize everyday life according to great narrative patterns. In that cell they would spend the few hours until dawn, alone—or, if it was allowed, with some fellow prisoners. Other political prisoners sent food, sweets, and cigarettes to the cell. The condemned wore clean clothes and spent their last night talking, eating, singing and dancing. The night before they were taken to the firing squad the female inmates in the Averof prison dressed in their best clothes, combed their hair, organized a dinner for their fellow inmates, and danced around the palm tree in the prison courtyard singing traditional folk songs like "Good-bye poor world, good-bye sweet life."[38]

It is difficult to interpret these rituals if the political practices are not placed alongside the popular beliefs and customs, where various perspectives (on marriage, farewell, and death) are interlaced. One might expect only political protest songs, but from the prisoners' memoirs we can deduce that traditional folk songs and dances were frequent during these rituals. For instance, prisoners sang the following: "Love needs a kiss / and war needs songs / flowers on the head / and glow within the heart. / Let the Reaper come and see / with what kind of bodies he is dealing / let him come and choose / and walk into the black land." Death as a struggle between the dying and the Reaper, signifying both the reluctance to leave the pleasures of life and the heroism of the dying person, is something found in modern Greek lament songs.[39] One should always bear in mind that the majority of the prisoners came from lower social strata and rural areas, where the traditional folk culture was dominant.

While waiting for dawn, those about to die also wrote their last letters to their families and often an illegal note addressed to their comrades and fellow prisoners. Some of the prisoners in death row had already written their last letters in advance, anticipating a probable execution. The tension escalated as dawn approached. The last moments before an execution, the noise of the vans arriving at the prison to transfer the condemned, and the cries of "Farewell, brothers" from both the remaining political prisoners and those to be put to death, are strongly impressed on the political prisoners' memory. Dimitra Mara-Michalakea recalls the last moments she spent with two women prisoners (Nika Martopoulou and Mairi Leontiadou) before their execution in the following arresting way:

> We hugged each other with sorrow, without saying a word. The door closed. I took some steps in the corridor. I held myself up against the wall so as not to fall down. I reached the iron grating. I thought of seeing them once more. It was not only I who had left, but also life itself. Absolute silence. I couldn't talk to them, so I whistled. They heard me. They took their hands out of the red blanket and waved farewell to me. Then, they covered themselves again, with their heads one next to the other, and closed their eyes.[40]

Even in these last moments before executions, the prison administration intervened. At the Cephalonia prison, first they prohibited the inmates from saying farewell to the condemned; later, the condemned were forbidden to say parting words as well. The time of the call for executions became unspecified: first, between nine and nine-thirty in the evening, later, between eleven and eleven-thirty, and, at the end, one hour before dawn (executions always took place at dawn), in order to protract the agony of the prisoners and leave them no time to prepare themselves for the farewell. As we shall see, in several prisons the political prisoners were repeatedly punished (letters, food parcels, and visits were suspended) because they shouted "farewell" to fellow inmates transported for execution.

From the few available last letters of the executed, I have selected three for purposes of discussing the meaning that the political prisoners attached to their deaths. Sergeant Nikos Braziotikos was condemned to death on 30 September 1946 and wrote to his family that day, a few days before his execution on 9 October 1946. This letter is interesting because it was written at the beginning of the Civil War, before executions became frequent. Perhaps not even he himself expected such a severe sentence, so for that reason he portrayed himself as a victim of circumstances

> It is true that the subjugation [of the occupation] has sown the seeds of hatred, of schism, of killing and of killing one another. The result of this is that I myself have become victim of this ugly schism and will fade from the face of earth. On 3 September our newly liberated motherland called me up to build our glorious and laurel-crowned army. But the awful schism occurred there too, because each one of us came from different organizations, left and right, the situation was troubled, and I with other soldiers, we decided to construct our ideology [*sic*] and

to vote for the Republic(…) I don't want you to cry or wear mourning clothes; just don't forget me. Ah! in this world all of us we are temporary; since we are born we are all gonna die, and I'm dying now. I'm sending you a picture of me to copy it to give to relatives and friends. I'm kissing you for the last time. Good-bye life, till we meet again in the other world. My mum, don't cry.[41]

Elli Svorou, twenty-six years old, was a dressmaker. She was arrested on 22 May 1948, sentenced to death, and before her execution wrote to her imprisoned fiancé on 7 June 1949:

My beloved. Be proud of me, as I am proud of you. And I wish that thinking of me will always bring you joy and happiness. I die like a real fighter should die. I die for those who hate me to live eternally with those who love me and I love. I know how painful it is for you that you will lose me. But you can find a girl like me and make your life in a way that you deserve. I will always be in your mind. The few books that once we bought together, luckily they still exist. I want you to take them from my cousin, who knows that they are for you, and to put them in the library that one day you'll make to remember me. A chess set as well, that I made for you. Say good-bye to all the guys. Be free soon. With love.[42]

The third letter was written from the Averof prison by Orestis Makridis a few hours before his execution on 25 June 1948, to his imprisoned wife Despoina:

My dear wife, I am sending you my last greetings from the death row. Despoina, our separation is cruel but I don't believe that you will be aggrieved because you know the reason I'm dying. And you should know that I die happy and proud. Despoina, look after your health (love your cell, eat your food, and read a lot). Despoina, my greetings to your parents, your siblings, and all our people. My dear Despoina, my last wish is, as soon as you are free, to find a nice man, one of ours, and to get married. I'm giving you my last kiss.[43]

The pain of the loss is overwhelming. And beyond, or after, the pain? The care of the executed for the people they leave behind endures. Be proud and do not mourn, just remember. On the one hand, this exhortation is a loving gesture to those who will live. The care for the other (especially in the letters to imprisoned partners) takes the form of encouraging them to endure the pain of death (take care of yourself) and to continue their lives (marriage). It is noteworthy that even in these last moments the care for the other is permeated by political considerations. The partner should get married to one of "us," or the care for the partner is worded using Secretary General Nikos Zachariadis' advice to prisoners ("love your cell, eat your food, and read a lot"). On the other hand, those who will live must not forget their duty to the political martyrs. The executed should be honored and remembered because they died for high ideals such as democracy and freedom are; they had a meaningful death. Meaningful death is somehow justified (no matter how hard it is to justify the death of a beloved person) and the fact of its significance alleviates the pain.

The most pressing question faced by the condemned was "how we should die."[44] Their answer to this question entails the concept of sacrifice, which is what underlies this meaningful death. To die for something (people, freedom, country, future generations, etc.) is an attempt "to render meaningful (indeed noble and desirable) what unless culturally processed would appear an unalloyed absurdity."[45] The very idea of sacrifice, handed down by religious beliefs, is in modern secular societies was related to the nation, the race and the party. To die for these causes is to gain access to the "collective immortality." Giving one's life for them, presupposes a symbolic universe whose demands have been legitimized, intermingled with a world-building enterprise that gives people a sense of identity, purpose, and place.[46]

Moreover, such an attitude toward death has as a prerequisite a subject that is not highly individualized. In Greece, the experience of occupation and resistance had provided this cultural and social background. The cultural background established by the resistance provided may be identified in particular in the similar pattern evident in the condemned prisoners' last letters and those written by resistance fighters before their execution by the occupation forces.[47] "The only way," wrote Dimitris Glinos, "to live and die like a *man*, is to live and die for an *ideal*."[48] Sacrifice opened the way to the pantheon of people's heroes and transformed death, which thousands of people faced every day inside and outside prison, into a comprehensible and justified contingency. Sacrifice as meaningful death gave the condemned the courage to face death, to cry out slogans for the Communist Party in front of the firing squad.[49] This was the way communist prisoners *should* die. States of powerlessness, fear and emotional emptiness, which are common among criminal prisoners on death row, are not absent in the case of political prisoners but are radically reframed.[50] By transforming death through sacrifice into a justified contingency, they situated themselves beyond the realm of death, in a sense negating it.

For the surviving political prisoners the day after an execution was a day of protest and commemoration. They refused to eat their daily prison mess and sometimes they played sports, to overcome the distressing mood prevailing after executions and to show to the administration that their morale was high. In the evening they organized rites in their dormitories to commemorate the executed. For half an hour, the political prisoners read the letters that the deceased had written for their fellow prisoners, recited poems, sang songs or gave lectures.[51]

The letters the executed prisoners addressed to their fellow inmates, were different from those they sent to their families. Vasileios Kafetzis left the following note to his fellow inmates at the Cephalonia prison before his execution on 5 May 1949:

(…)Come on brothers! United, disciplined, your chests hard as a rock, become as hard as granite, so that the filthy snake won't get into our fortress. Victory has arrived, comrades, hold our fortress and the people will break our chains. And be sure that I, from my grave I'll stand by your struggles. I curse him who yields an inch and forgets these moments (…)[52]

The message of this strongly worded, emotionally charged note to his fellow inmates is clear. The "filthy snake" is the declaration of repentance that threatened the "fortress," that is, the prisoners' collectivity. He addresses his fellow inmates as a group not as individuals. The individual appears only in the form of the repenter, who is not just deplored but cursed, an absolute condemnation for the rest of his life. The purpose of the note is to boost the morale of his fellow inmates. Again, the tense is not the present but the future. Kafetzis in his note places his sacrifice beyond the present, which is dominated by the fear of death; it belongs to the future, which is presented as imminent and specific (the hope of victory).

The "bureau," which was behind all these initiatives, could not let the mourning prevail for long because mourning could nurture pessimism and, most importantly, fear. Under the specter of death, commemoration, as the imaginary unity between the collectivity of those who live (political prisoners) and the collectivity of those who have died heroically ("people's heroes"), had the purpose of diluting the fear of dying, of justifying and attaching meaning to death. The instructions of the party to its cadres were "to develop the tradition of heroism and self-sacrifice."[53] The fear that threatened the coherence of the political prisoners' collectivity should become heroism, the glorification of the collective spirit.

Notes

1. Manousakas, *To chroniko enos agona,* 33.
2. Elaborated data from the review *Sofronistikai Pliroforiai* of the years between 1936 and 1939.
3. Flountzis, *Akronafplia,* 468.
4. Municipality of Lavreotiki, List of those who died in Makronisos from 6 June 1949 to 22 November 1951 and are registered in the registry books of the municipality, Lavrio, 28/2/1988. In Vardinogiannis and Aronis, eds., *Oi misoi sta sidera,* 202-205.
5. Ibid., 143-147.
6. Ibid., 226-227.
7. Aegina Prison Archives, Hospital Record no. 1582.
8. UNRRA PAG 4/3.0.12.2.0., Box 6, File W/17 (1), Prison reports, Report on prisons in Athens and Piraeus, 2 March 1946.

9. Ibid., Report on Trikala prison, 30 August 1945; UNRRA PAG 4/3.0.12.2.3. Box 12, File W/17 (1) Visit to the Prison at the Italian School, 30 April 1946; (in the same file) Report on the Nauplio Prison
10. Ethniki Allileggyi, *Sta xeronisia*, 55, 64; Commission internationale contre le r(gime concentrationnaire, *Livre blanc sur les camps d' internement en Grèce* (Paris, 1953), 107.
11. ASKI, box 423 F25/5/6, Report on prisons 16 December 1951; ASKI, box 423 F25/5/85, Appeal of tubercular political prisoners from Amfissa preventorium.
12. ASKI, box 422 F25/4/205, Letter of Vasilis Kalaras, Sotiria hospital, 20 December 1958.
13. UNRRA PAG 4/3.0.12.2.0, Box 6, File W/17 (1), Prison reports, Infirmary at Averof prison, 25 October 1945.
14. ASKI, box 421 F25/3/36, Letter of A. Berdebes from Giaros, 11August 1950.
15. ASKI, box 423 F25/5/27 Memorandum of Panagiotis Timogiannakis, detainee at the Argostoli prison to the honourable Minister of Justice, 7 July 1953.
16. FO 371/87647 RG1016/6, Athens to FO. BMM to Greece. Report on Makronisos, 20 January 1950.
17. ASKI, box 422 F25/4/40, Letter of Nikos Andrikidis, 16 February 1953.
18. Margaris, *Istoria tis Makronisou*, vol. 1, 609-634 and vol. 2, pp. 1-31, 129-193; Mavridis, in Vardinogiannis and Aronis, eds., *Oi misoi sta sidera*, 153-160. Needless to say, the official version of the incidents was quite different. According to General Director G. Bairaktaris, the incidents were a plot of KKE members "who insulted the staff most vulgarly and caused a state of disorder during which they kicked and injured several members of the staff who were then obliged owing to the situation to enforce order by all means." The general director did not mention in his report either what happened the next day or that several soldiers were killed. NARA 868.00/6-248, The Greek "concentration" camp at Makronisos, 2 June 1948, FO 371/87647 RG 1016/18, General Director's report on the Makronisos Reformative Organisation, 24 January 1950.
19. *Rizospastis*, 26 January 1947.
20. Giorgos Margaritis, *Istoria tou ellinikou Emfyliou Polemou*, vol. 1, 527;Close, *The Origins*, 192.
21. *Rizospastis*, 3 June 1947.
22. Foivos Gregoriadis, *Istoria tou emfyliou polemou (1945-1949). To deftero antartiko* (Athens, n.d.), vol. 4, 1146-1147.
23. ASKI, box 423 F25/5/6 Report on prisons, 16 December 1951.
24. Foot, "The Tale of San Vittore," 25-48. In the two-day incidents at the Makronisos camps, according to the commander of the First Battalion, ten "loyal" soldiers were injured heavily and thirty-nine lightly. See Margaris, *Istoria tis Makronisou*, vol. 2, 175. Generally speaking, no prison riots, in the current sense of an assault on staff and damage of prison property, were organized by political prisoners during the Civil War.
25. FO 371/67076 R10153, British Consulate-General, Salonica to Athens, 7 July 1947.
26. See above, chapter 3.
27. FO 371/72355 R10822, Letter by the Minister for Press and Information to Mr. Vincent Tewson, General Secretary, Trade Union Congress, 11 September 1948.
28. FO 371/87668 RG 10113/11, Prison population of Greece, 6 April 1950.
29. See chapter 2.
30. The government had issued instructions to the prosecuting officers of special courts-martial to suspend the execution of persons sentenced to death by a majority of three to two. See FO 371/67079 R15861, Salonica to Athens, 1 December 1947. The Minister of Justice and the Board of Pardons, consisting of six members (judges and higher officials of the Ministry of Justice), submitted their individual recommendations to the king, who decided whether or not to reprieve and commute the death sentence. See Oikonomopoulos, *Ektakta stratodikeia kai nomothesia*, 172-182.

31. NARA 868.00/6-548, Athens to Department of State, 5 June 1948. The total number of those executed between 1 May and 11 May 1948, according to the U.S. Embassy, was 107, of whom 61 were condemned by civil courts and 46 by military courts.
32. FO 371/67076 R10153, British Consulate-General, Salonika to Athens, 7 July 1947.
33. See, for instance, the letter of Dwight Griswold, Chief of the American Mission for Aid to Greece, a reply to a report by Homer Bigart, *New York Herald Tribune* journalist, in the *New York Herald Tribune*, 2 May 1948. See also Wittner, *American Intervention*, 143-151. For the French press in general, see Nasi Balta, *O ellinikos emfylios polemos (1946-1949) mesa apo ton galliko typo* (Athens, 1993).
34. Following the recommendations of U.S. officials and facing a wave of strong criticism after the mass executions in May 1948, the government gave details concerning the prisoners in death row. Almost all of them were condemned after the liberation for murders committed during the occupation and the December events. It is interesting that in that list, though the dates and places where the murders had been committed were given, and the decisions of the courts were cited, any information that might have revealed the motives for the murders (such as the profession of the victim) was omitted. See NARA 868.00/3-448, Department of State to Athens, 4 March 1948; NARA 868.00/3-1748, Athens to Department of State, 17 March 1948; NARA 868.00/5-2648, Athens to Department of State, 26 May 1948.
35. FO 371/72354 R6123, Athens to FO, Undersecretariat of State for Press and Information, Facts about the execution of common criminals, 14 May 1948.
36. From the the Averof prison eight political prisoners were transferred for execution in 1947, 185 in 1948, and 111 in 1949. See, Averof Prison Archives, Register of convicts of Averof prison. From the Corfu prison, eleven were transferred for execution in 1947, sixty-three in 1948, thirty-seven in 1949. See, *Fylakes Kerkyras-Lazareto....*, 117-127. From the Cephalonia prison forty-three in 1948 and sixty-one in 1949. See, ASKI, EDA Archives-National Resistance Archives ("Phoenix").
37. Mitsos Roupas, "I ektelesi tou Filippa," in Vardinoyiannis and Aronis, eds., *Oi misoi sta sidera*, 282-286.
38. Eleni Kyvelou-Kamoulakou, "Kalo voli adelfes," in Vardinogiannis and Aronis, eds., *Oi misoi sta sidera*, 421-433. It is interesting to notice that criminal prisoners on death row had similar rituals, that is they spent the night before the execution with their fellow inmates eating and drinking and they distributed their belongings to them. Petrounakos, *Ai fylakai mas*, 139.
39. Margaret Alexiou, *The Ritual Lament in Greek tradition* (Cambridge, 1974), 37-38, 185-205.
40. Dimitra Mara-Michalakea, *Gynaikeies Fylakes Averof. Athina, 12-13 Apriliou 1949* (Athens, 1995), 25-26.
41. ASKI, box 421 F25/3/6, Letter of Nikolaos Braziotikos, 30 September 1946.
42. ASKI, EDA Archives, National Resistance Archives, Letter of Elli Svorou, 7 June 1949.
43. ASKI, EDA Archives, National Resistance Archives, Letter of Orestis Makridis from the Averof prison, 25 June 1948. One has to notice the similarity of the letters written by men and women awaiting execution. See chapter 11.
44. Lambropoulou, *Grafontas apo ti fylaki*, 74-87.
45. Zygmunt Bauman, *Mortality, Immortality and Other Life Strategies* (Cambridge, 1992), 27.
46. Peter Berger and Thomas Luckmann, *The Social Construction of Reality. A Treatise in the Sociology of Knowledge* (London, 1971), 110-122. The authors argue that "(t)he symbolic universe is conceived of as a matrix of *all* socially objectivated and subjectively real meanings; the entire historic society and the entire biography of the individual are seen as events taking place *within* this universe" (p. 114). See also Philip A. Mellor, "Death in High

Modernity: The Contemporary Presence and Absence of Death," in *The Sociology of Death,* ed. David Clark (Oxford, 1993), 3-30.

47. See *Ethniki Antistasi 1941-1944, Grammata kai minymata ektelesmenon patrioton* (Athens, 1974). The emphasis in the resistance members' last letters before execution by the occupation forces is on honorable death, dying for freedom and the country (explicit references to the Communist Party are few).
48. Note of Dimitris Glinos, cited in *Elefthera Grammata* 32-33 (21 December 1945): 1 (original emphasis).
49. FO 371/67079 R14325, Salonica to Athens, 24 October 1947. The British consulate in Salonica complained because the newspaper *Macedonia* had published pictures of prisoners just before their execution, with the "condemned group looking like a picnic party, their faces wreathed in smiles and displaying superb courage."
50. Robert Johnson, "Life Under Sentence of Death," in Johnson and Toch, eds., *The Pains of Imprisonment,* 129-145.
51. Interview with Takis Benas on 24 February 1998. See also, FO 371/78497 R9888, Report on Kalamiou prison visited by W. E. Newton PSO II on 27/9/49, 3 October 1949.
52. ASKI, EDA Archives, National Resistance Archives, Vasileios Kafetzis, Cephalonia prison, 5 May 1949.
53. "Merika symperasmata kai kathikonta," *Kommounistiki Epitheorisi* 1 (January 1947): 14-17.

Part Three

PRISON AS A FIELD OF CONFLICT

Chapter 9

Transforming Prison

It is Christmas day. Our committee went to the commander and gained permission to go to the village. The night before our choir went to the village and sang Christmas carols. The next day the whole battalion (one might have thought that it was a demonstration) we organized a dance in the square of the village. It was real pandemonium. Civilians, women, girls, children, and soldiers were hugging and dancing. They were shouting to each other, "Dance, brothers," and were starting to dance once more. Around five o'clock in the afternoon when we returned to the camp, their schemes against us unraveled. They started beating our fellow soldiers and dragging them to the dungeons. At that moment our anger became unrestrained; some of us dashed and released our fellow soldiers.[1]

What happened at the Agios Nikolaos camp on Crete on Christmas 1946 was not unique. A holiday feast organized by detained soldiers became an occasion for acting out of otherwise hidden and repressed sentiments and needs, for allusion and remembrance, for the reassessment of the boundaries between political prisoners and the free community. Dances, songs, music, an extra portion of food; the remembrance of past Christmases with friends and family, but also the joy and the excitement of participating in a demonstration; meeting free citizens and reminding each other of the very fine line dividing the inside from the outside of the prison: this confluence of circumstances transformed the prison world and probed its limits.

The committee, the feast, and the conflict with the administration are typical concomitants. Though the prison or the camp may seem a realm of total heteronomy, actually, given the restrictions of the institution as such and its interrelation to the sociopolitical situation, it is a field of continuous conflict and negotiation between the prisoners and the administration. I will to explore this field in the third part of the book. More specifically, I will discuss the informal organization of everyday life by the prisoners, the various forms of conflict between the political prisoners and the administration, and finally, the Communist Party mechanism inside prisons.

Notes for this section begin on page 179.

Starting with the informal organization of everyday life by the prisoners, I will discuss the ways in which they transformed prison—concretely when the informal organization of prison by the prisoners themselves tested the limits of the prisons' rules and regulations, and imaginarily, when prison became the field on which prisoners acted out their wishes, hopes, and fears, and thus broke the isolation and restrictions of the penitentiary. Actual and imaginary did not collide; on the contrary, they were different ways of transforming prison. Their interplay created multiple locations for the subject's enactment, locations that undermined, contested, and escaped the restrictions and the ordeal of institutionalized prison life.

Activities

Back in 1937, when the first prison for political prisoners was established in Akronafplia, lessons and the organization of routine duties by the prisoners themselves constituted the basic features of their everyday life. Prisoners attended classes in literature, mathematics, geometry, geography, physics, foreign languages, music, dance, and for many of them, vocational training; they also performed routine duties such as cooking, cleaning, and maintenance and repairs.[2] In exile, political prisoners organized their lives according to a similar pattern. The exiles' collective assigned duties to its members according to their professions, and organized classes, lectures and leisure activities alike.[3] Insofar as the same pattern was adopted during the Civil War, we can assume that it originated in the experience of collective life in prisons and exile under the Metaxas regime. Many people who had been in prison in the prewar era and found themselves incarcerated after the liberation of the country conveyed their social experience of organizing collective life in prisons to the new inmates.

Obliged to spend more than half of day inside crowded cells and rooms, in very unhygienic conditions, the first issue that interested the inmates was the care of the body. After the morning roll call, the prisoners gathered in the prison courtyard for exercises. A gymnast could always be found among the prisoners to instruct them in simple exercises. The prisoners, even the elderly, were very eager to be out in the courtyard after spending the night in the stench of the chamber pot and the suffocating atmosphere of the cell, and many of them did exercises. For the same reason sporting events were often organized on Sundays inside the prisons, for instance volleyball games or tennis matches. Care of the body was also the motivation for a whole set of practices: exhortations to fellow inmates to take frequent showers, signs on the walls about the significance of cleanliness and hygiene, medical tests conducted by inmates who were doctors, protests for the improvement of meals.

One issue that attracted special attention from the political prisoners was their education. In almost every prison or exile camp political prisoners organized classes for some time, and the reminiscences of those classes are salient in their memoirs. The classes were organized by the prisoners themselves despite the authorities' prohibition. Students were divided into classes according to their level of literacy, and educated prisoners stood as teachers. In the Averof women's prison the inmates studied literature, mathematics, and foreign languages (Russian, English, French), and the illiterates learned to read and write. A choir was formed and songs for national holidays and feasts were taught; actresses instructed the detainees who acted in theatrical plays. The imprisoned schoolteachers were also occupied with the ninety or more children of detainees. There was also vocational training in bookkeeping and dressmaking.[4] The way that the lessons and the classes were organized differed according to the situation in the prison. If lessons were tolerated by the administration, they took place in the dormitories; if not, they were organized in small groups. Exercise books and writing materials were sent by mail, or the prisoners used what materials they could find inside the prison.

The older prisoners, women in particular, had the greatest difficulties since the vast majority was illiterate.[5] For them, literacy meant being able to write and read the letters from their families. Some women anticipated a new necessity, knowing that after the death or flight of their husbands or sons they would have to take over the finances of their households. Many political prisoners in their memoirs recall the efforts and eagerness to learn of these elderly women (the so-called "black cloud," for they wore mourning clothes), and, of course, how proud they were when they managed to write letters themselves. "My grandson will read the letter, like you did?" a surprised elderly detainee once asked the teacher, who had read her letter aloud for corrections. Writing a letter posed difficulties for illiterate prisoners, who had not only to find a literate prisoner available to write a letter, or to correct it (and correction might imply a change in the content of a letter), but also to think and express their message not orally but in the written form of a letter.[6] The writing of a letter was often their first encounter with the world of writing. The "mystery," after years of exclusion from the literate and dependence on shrewd go-betweens, was dispelled.[7]

Classes in prison organized by the prisoners themselves were not a phenomenon unique to Greek political prisoners. On the contrary, they were a common feature of prisoners' lives in quite different contexts, like British prisoners of war in Nazi camps, interned foreigners in British camps, Jews in Italian concentration camps during the Second World War, and Salvadoran or Peruvian political prisoners in the 1980s.[8] Classes organized by the prisoners themselves presupposed a sense of community. Embedded in an ideological framework, they served as an orientation towards the future. Political prisoners, like prisoners of war, shared an identity and referred to a community that was outside prison. The bonds among the prisoners and between the prisoners and the outside community were reinforced by their ideological commitment that underlay the classes they organized. In the case of political prisoners, we can trace several trends of that ideological framework: the teaching that lack of education symbolized the oppression and deprivation of the lower classes; the project of the Enlightenment, which held that the source of human misery was illiteracy, and assumed that people became would understand the social origins of their misery as soon as they became literate; the conviction that education was part of the political struggle inside and outside prisons. Moreover, classes in prisons had explicit future-oriented purposes. A more vague and ideological one was that the prisoners should be educated in order to be able to run the new socialist society. But for political prisoners as individuals, imprisonment was a parenthesis in their lives, sooner or later they would be released and they would have to finish their studies or find a job. Classes, individual study, or learning a craft, was a way to plan their lives ahead, to prepare themselves for their future as self-employed—they knew that they would not find a job in the civil service. And indeed, it was common after their release for political prisoners to become accountants, a profession they had learnt in prison.

Prison was mainly an oral world. Prisoners carried and communicated news, information, and knowledge by talking rather than by reading or writing, not only because many prisoners were illiterate, but also because a piece of paper could be a piece of evidence as well. Take, for instance, another educational activity, what the prisoners called "collective reading." This would actually be better termed collective listening, because one prisoner read a book while the others listened. When new restrictions were imposed, lessons were taught orally, without written material, when the prisoners were walking in the yard. For the classes, as for other activities, political prisoners' mnemonic capacity, not printed material, was their best equipment.

Books, however, were introduced into prisons. Books with "reprehensible content" were not allowed in prisons and were to be confiscated.[9] But there were always ways to smuggle a book inside prisons. The archives of the Aegina hold a number of books that belonged to political prisoners and were confiscated by the guards; from them we may get an idea of what they were reading in the late 1940s and in the 1950s. One may find among them dictionaries, André Maurois's *Histoire des États-Unis*, Joseph Stalin's *Les principes du léninisme*, a *World History* and *The theory of historical materialism* edited by the Academy of Sciences of the USSR, a biography of Lenin (in Russian), Lenin's *Collected Works* (in Russian), the review *Économie et Politique*, the *Communist Manifesto*, and Leo Tolstoy's *Anna Karenina* (in Russian), to name a few titles.[10]

Political classes were taught alongside the educational ones. In a letter sent from the Zakynthos prison to the communist daily *Rizospastis*, political and educational activities are intermingled:

> We have a school for illiterates and another one for the literate. We have a class for all the EPONites with lessons on the struggle of our organization and on

several issues concerning the young. We also give a talk every week on issues about the young. We also have a school for cadres, which 30 EPONites attend; they are taught lessons on organization and leadership, and on the problems of the Younger Generation. There is also a theater and an elocution class. We have the main theater, where every Sunday there is a play for all the prisoners in the central dormitory. We have clubs in which we play chess, read and dance. We have a ball and we play volleyball, as well. Every morning we do exercises with a gymnastics teacher.[11]

This letter, indicative of the enthusiasm of EPON youths, was not only a report on the political prisoners' activities but also an example of what they should do once they entered the prison gate. The inventory of activities and the authoritative style of writing illustrate the vacillating nature of prisoners' self-organization: they were initiatives spontaneously undertaken, and at the same time, tasks to be performed with discipline. I shall return to this question later.

Political exiles had relatively more freedom to organize themselves. On Ikaria, the OSPEs (each village had its own OSPE) undertook the management of the exiles' accommodation. Newcomers presented themselves to the bureau of the local OSPE at the port of the island and from there were dispatched to the various villages. The Coordination Committee with its subcommittees had to solve the problems and meet the needs of the exiles in different villages of the island: they assigned the exiled doctors to the local OSPEs, and distributed medicines, animals for transportation, food, and blankets among the villages.[12] Just as the teachers were assigned teaching positions, all the political prisoners were charged with different kind of jobs according to their expertise, and there was a rotating system for the duties (cleaning, cooking, transportation, and so on). These activities usually fell under the scope of political prisoners' organization. In any case, under whose authority the prison activities would be directed was always an issue of negotiation or conflict. Since any form of prisoners' organization was banned, the administration could intervene and impose new restrictions at any time.

The report of a British officer who visited the camp on Chios in January 1949 gives us a picture of exiles' self-organization. At that time, 1,316 women and 52 children were interned at the camp. The women controlled the distribution and use of the water supply. Mainly two deportees provided medical attention, since only one doctor visited the camp three times a week. The detainees did the purchase (from the local market), distribution, and preparation of such commodities as food themselves. However, the struggle of the political detainees' community to exert control over the whole life of the camp had provoked a reaction from the administration. For instance, the distribution of clothes was in dispute since the women had challenged the gendarmerie's authority over this issue; the detainees had also demanded to inspect the books and the accounts of the administration.[13]

The distribution of money and goods fell within the scope of the collectivity's activities. The prisoners had to give a share of any checks and foodstuffs they received to the "cashier of the group." In this way the collectivity tried to solve problems such as the following: the allowance that exiles—but not prisoners—received was meager (in 1950 the daily allowance was 2,700 drachmas), the support that prisoners received from their homes was dependent on their finances, and prisoners incarcerated close to their hometowns were more privileged because they had more visits. For these reasons and in an attempt to strengthen solidarity by blunting differences, the "cashier of the group" collected a portion of foodstuffs that could be used in common (coffee, for instance), and money for the purchase of goods to support the poorest among the prisoners. In a similar vein, in prisons small companies of eight to ten people were created, in which prisoners native to the city where the prison was situated (who thus had regular visits) shared their food parcels with the other prisoners. At the Kastor women's prison in Athens, the political prisoners found an additional way to overcome their financial difficulties. With the administration's permission, gloves, caps, or socks knitted by them were sold at the market. At a certain point, the women prisoners no longer had enough time to carry out all these organized activities (lessons, labor, duties, and so on). Realizing this, the "bureau" took a unique and unprecedented step: they changed the division of time. Time was no longer divided into weeks but into ten-day periods, and the names of the days were changed (first, second, third, instead of Monday, Tuesday, Wednesday, and so on)! Since there was not enough time, what they changed was the measure of time rather than the schedule, thereby reducing the number of holidays.[14]

The self-organization of collective life was important because it was directly related to the improvement of living conditions. The prisoners in charge did their best to meet the needs of their fellow inmates because the prosperity of the collectivity was dependent on them. The principles of solidarity among them and devotion to the collectivity were prevalent. This kind of "superego of the group" is illustrated in one "newspaper" published by political exiles on the island of Sikinos. "Everyday," the newspaper says, "the member of the OSPE should not *forget* to think of what he did for the group and to examine himself without fear."[15] The same newspaper gave an example of what that meant:

> For instance when it is my turn to work in the kitchen, I bring wood to cook the food, I wash the dishes, and I see, so to speak, to the preparation of the food without complaining. In this case, I salve my conscience for I've done my duty and I have the right to eat my food without being ashamed in front of those who are going to prepare the food that I'm going to have. If each one of us considers all his duties in this way, then all the needs of our group will be fulfilled, without any misunderstandings that do harm and undercut our unity.[16]

It was true that whenever the detainees were permitted to take initiatives, living conditions were improved and collective life was sustained. Idleness was the worst enemy of the inmates. Labor, like all the other organized activities in prisons and exile, served the dual functions of preventing them from thinking of their long sentences, their relatives, and the misery of life in prison, as well as forging bonds of solidarity among the detainees. All these activities were a way to beguile time, to change the monotony and boredom of prison life, to give expression to their creativity, and to learn or practice a skill. "It is such a worrying thing to be inside the tent"[17] crowded and inactive, when labor, lessons, lectures, and sports provided an escape from this suffocating environment. When Richard Lippincott, a UNRRA official, asked several political exiles what they did with their spare time, he noticed that "Communist exiles invariably found their spare time much less oppressive than non-communists, who were always among those most vehement in condemnation of the bitterness of their lot."[18]

Feasts

Feasts, which were organized on certain occasions—national or religious holidays, for instance—represented a special feature since they transgressed the limits of routine in prisoners' everyday life. At feasts they had the opportunity to express themselves more or less explicitly, to communicate beliefs and feelings, and to entertain or to instruct their fellow inmates in public. In this section I will discuss both official and illegal feasts as attempts by the political prisoners to confirm an identity and to draw symbolic boundaries between themselves and the authorities.

Official feasts interrupted the depressing routine of life in prison. The prisoners were not locked in at noon, and so were able to spent the whole day out in the yard. The administration provided the prisoners with musical instruments, the food was better for the occasion, and restrictions were slackened. The political exiles on Ikaria took many initiatives to celebrate the Easter of 1947. Exiles' choirs chanted in the various churches of the island, they had a festive lunch together in large groups, they decorated the buildings, they exchanged visits and presents with the islanders, and they performed songs and plays.[19]

The occasions for such feasts were official holidays. Besides Christmas and Easter, political prisoners also celebrated the other two official holidays: the 25th of March (the outbreak of the war of independence against the Ottoman empire in 1821) and the 28th of October (the outbreak of the Greek-Italian war in 1940). Sometimes even plays were staged; in these cases the political prisoners prepared for weeks before the performance The scenery was constructed out of cardboard and paper and prisoners who were tailors made costumes out of the prisoners' clothes and the sheets. Hours of voluntary work and ingenuity made possible the staging of such performances as *Mesologgi lives* on 25 March 1948 at the Chios camp or *Rigas Velestinlis* on 25 March1950 at the Itzedin prison.[20] Neither the playwright nor the plays were chosen at random. Vasilis Rotas, the author of the two plays mentioned above, was one of the intellectuals imprisoned during the Civil War. His play *Rigas Velestinlis* referred to an eighteenth-century revolutionary and intellectual who influenced the war of independence and represented the radical liberal version of nationalism. The other play referred to the heroic exodus of the Greek independence fighters after a twelve-month siege by the Ottomans in April 1826—the prisoners could easily identify themselves with the besieged Greeks.

But even for these official holidays the permission of the administration was not presumed; in many cases the feasts that the prisoners had organized were prohibited or stopped. Still, the detainees could find ways to overcome the prohibition. In the Larisa camp in 1946, for instance, the political detainees wished to celebrate the 28th of October, but the administration prohibited it. The detainees, however, were determined to commemorate that day, because, as they claimed, "it is *our* feast."[21] And they celebrated *their* 28th of October inside the dormitories with a brief talk on the meaning of that day, the national anthem, folk songs, and poems.

The celebration of a national holiday was actually a struggle over the meaning of that day. What was supposed to be celebrated on the 28th of October? The political establishment was celebrating the rejection of the Italian ultimatum by the dictator Metaxas and the virtues of the Greek army. The political prisoners were celebrating the Greek people's will to fight for the independence of the country, as it had been demonstrated in the Greek-Italian war and the resistance against the Axis occupation. Within this context, the national holidays were ambiguous or invested with a double meaning. In the commemoration of the 25th of March the similarity between the 1820s and the 1940s was established through analogy, whereas in the celebration of the 28th of October political prisoners stressed the continuity between 1940 and the postwar years. Just as, the fighters of the 1820s had been called *klefts* (bandits), Vasilis Rotas argued in 1946, the resistance fighter were being defamed in the same way as "rebels, mountaineer thieves, a mob."[22] In the same vein, political detainees sang folk songs on the occasion of the 25th of March to underline that "In the *armatolos* and *klefts* of 1821, whom the *kleft* songs praised, we see the ELAS fighter or today's guerilla."[23] On 25 March 1945, the nine hundred prisoners at the Chatzikosta prison (Athens) went on a twenty-four-hour hunger strike, to demonstrate that on the day that the war of independence was commemorated, thousands of people who had fought in the resistance for the liberation of the country were in prisons.[24]

The struggle over the meaning of these national holidays transformed them into a field of contest between the authorities and the prisoners. The holidays gave political prisoners the opportunity to complement to their celebrations with a form of protest. The content of the celebration itself was equally challenging. The celebration of the 25th of March reenacted the struggle for the liberation of Greece, and moreover created the opportunity to construct the genealogy of the Greek communist movement. The war for the independence of Greece was represented as an unfinished project that the communists undertook to complete.[25] In this way political prisoners contested the unity of the national past and revealed its ambiguity. However, the real issue was not the past but the present. Giannis Zevgos, a member of the Central Committee of the KKE, made this quite clear on the occasion of the commemoration of the 25th of March at the Akronafplia prison in 1942, when he argued that "The KKE is (…) the sole heir of the glorious traditions of 1821."[26] This genealogical approach provided continuity with the past and legitimacy for the present. Within the context of the conflict and civil strife political prisoners viewed the past in terms of exclusion rather than of unity: it was "their" feast because they were the "sole heirs."

To illustrate the discussion of prisoners' feasts, I would like to focus on a specific one, a revue staged at the carnival of 1949 by the women in the Averof prison. The script took the form of verses written exclusively by them, and matched the rhythm of well-known melodies and songs. Thanks to Olympia Papadouka's book *Averof Women's Prison*, we have the text of that revue.[27] It is divided into eleven acts, each one dedicated to one aspect of the women's daily life in prison.

These verses bring together the expression of the difficulties of prison life, and the goals of instruction and entertainment. "They put us in jail / to be wasted away / and from the fatigue duties / to drive us insane." The "they" is never defined; it may be the government, the prison administration, or the British and the Americans among others. Perhaps it is all of them who are comprised in the pronoun "they," which facilitates the juxtaposition of power and the prisoners: "they" as a whole are confronted with "us" as a whole; the dividing line is more than clear and there is no space in between. When the others are specified, they are personified. Froso was the name of one of the female guards, not the most powerful but one who had everyday contact with the detainees. Severe and shrewd, she became the object of the revue. The parody of her is based on gender connotations: "Your screams at us / no wonder you can't have a baby." One feature is isolated and exemplified to demonstrate the general (women as mothers) and the particular (what kind of women can give birth), and to draw the dividing line between "us" and "them" according to gender terms (we can give birth to a child, she cannot).

The main characteristic of these lyrics is the light-hearted mode. The tempo is fast, the women on stage all dance together, the mood is optimistic, the mockery is self-directed: "If you pass by once / the door of the scullery / four will bring you out / like a plucked chicken" or "Everything is as clean as a mirror / I alone will be the nigger"[28]; or "How, my daughters, / do they scrub the cement? / How do they scrub the cement? / Look at us and have a little fun". Even when the verses refer to unpleasant and sorrowful feelings, then are coupled with joyful ones. The following lines pertain to the cleaning of the visiting room and are sung according to the sad *mantinada* rhythm of traditional Cretan folk songs: "Ah! Among all these duties / is another one / that whenever I start … / the laugh, the joy stops. / It is the visiting room / I have to clean / that was surrounded by so many faces / that I'll never see again." These wistful reflections are is coupled with the following rejoinder, sung in fast *mantinada* rhythm: "But my heart is raised / the hands work. / We are of Freedom / and of labor the masters."

The purpose of the revue was both to entertain and to boost the prisoners' morale. For this reason depressing issues, such as executions or diseases, are not commented on, and the light-hearted mode—a constitutional element of the revue as a theatrical genre—is chosen. Within the context of the aim of boosting the women's morale the importance of unity and respect for the rules of conviviality are emphasized. The women danced and sang on stage in groups, and the plural "we" is prevalent in the text. The same purpose is implicitly served through the didactic style of some of the lyrics. Commenting on the scarcity of water, the players singing "You will fill it very well / as long as you get in line;" on the duties to be carried out they urge "Scrub well, scrub well, to be clean as a glass / tile by tile till the yard shines." I think that the last verses of the revue are indicative of the whole spirit: "All together / hand by hand let's hold each other / and united this way, in one heart / sorrows and joys to live on."

Illegal feasts, unlike the celebrations of official holidays, were directly related to the political identity of the prisoners and for that reason were forbidden by the administration. Occasions for such feasts were the commemoration of the Bolshevik revolution, of the foundation of the EAM, or the EPON, and the mass executions of resistance fighters by the Germans. On those days, after the lock-in and before lights out, the prisoners gathered in the cells and, always with lookouts, organized a small feast. Someone gave a short talk on the meaning of the day, someone else read a relevant story or recited a poem, and at the end the prisoners whispered revolutionary songs. Those small feasts were not as entertaining as the official ones but were equally exciting and important (even more so, given their secrecy).Besides the illegal feasts, a whole range of clandestine but festive events took place in the evenings. When they were not reading books or playing chess, their cells or dormitories were transformed into small stages. Jokes, songs, stories, bantering exchanges, and short sketches were performed to pass the time, to tease a fellow inmate, to ridicule the guards, to remember their free life. They told stories from the "good old days," their glorious past as resistance fighters during the occupation, they organized what they called "literary evenings" (small talks dedicated to famous writers), or they danced to the rhythm of a strange music made by the sound of spoons and hands.

Tearing Down the Walls

Dimitris and Eirini Sotiropoulos were a couple that experienced the calamities of the civil war in full measure. They found themselves in the Averof prisons, two different buildings for men and women, one next to the other. They had several problems to solve. They had left behind two young daughters, and their financial situation was deteriorating. The shoe factory that Dimitris owned had been closed down, and it had come time for their house to be sold to raise money to live. They had also to find a way to talk about these issues, which led to their discovery of the "telegraph." Two handkerchiefs, one hung from a window of the men's prison and one from a window of the women's prison just opposite, were enough. With the handkerchiefs they drew capital letters in the air. The initial problem was that the receiver had to read backwards. Later, when this form of communication became known amongst the prisoners, the problem was the plethora of messages; the Sotiropoulos couple had to "instruct" a second "telegraphist." Their device can be perceived as a way in which the cell becomes a larger space and the walls separating the prisoners are rendered less visible.[29]

In this part of the chapter I shall discuss the ways in which the political prisoners overcame the restrictions of prison and restored, mostly illegally, their communication with the free community. I shall begin with the imagination of the prisoners and the imagined transformation of prison, then I shall discuss illegal ways of gaining information from outside, and, finally, how the free community expressed its solidarity to the political prisoners. The walls separating the political prisoners from the free community, even in the hard times of a civil war, were very thin. Although they were in jail, political prisoners were not marginalized, nor did they experience their incarceration in this way; on the contrary, they constituted a numerous division of a revolutionary movement upon whose success their future depended. The awareness of belonging to a collective agent outside prisons and the close interrelation of the situations outside and inside prisons made prison walls permeable.

It is interesting to discuss the impact of news on prisoners' imagination. Nobody knows how the news that Shanghai had fallen into the hands of the Chinese Red Army reached the Makronisos camps in 1949—perhaps someone had glimpsed a newspaper held by an officer. Nobody knew what had exactly had happened in Shanghai; still, the excitement was great. The prisoners had seen no picture of the arrival of the Chinese Red Army in Shanghai, yet a detainee on Makronisos could imagine it as he wrote in his memoirs: "Workers run, embrace each other and carry the liberators in their arms (...) millions of kids run onto the roofs to see the legendary People's Army coming from the Great March."[30] Onto the arrival of the Chinese People's Army in Shanghai, the detainee projected his own hope, that of the arrival of the Democratic Army in Athens or Salonica. In fact, was perfectly able to picture it because not even five years had passed since 12 October 1944, when ELAS units had actually marched through the center of a just-liberated Athens.[31]

The prisoners' imaginations could not be confined to the prison, because that would mean acceptance of defeat, and loss of hope. As had been the case under Metaxas' dictatorship, when political detainees "fought" with the antifascists in the Spanish Civil War, in the Greek Civil War political prisoners' imaginations transforming the given place, time, and reality. The imagined places were China or the newborn people's republics in Eastern Europe or the mountains of the territories controlled by the Democratic Army of Greece. In the Averof women's prison a new dance (*noutikos*) was introduced, one that was said to be the favorite of guerillas. It represented the return from battle of a group of male and female guerillas. Because it was a dance without singing, the imaginary bonds became even stronger; whereas the guerillas remained silent to avoid being tracked down by the national army, the women in prison did the same to elude the guards' attention. The spatial dimension is coupled with a temporal one; the place imagined is the country of the future. The future was the only perspective that political prisoners could have. The present was perceived as a transitory phase, a forced reality that could not last for long. The revival of the past and the invention of the future were the agreeable realities. Political prisoners' imaginations made sense of their lives along the lines of a drama: action in the past, hardship for the hero in the present, redemption in the future.

Olympia Papadouka, in the book mentioned above, tells the story of Zoe Mamali, an eighty-year-old woman from Arachova. Her three sons, Stathis, Giorgos and Stergios (*nom de guerre* Demos), participated in the resistance and after the liberation shared the fate of all leftists. Zoe Mamali was in prison, sentenced to life, allegedly for helping her son Demos, who was a guerilla captain. Happy and very proud of her sons, she repeated to her fellow inmates "I have three brave men (*pallikaria*). All of them are in the ELAS and I, I'm close to them." Giorgos was arrested and tortured, signed a declaration of repentance, and was sent into exile. He died a few years later, after his release. Stathis was arrested, sentenced to death, and imprisoned on Corfu. From that moment on Zoe Mamali was very worried. She received regular letters from Stathis, but her fear was not abated: "I feel it. They killed my Stathis." Her Stathis, aged thirty-one, had been executed on 11 March 1948. In his last letter, he wrote: "Don't be resentful. Say it is for the cause, and Demos will take revenge." Many in the Averof women's prison knew that Stathis was dead, but they were loath to tell his mother and left her unaware, except for her unpleasant feeling. She continued to receive letters from him; before his execution Stathis had written a number of letters to his mother and asked his cellmate to send one at a time. As soon as she learned of her son's death, she burst out "Do you think I'm gonna give up? My Demos is over there. Demos will make 'em pay for all these things." However, her attitude changed. Now she was more nervous and angry. She would pace in the yard, staring at something beyond the wall, murmuring "Come on my Demos, beat 'em, beat ' em … Make 'em pay …" The end of the Civil War was near, and a group of recently arrested guerilla women arrived at the prison bringing bad news. Villages were burnt, people were killed and Demos was one of them; they had brought his head into Arachova and rolled it in the dung. From that day forth, Zoe Mamali did not talk to anyone and stopped walking in the yard.[32] While her body was in prison, in her imagination was on the mountains with her son and the guerilas, fighting with them to avenge Stathis' death. She did not call her son by his Christian name, Stergios, but by the name his comrades used, Demos. It was a reaction to the inertia and powerlessness imposed by imprisonment, up to the moment that the hope that fueled her imagination was shattered.

The lives of the political prisoners like Zoe Mamali were tied to what happened beyond the prison walls. Their powerlessness and anxiety were increased by the lack of information about the course of the Civil War and the fate of their beloved persons. News, however, as we have seen, traveled despite the various restrictions. Since correspondence was censored, and radios and newspapers were forbidden, the inmates had to find other, non-officially controlled means of communication.

Visits, if the circumstances allowed, would provide the opportunity for a short private talk. News about the prisoners' families and comrades, information about their cases, and the general political situation would be discussed within a few minutes with relatives or lawyers. Sometimes a message would pass through prison walls—a small piece of paper hidden in food or sewn into a bag. Many of the letters concerning living conditions and torture that were published in newspapers had been handed to visitors. On one occasion, in 1955, visits provided the prisoners at the Vourla prison with the materials for their escape. Eirini Petroulaki, the visitor who helped her fiancé Theodoros Vasilopoulos and his fellow inmates to escape, knew how to read his notes. In between the lines concerning a safe issue, like asking for his favorite food, he had written his real request in lemon juice: a drawing of the prison. All she had to do was to iron the letter and the message was revealed. Civil War-era prisoners and their correspondents used the same trick in their letters.[33] Transfers of political prisoners presented another opportunity for gaining information. Newcomers had many things to say about their experience in other prisons, or about what had happened up until their arrest. For this reason the other prisoners welcomed them upon their arrival; the monotony of prison life was interrupted and news about individuals and events was spread.[34]

A third information source was the guards. Good relations with a guard proved to be very useful and helpful in many cases. A brief talk with him could provide valuable news. When political prisoners could not count on the sympathy of the guards, bribery was the solution. Smuggling a newspaper or a small radio into a prison, or handing a note to a lawyer was, for many guards, a lucrative enterprise. Furthermore, the rest of the prisoners (common criminals or *dilosies*) sometimes were an important source, telling the political prisoners what they had heard in the offices of the administration or on the radio.

Under these circumstances the news reaching a prison was fragmentary, something of a patchwork rather than a complete story. The news was to be "created," as one prisoner put it, rather than communicated.[35] Different news from different sources, each with its own bias, was circulated, discussed, checked, and confirmed, so that in the end the prisoners were able to get an idea of "what really happened." News became rumors and vice versa in this endless quest for fresh information. In jail, where nothing happened and everything followed the same routine day after day, news was a break, a change. This situation reflected the prisoners' desperate attempts to establish contact with society. News reports were vague not only because of the variety of the sources, but also because the transmitters projected onto the news their own wishes or fears. In this sense, to a large extent they "created" news because they needed news. Anything that might have happened was becoming news for the prisoners, because once in prison their hopes for release were linked to a parliamentary debate, a United Nations plenum, a press conference—anywhere and anything outside the prison.

After 1949 the images of the future would become grimmer, and the account of what was lost throughout these years more painful. The need to finally be released, since the Civil War was over, became ever more urgent. This task could no longer be accomplished with arms, but with the help of family and the solidarity organizations. The families of political prisoners had a clear conception of the ordeal of political persecution. The arrest of one member of a family could easily result in the persecution of the rest of the family, ranging from frequent house searches or interrogations at the police station, to pressure to sign a declaration of repentance renouncing the political prisoner, to the stigmatization of the whole family, or even to exclusion (dismissal from their jobs, for instance). Nevertheless, prisoners relied heavily on their families and both were aware of it. The family had to find lawyers, money, witnesses, or persons who could influence the decree of the court. It was often incumbent on them to bribe members of a court-martial, or to take care of the persons or possessions the prisoner had left behind. Time and again, during imprisonment, prisoners considered their families to be in a privileged position, since they were free, and had many expectations of them:

visits, letters, money, parcels, and so on, even though the conviction of one member of a family usually meant additional financial difficulties for the rest. For many prisoners, family was perhaps the only link to society, the first and last resort for immediate help. Thus assuming full responsibility for the fate of the prisoner, family became the first nucleus of solidarity with the political detainees. Moreover, internment became a shared experience for the prisoners and their families alike, though from different positions, and a serious test of family bonds.

Many relatives sought not only individual but collective solutions as well, like the foundation of solidarity organizations. The PEOPEF (*Panellinia Enosi Oikogeneion Politikon Exoriston-Fylakismenon*, or Panhellenic Union of Political Exiles'-Prisoners' Families) was the most influential among them, after the ban on *Ethniki Allileggyi* in 1947. It was officially established in October 1950 in Athens by women relatives, mostly mothers, of political prisoners. Its objectives were to organize campaigns for a general amnesty and to press the government for the amelioration of living conditions in prisons. Hundreds of memoranda, appeals, and complaints were handed to international organizations (the International Red Cross, the United Nations, etc.), foreign embassies, newspapers, political parties, the Church, and government ministers, concerning issues such as the granting of general amnesty, the abolition of the death penalty, the abolition of the Giaros and Makronisos camps, the release of tubercolars, and other such issues. Another important activity was the collection of money and goods for prisoners. The PEOPEF assisted the International Red Cross in the distribution of aid material to the political exiles, kept contact with solidarity organizations abroad, and established branches in big cities like Patras and Salonica. However, the post-Civil War atmosphere did not encourage such activities. In 1952 the PEOPEF was brought to trial and ran the risk of being outlawed because it had "swerved from its purposes." Still, it managed to exist until 1954.[36]

Solidarity organizations were formed abroad as well. The London-based "League for Democracy in Greece," founded on 25 October 1945, was the first solidarity organization established abroad. Among its principal aims was "a general amnesty for all Greek democrats imprisoned for political reasons." Other such organizations were the Swiss Committee for Aid to Democratic Greece, in Geneva, the Swedish Committee for Aid to Democratic Greece, in Stockholm, and the French Committee for Aid to Democratic Greece, in Paris. They published bulletins on Greece, organized informational campaigns and pressed their governments on issues concerning the political prisoners and the state of democracy in the country, and organized the International Conference for Aid to Democratic Greece, which was held in Paris in April 1948.[37] For the prisoners themselves, support from foreign solidarity organizations not only improved their material conditions, but was also a sign that they were not alone, "a message of hope from far away."[38]

The KKE, overtly or not, provided the major support to the political detainees. The front pages of its daily *Rizospastis* were frequently covered with reports, letters, and articles concerning the situation inside prisons; political rallies were organized in Athens and other large cities to demand a general amnesty; members of the Politburo visited political prisoners in several prisons; and the local KKE organizations took initiatives to support the political prisoners, like raising money, or collecting clothes and food. The front organization *Ethniki Allilegyi*, a welfare organization established during the wartime resistance, was the main solidarity organization for political prisoners until 1947, when it was banned. *Ethniki Allileggyi* published a bulletin concerning the situation in prisons and exile, sent memoranda and appeals to the government and international organizations, provided legal assistance to the detainees, exerted pressure on the UNRRA to channel its supplies directly to the prisoners rather than through the state, and so on. Most importantly, *Ethniki Allileggyi* managed to substantially improve prisoners' and exiles' lives by sending large quantities of foodstuffs, clothes, shoes, medicine, cigarettes, and even books and writing materials.[39]

The prioritization of the party's objectives was inextricably related to the political situation. Political prisoners were on the political agenda as long as the KKE was aiming at its reincorporation within the political life of the country. The issues of political prisoners and political persecution were means to urge the government to purge the state apparatus of extreme rightists and royalists, and to press for the respect of civil liberties, for the abolition of undemocratic laws, and for fair elections. The decision to abstain from the elections of 1946 and form guerilla units became the point of no return. On the one hand, the perspective of reincorporation was abandoned and the consequences were very serious (emergency laws, the ban on the KKE and resistance organizations, prohibition of newspapers); on the other, guerilla warfare imposed a new set of priorities; political prisoners were no longer at the top.

A network of solidarity and support was reconstructed after the end of the Civil War. Since the ban was not lifted, KKE members had to work through broader organizations such as the PEOPEF, or political parties like the EDA. In the people's republics too, the party mechanism was utilized directly to support political prisoners. This mechanism linked political refugees in Poland, Hungary, Czechoslovakia, Romania, and the Soviet Union with their relatives in Greek prisons. Greek political refugees in these countries organized the collection of clothes, which were distributed to the political prisoners through the International Red Cross and also raised funds for them.[40] In many cases prisoners wrote to friends behind the Iron Curtain, asking for economic support for their families. These letters were forwarded to the local party committees, which were responsible for raising the necessary funds. The addresses and names underlined in these letters, and the notes on the envelopes of the person in charge as to whether the prisoner was given the money or not, may give an inkling of the way the whole network developed.

Notes

1. ASKI, box 421 F25/3/9, Letter of Airman Giannis Skartsatos, 27 December 1946. On the same incident, see also ASKI, box 421 F25/3/11, Letter of Konidis, 12 January 1947. The Agios Nikolaos camp was one of the camps established in 1946 for suspect soldiers. In 1947, all inmates were transferred to the Makronisos camps.
2. Flountzis, *Akronafplia*, 106-108; Manousakas, *To chroniko enos agona*, 177-180; Giannogonas, *Akronafplia*, 35-37
3. Kenna, "Making a World: Political Exiles in 1930s Greece," 33-40.
4. Papadouka, *Gynaikeies Fylakes Averof*, 16-21.
5. The official estimate in 1940 was that 10 percent of the men and 44 percent of women in Greece were illiterate. Greek Office for Information, *Greece: Basic Statistics* (London, 1949), 12.
6. Hebrard, "La lettre representée", 279-365.
7. Papadouka, *Gynaikeies Fylakes Averof*, 36-39; Stasa Kefalidou in Theodorou, ed., *Stratopeda Gynaikon*, 100-101; Panagiotis Aronis, "Mathimata sto Itzedin," in Vardinogiannis and Aronis, eds., *Oi misoi sta sidera*, 462-464. An idiosyncratic economy of writing was developed among the prisoners. Stamatia Babatsi, now an old lady in her seventies, sentenced by special court-martial to life imprisonment, and spent ten years in prison, where she learned how to read and write. After interviewing her, she insisted on writing the story of her life in prison for me. Her eight small pages of text are an example of the economy of close writing. The letters are very small, the words are hardly separated, and the writing covers the whole length and breadth of the page.
8. David Rolf, "The Education of British Prisoners of War in German Captivity, 1939-1945," *History of Education* 18, no. 3 (1989): 257-265; Maxine Schwartz Seller, "Filling the Space: Education, Community and Identity in British Internment Camps during World War II," *Pedagogica Historica* 32 (1996): 685-707; James Walston, "History and Memory of the Italian Concentration Camps," *The Historical Journal* 40, no. 1 (1997): 169-183; John L. Hammond, "Organization and Education among Salvadoran Political Prisoners", *Crime, Law and Social Change*, 25 (1996): 17-41; Tina Rosenberg, *Children of Cain: Violence and the Violent in Latin America* (New York, 1991), 195-199.
9. Ypourgeion Dikaisynis, *Egkyklioi kai apofaseis 1945-1953*, 82.
10. In order to avoid the confiscation of illegal books and the penalties possession of them incurred, the prisoners tried all sorts of tricks to deceive the guards. At the archives of Aegina prison, the book *Collected Works* of Lenin was covered with newspaper and a page from the Michael Scott book, *Shadow over America* was glued over the first page of the original. Some further related remarks on the books in general are that the books were all covered so that their titles would not be visible, the title page was torn from many of them so that they could not be identified, and the pages lack underlinings or comments, which suggests that they were books from the political prisoners' "library" rather than private ones.

11. *Rizospastis*, 8 August 1947.
12. *Rizospastis*, 23 September 1947.
13. FO 371/78369 R1617, British Police Mission on Mytilene to Chief of Mission, 22 January 1949
14. Sasa Tsakiri, "Stis fylakes Kastoros – "I arachni," in Vardinogiannis and Aronis, eds., *Oi misoi sta sidera*, 552-554.
15. *Adouloti Foni*, no 4, 16 November 1946, in ASKI, box 422 F25/4/216 (original emphasis).
16. *Adouloti Foni*, no 2, 2 November 1946, in ASKI, box 422 F25/4/214.
17. Andreas Nenedakis, *Apagorevetai* (Athens, 1964), 22.
18. NARA 868.00/11-2746, Political exiles in the Cyclades islands, 27 November 1946.
19. *Eleftheri Ellada*, 22 April 1947
20. Natalia Apostolopoulou, *Grothia sto skotadi. Apo tin politistiki zoi ton exoriston gynaikon* (Athens, 1984), 31; Benas, *Tou emfyliou*, 161
21. ASKI, box 421 F25/3/10, Letter of Giannis Flogeros from the Larisa camp, 10 January 1947 (my emphasis).
22. Vasilis Rotas, "Kleftika tragoudia," *Eleftera ammata* 39 (22 March 1946): 76-77.
23. Konstantopoulou in Theodorou, ed., *Stratopeda gynaikon*, 57.
24. *Rizospastis*, 28 March 1945.
25. "1821-1947," *Kommounistiki Epitheorisi* 3, (March 1947): 1-2.
26. Lecture of Giannis Zevgos on 25 March 1942 at the Akronafplia prison, published in, *Akronafplia – Dialexeis* (Athens, 1945), 54.
27. Papadouka, *Gynaikeies Fylakes Averof*, 23-65.
28. The word "nigger" (*arapis*) in Greek folktales, songs, and sayings was a metaphor for the dark and the dirty. In this particular song means also the hard-working person, the slave. In prison jargon, solitary confinement and the toilets were called *arapis*.
29. Papadouka, *Gynaikeies Fylakes Averof*, 85-90.
30. Vardinogiannis, *Makronisos*, 104.
31. The imaginary transfer, a sign of the internationalist solidarity among communists, was prompted by the news reaching the prisoners. See, for instance, the impact of the December events upon the prisoners in the Buchenwald concentration camp, in Jorge Semprun, *Quel beau dimanche!*, (Paris, 1980, Greek translation, Exantas, 1989), 37, 299-302.
32. Papadouka, *Gynaikeies Fylakes Averof*, 95-103. See also Skourtis (*Autoi pou dropiasan*, 99) who was in the same prison with Stathis Mamalis.
33. For the escape from the Vourla prison, see Theodoros Vasilopoulos, *Pos apodrasame apo ta Vourla* (Athens, 1983); Kyriakos Tsakiris, *Vourla. I megali apodrasi* (Athens, 1994).
34. Takis Benas recalls very vividly his reception at the Vourla prison in 1948: "I don't know who was the first who thought it, but with this ordinary gesture you were becoming human again. It was not something special, a dessert-spoon with a home-made sweet, grape, morello and the like, and a glass of cold water from the pitcher. (…) [I]t was something chosen to address your soul, that was brought you back to humanity, a treat that reminded you of your mother during the holidays. Almost fifty years have passed, and I recall with gratitude how sweet they made my first day of imprisonment." Benas, *Tou Emfyliou*, 85-86.
35. Ydraios, *Grammata apo ti fylaki*, 24-28.
36. ASKI, PEOPEF Archive, PEOPEF, *Dyo chronia agonon gia ti sotiria ton desmoton*, a brochure published in Athens in October 1952, and the report of the PEOPEF directory board in 1951. See also Ourania Papadopoulou, "Femmes et politique dans les années de répression en Grèce. Le cas de la PEOPEF (1948-1954)" (M.A. dissertation in social sciences, École des Hautes Études en Sciences Sociales - École Normale Superieure.) Maria Karra, who was on the directory board, gives important information in her book, *Emeis oi ap'exo*.

37. For the *Comité Francais d'aide à la Grèce démocratique*, which was founded in 1948 in Paris, see Nasi Balta, *O ellinikos emfylios polemos*, 181-184. For the League for Democracy in Greece, see Diana Pym and Marion Sarafis, "The League for Democracy in Greece and Its Archives", *Journal of the Hellenic Diaspora* 11, no. 2 (1984): 73-84. For the Swiss Committee for Aid to Democratic Greece, see NARA 868.00/4-1348, Bern to Department of State, 13 April 1948.
38. MGA/LDG, Info XI, Individual dossiers, Letter from Maria Mouratidou to Diana Pym, 26 January 1951.
39. Ethniki Allileggyi, *Sta xeronisia*, 60-63.
40. The ASKI Archives contain lists of names of political prisoners eligible for financial support from the Greek Communist Party mechanism in Romania (box 423 F25/5/111), Tashkent in the Soviet Union (box 423 F25/5/112), Bulgaria (box 423 F25/5/113), and Czechoslovakia (box 423 F25/5/114).

Chapter 10

Forms of Resistance

In September 1949, Captain W. E. Newton visited the Itzedin (or Kalami) prison on Crete to investigate alleged maltreatment of the prisoners. The political prisoners in this prison had gone on hunger strike three times between February and March 1949 to protest against executions. After having recovered from his initial shock at the lax discipline and absence of surveillance in the prison (for instance, there was but one unarmed guard for more than three hundred prisoners who were circulating freely in the exercise yard), he visited the dormitories, where 250 unrepentant political prisoners were accommodated. "I asked the prisoners," Captain Newton wrote, "if any of them would like to see me on any matter regarding the administration of the prison or any private matter. Their reply was a definite *no*"(original emphasis). A second attempt at discussion with the political prisoners proved equally unsuccessful. The officer, however, was not discouraged. At the Chania prison, he called a certain Kalaitzakis, who had been transferred from Itzedin prison, to the director's office. "I put," Captain Newton continued, "several questions to him regarding Kalamiou prison but he was quite *insolent* and *openly laughed at me*, and said that it was of no use asking questions as he did not intend replying. In the circumstances there was nothing I could do but send him back to his section."[1]

There are various forms of resistance between the extremes of refusal to cooperate with the authorities and open confrontation with them; just as there are different ways of acting them out, from laughter to hunger strikes. The various ways in which political prisoners transformed prison through the organization of their everyday life provided them with what James C. Scott called the infrapolitics, that is, the necessary conditions, for overt, public confrontation with the authorities.[2] It is unlikely that the occurrence of open resistance was solely dependent on these infrapolitics—if it were, it would be very difficult to explain why a hunger strike occurs in one prison and not in another. It was rather a question of correlation of power between prisoners

---

Notes for this section begin on page 196.

and the administration, and of the particularities of each prison. However, I do suggest that a prerequisite, for any form of resistance, was the articulation of these infrapolitics.

In this chapter I shall discuss the various forms of resistance to develop two arguments. The first, which is obvious, is that political prisoners' resistance cannot be understood unless it is placed in the context of the Civil War. For the political prisoners, protests in prisons demonstrated that they were part of the broader movement engaged in the Civil War, that prison was "a new arena for the same struggle."[3] But things were not always so simple in this "part and whole" relation. Protests in prison were not always possible, and most importantly, political prisoners were often reluctant to pay the high price of a protest. One may even be tempted to mention compliance of political prisoners. This is related to the second argument, which suggests that instead of applying the dichotomy of resistance-submission, one should explore the various subject-positions in relation to power, the "ambiguity of resistance and the subjective ambivalence of the acts" of the dominated.[4] Protests in prisons were not the rule but the exception, so when studying the microlevel of everyday life and of individual, then one faces acts that cannot simply be categorized as either resistance or compliance, acts that pose the problem of intentionality on the part of the subject and interpretation on the part of the historian.

I will start by examining the more implicit, spontaneous, and often individual forms of resistance. Then I shall turn to the discussion of more open, organized and collective actions that demonstrated the prisoners' disobedience. Finally, I will discuss what the political prisoners regarded as the highest and most important form of struggle inside prisons, the hunger strike. However, before discussing the forms of resistance, I would like to draw attention to the absence of the most characteristic act of prisoners' defiance, escapes. From this viewpoint, the escape of twenty-seven political prisoners from the Vourla prison on 17 July 1955 was unique. It is not a coincidence that it was organized without the permission of the Communist Party. The Communist Party did not allow prisoners to escape because it was considered to be an individualistic solution that did not take into account the consequences of such an act for the rest of the prisoners. The few organized escapes concerned only members of the higher echelons of the party.[5] Attempts of guerilla units to attack prisons and release political prisoners were very few. Such operations involved high risk because prisons were in the cities. The release of 220 prisoners from the Sparta prison on 13 February 1947, and of about forty prisoners from the Gytheion prison on 20 February 1948, should be regarded as exceptions rather than the rule. These two incidents had the additional objective of serving as a demonstration of force on the part of the guerillas in right-wing regions, and a way to recruit guerillas for the Democratic Army.[6] Political prisoners, with very few exceptions, obeyed the party line and did not attempt to escape even when they had the chance.

"Not struck by the enthusiasm of the audience"

The ordinary questions that a soldier on Makronisos should ask himself, according to the administration, were

> What have I done today? What good, that I didn't know, have I learned today? What have I heard from my colleagues? What have I said? Did I send a letter today, and what did I write? Did I write about what is going on this little island, in this port, where our souls are washed and are given back to society so white, like the white seagulls that accompany us? Did I show my new colleagues the real way, the Greek way? If the answer is yes, then I can sleep well. If no, then I have to think about what I shall have to do tomorrow. It's never too late.[7]

Many prisoners were not eager to follow the Greek way. They refused to sign declarations of repentance, or to send letters to their hometown mayor or priest renouncing communism or praising, as in the above quotation, the Makronisos camps. The detainees very well knew the consequences of a refusal: torture and hardship, a death sentence or even execution. If they signed, they could hope for better treatment, and perhaps their sentence could be commuted to life or ten years of imprisonment. They would not spend their term on death row. The question then, is why many people did not sign. What made them endure tortures or face the firing squad?

Many of them were devoted members of the KKE. They were ready to die rather than betray the principles of the party. Koula Eleftheriadou was one of these devoted party members. In her last letter before her execution, she wrote that "it is better to die honestly, for my ideals, which are the ideals of all workers, than to live dishonestly, betraying my party."[8] Communist prisoners, like Koula Eleftheriadou, who preferred to die rather than sign a declaration of repentance, consciously acted as the vanguard of the movement by setting the example and the standards for the others. The ideological conviction that the declaration of repentance was a betrayal of the party and that refusal to sign constituted an example for the rest of the inmates, gave them the moral strength to endure the ordeal of torture or face death. The communist ideology shaped their worldview and practices, their way of being.

However, not all the prisoners were members of the KKE. Thousands had been arrested, tortured, and condemned because they were related to guerillas, or only suspected of holding leftist views, or had participated in the resistance. Others were members of other parties, like Taxiarchis Psaromytas, a member of the socialist party SK-ELD who was sentenced to death unanimously because he was spreading "communist propaganda".[9] And even for the devoted party member, there was something besides party loyalty, what Koula Eleftheriadou in her letter called "dishonesty". Motives for refusal included not only ideological conviction but a sense of dignity in the preservation of the self, "the recognition of itself *as such*".[10] The declaration of repentance was, for members and non-members of the KKE alike, a public renunciation, a negation of the constituents of the self: of past, memory, identity, personal and societal ties. In the social construction of the self in Greece, the concept of honor was a constituent part of an individual's integrity. In this sense, the refusal did not spring only from a sense of duty, a loyalty to the cause, but also from the prisoners' resolution to be recognized as themselves and to preserve their integrity, the bonds between the self and the collective.[11]

What about the thousands of repentant prisoners, then, who were in fact the majority? If the authorities' aims were to construct a passive consensus to bolster the regime by means of coercion, and to dissolve political detainees' collectivity, the reality, even under the extreme conditions at the Makronisos camps, showed that both goals were always at stake, never guaranteed. This passivity could be deceptive, ambivalent, temporary, and in fact could amount to no consensus at all; the collectivity was shattered but nonetheless many detainees as individuals could find ways to reveal the bonds that held the political detainees together.

Though the ministers of War and Justice, the press, the king, and army officers praised the "National School," rhapsodizing that "on this barren island a Greece more beautiful than ever sprang up,"[12] the results were ambivalent. The general director of Makronisos camps could claim "wonderful results for the State and disastrous to the communists and their followers because out of these [soldiers] the State took back 80%-90% purified Greeks free from the nightmare and terrorism of the instructor",[13] but the reality was more complex. The production of declarations of repentance and national-minded soldiers was achieved by means of sheer coercion. When the coercion waned, a different picture came to light. In the elections of 5 March 1950, more than a third of the soldiers and civilians on Makronisos vote for the *Dimokratiki Parataxis*, the left-wing coalition. The deportees did not vote for the Populist Party, that was closest to the Makronisos reformative principles, but for the party that represented the Left in the elections and was the most vehement critic of the Makronisos camps.[14]

The flaws in the prisoners' reform were visible already before the elections. In January 1950, when Lieutenant Colonel D. I. Strangeways visited the Makronisos camps was present at one of the ordinary ceremonies of the camp. Unlike the Minister of War Georgios Stratos, who a few years earlier on Makronisos had been struck by the soldiers "who carried us in their arms for one thousand meters cheering for the nation,"[15] the British officer conveyed a somehow different picture:

> Before breakfast had been over ten minutes, the men and boys were assembled in front of their tents and squatting on their haunches commenced a "lesson." They were formed into company groups and there were some 7,500 on parade. The first item was the singing of the battalion song. This was led by a choir which was

broadcast over the loudspeakers, the internees joining in a somewhat half hearted and mechanical manner. There followed a series of talks which were interrupted by well disciplined clapping. I felt that the actual number of claps had been laid down as they commenced and finished with remarkable precision. I watched the men's faces and though there was complete silence during the item I was *not* struck by the enthusiasm of the audience.[16]

He "was *not* struck by the enthusiasm of the audience", consisting of reformed prisoners, because the halfhearted singing and disciplined clapping were a disguised disapproval of the ceremony. Their compliance with the rules of the show was undermined by their aloofness from the role they were charged to play. It was an ostensible compliance that revealed the ambiguity of the detainees' performance. The attitude of the audience blurred the boundaries between resistance and compliance.

Michalis Kyrkos had been elected a member of Parliament and held ministerial positions, during the interwar era, in governments formed by the Liberals. During the occupation he joined the EAM, and after the liberation, together with Alkiviadis Loulis, formed the Democratic Radical Party, which participated in the Political Coalition of the EAM Parties and was the director of its daily, the *Eleftheri Ellada* (Free Greece). He and Alkiviadis Loulis were tried for "high treason" by the special court-martial of Athens in 1949, but the trial was adjourned indefinitely. Notwithstanding, in June 1949, the two friends found themselves on Makronisos. In his memoirs, Kyrkos recollected that when he was being held in solitary confinement inside a tent, he had some visitors. Although it was strictly forbidden for anyone to talk to him, at night soldiers came to talk to him and bring him food. The soldiers concealed these acts from each other so that if they were arrested, they would not inform against their colleagues; they knew that they were violating the rules by visiting him and would be severely punished if arrested. Michalis Kyrkos commented that "These young men were subjected to horrible corporal and moral torments. They couldn't bear them and signed. Still, they lost neither their humanness, their dignity, nor their psychic politeness."[17]

Many former detainees on Makronisos recall events that typify the constant interchange between reformed soldiers' conformity to and undermining of the administration's dictates. Such was the case, for instance, of a group of detainees in the Makronisos Military Prison who underwent the torture of standing naked on a cold winter night while military policemen emptied pails of cold water on their backs. As soon as the military policemen and their chief left the soldiers to continue the torture, they emptied the pails on the ground as the detainees were "cried out."[18] The imitation of the duty replaced the duty itself, revealing a double reality: one onstage, and the other offstage. The offstage reality was the only one that permitted the two sides (repentant and unrepentant) to approach each other and to trace the bonds that united them.

Let us return to the British officer who visited the Itzedin prison in late September 1949. He reported that the political prisoners were circulating freely in the yard, others lay on their beds talking, others read a newspaper, and "in the barber's shop I found a prisoner shaving himself entirely without supervision". [19] As insignificant as a shave might seem, his comment reveals the ambiguity of the act, contested by different intentions and interpretations. The British officer would probably have thought that a razor in a prisoner's hands was a weapon. Moreover, he was alone in the barbershop. Recording that incident among other violations of prison regulations, he categorized it as a breach of discipline. But for that political prisoner, the razor was not a weapon: he used it to enjoy a morning shave. The intention and the motive of the prisoner were not to demonstrate his disobedience, not to break the rules. Due to the lax discipline this prisoner could at last have the joy of a morning shave precisely because he was alone, could enjoy a few minutes of privacy, a rare privilege in jail, and take care of himself entirely without supervision. Taking care of himself and enjoying a few moments of privacy (in a prison where 250 prisoners were accommodated in five dormitories) may be construed not as an act of resistance but a moment of transgressing the prison world and getting closer to the everyday life outside the prison walls. From a domain of deprivation or ill treatment of his needs, prison for a moment was transformed into a place where he could fulfill them.

Protests in Prisons

How long did it take to transport political prisoners from the Chatzikosta prison to the Averof prison? Usually not more than half an hour. On 30 July 1945, however, it took considerably longer. The situation began when the political prisoners at the Chatzikosta prison decided to make the windows in their dormitories larger, and for that reason started to remove bricks from the windows. The director and the chief of the guards were alarmed and tried to dissuade them, but their efforts were futile. The situation deteriorated, and at some point the guards started shooting. Three prisoners were wounded, and after protests the prisoners returned to their dormitories. The following day, the Ministry of Justice, considering that there was an "inclination towards revolt," decided to transfer 189 prisoners to the Averof prison, among them those who were considered the "instigators." The necessary numbers of policemen were dispatched to the prison. The prisoners, however, were very suspicious and reluctant after the incidents of the previous day. They formed a committee and met with the deputy district attorney, asking for clarification of the purpose and the destination of the transfer. Only when they were assured that their fellow inmates would be transported to the Averof prison did they consent to it. Even then, many prisoners were not very willing to cooperate with the authorities. As the minister of Justice Soliotis stated, "The transfer was carried out with great difficulties due to the prisoners' strong opposition. (…) The transfer, which with the means at our disposition would have been accomplished within half an hour, required nine hours, i.e. from 7 P.M. to 4 A.M., and engaged the force of seventy policemen, fifty gendarmes and the whole of the external guard altogether".[20]

Protests were very frequent, particularly in the early postwar years. Living conditions (quality of meals, hygiene conditions, behavior of guards, restrictions on visits, and so on) were the major issue on the political prisoners' agenda, as well as a replacement of autocratic directors, the introduction of stricter rules, and unannounced transfers. Save hunger strikes, very few of the prisoners' protests reached the pages of newspapers, instead remaining confined within prisons' walls. Nevertheless, political detainees' aim was to break their isolation and segregation from the free community. In an attempt to examine the forms of protest, I shall relate them to the addressee to show that the diverse addressees required diverse contents and forms of protest. Letters of accusation to authorities and organizations, protests aiming to communicate to civilians what was happening inside prisons, and the semiotic struggle at the microlevel of everyday life inside prisons will be discussed respectively.

Thousands of letters were sent to international organizations, foreign governments, ministers, the prime minister, the Church, and other empowered agents. The majority was letters of accusation and memoranda that stressed the wretched conditions in prisons and exile, the unjust and politically motivated detention of prisoners and exiles, and the profile of detainees presented through individual cases. They had a collective character. They were signed either anonymously, as political prisoners, or by a number of prisoners who gave their names, which gave a sense of representation and, perhaps, responsibility for the initiative.

The purpose of such appeals was to exert pressure on the government or organizations at a high level, not through social solidarity but through international interest and political pressure. The writers sought to inform those who had power and could have an influence on the interests of the detainees. These letters and memoranda attributed to the addressees the "neutral" status of the ignorant. Political prisoners informed them about their past in the resistance, their unjust prosecution after the liberation, and the ordeal of imprisonment and exile. They asked these agents to intervene not on grounds of political sympathy but of universal human values. The political exiles on Agios Efstratios, for instance, argued for their immediate release because "[i]t is imperative from a legal, moral and international point of view and for the honor of humanity."[21] The single most important aspect of the memoranda and appeals was that through them, prisoners sought to establish themselves as political prisoners. In one appeal to the United Nations and its Security Council requesting general amnesty without conditions and for all political crimes the senders started by identifying themselves as "Political prisoners at the Akronafplia prison, most of us fighters in Albania [the Greek-Italian war in 1940] and all of us members of the National Resistance."[22] Since the government did not recognize the existence of political prisoners in the Civil War, political prisoners sought to establish this category. They differentiated themselves from common prisoners (their past in the resistance), made explicit references to the emergency laws that had driven them into prisons, and asked for the enforcement of measures that applied to political prisoners only (amnesty, for instance).

If the written appeals presuppose some rules, the same can be said of the verbal ones. Both presuppose a form of prisoners' organization, are addressed to a receiver, rely on a text, meet a need, and represent a form of reaction and resistance. In the case of written appeals, the author is the "bureau" of the group; the message is addressed to official institutions; the text follows the rules of literacy and the canon of sophisticated wording; the need is to inform in order to press the higher echelons of the government. Verbal protests, however, followed different rules.

From 1947 to 1949, when executions became frequent, transfers of political prisoners at night signaled that another group of prisoners was being taken for executions. At that moment, when the prisoners saw their comrades, fellow inmates, or friends leaving the prison, the only thing they could do to protest executions was to cry out at the sleeping city. In the Averof prison after the evening roll call on 11 September 1951, eight political prisoners were called to present themselves at the secretary's office. Though executions had stopped, the eight prisoners were alarmed. They met with the "bureau" of the group and together decided not to present themselves at the secretary's office, but instead to delay the return of the prisoners to their dormitories. The eight prisoners would change dormitories in order to impede their being tracked down, while the other prisoners would demand the presence of the director for a discussion of the issue and call out from the windows of their dormitories to inform passers-by what was happening behind the walls. One of the eight prisoners recalls the words they cried out:

> People of Athens, democrats, patriots! Two days after your verdict in the elections, the forces of instability and schism are preparing a new crime. They are taking eight fighters for execution. Mobilize to stop the crime that the American imperialists and the native forces of instability are organizing. Block the way to a new massacre! Save the fighters! Save the normality of the country! No more blood![23]

After a while, the women prisoners from the adjoining building followed, calling on the people to mobilize. "Tonight, tonight!" they cried, "Tomorrow will be too late." People started to gather around the prisons, journalists came, deputies called ministers to verify the rumors about imminent executions. Six hours later, the director of the Averof prison Stylianos Voutsinos came to the prison to announce that the executions had in fact been planned, but after the uproar had been suspended. Voutsinos himself had been dismissed.

Focusing on these verbal appeals, we can see the difference in comparison with written appeals. They were organized, but their success was heavily dependent on the actual and wholehearted participation of the prisoners; the recipients were the passers-by, the citizens; the texts were direct and explicit, and were directed at the sentiment and memory of the people, in an attempt to gain their support; the need was not only to inform but also, and more importantly, to mobilize. This form of protest can be construed as an attempt to directly undercut the basic precondition of prison, that is, the segregation of the outside from the inside of the prison.

The need to overcome the reality of segregation lies behind this form of protest. From this viewpoint, the incident in the Averof prison in 1951 was an exception. The facts that this prison was in the capital of the country, which was also the center of political life, and that it was September 1951, two years after the end of the Civil War and two days after the elections that opened the road to a less conservative government, made the exception possible. It was the sole occasion on which prisoners' protests succeeded in mobilizing the people and suspending executions. Yet, it was the only way for the prisoners to overcome a strong feeling of powerlessness, to find a way to express their wrath and sorrow. The cries read off of twists of paper were addressed to the citizens, to make them participate in the event, were addressed to those transported for execution as an ultimate greeting and sign of solidarity, and, finally, were addressed to the criers themselves. Their voice could at last be heard beyond the prison walls.

Needless to say, the authorities regarded these protests as a breach of discipline. Stylianos Voutsinos, before his appointment as director of the Averof prison, had been director of the Aegina prison. For him any farewell that the inmates addressed to someone before he was taken for execution was a breach of discipline. On 10 August 1949, when one prisoner on Aegina was being taken away for execution, the other prisoners from his wing shouted collectively "Farewell!" in unison two or three times. "As a result of this demonstration the above mentioned privileges [food parcels, letters and visits] for these prisoners were immediately withdrawn, and the prisoners were informed that the restrictions would be for a period of forty-five days. However on the 22nd August the prisoners apologized for their misbehavior, and as a result of this the Director immediately restored all the privileges."[24] We do not know whether they in fact "apologized for their misbehaviour," but one month later the same prisoners, for the same reason, committed the same breach of discipline and were punished again in the same way.

Anything that could be perceived as sign of solidarity and collective identity had to be banned. The little black handkerchiefs that the women prisoners at the Themistocleous Street prison (Athens) hung in their dormitories in commemoration of the two hundred patriots executed by the Germans in Kaisariani in May 1944, were torn up by the guards.[25] At the microlevel of everyday life any act by the detainees that transformed the prison was perceived as a potential threat. Political prisoners staged numerous protests concerning the decoration of dormitories: they were forced to remove posters of heroes of the resistance, and flags or insignia of the Allied countries.[26] We can assume the political orientation of these decorations, but it is something else that is important: one elementary form of resistance was the gradual appropriation of the prison by the political detainees. In the case of the posters, the prisoners revived their glorious common past, confirmed their political identity, and transformed that place into *their* place. The administration's measures, too, were signs in that semiotic struggle. One night in September 1946 at the Aegina prison the political prisoners of a wing were singing songs of the resistance. A guard heard them and demanded that they stop, but they refused to comply. The director punished the nineteen prisoners with deprivation of visits for fifteen days. The director' decision was, however, unusually delayed, coming into effect two weeks after the incident had happened. The punishment was imposed four days before the 27th of September, the anniversary founding of the EAM. The purpose of the delaying the punishment was to dissuade political prisoners from commemorating the EAM and, at a semiotic level, to demonstrate who was in power in prison and in Greece as well.[27]

Like the black handkerchiefs at Themistocleous Street prison, the black flags in the Akronafplia prison,[28] and the "revolutionary and menacing battle-songs" in the Kyparissia prison,[29] were signs of political prisoners' identity. These signs demonstrated that prison, like society, was in a state of conflict, but also that the limits of freedom in prison and in society alike were ambivalent, wavering. Prisoners in their verbal appeals used twists of paper, but the police had prohibited citizens to use them because they could disturb the public order.[30] The prisoners in Kyparissia sang "battle-songs," something that would have been impossible for anyone else to sing in the streets of this provincial town without the risk of finding themselves immediately arrested by the local gendarmerie. This situation was described by a political prisoner as a paradox in the following sense: "We, the interned, felt ourselves to be free and on the contrary for us, it was the free citizens who were interned."[31]

On 29 December 1949, the day of commemoration for the "children's abduction" by the guerillas, the administration of the Corfu prison ordered the political prisoners to stand at attention while a special radio program was broadcast over the loudspeakers. The prisoners decided to disobey by continuing to walk in the yard during the broadcast. The guards attacked them and several were severely beaten.[32] What made the prisoners disobey? One aspect of the explanation is the already discussed semiotic struggle inside prisons. The day of "national mourning" became a field of conflict between two different interpretations of the issue of the "children's abduction." However, I think that the other aspect is the value of conflict *per se*. Memoranda and letters to the press could help only in the long run. Protests, on the other hand, gave political prisoners the opportunity to overcome their powerlessness, for even for a day or just one-hour, and to directly challenge the administration. Such protests were motivated by the desperate need to do something about their life in jail, to reveal their power to the administration. In the routine of prison life, protests transformed underground political activities into direct action. Open political action was precisely what the imprisoned leftists missed in prisons. The importance of open political action is denoted in the words of a former political prisoner recalling a protest: "I don't remember what we were demanding, I remember what we were doing."[33]

Hunger Strikes

Hunger strikes represent one of the most frequent forms of protest by political prisoners during this era. Nevertheless, they were not all the same. From 1945 until 1948, hunger strikes lasted a few days, and the demands concerned living conditions in prisons. Political detainees went on hunger strike at the *Kapnergostasio* (Tobacco Industry) prison demanding visits, mess hall, newspapers, and unrestricted circulation in the yard; at the 9th police station of Thiseio in Athens to protest against the conditions of detention; in the Volos prison demanding their transfer to other prisons because theirs was flooded; in the Military Prisons of Air Force because the detainees were forbidden to circulate in the yard and in the corridors, and so on.[34]

From 1948 until the end of the Civil War, however, the character of hunger strikes changed. The hunger strikes were fewer but lasted longer; the demand was to stop executions, and the strikes actually were directly related to executions in the double sense of place and time. Political prisoners went on hunger strikes in prisons from which political prisoners were transferred for execution, and the strikes often commenced when such transfers were taking place.

The leadership of the political prisoners, the "bureau," decided whether there was going to be a hunger strike and then the prisoners discussed the issue dormitory by dormitory. The majority usually voted for the proposals of the leadership and those who disagreed had to comply with the majority (the principle of democratic centralism). The high percentage of prisoner participation sustains this view, as in the case of the Aegina prisons where 530 of 660 political prisoners went on hunger strike in 1948.[35] A strike committee was appointed, with representatives from each dormitory or wing that was not on strike, to help the strikers, coordinate the strike and maintain contact with the administration. Two examples from hunger strikes in the spring of

1949 will help me to discuss this form of protest in further detail. The first is based on the account of Pericles Rodakis, held at the Cephalonia prison at that time.

Cephalonia, an island in the Ionian Sea near the Peloponnese, was the site of one prison where several hunger strikes occurred. More than one hundred prisoners were transported from the local prison and executed on this island within a span of about one and a half years.[36] In March 1949 the "bureau" was informed that the leading cadres of the Communist Party interned at the Averof prison had reached a decision: prisoners on death row in the major prisons were to go on a hunger strike. The demand was the cessation of executions. For the hunger strikers, it was also a symbolic gesture of solidarity with the Democratic Army, which was fighting hard battles on the Peloponnese. Later they discovered that the hunger strikes were not well coordinated and that the Democratic Army had been defeated on the Peloponnese before the hunger strike had even begun.

The execution of Stelios Balas on 28 May 1949 was the occasion for the beginning of the hunger strike. The strike committee had already been formed and on the night of Stelios Balas' execution, the prisoners refused tea and stated to the guards that as of that moment they were on hunger strike. The political prisoners removed from their cells any food they had (save lemons). One appointed prisoner from every wing did not go on strike in order to help his fellow inmates. The administration (the director of the prison at that time was Ioannis Vizirtzis) decided to adopt a hard line. Four more political prisoners were taken for execution and the cadres held responsible for the strike were moved to the solitary confinement wing. The worst was yet to come. After a week of the hunger strike, the director moved one step further: the prisoners had to face the torture of forced feeding. Five or six guards held the prisoner while a doctor passed a rubber tube into the prisoner's nose to feed him with milk. The sight of the forced feeding (the rubber, the struggle with the guards, the blood from the prisoners' noses) terrified the prisoners and led many to stop the hunger strike. Unfortunately, the forced feeding caused not only horror, but death as well. As the prisoner was not breathing normally and the rubber tube reached the point where pharynx and larynx met, there was the danger that a few drops of liquid might pass into the lungs and cause a very dangerous pneumonia. Many prisoners fell sick in the following days with a high fever, and five of them died. Faced with this situation the director decided not to stop the forced feeding but to change the method. Instead of feeding via rubber tube, the guards should forced the prisoner to open his mouth, placed a piece of wood in it to keep it open, and then emptied a glass of milk into his mouth. On the fourteenth day, the prisoners exhausted, sick, and frightened, decided to stop the hunger strike. The next day another prisoner, Takis Feidaris, was taken for execution.[37]

In the framework of the coordinated hunger strikes in the spring of 1949, another one broke out and was recorded in the prison administration files. On 11 May 1949, a hunger strike began at Aegina prison and lasted for fifteen days. At that time the prison held 799 prisoners, of whom 603 were on death row. The hunger strikers were the prison's 439 unrepentant political prisoners, who were concentrated in the three of the five wings of the prison. In an attempt to confuse and disorganize the strikers, the administration transported twenty strikers to other prisons, and thirty-one political prisoners, all but two of whom were *dilosies*. Though a number of political prisoners were fed forcibly, the doctor of the prison reported nothing except that he had visited the three wings on strike. As the hunger strike reached its climax, the number of guards was increased. To the sixty-four permanent personnel, another thirteen guards were added on 24 May, and four more the following day. This was not a good sign, because the hunger strike was about to stop. The reason for the increase of guards was perhaps that on 25 May 1949 the same day that the hunger strike stopped, six prisoners were transported for execution, and on the following day four more. The ten executed men were sentenced to death for crimes committed in the period between the occupation and the *Dekemvriana*, and had already been in prison for some years.[38]

All these hunger strikes were directly related to the execution of political prisoners, explains the fact that strikes were localized in certain prisons, like the Corfu, Aegina, Cephalonia, Itzedin, Averof, and Akronafplia prisons. They started after one or more prisoners were taken for execution, and the strikers' major demand was the cessation of executions, which to be confirmed by the Attorney General and the Inspector of Prisons from the Ministry of Justice. Since there was no such official undertaking and executions were not stopped, hunger strikes were repeated. At the Corfu prison, for instance, political prisoners went on hunger strikes for eight days in July 1948, for nine days in November 1948, and again for fifteen days in February-March 1949.

Yet there remains the question of whether these hunger strikes were successful. Sadly, hunger strikes as a means to exert pressure on the prison administration on the issue of executions had little success. The administration did not allow the prisoners to meet the Attorney General and often adopted a hard line, mandating forced feeding, the transfer of cadres to solitary confinement or other prisons, the suspension of prisoners' rights (letters, parcels, visits), and the refusal to transport weak prisoners to hospital. All these measures made this form of protest even more difficult. Moreover, the executions following hunger strikes showed that the authorities had no intention of yielding to the prisoners' demands.

The wave of hunger strikes in the spring of 1949 showed that there was some loose coordination among several prisons. When the prisoners on Cephalonia started to discuss the possibility of a hunger strike, protesters in the Corfu prison had already ended a hunger strike that lasted fifteen days (from 23 February to 9 March 1949). The prisoners at the Aegina prisons went on strike two weeks before those at the Cephalonia prison; the prisoners at the Itzedin prison went on hunger strike from 15 April to 22 April 1949. The prisoners at the Akronafplia and Averof prisons also went on strike in the spring of 1949. If there was a degree of coordination among these major prisons, which implies a communication and information network, the same cannot be argued about the rest of the prisons. News of the hunger strikes reached other prisons several weeks after they had ended.[39] Hunger strikes as a form of protest remained rather localized and confined to very few prisons, and did not become a common cause of all the political prisoners.

Hunger strikes were one of the few ways that the strikers' main demand, the cessation of executions, would get some sort of publicity. It may be argued that while hunger strikes did not stop executions, they did contribute to the pressure exerted on the government. But because visits and correspondence were not allowed during hunger strikes, the news was unlikely reach relatives or journalists. Moreover, the left-wing newspapers were banned, and since the progress of the Civil War was the big issue, no room was left in the mainstream media for strikes in prisons.

In sum, the price of hunger strikes was disproportionately high and their impact on prisoners' health and morale should not go unnoticed. Given the poor health of the prisoners, hunger strikes represented a real ordeal, especially for those who went on strike for more than once. Three political prisoners were admitted to hospital during the aforementioned hunger strike at the Aegina prison, but the days following the end of the strike saw admission of a further nineteen. For all of them, the diagnosis recorded was "hunger strike."[40] And after two weeks of virtual starvation how could all these people be dissuaded from eating and persuaded instead to drink only milk in order not to damage their stomachs? In the end, the fatal blow to prisoners' morale was not their corporal exhaustion but seeing their fellow inmates and strikers dragged away by the guards for execution. They must have realized, at very same moment they stopped a hunger strike, that they had failed not only to stop the executions in general but even to save their fellow inmates from the firing squad.

The problems for the prisoners started when the strike was prolonged and the administration adopted a hard line. In this case, the unity of the prisoners was at stake, since a number of prisoners would stop the strike out of sickness, exhaustion, or terrorization. Their fellow inmates would label them as "broken" and the strike would continue, or, as in the strike on Cephalonia, their stance would be perceived as a sign that the strike should stop. It was a very difficult decision for an individual to stop the strike. It was a breach of the party discipline, and discipline was one of the praised virtues of the party ideology. This spirit of discipline and of self-sacrifice is reflected in a passage from a text that was distributed among political prisoners at the Aegina prison concerning a hunger strike at the Averof prison:

The discipline and trust of the strikers in the strike committee, their coherence and endurance, was the most important lesson for the morale and the power of the group, and showed that in the future they could endure any hard struggle, any self-sacrifice whatsoever. (…) When on the seventh day the strikers were asked whether they would continue or stop the strike, all the Averof fighters stubbornly hung onto their beds and stated their irreversible decision not to get up from their beds unless their main demand was satisfied unconditionally.[41]

For the party leadership at the Aegina prison, the hunger strike at the Averof prison served as an example to demonstrate the preconditions of a successful struggle. Discipline and unity, or to be more accurate, unity through discipline, were the necessary conditions. Who would dare to be stigmatized as "antiparty" and undergo the consequences?

Notes

1. FO 371/78497 R9888, Report on Kalamiou Prison visited by Captain W. E. Newton PSO II on 27/9/49, 3 October 1949 (my emphasis).
2. James C. Scott, *Domination and the Arts of Resistance. Hidden Transcripts* (New Haven and London, 1990), 183-201.
3. Hammond, "Education among Salvadoran Political Prisoners," 21.
4. Sherry B. Ortner, "Resistance and the Problem of Ethnographic Refusal", *Comparative Studies in Society and History* 37 (1995): 173-193.
5. One such instance was the escape of Dimitris Partsalidis and Dimitris Paparigas from the island of Ikaria on 24 December 1947, when the guerillas were forming their Provisional Government.
6. Margaritis, *Istoria tou ellinikou Emfyliou Polemou*, vol. 1, 535-537, 567.
7. *Scapaneus* 9 (1 September 1948): 23
8. FO 371/67019 R7957, Report of Mr. Francis Noel-Baker M.P., 6 June 1947; ASKI EDA Archives, National Resistance Archives, Letter of Koula Eleftheriadou from the Eptapyrgio prison, 5 May 1947.
9. FO 371/87683 RG10134/6, Athens to FO, 6 October 1950.
10. Terrence des Pres, *The Survivor: An Anatomy of Life in the Death Camps* (New York, 1976,) 66.
11. The moral grounds for not signing a declaration of repentance as a matter of dignity versus shame are also found in other, similar cases. The poem "Recantation," was written in 1963 by the Iraqui opposition poet Muzaffar al-Nuwwab, concerned those who renounced their political beliefs. In this poem, a sister says to her brother, a political prisoner who recanted his political beliefs: "How can I face, with this recantation, every sister, who awaits / from you, brother, revenge for her injured honor! / How can I face, with this recantation, the mothers and share / my cares with them." And the final line is: "Oh People! The one you see is not your son." Cited in, Harlow, *Barred*, 75.
12. Speech of Minister of War Panagiotis Kannelopoulos to the soldiers on Makronisos on 23 March 1949, *Skapaneus* 16 (1 April 1949): 17.

13. FO 371/87647 RG1016/18, Athens to FO, General Director's report on Makronisos Reformative Organisation, 24 January 1950.
14. Elias Nikolakopoulos, "Ekloges sti Makroniso," Proceedings of the conference *Istoriko Topio kai Istoriki Mnimi*, 329-336. Out of the 10,036 soldiers and civilians who voted, the *Dimokratiki Parataxis* polled 35.3 percent; the EPEK, a new centrist liberal party, 24.7 percent, the Liberal Party 17.5 percent; and the Populist Party, just 9.5 percent. It should be added that the soldiers at the Makronisos camps could vote, because regular conscripts retained their voting rights while in military service. The deportees were eligible to vote because their penalty was "administrative," which means that, from a legal viewpoint, they were not deprived of their freedom and their political rights were not suspended.
15. *Acropolis*, 1 October 1947.
16. FO 371/87647 RG1016/6, BMM to Greece, Report on Makronisos, 20 January 1950 (original emphasis). See also chapter 5 for some other remarks Strangeways made on the Makronisos camps.
17. Michalis Kyrkos, *Piso apo ta kagkela* (1961, reprinted Athens, 1995),147-149.
18. Vardinogiannis, *Makronisos*, 57-62.
19. FO 371/78497 R9888, Report on Kalamiou Prison visited by Captain W. E. Newton PSO II on 27/9/49, 3 October 1949.
20. *Acropolis*, 29 July 1945 and 31 July 1945; *Rizospastis*, 31 July 1945
21. Memorandum of political exiles on Ai Strati, 17 September 1950, in *Ta thymata tou monarchofasismou*, 69.
22. Appeal of the political prisoners at the Akronafplia prison to the United Nations, 23 September 1950, in *Ta thymata tou monarchofasismou*, 31.
23. Vasilis Papagiannopoulos, "Pos mataiothike i ektelesi mas," in Vardinogiannis and Aronis, eds., *Oi misoi sta sidera*, 347. In the elections that had taken place two days before the leftist EDA had won 10.6 percent, and the right-wing (*Ellinikos Synagermos*) 36.5 percent. The formation of a more moderate government by the centrist parties (the two major centrist parties together had polled 42.5 percent) was possible (the executions were meant to torpedo that prospect. The concept of "schism" is also remarkable. As we have seen in chapter 2, in Greek history, the term "National Schism" was coined to describe the rupture between the Liberal party of Eleftherios Venizelos and King Constantine. By referring to "schism," the prisoners tried to establish an analogy with that troubled period and draw support from any non-royalist citizen.
24. FO 371/78497 R9888, Report on Aegina prison, visited by Captain W.E. Newton on 24 September 1949, 3 October 1949.
25. *Rizospastis*, 4 May 1945.
26. *Rizospastis* 4 April 1946 (Chatzikosta prison); *Rizospastis* 11 April 1946 (Akronafplia prison); MGA/LDG, Info IV, *National Solidarity Bulletin of press*, 5 November 1946 (Averof prison).
27. Aegina Prison Archives, Director's disiplinary decrees, 1277, Decree no. 40, 23 September 1946.
28. *Rizospastis,* 23 November 1945.
29. *Acropolis,* 4 November 1945.
30. Georgios Papastratos, *Apasai ai astynomikai diataxeis kai apofaseis tis dieythinseos Astynomias Athinon* (Athens, 1948), 324.
31. Kyrkos, *Piso apo ta kagkela*, 53.
32. Memorandum of the families of the detainees at the Corfu prison, 19 March 1950, in *Ta thymata tou monarchofasismou*, 28-30. Interview with Dimitris Mouratidis on 27 February 1998.
33. Interview with Stamatia Barbatsi on 20 February 1997.
34. *Rizospastis,* 14 March 1945, 20 June 1945, 15 September 1945, and 20 March 1946.

35. FO 371/72355 R 13921, Prisons Dept. of BPPM to Chief of Mission, Enclosure to a report on hunger strike at Aegina prisons, 30 November 1948.
36. 104 political detainees were executed between January 1948 and September 1949. Almost every week or two weeks, one or two prisoners were executed; sometimes even a group like on 9 February 1948 and 3 March 1948 when eleven and twelve prisoners were executed respectively. ASKI, EDA Archive, National Resistance Archive ("Phoenix")
37. Pericles Rodakis, "I apergia peinas – Anagkastiki sitisi," in Vardinogiannis and Aronis, eds., *Oi misoi sta sidera,* 313-334.
38. Aegina Prison Archives, Prison logbook, no. 746; Record of incoming and outgoing prisoners, no. 566; Prison record of number of prisoners, no. 530; Record of sick prisoners, no 1483. For the executed political prisoners, see, Individual files, f. 51, Koutsougeras Michail, no. 3518/317, Koulakiotis Ioannis, no. 3519/402, Koulakiotis Andreas (Ioannis' brother), no. 3520/362, Pantazis or Pantazopoulos Spyridon, no. 3521/405, Pantazis or Pantazopoulos Ioannis (Spyridon's brother), no. 3522/406, Andritsos Athanasios, no. 3523/665, Michalopoulos Georgios, no. 3524/352, Tserkezis Panagiotis, no. 3525/661, Liaskos Stamatis, no. 3526/662, Georgakopoulos Christos, no. 3527/953.
39. When Takis Benas arrived at the Aegina prison on 19 May 1949 and found the prisoners on their ninth day of a hunger strike, he did not know anything about the strike, despite having been transferred from the Vourla prison, a transit prison in Piraeus, not far from the island of Aegina. Interview with Takis Benas on 10 March 1998.
40. Aegina Prison Archives, Hospital Record, no. 1582.
41. Notice of the Cohabitation Group of People's Fighters at the Aegina prison on 25 May 1948, in *Matomeni Vivlos* (n.p., 1949), 73-78.

Chapter 11

The Politics of Counterpower

After the visit of the minister of Justice Vasileios Kyriacopoulos and Colonel Chris Woodhouse to the Averof prison on 27 September 1945, the British ambassador, Reginald Leeper, cabled a telegram to London reporting:

> The entire internal organisation of prisoners is in the hands of a small Communist committee. The gaolors seem glad to be relieved of responsibility. The Communist committee runs a newspaper, a theatre, a workshop for producing E.A.M. posters and portraits of Stalin, a discussion group and a mutual benefit insurance society. (…) When M. Kyriacopoulos began to address them silence was imposed not by the gaolors but by [the] Communist committee. They punctuated his speech with ironic cheers, catcalls, slogans of songs, which were taken up with well trained spontaneity by the entire crowd of prisoners under guidance of [an] expert cheer leader. Committee replied with several violent speeches, which were wildly cheered. It was difficult to guess who was supposed to be reforming whom.[1]

Though he gives a very vivid and perhaps exaggerated picture of the Averof prison, it must be noticed that the situation in prisons, from the point of view of political prisoners' organization, changed dramatically after 1947, when severe restrictions were imposed on the prisoners. However, the point that he makes is interesting. The ambassador argues for the decongestion of prisons because "that prison has become a Communist training school sponsored by the Government" and the prisoners "were arrested for being Communists which they were not but soon will be," an argument taken up by other scholars of the era as well.[2] In other words, the question is: what was the role of the Communist Party mechanism in the shaping of political prisoners as a subject?

The majority of political prisoners during the period under examination were involved in politics for the first time in their lives during the resistance and through its mass organizations. It is important to remember that the

---

Notes for this section begin on page 219.

KKE had between ten and fifteen thousand members in 1936 and was actually dissolved during the Metaxas dictatorship. The occupation dramatically changed the political landscape. It is difficult to assess the membership of the leftist resistance organizations, although leading cadres of the EAM claimed that toward the end of the occupation, at a time when the country had about seven million inhabitants, between one and one and a half million people supported, as members or sympathizers, the EAM organizations.[3] While it is certain that a very large part of the population was involved in leftist politics during the occupation and, one can argue, had active role in politics and entered the political arena for the first time in the history of modern Greece, the question of the political views of these people is less clear. The same holds true for the resistance. Though the role of the KKE in the formation and leadership of EAM organizations was undoubtedly prevalent, their political profile and program was vague. National independence and democratic social reform, as it was phrased in the vague slogan of *laokratia* (people's rule), were the major issues.[4]

The power of the EAM, however, waned after the liberation. The continuation of the civil strife after the German evacuation and the *Dekemvriana*, with the excesses of "revolutionary violence" in Athens and the provinces, distanced many people. Moreover, the "white terror" made clear that the tables had turned and that participation in the resistance was not a good credential in postliberation Greece. The Communist Party of Greece in December 1944 had 420,000 members, but by September 1946 its membership waned down to 295,000.[5] In 1947, U.S. sources estimated that the party had 200,000 members.[6] In the process of polarization, which reached its climax with the Civil War, the dividing lines became better defined. The people who had participated in the resistance had to be either "communists" or "national-minded".

Prisons are the places where opposition and resistance movements are schooled.[7] From this viewpoint, political prisoners' organization can be regarded as a process of transforming prisoners into communists. It is a process of homogenizing multiplicity, imposing and legitimizing a hierarchy, and excluding the difference. At the beginning of this chapter, the organization of everyday life will be analyzed as a sociocultural process that attempts to homogenize diverse social and cultural backgrounds and incorporate them into the dominant party culture. Next, the consolidation of the party authority in prisons as the organizing nucleus of prisoners' activities, which imposes a certain type of hierarchy and supervises the individual prisoners, will be examined. Finally, the process of punishing and excluding those who do not conform to the party legitimacy and authority, namely the dissidents, will be discussed.

Political prisoners are both a single and a multiple subject. They share certain characteristics that give them the sense of belonging to a collectivity and having a common identity, but meanwhile, the subject and its identity are in the making. From many perspectives, political prisoners in the Greek Civil

War were a new subject, one that lacked the historical depth that would enhance it with coherence. The fact that thousands of political prisoners, especially on Makronisos, denounced the Communist Party revealed that it was not a solidly made subject and that the influence of the Communist Party among them had limits. Very few of them had been in prison during the Metaxas years. The common political background held by most of them was the three years of struggle against the occupation. The political socialization produced by the resistance became increasingly outdated in the Civil War and was also problematic in the eyes of the Communist Party. The Communist Party in the Civil War years regarded the political culture of the resistance movement as too "liberal," one that needed to become more Bolshevik-like. Finally, we should always keep in mind that a huge number of people were incarcerated for a relatively brief period of time in different places of internment, for different reasons and under different conditions. The leadership in prisons sought to homogenize the political prisoners, to create a single and uniform identity, but this remained an unfinished process due to the diversity of the subject. Prisoners with different class and cultural backgrounds and political experiences made up a multiple subject, an "organized multiplicity."[8] However, in the relation between the uniformity and multiplicity of the subject, identity politics matters. To the public and the administration the subject appeared (as in the case of the Averof political prisoners at the beginning of the chapter) as a unified and disciplined subject. It is only when one studies political prisoners from within and offstage that the hidden internal tensions, conflicts, and differences come to the fore.

Becoming Communist

To draw the social and class profile of the political detainees, based on statistical data, is rather an unattainable task. In 1952 an American scholar, R. V. Burks, visited Greece and carried out research on Greek political prisoners. He interviewed and persuaded 586 "repentants" to fill out questionnaires. Although the representativeness of such a sample for the whole political prisoners' population is questionable, his conclusions were interesting. Burks argued that "instead of a movement representing a single social class, there is very clearly a movement representing all social classes."[9] But mostly the lower and lower-middle classes, one might add. In his small sample, 42.2 percent were skilled and unskilled urban workers and 33.8 were peasants. The large proportion of peasants among the political prisoners seems to be undisputed. In 1946, out of a sample of 811 exiles, 262 men and 143 women were peasants, and 183 were workers.[10] From a report written by prisoners in 1951 concerning the overall political prisoners' population, we learn that 60 percent were peasants, 7 percent women, and 15 percent youths below the age of twenty-five.[11] From a different viewpoint, it is significant that the KKE was alarmed by the fact that the majority of its members were peasants and employees, and only 18 percent were workers.[12]

Illiterate among literate, peasants among city-dwellers, party cadres among the rank-and-file and "fellow travelers:" the prison brings together different worlds. The connecting links among those worlds are the glorious past of the resistance, the experience of persecution, and their actual situation in prison. These connecting links (and family or local ties should be added as well) stand as a counterbalance to the social and cultural diversity. From this point of view, the prisoners' organization can be seen as an attempt to minimize the differences by providing a pattern for the ideal political prisoner. I suggest considering the organization of prisoners' everyday life as a sociocultural process of homogenization, with the leading part in this process played by the imprisoned party members. This process aims to develop a specific way of life and to cultivate a cosmos, a symbolic universe that characterized the communist political prisoner. In this sense, organization of everyday life is a sociocultural process of introduction to communism as a way of life and a cosmos. This sociocultural process operates at two levels. The first is the level of the shared past, experience and actual situation; these common elements are developed, commemorated, and established as features of a particular identity. The second is the level of synthesizing, providing or sometimes imposing the pattern of the political prisoners' culture, a combination of the educated individual and "people's fighter" characteristics.

Often the concept of time is revealing of a collective identity. Even nowadays, many political prisoners refer to the 1940s as an era of "war." They do not distinguish between the period of occupation and the years following the liberation. They establish a continuum based on their experience of persecution, violence, and death, which contradicts a conventional historical periodization. Manolis Glezos, who in 1941 became the symbol of the resistance because as a youngster together with his friend Apostolos Santas, he had hauled down the swastika flag from the Acropolis, wrote in 1949 from prison:

> I am committed for trial before court-martial for the seventh time since the Nazi occupation of Greece. I was tried three times during the occupation and the fourth condemned me to death, by default, after an especial order by Hitler himself. In the last three I was condemned by the new fascist regime of our country to various punishments, one of which is the death penalty. [...] I hope that this time also they will not allow the Greek fascists to execute Hitler's order.[13]

The differences between the occupation and the postliberation era are minimized so that a continuity can be established. It is the continuity of persecution that enables Glezos to draw a parallel between the occupation and the "new fascist regime". Communists referred to the postwar situation as a "second occupation" and the political establishment as "monarchofascists" to emphasize the similarities between the two eras. In a similar vein, nationalists referred to communism as "red fascism." The continuity is established through the analogy. After the liberation, they continue to call themselves "resistance fighters" while the others are called "monarchofascists"; the juxtaposition between "resistance" and "fascism" underlines the continuity and justifies the prisoners' cause. By the same token, whereas during the occupation they were fighting for the country's liberation from the Axis forces, in the postwar era was they upheld the struggle against American rule *(amerikanokratia)*.[14]

The identity of the resistance fighter is celebrated, commemorated, and confirmed on every possible occasion. Prisoners sang songs from the resistance, and commemorated the founding anniversaries of the resistance organizations. The walls were decorated with pictures and slogans from the resistance, and in the appeals they send, the political prisoners describe themselves and sign as "fighters of the National Resistance." The construction of identity is also a question of self-recognition and recognition by others.[15] In that case the identity of the "fighter of National Resistance," is prerequisite for their recognition not as prisoners but as political prisoners. Differences, discrepancies, mistakes, contradictions of the policies followed by the EAM or KKE are discussed but are presented as insignificant. Only after the end of the Civil War, in an attempt to overcome the crisis following the defeat, would a reevaluation of the common past of the resistance be put forward, mainly as criticism of the party line and the higher echelons of the party. Be that as it may, during the Civil War, the resistance was the cornerstone of political prisoners' identity and a key element of their profile.

Last but not least, the political identity of the political prisoner is superimposed and dominates all the other identities of the prisoners. From this viewpoint, the similarity of political prisoners' discourse is striking. When someone reads, for instance, the last letters of those condemned to die, it is very difficult to trace gender differences between male and female political detainees. In these letters, their common discourse on the honorable death of a people's fighter overshadows the gender of the fighter. The prevalence of the political identity over that of gender stems both from the experience of the struggle for a common political goal during the occupation, i.e. the liberation of the country, and on the other from the ideology of the Communist Party.[16] Chrysa Chatzivasileiou, who wrote on the women's question, although she criticized the backward views of male communists, nonetheless maintained that the "partial" and "social" goal (women's liberation) depended on the "total" and "political" goal (the socialist transformation of the country).[17] In this way prisoners' multiple identities, mainly class and gender but also ethnic identities (for Slav Macedonians and Muslims) are subjected to the political one. The political identity of the prisoners becomes prevalent not only because of the political character of their persecution by the regime, but also because it is cultivated within prisons as the feature that can unify all the detainees. Nevertheless, identities are not fixed but fluid and contested. The defeat of the Democratic Army, the Communist Party thesis for the "complete national restoration" of the Greek Slav Macedonians,[18] and the establishment of the Macedonian Republic in Yugoslavia, would create a "conflict of loyalties" and give rise to an identity hitherto suppressed or silenced, that of the Slav Macedonian prisoners, who formed their own groups inside prisons to the dismay of the rest of the political prisoners.[19]

Social and cultural diversity had to be regulated, controlled, and normalized at the microlevel as well. Needs, drives, and habits are situated at the center of this cultural process. The following letter, written by a peasant woman and guerilla, is significant because it captures the social and cultural differences among political prisoners in an impressive way. Loula Derveki writes to her brother Giorgos:

> When we first came here we slept on the floor because we didn't have anything but the trousers we were wearing. Giorgos, they didn't pay any attention to us, the guerillas, and they said to us that we didn't go to the mountains to fight but to do something else, you know what ... They want us to cook their food, to wash their dishes while they hang around and pretend that they are the leaders in the Averof prisons. If, Giorgos, it is to be like this, well, it is a pity that so many brothers have died; some of the educated tell us that the greater the number of us who die the more they become famous. (...) Amalia Rirri fell sick with serious pleurisy and we had nothing to offer her, not even an apple. And some "ladies" here, while they receive bags so full that they cannot carry them, they didn't give a single apple to this mother, instead they eat all alone to take care of their skin. (...) Well, Giorgos, they organize dances and several sketches but they haven't even once invited us to participate. Certainly they are right, Giorgos, because we do not have silk panties nor jersey underwear; the only things we have are the trousers and the jackets we had on the mountains, and, you know, this is improper and so you have to understand how tough our life here is and that what we are doing is a double struggle.[20]

Us and them: the peasants and the city dwellers, the illiterate and the educated, the guerillas and the party cadres. Or, "trousers and jackets" on the one hand, and on the other "silk panties and jersey underwear," those who went to the mountains and those who "take care of their skin." The directness of the writing style, the clear distinction between "us" and "them", the irony and the exaggeration, give a picture of this cultural confrontation among the prisoners. Different concepts of femininity go together with different habits that reflect cultural and class distinctions. Loula Devreki had to fight a double struggle while in prison, against the administration as well as against the discrimination and prejudices of her own comrades.

The leadership undertook to normalize the diversity and the differences. It provided a cultural pattern that combined the conduct of the educated city-dweller with the ethos of the "people's fighter." On the walls of the Pavlos

Melas camp (Salonica), prisoners had written the slogan "Good conduct is characteristic of civilized individuals".[21] What did "good conduct" and "civilized individual" mean? KKE Secretary General Nikos Zachariadis, in a leaflet published in 1946 under the title *The Communist, people's fighter, member of the KKE*, outlined the profile of the ideal communist. For his bodily health, the communist sleeps with window open, takes showers often ("he loves water, large quantities of water"), exercises every morning, practices sports, and hardens his body. What Zachariadis called "health of the psyche" is "mental equanimity, lucidity, and readiness; composure and revolutionary courage; correct estimation and determination; moderation, calmness, restraint; no pointless and excessive enthusiasm, no sudden ups and downs." The character of the communist concentrated "the most decent national-popular virtues and advantages, which characterize the Greek, the *Romios*": honor, dignity, straightforwardness, consistency, honesty, unselfishness, integrity, taciturnity and modesty. With regard to his intellectual interests, he is interested in literature, theater, music, fine arts, goes to the movies ("the production of the progressive ones"), listens to radio, and learns foreign languages ("first of all Russian"); "all these in the golden mean and always from the viewpoint of the party expediency."[22]

For the lower strata and the peasants, it was a cultural transformation in line with the way of life of the educated city-dweller. The cultural transformation went along with the construction of a specific reality. Greece in the 1940s was absurdly represented as a country with an educated urban population who enjoyed leisure activities, whereas Greece was in fact a country nearly destroyed by war, where 60 percent of the population were peasants. The construction of that particular reality also revealed something else: peasants were seen as a backward social class. Marxist-Leninist ideology, together with other modernist ideologies, viewed the peasants as an element of the past, a constituent part of a traditional society which was declining under the impetus of capitalism, something that had not yet become what it should be, i.e. the working class. The role of peasantry is described very well by Zachariadis: "The peasantry only in its alliance with the revolutionary proletariat and under its [revolutionary proletariat's] hegemony may find and finds its revolutionary orientation, revolutionary mission and social redemption as well. In this way only can we detach the peasantry as the reserve of the bourgeois class and make it the reserve of the revolution."[23] Even when "redeemed," the peasantry was to remain a "reserve."

It would be a mistake and an oversimplification to analyze the whole cultural process as indoctrination. Certainly, there were in-prison activities that may be described as indoctrination. Political lessons are such an example. In the Zakynthos prison, as we have already seen, there was a class for the forty-five imprisoned EPON members, in which lessons on the struggle of the organization were given, and a class for cadres, thirty of whom attended lessons on organizing and leading. It is plausible that many of the activities which were addressed to all the political prisoners, like the theater, the feasts, or the reading groups, had a political content as well.[24] But these diversions were complementary and intermingled within the whole nexus of everyday life activities.

A leftist literary theorist described resistance organizations as a "school" where "a new type of man" was created.[25] That characterization holds true for prisons as well. Prisons were like a laboratory of cultural transformation in the broad sense. Dimitris Glinos in 1937 gave three lectures at the Akronafplia prison on the topics "How we should read," "How we should talk," and "How we should write". These lectures were not a blueprint for communist agitation and propaganda but rather an introduction to intellectual discipline, positivist thought, and a modernist worldview. Moreover, they inculcated a certain culture and habits. Glinos categorized reading, for instance, into four types: to kill time, out of curiosity, for "artistic excitement," and for knowledge. He dismissed the first two (represented by newspapers and magazines) because they tend to be a "drug, pseudo-education," "superficial reading" that "weans us from serious work." On the contrary, the last two kinds of reading had "value for a human being."[26] From that point of view and in the big picture, in the Greek society of the 1940s the Left was both a revolutionary and a modernizing movement. The intersection of these two features is demonstrated in the following note from the leadership at Averof women's prison. The first task that the leadership had set: "The struggle against the general and political backwardness (in our prison too many women were illiterate). Many old women had never had a shower in their lives. Others didn't know what USSR means".[27] The fight against illiteracy (an explanation for political backwardness), modernizing the habits of the political prisoners, and their political instruction were interwoven in the organization of everyday life.

In collective prison life, prisoners who came from cities, intellectuals and party cadres set the examples for this cultural transformation. Indeed, they were the agency of the cultural transformation. The peasant woman watched the educated woman from the city, who had her hair cut short and took care of her face, and imitated her, or was embarrassed when she saw her smoking.[28] At the Averof prison, the women prisoners often played volleyball in the yard; it would be reasonable to ask how many women prisoners had ever seen women playing volleyball before and who in fact were playing. Very few women played, mainly the educated, and many of the volleyball matches were organized by the eighteen women prisoners who were segregated as leaders of the prisoners. The very idea of sports was introduced to the other prisoners as paradigmatic, in the sense that it represented a specific care for the body and leisure activity, and was a behavior to be emulated, since it was performed by the educated and individuals high up in the prisoners' hierarchy.

However, the endeavor undertaken by the party members was an incomplete cultural process. Feasts are a good case in point. A wide variety of entertainment was included in their repertoire, from playwrights like Vasilis Rotas to Molière, from Rossini's *The Barber of Seville* to the traditional folk song "Forty brave men." Generally speaking, three distinct cultural trends may be identified in their songs, theatrical plays, and musical themes. The first is traditional folk culture, especially in connection with rural areas, seen in *kleft* or other folk songs, dances, and pastoral dramas performed by prisoners coming from these areas. The second is what can be considered high culture, such as plays by Shakespeare or ancient Greek dramas, and *oeuvres* of Beethoven, Mozart, and Schubert. The third is the leftist or, in broader terms, committed culture: poems of Kostas Varnalis, Luis Aragon, and Paul Eluard, songs of the resistance, plays by Vasilis Rotas or Soviet authors were often performed.

This combination corresponded to the cultural profile that was being constructed and promoted by the party: respect for the popular culture, knowledge of the standards of the educated individual, and revolutionary spirit. What was, perhaps, more interesting is the first trend, respect for popular culture, which in many cases seemed at first sight to clash with the communist worldview. The women detainees on Chios in 1948, at the insistence of the old women, asked and got permission from the administration to go to church. A group of them formed a choir and chanted together with the cantor of the church; later, at Christmas, a number of them went to church for holy communion.[29] Respect for popular culture, even for attitudes like that above, which otherwise could have been labeled by the Party as "retrogressive," mirrored not the openmindness of the party but the diversity of the social subject. Educated people and illiterates, villagers and city-dwellers, the young and the elderly found themselves confined in the same place, and their social diversity was expressed in the variety of cultural life in prisons.

Prisoners' culural life can be described as a hybrid, as pastiche of several patterns due to the prisoners' mobility, the small number of people who could undertake such cultural activities, the party's respect for popular culture, and tolerance of the coexistence of different cultures. The women exiles on Trikeri island dressed in local garbs organized feasts with local folk dances, staged the ancient tragedy "Prometheus Bound," and gave choral performances of German, French, Russian, and Greek popular songs, as well as Dvorák, Gluck, among many others.[30] This hybrid cannot be easily categorized but rather induce us to consider prison as a field of cultural interaction. What is beyond doubt is the fact that most of the prisoners had never before encountered these poems or music. For these women, as contradictory as it may seem, imprisonment opened up new horizons, broadening an experience that theretofore had been limited to cultivating a field or living in a small village. Vice versa, the prisoners from cities had no idea about life in rural areas and looked down upon their culture. Prisons were a "map of Greece personified" by the social experiences of their fellow inmates and their places of origin.[31]

Constructing Power: The Party Mechanism

Behind the prisoners' organization of everyday life there was always the party mechanism, the "bureau" (*grafeio*), as it was called. The bureau maintained contacts with the prison administration, organized feasts, led prisoners' struggles, managed the division of labor of the detainees, controlled the contacts with political prisoners from other prisons, made out petitions and appeals, and decided on individual matters or collective issues. Since the power of the Communist Party among the leftist parties and organizations of the era was overwhelming, the party mechanism remained unchallenged within prisons. Three issues related to the construction of power of the party mechanism will be put forward: first, the structure of the mechanism, second, the establishment, and finally, the enactment of this power. These three issues, which can be codified as hierarchy, knowledge, and supervision, served the same purpose: the striving of the party mechanism to expand the domain under its control, i.e., the political prisoners.

In the first two years after the liberation (1945 and 1946), the prisoners' self-organization was quasilegal. The political prisoners were organized in the *omada symviosis* (cohabitation group), and they enjoyed a great degree of freedom inside prisons to organize their daily life. The prisoners' representatives were elected and prisoners regularly held meetings. From 1946 on, however, the situation changed. A circular issued by the Ministry of Justice in March 1946 forbade "the existence of all prisoners' committees" and considered "as a heavy disciplinary offense any toleration of Prisoners' Committees in the future or any mass submission of complaints or any other interference in internal prison administration on the part of the prisoners".[32] The circular was not put in force immediately, but took effect gradually until the end of 1946. A similar process of "restoration of law and order" for the political exiles came into being in 1947, when the communities of exiles were transformed into "camps of disciplined living" and Emergency Law 511 concerning the living conditions of exiles was passed.[33]

Under the new circumstances, the *omades symviosis* were dissolved. The bureau appointed the representatives, and prisoners' meetings ceased to exist. What remained from that phase of organization was a certain type of economic solidarity—political prisoners continued to give a share of their parcels or income to the group. A type of informal prisoners' representation was retained because prison administrations preferred to arrange everyday routine issues with a few representatives rather than the whole prison population. There were three so-called representatives. The first was the "representative" (*ekprosopos*), who was responsible for the various working parties and presented to the administration the political prisoners' problems; the second was the "mayor" (*dimarchos*), who was responsible for cleaning duties; and the third was the *thalamarchis*, the person in charge of the dormitory, who counted the prisoners and informed the guards. The informal representation was welcomed by the administration and the prisoners alike because it lessened tensions (between the administration and the prisoners, and among the prisoners as well) that might have arisen over issues of everyday life.

Besides the informal organization, there was the underground organization of the Communist Party as well. At the top of the party organization was the *grafeio* ("bureau") of the prison, consisting of three people more or less. Among them was the "secretary," the leader of the party organization in prison. However, it should be added that the term "party organization" is not the most accurate. The party organization inside prisons was not officially recognized by the party as such, though it did keep contact with the party outside prisons. The first reason for that non recognition was that the formation of a party organization inside prisons was prohibited by the emergency laws of the Civil War and the outlawing of the Communist Party, and hence would have brought new and heavy indictments upon the political prisoners in jail. The second reason was that when party members were arrested, their membership was put on hold. Their cases would be reviewed based on their conduct during the ordeal of arrest, trial, and imprisonment, and on whether they signed a declaration of repentance or not. The review would result in the ranking of a prisoner in the hierarchy of the organization.

The *grafeio* operated within a small circle of prisoners who were called the "narrow" (*steni*) because they had close contact with the leadership. Those were the prisoners who had signed declaration of repentance and were irreproachable, "clean." Below that small circle there were various categorizations of prisoners, and a system of stratification was meticulously elaborated as years passed. Below the "narrow" was the "wide" (*platia*), for those prisoners who had signed declarations of repentance while on trial or in the Makronisos camps and later withdrew them. Below that was a third category, the "influence" (*epirroi*) or the "contact" (*epafi*), for those repentants who had signed declarations of repentance or collaborated with the authorities in order to mitigate their position while on trial. The final category comprised the "suspects" (*ypoptoi*), prisoners for whom there was no information whatsoever. They were considered "stool pigeons" and sooner or later they were expelled from the political prisoners' dormitories.[34]

The role of the bureau depended on the situation in each prison, but, in any case, it was the "shadow" power. By "shadow power," I mean that it was a leadership that remained secret from both the prisoners and the administration, one that constituted a parallel and underground structure of power. The reasons for secrecy were obvious. Since the emergency laws prohibited the Communist Party organizations, the discovery of such a mechanism would have as a consequence the transfer of its members to other prisons or, even worse, their court-martial, which would disrupt of underground network. The bureau appointed the three aforementioned informal representatives (the *ekprosopos*, the *thalamarchis* and the *dimarchos*) as well as a "party responsible" in each dormitory or wing of prison, who organized and supervised the political prisoners' every day life and activities.[35]

The hierarchy in most cases was not connected to material privileges. Sometimes the leadership had better food or accommodation, but these privileges were not institutionalized. However, there were cases when the "bureau" took advantage of its power. The situation that Konstantinos Georgantis found in the Mesologgi prison in 1945 is described in his report to the party as "the most miserable." The cadres had isolated themselves in a dormitory and the other prisoners, who were left to "play cards and have drinks", called them "Kolonaki" (the bourgeois district of Athens).[36] The "bureau" was held responsible for the prisoners' everyday life, and, as this report shows, was supervised by the party mechanism on whether it performed its duties or not.

By and large, the categorization of prisoners was established on a hierarchical model connected to differentiated access to knowledge. Access to knowledge meant that the bureau of the group controlled the prisoners' information. The bureau regulated and controlled the informal network of communication that prisoners maintained, mainly through visits, correspondence, rumors, talks with the guards, and random access to newspapers or radio broadcasts. Control of information was, thus, production of the proper, according to the bureau, knowledge. Whenever it was possible, in exile in particular, political detainees published their own newspaper. On Sikinos island, for instance, the exiles published their newspaper *Adouloti Foni* (Unconquered Voice), because

> We should not regard the issue of the circulation of news with frivolity. It is rearranged in such a way as to one day make us believe that within few days we will return home, and on another, that all is in gloom and doom. (…) But you may say … shouldn't we keep up with the political situation, as long as we have the opportunity to do so? Of course, but there is a better way, which will help us to sharpen our political minds. We have our newspapers, which they can teach us many things. If we study them, and, if it is possible dormitory by dormitory, analyze them, then we will draw the conclusions that will shed light on the intrigues of the fascists, natives and foreigners.[37]

To control and regulate the flux of information by publishing their own newspaper was a difficult task. Usually, the bureau bribed the guards and got a radio or newspapers inside the prison. The news mechanism set in motion may illustrate how the whole mechanism worked and which purposes prisoners' categorization served. The bureau gave a full account to the "narrow" circle. Each prisoner of the "narrow" circle kept contact with two or three prisoners of the "wide" one and informed them, neither revealing the source nor giving a full account, of the news. The prisoners of the "wide," in their turn, were in touch with two or three prisoners classified as "influence" or "contact," and provided them with even less information. The "suspects" were isolated and nobody talked to them.

Thus, it may be argued that part of the bureau's power was based on the knowledge that it possessed. By controlling all the "external" (outside prisons) sources of information, it channeled and filtered the news that reached prisoners. The pyramidal structure of the organization corresponded rather to the power that the differentiated access to knowledge implied than to the material privileges that the bureau could have enjoyed. Taking into account how important news about the course of the Civil War was to the prisoners, lack of information rendered them even more powerless over their own lives. Or, to give a more specific example, the fact that the political exiles at the Makronisos camps had not been informed by the leadership about the harsh treatment they would receive when being incorporated into the military camps in the winter of 1949, rendered them unprepared and defenseless toward their tormentors.[38] The paternalism of the leadership (divulging no news that might undermine prisoners' morale) was nothing but a euphemism for the power relations.

Besides the "external" information, the bureau was aware of "internal" information as well. In this case, knowledge facilitated the supervision of the prisoners. By "internal" information I refer to the classification of political prisoners and the supervision of everyday life. The bureau was in contact with other prisons and was informed about the individual prisoners. In a sense, the bureau kept a "party record" for every political prisoner. How did the individual "party record" circulate from prison to prison? Mostly through transfers. In a transfer from one prison to another or after a trial, a trusted prisoner was assigned to forward to the bureau of the prison of destination all the information for each individual of the group transported. The bureau, based on the information about every prisoner (whether, for instance, the newcomer had signed a declaration of repentance or had informed against other members) classified him or her in the respective group: "narrow," "wide," and so on.

Moreover, the bureau kept a close eye on the individual prisoners inside prisons. Conversation, jokes, gossip, complaints, and private matters fell under the bureau's supervision. It approved individual petitions or appeals; before their trials, prisoners discussed with it what they were going to in court; the prisoners' outgoing mail was checked by the bureau prior to the administration's censorship; "vigilants" (*epagrypnites*) monitored was said during the visits.[39] An amusing sketch will help to illustrate the way in which surveillance was realized. The sketch performed at the Averof women's prison goes like this: as women stroll by twos in the yard of the prison talking about their boyfriends, a third woman approaches them, pretending to be knitting; she tries to get close to them and is obviously eavesdropping, as the knitting needles are tangled in her hands.[40]

Nonetheless, it would be an oversimplification to argue that the authority of the bureau inside prison was maintained by imposition or, even worse, coercion. It would also be a mistake to depict political prisoners as passive, they were disciplined. The political prisoners supported the leadership, but at the same time they were able to test the limits of the bureau from within without directly challenging its authority. I think that the phrase "from within" allows us to understand the prisoners' position. They conceded the legitimacy of the leadership. The idiosyncrasy of that legitimacy was that it was based both on the communist political culture and the role of the bureau inside prisons. Compliance with the leadership and discipline had been inculcated in the habits of the communists and were integral parts of the communist political culture, I shall return to this point later. The bureau was the sole organized nucleus within prisons that would provide the political detainees with a pattern for the organization of their everyday life; and the political detainees knew that this was the only way to improve their living conditions. The bureau assigned duties, arranged feasts, organized lessons, led struggles, and in brief was behind any aspect of the collective life. A consensus was manufactured, since all these activities met the prisoners' needs. At the same time it was a consensus tested and negotiated by the prisoners, for it implied the uniformity of their subjectivity. We have already seen how prisoners' cultural differences created a hybrid inside prisons.[41] Another example of this negotiation was that although the individual prisoners' contributions delivered to the collective treasury from the parcels and the checks they received was never questioned, the percentage remained, throughout the era, a thorny and contested issue. Relations between the leadership and the political detainees were based on a consensus, questioned, negotiated, and undermined both by the bureau's striving for absolute control of the prisoners' life and by the prisoners' demonstration of their subjectivity. The turning point, however, came when the leadership felt that the contested consensus threatened its authority and questioned its legitimacy. There lay the fragile dividing line between within and without.

Us and Them: The Dissidents

Many prisoners could not test the limits of the party authority from within. Some were excluded from the beginning, while others were segregated and isolated by the political prisoners' collectivity in the process of being removed from the collectivity. These prisoners were the repenters, who after having signed declarations in prison were transferred to different dormitories; the criminal prisoners, who by definition were excluded from the political prisoners' collectivity; and finally, the dissidents, who mostly remained within the political prisoners' collectivity but were isolated. In the following pages the last two cases will be discussed. Although one may argue that criminal prisoners were of no importance in the formation of the political prisoners' identity since they were excluded from the beginning, nonetheless their presence inside prisons constituted a negative example for the political prisoners. Criminal prisoners represented the threat of exclusion from the political prisoners' collectivity, and a first step in that direction was the isolation of the dissidents. The dissident was isolated so that he or she would have to leave the political prisoners' dormitories and go to those of the criminal prisoners. In this sense, criminal prisoners and dissidents constituted two distinct but negative examples.

To discuss the relations between political and criminal prisoners is to study the boundaries of the nonrelation between them. Common criminals were separated from the political prisoners in a double sense. They were, literally speaking, segregated because they were interned in different cells or dormitories. They constituted two different worlds coexisting in the same place but with a limited contact, on an individual basis. The escape of ten juvenile prisoners (six thieves and four political detainees, all of them awaiting trial) from the Kifissia prison in Athens in August 1945 has all the features of an exception: it is probably the sole case of common action between commonlaw and political prisoners mentioned in the press, one of the few cases of escapes by political prisoners, who, in addition, were minors.[42] On a different occasion, as one political prisoner recollects in his memoirs, again in the same juvenile prison of Kifissia, political and criminal prisoners went on hunger strike together; not surprisingly, one of the demands of the strikers was the segregation of the political from the criminal prisoners.[43] Though commonlaw prisoners are described in political prisoners' memoirs as individuals who respected the political detainees, the encounters between them were limited due to the fear of a demoralizing effect, that contact with delinquents such as murderers, drug addicts, or prostitutes would be detrimental. Moreover, political prisoners wanted to differentiate themselves from the common prisoners in order to remove the stigma of the prisoner. As the communist poet Kostas Varnalis put it, describing a transfer of criminal and political prisoners: "Together with us, last, in the ship / junkies, bums and smugglers / on purpose, so that it may seem / that it is the same thing Freedom and hashish."[44] The image of the commonlaw prisoners, as it emerges from political prisoners' memoirs, is that of miserable human beings, regarded with either compassion or repulsion. The latter was especially likely when criminal prisoners were made assistants of the administration in the running of the penitentiary, like at the Giaros camps. The boundaries in that case were redrawn. Political prisoners identified criminal prisoners with the administration, attributing to the guards the negative denominations of the criminals (thieves, homosexuals, drug addicts, etc.).

Nevertheless, there was contact, and often, political prisoners were informed about transfers or executions by criminal prisoners who frequented the administrative offices. The presence of political prisoners with their discipline and organization made the lives of all the prisoners more bearable. Despite the segregation, there was osmosis between them; sometimes detainees even exerted a political influence upon the criminal prisoners. Why else would a drug-addicted prisoner at the Aegina prison tell the guard "It is not a dictatorship now, leave the fascist things you know, and don't provoke us," instead of simply swearing?[45] The political culture of the resistance was spread throughout the society and the presence of political prisoners had an influence in the prison culture.[46]

Let us now return to the political prisoners who were within and without the prisoners' collectivity. Eleni Skarpeti, a young woman sentenced to death, was brought to the firing squad but at the very last moment escaped her execution.[47] Her father, an old politician, managed to suspend her execution through his influence and contacts. Eleni Skarpeti herself knew nothing about the suspension of her execution when she was brought to the firing squad. The fact that she escaped her execution made her immediately a "suspect" in the eyes of the other political prisoners. When she was transferred back to the prison in a state of shock, a doctor who was a political prisoner herself refused to treat her. It was the beginning of her isolation. The bureau did not even discuss her explanations, and Eleni Skarpeti spent the next thirteen months isolated at the Averof women's prison. Her fellow inmates scornfully called her "Angel", because the nuns of the administration believed that a miracle had saved her life.[48]

In the case of dissidents and suspects, there was again a process of stigmatization and exclusion, but it was different from the one applied to the repenters. The diffused suspicion may be a starting point to illuminate this process. The very fact of someone's arrest was a source of suspicion for the party. The arrest meant that the member did not keep the rules of underground life and action. Moreover, as September 1947, when the party decided to launch a full-scale war and called its members to join the guerilla forces on the mountains, it looked with suspicion upon those who remained in the cities acting "passively," and then "found themselves" in prison.[49]

Being suspicious was a duty; being aware of nuances in behavior that could classified as suspicious was a requirement. The report written by the bureau of the Averof women's prison that referred to the prisoners who were illiterate, didn't take showers, and didn't know what USSR meant, continued that "[o]thers [prisoners] could not imagine that there might be agents of the enemy among the prisoners. The mass of the prisoners presents all the problems of the mass and incessant, tireless effort is required to raise them to the level of the conscious fighter." It concluded by setting the task of "[t]he struggle against the agents of the enemy and their slogans, the struggle for mass political vigilance, for the unmasking and the isolation of the agents."[50] This report is interesting because it illustrates how the atmosphere of diffused suspicion was enacted. The political instruction entailed the introduction and implementation of the category of "suspect" to the rest of the prisoners. A "conscious fighter" was one who was vigilant, who was educated to understand what an "agent" is, and to identify certain conduct as "suspect."

The years that the party spent underground and the bitter experience under the Metaxas dictatorship may be helpful to contextualize but do not suffice to explain what has been called "stool pigeon phobia". At that time it was already evident that anyone who criticized the leadership was likely to become a suspect and be accused as a stool pigeon. In 1939 at the Akronafplia prison, the tension between the bureau and several political prisoners was extremely heightened. One issue was the control of information on the part of the bureau. Giannis Ioannidis, a member of the Akronafplia bureau and member of the KKE Politburo, had hidden an issue of *Rizospastis*, in which it had been published that his wife had been expelled from the party because after her arrest she betrayed several party members. A second issue was the privileges of the bureau. The members of the bureau did not have duties like the rest of the prisoners, and notwithstanding had better food. The situation worsened upon the arrival of Dimitris Paparigas, member of the Central Committee of the KKE. While he was returning from a trip to the Soviet Union, he had introduced the wife of Kostas Votanis, at that time a prisoner in Akronafplia, as his wife. Many political detainees considered this act immoral and questioned Paparigas' position in the bureau. The bureau isolated a number of detainees as suspects and factionalists; two of them, Thanasis Gakis and Thanasis Kapenis, were beaten by their fellow inmates and kicked out of the political prisoners' dormitories in 1939. Later in the occupation, though both Gakis and Kapenis were active in the resistance movement, they were killed by the guerillas. The orders for their execution had come from people who were in the Akronafplia bureau in 1939.[51]

Since discipline and compliance with the decisions of the leadership were among the most praised virtues of a communist, anyone who dared to question the leadership was accused of undermining unity and spreading the confusion, and was regarded as a probable undercover police agent. The power of the bureau as a mechanism rested to a large extent upon surveillance of the individual prisoners. Surveillance in that case had a specific name, it was called "vigilance." "Vigilance," wrote a leading cadre, "is the *quintessence* of our proper policy for the appointment of our cadres."[52] "The basic element in the cadre policy", Zachariadis wrote, "is their selection, promotion and their appointment, after consideration and supervision of their whole course—consideration and supervision that never stop."[53] This held not only for the cadres but for the rank-and-file as well. In exile camps and in prisons the bureau assigned the duty of vigilance to its trusties, who supervised the everyday life of the rest.[54] Their duty was to "watch out, to observe" the individual life of the prisoner, to become "*a living register.*"[55]

The bureau organized the surveillance but it was the political prisoners those who actually supervised. In this way, they became part of the whole system in a double sense. First, they knew that the supervisor might become one of the supervised some day, if he or she failed to comply with the rules of the game: "listen, watch, keep silence."[56] Through supervision the prisoner learned what to avoid, whom to be afraid of, with whom to talk, and so on. Second, that situation created an atmosphere of diffused suspicion and mistrust among the prisoners. Political prisoners were rendered unable and unwilling to question the authority of the bureau—unable because as supervisors themselves they were accomplices in the exclusion of their fellow inmates; unwilling because they did not want to undergo the consequences of being excluded.

From the moment that a prisoner began to be considered a suspect, the ordeal began. The prisoner was first relieved from his or her duties in the prison and then was isolated. Isolation meant that no one talked to him or her, except one person who informed him or her about routine prison events like mess, visits or correspondence. To make the lives of the isolated even more difficult, other prisoners were instructed to harass them: they did not let them sleep, pushed them so that their food or water would spill, turned their backs when the isolated talked to them.[57] This was perhaps the worst ordeal that could have ever been invented: to be in jail and at the same time isolated by one's comrades and fellow inmates—segregated from both society and the prisoners' collectivity. Dina Katopodi was isolated at the Averof women's prison, because as a guerilla had surrendered her arms without prior consent of the Party; after spending eight years in isolation, it was found out that this was not true and she was "rehabilitated." Another example of isolation was that of Evgenios Charalambidis, an accountant who had been "people's mayor" of the Peristeri district in Athens after the liberation in October 1944. Charalambidis did not only question the high-handed manner of the "secretary" at the Corfu prison. He knew also that the "secretary" had not behaved properly in his trial (he had burst into tears upon his sentence to death), and he had become "secretary" despite the opposite directions of the party (he had destroyed the note that suggested that he should not take any leading posts in the prison). He was isolated although he was in the death row; the rumor had it that he was about to sign a declaration of repentance. Charalambidis was executed on 22 July 1948 and upon his transfer he urged his fellow inmates to keep an eye on the "secretary." He was right; after a while the "secretary" signed a declaration of repentance. Prisoners awaiting execution, like Charalambidis, did not escape the consequences of isolation. The bureau ordered that no one should reply to the farewells of prisoners who were transferred for execution, if they had been punished with isolation.[58]

When the "offense" was not severe, the bureau asked the isolated to perform "self-criticism": a humiliating practice that included, as Luisa Passerini pointed out, "tones of self-destruction and self-denigration" and justified and legitimized the leadership's authority.[59] Quite often the punished one was not aware of the reasons for his or her punishment; nor were the rest of the prisoners. There were "rumors," but no specific accusation. The "rumors" could concern anything; they could range from purely political (like anti-Party behavior or defeatism) to moral issues (alleged homosexuality).[60] The fact that the accusations were vague and took the form of "rumors" deprived the isolated of the opportunity to defend themselves, and spread suspicion and distrust among the prisoners. Most of the prisoners participated in isolating someone without knowing the exact reasons, out of obedience to the bureau. The political prisoners' basic premise for the punishment of a fellow inmate was: "The isolated must have done something wrong and the Party knows it."

The bureau by controlling the information and possessing the knowledge of what was happening inside and outside prisons, was the source of knowledge and truth. The political prisoners' discipline and obedience to the leadership strengthened its power, investing it with the feature of party infallibility. The specific history of communist prisoners' discipline and compliance with the leadership is, on the one hand, common to all the Communist Parties' history of "bolshevikization" in the interwar era, which created the long tradition of infallible leadership and disciplined members.[61] On the other, the Greek case had one peculiarity: the very fact of the Civil War reinforced the need for discipline and unreserved unity. The predisposition for discipline could hardly find any better conjuncture to be enhanced than the Civil War.

The aspects of exclusion and isolation of suspects and dissidents were even more evident and, sometimes, appalling in internment institutions run by the Communist Party. These were prisons in the territories controlled by the Democratic Army and camps in neighboring countries during the Civil War. I shall examine them only briefly because the available information is inadequate and further research is required. The main prisons of the Provisional Government of the Democratic Army of Greece were established in 1948 in the Grammos mountain range (later were transferred to the Vitsi Mountain). The prisoners came from territories controlled by the Democratic Army and were mainly villagers held as "suspects." Those prisons combined labor and indoctrination. The prisoners were put to work cultivating fields or building roads in those territories. The daily program included the reading of the Democratic Army newspaper, listening to the guerillas' radio broadcast, and attending lectures organized by the authorities. The suspects were interned there in order to "be corrected, to become better men and contribute to the victory." Like the governmental rehabilitation camps, the goal of the prisons administered by guerillas was to ensure that the released prisoners had one "sole aspiration: not to commit the same offense again, and like good citizens and fighters to contribute with a spirited effort to the liberation of the Motherland."[62]

One of the main guerilla camps in a neighboring country was in Bulkes, a village in the region of Voivodina in the former Yugoslavia, where a camp had been set up by the Communist Party of Greece in 1945. In the beginning this camp hosted former members of the ELAS who had fled Greece due to the "white terror." It later became a training center for guerilla officers and soldiers. The camp developed its own security mechanism, the *Ypiresia Taxis Omadas* (Group Order Service), which supervised the camp and arrested and imprisoned the suspects. In the spring of 1946 the leadership of the camp decided to address the problem of about a hundred suspects by transferring them. When the suspects were taken to the train station, they found the whole population of the camp, about three thousand people, waiting for them. The crowd spat on the suspects, beat them, and called them names like "worms" and "traitors". The suspects were delivered to the Yugoslavian secret police, and then forwarded to the Yugoslav-Greek frontier so that they might be arrested by the Greek authorities! Other less lucky suspects from that camp were ruthlessly murdered by the *Ypiresia Taxis Omadas* on a small island in the Danube river.[63]

The party discourse provides a class explanation for the dissidents. Dissidents are most commonly characterized as petit bourgeois or intellectuals. The petit bourgeois, often described as "vacillating," is juxtaposed with the revolutionary worker. Nikos Zachariadis formulated the "vacillation" in this way:

> In such moments, one way or another, the individual aspirations for career, the petit bourgeois ambitions and residues, the petit bourgeois selfishness, the vanity, the intellectualist individualism will clash with the bolshevik partisanship, which intransigently, without surrender, concession or compromise, demands and imposes that the individual to be subjected, and even sacrificed, when this is necessary, to the party.[64]

Behind the rhetoric on "vacillating petit bourgeois" and intellectuals, lay the problem of the individual and its relation to the collectivity.[65] Whereas the party resolved the issue by prioritizing the collective and rendering the individual to a subject under the authority of the leadership, many prisoners resisted this subjugation. Aris Alexandrou, a poet who in 1948 was isolated as a "defeatist" during his exile on the island of Limnos, wrote: "For the group I / had always been a suspect / like truth is."[66] By questioning the infallibility of the leadership, the dissidents challenged its power as a regime of truth. To use Bourdieu's terms, what was called into question was the *doxa* of the group in an attempt to form heterodoxies and orthodoxies.[67]

Despite the dissidents and even though their isolation constituted a negative experience for many political prisoners at that time, the *doxa* of the political prisoners did not waver during the Civil War. The close interrelation between the situation outside and inside prisons has to be pointed out again. During the Greek Civil War, political prisoners lived with the hope of the victory, and the preservation of their unity was an undisputed task. The leadership inside prisons was seriously challenged only from the moment that the leadership of the whole movement failed. Only after the end of the Civil War in the 1950s, in the context of the discussions about the defeat of the Democratic Army and, later, about the "Stalinist phenomenon," were prisons transformed into a political laboratory where orthodoxies and heterodoxies clashed.

The deterrent effect of the isolation of suspects and dissidents secured the power of the party mechanism from possible challenges. The pain of imprisonment was worsened by rejection on part of comrades and fellow inmates. The dissident was no longer a "people's fighter" like all the other political prisoners, but a stool pigeon. His or her past as a member of the EAM/ELAS was silenced and a newly invented petit bourgeois history was invented and attached together, with the inventory of the anti-Party qualities. The dissidents did not deny their past, nor did they "repent." They were deprived of it; their past was negated by their fellow inmates.

Notes

1. FO 371/48282 R16619, Athens to FO, 29 September 1945.
2. Ibid. See, for instance, a right-wing politician who claimed that prisons were "excellent universities of Communism" in Evangelos Averof-Tositsas, *Fotia kai tsekouri* (Athens, 1975), 193-194.
3. Lars Baerentzen, "I laiki ypostirixi tou EAM sto telos tis katochis", Mnemon 9 (1984):157-173. For the difficulties in assess the figures of membership to the Resistance organizations, see Hagen Fleischer, "The National Liberation Front (EAM): 1941-1947. A Reassessment", in Iatrides and Wrigley, eds., *Greece at the Crossroads*, 69-70.
4. Mazower, *Inside Hitler's Greece*, 310-315.
5. The KKE had 45.000 members and the other 250,000 members from the provinces were channeled to the Agrarian Party of Greece. Between 20,000 and 25,000 members were expelled from it as *dilosies* and suspects. See the report of Giannis Ioannidis to the twinned parties and the Communist Party of the Soviet Union on 12 September 1946, in *I trichroni epopoiia*, 585-597.
6. NARA 868.00B/12-2647, Athens to Secretary of State, Report on Communist Party of Greece and its activities during month of November 1947, 26 December 1947.
7. Harlow, *Barred*, 10.
8. Lambropoulou, *Grafontas apo ti fylaki*, 127.
9. Though the findings of his research should not be taken at face value, given the context of the Cold War and the limitations of a study concerning political questions put to political prisoners still in prison, two points are noteworthy. First, out of the sample only 28.2 percent admitted membership in the KKE, and 14.8 percent "denied any contact with the Communist movement or simply left the particular question unanswered;" the rest were members of the resistance organizations. Although "it was agreed by prison

authorities, police officials and repentant leaders that 28 percent was too low for party membership," what the figures derived in study tell us is that a large number of the political prisoners, but not the majority, were communists and members of the KKE. If it is also taken into account that in that period the number of political prisoners was steaadily decreasing, we may assume that in the previous years the relative weight of party members was even smaller. R. V. Burks, "Statistical Profile of the Greek Communist", *The Journal of Modern History* 27, no. 2 (1955): 153-158.

The second point is related to the political ends of scientific research in the Cold War years. Burks, upon finishing the project on the statistical profile of political prisoners, suggested another project on psychological war. The focus was on the Averof prison, and the project concerned the preparation of pamphlets and other psychological devices to test the degree of disorganization and defeatism that they could create among political prisoners. A measure of success would be to achieve the defection of 360 of the 600 political prisoners in the prison. To show the significance of his projects, Burks added that "[m]ethods learned by work in the Greek prisons might well be applicable to other communist parties." Cited in Hagen Fleischer, "Makronisos 1950: Protypo gia ti Germania tou Psychrou Polemou? Amerikanikoi provlimatismoi kai syntages gia ti dimokratiki anamorfosi," in Proceedings of the Conference, *Istoriko topio kai istoriki mnimi*, 199-224.

10. MGA/LDG, Info X, National Solidarity Press Bulletin, 15 November 1946. The 811 exiles were on the islands of Folegandros, Gavdos, Fournoi, and Agios Efstratios.
11. ASKI, box 423 F25/5/6, Report on prisons, 16 December 1951.
12. Petros Roussos, "Koinoniki synthesi kai diafotisi ton melon," *Kommounistiki Epitheorisi* 40 (August 1945): 8-11.
13. MGA/LDG, Info V, Letter of Manolis Glezos from the Averof prison to the *Daily Worker*, 19 February 1949.
14. See, for instance, the radio broadcasts of the Democratic Army from 30 November until 14 December 1947, published under the telling title *"Slavikos kindynos" i Amerikanokratia kai ethnikos afanismos* ("Slav danger" or American rule and national havoc) (n.p., 1947).
15. Craig Calhoun, "Social Theory and the Politics of Identity," 20.
16. For the EAM women's participation in the Resistance should serve only one objective, the liberation of the country. See, *Pos prepei na doulevei I gynaika sto Ethniko Apeleftherotiko Metopo* (n.p., 1943).
17. Chatzivasileiou, *To KKE kai to gynaikeio zitima*, 27-28, 37.
18. Decree of the Fifth Plenum of the Central Committee of the KKE, 30-31 January 1949, in KKE, *Episima Keimena*, 337.
19. Interview with Spyros Andreadis on 6 April 1998.
20. ASKI, box 422 F25/4/8, Letter of Loula Derveki, 16 September 1950.
21. MGA/LDG, Info X, *Symfiliotis*, 14 November 1946.
22. Zachariadis, *O kommounistis*, 14-22. When Nikos Zachariadis writes for the ideal communist, he has always in mind the male communist; for that reason he uses the pronoun *he*. As we have already seen in chapter 6, different properties were required from the female communists.
23. Nikos Zachariadis, *Provlimata kathodigisis sto KKE*, (n.p., 1953), 70.
24. *Rizospastis*, 8 August 1947.
25. Markos Avgeris, "Enas neos kosmos," *Elefthera Grammata* 22 (5 October 1945): 1-2.
26. Dimitris Glinos gave these lectures on 21 May, 4 June, and 11 June 1937 at the Akronafplia prison. His notes were later published under the title "Odigos sti morfosi", in *Sti mnimi tou Dimitri A. Glinou*, 157-164. See also, *Pos na meletame. Praktikos odigos gia tin aftomeleti mas* (n.p., 1948).

The Politics of Counterpower   221

27. ASKI, box 421 F25/3/54. Some problems from the life of prisoners in Greece, 22 August 1953.
28. Marigoula Mastroleon-Zerva, *Exoristes. Chios, Trikeri, Makronisi* (Athens, 1986), 35-37; Stefanou, *Ton afanon*, 68; Karra, *Emeis oi ap'exo*, 65-66.
29. Stasa Kefalidou, in Theodorou, ed., *Stratopeda gynaikon*, 108. See also Nikos Marantzidis, *Oi mikres Mosches. Politiki kai eklogiki analysi tis parousias tou kommounismou ston elladiko agrotiko horo* (Athens, 1997), for the fusion between communism and Christianity in the case of Mantamados village on the island of Lesbos, 39-64.
30. Apostolopoulou, *Grothia sto skotadi*, 44-50, 58-65.
31. Interview with Cleopatra Chatzisavva on 3 July 1998.
32. UNRRA PAG 4/3.0.12.2.3., Box 12, File W/17 (1), Individual prisons, Confidential circular to the Prison Directors of the State Prisons, 13 March 1946.
33. See above, chapter 4.
34. The information on the political prisoners' organization was based mainly on interviews with former political prisoners: with Panagiotis Aronis and Dimitris Mouratidis on 20 February 1998, with Takis Benas on 24 February and 10 March 1998, with Spyros Andreadis on 2,3, and 6 April 1998, and with Stelios Zamanos on 9 September 1998. See also Minos Stavridis, Kataggelies," in Vardinogiannis and Aronis, eds., *Oi misoi sta sidera*, 539-547; Tsakiris, *Vourla*, 43-46; Takis Benas, *Tou emfyliou*, 205-210.
35. One should also mention that in the framework of political prisoners' informal organization, prisoners were often organized in subgroups according to the geographical region of their origin or the resistance organization they belonged to (this applies mainly to the EPON members).
36. ASKI, box 589, Report of Konstantinos Georgantis, 10 May 1946
37. *Adouloti Foni*, vol. 3, 9 November 1946, in ASKI, box 422, F25/4/215.
38. Flountzis, *Sto kolastirio tis Makronisou*, 105-107
39. Tsakiris, *Vourla*, 43-46; Stamatis Skourtis, *Ospou na ximerosei* (Athens, 1993), 161.
40. Papadouka, *Gynaikeies fylakes Averof*, 117-118.
41. From this viewpoint, an event from the cultural life in prisons that Takis Benas recalls in his memoirs is telling. The topic of discussion among the prisoners in the Corfu prison in 1955 was what kind of songs and dances were appropriate for them. After many discussions and disagreements, they rejected "foreign" culture, like tango and waltz, and the *rebetika* songs (urban popular songs) were discredited as "decadent," though they were very popular among the prisoners, so by *reductio ad absurdum* they ended up with traditional folk songs. "Thus, the *rebetika* songs went … underground. We sang them of course, but with … look-outs." Benas, *Tou emfyliou*, 233-234.
42. *Acropolis*, 30 August 1945.
43. Missios, … *kala esy skotothikes noris*, 87-103.
44. Kostas Varnalis, "Stin exoria." Cited in Flountzis, *Akronafplia*, 32.
45. Aegina Prison Archives, Disciplinary decrees of the director, 1277, Decree no. 44, 8 October 1946
46. For a discussion of the common prisoners in the communist political discourse and imaginary, see Georges-Panayiotis Panagiotopoulos, *Réclusion et ideologie. Une sociologie politique de la réclusion a partir de l'expérience des communistes grecs*, Mémoire du DEA de Sociologie, École des Hautes Études en Sciences Sociales, (Paris, 1994).
47. See above chapter 8.
48. Antoniou and Skarpeti-Tsali, *Apofasi 225A/1948*, 146-160. Interview with Cleopatra Chatzisavva on 3 July 1998.
49. Decision of the Third Plenum of the Central Committee of the KKE, 12 September 1947, in, *I trichroni epopoiia*, 257-261, 637-639.

50. ASKI, box 421 F25/3/54. Some problems from the life of prisoners in Greece, 22 August 1953.
51. Flountzis, *Akronafplia*, 236-257; Giannogonas, *Akronafplia*, 43-44, 47; Nefeloudis, *Achtina*, 127-128. Some years later, as it is often the case in the history of the communist parties, the accusers became the accused. Nikos Zachariadis criticized the leadership in Akronafplia prison because "their example and actions had a negative influence" among the prisoners. Zachariadis, *Provlimata kathodigisis*, 224-225.
52. "To provlima ton stelechon", *Kommounistiki Epitheorisi* 9 (1 September 1947): 402 (original emphasis). The article was probably written by Vasilis Bartziotas.
53. Zachariadis, *Provlimata kathodigisis*, 252.
54. *Vasikoi kanones epagrypnisis*, 16.
55. "Organosi kai periechomeno tis epagrypnisis," *Kommounistiki Epitheorisi* 4 (1 April 1947): 171 (original emphasis). The article was probably written by Vasilis Bartziotas.
56. Giannogonas, *Akronafplia*, 47.
57. Andreas Xyftilis, "Afigisi," in Vardinogiannis and Aronis, eds., *Oi misoi sta sidera*, 548-550.
58. Papadouka, *Gynaikeies Fylakes Averof*, 159-160; Skourtis, *Ospou na ximerosei*, 287-289; idem, *Aftoi pou dropiasan*, 56-60; Tsakiris, *Vourla*, 46-49.
59. Luisa Passerini, "Lacerations in the Memory," 206.
60. Fani Manolkidou-Vetta, *Tha se leme Ismini*, 91-94.
61. See for instance the brochures, KKE, *Apla mathimata. Mathima proto* (Athens, 1944), the chapter titled "Bolshevik discipline and monolithicity," (p. 5), and the next one, KKE, *Apla mathimata. Mathima deftero* (Athens, 1944), the chapter titled "Conscious, out of iron discipline," (p. 4).
62. *Deltio Eidiseon tou Dimokratikou Stratou Elladas*, 10 January 1949, *Pros ti niki*, 7 March 1949. These prisons were for civilians. Soldiers of the Democratic Army were interned in the guardhouses of the military divisions. For serious offenses were court-martialed by guerilla military courts. If sentenced to death, they were executed. See *Deltio Eidiseon tou Dimokratikou Stratou Elladas*, 5 February 1949.
63. Christos Kainourgios, *Sta stratopeda Rubik kai Bulkes. Periplaniseis kai peripeteies laikon agoniston 1945-1947*, (Athens, 1991), 89-91; Kostas Siaperas, *Mystikoi dromoi tou Dimokratikou Stratou* (Athens, 1990), 73-87, 123-126, Alekos Sakalis, *Mnimes* (Kozani, 1997), 106-112.
64. Nikos Zachariadis, *Provlimata kathodigisis*, 233.
65. Some leading party cadres regarded internment as a means for the rehabilitation of intellectuals. Hence, in one article the author spoke for "a cadre from Trikala that I hope in exile now is himself again." Vasilis Bartziotas, "Provlimata kathodigisis," *Kommounistiki Epitheorisi* 2, (February 1947): 63.
66. Aris Alexandrou, "Alexandrostroi," *Agonos Grammi*, 1952. Cited in Dimitris Raftopoulos, *Aris Alexandrou, o exoristos* (Athens, 1996), 159-165.
67. Pierre Bourdieu, *Outline of a Theory of Practice* (Cambridge, 1977), 159-170.

Epilogue
After Prison

The Civil War ended in August 1949, at least on the battlefield. The death toll was very high. The Greek General Staff estimated that 12,760 soldiers and officers, and 36,558 guerillas were killed (the latter figure, however, seems to be inflated; perhaps a figure of about 25,000 losses on the part of the Democratic Army of Greece would be closer to the reality). It was the bloodiest war in the history of modern Greece, and its losses can be compared only with the expedition to Asia Minor in 1922.[1] But even after such a disastrous war, Greece like other post-Civil War societies, hastened to return to a certain kind of political normality and appeasement. In October 1949, two months after the last battles of the Civil War, the executions of political prisoners stopped.[2] In 1950 the Makronisos camps for civilians closed down, and within the next years the number of political prisoners in Greece steadily decreased. In 1955 there were 4,498 political prisoners and 898 exiles; in 1962 there were 1,359 prisoners and 296 exiles.[3] A similar tendency for abandoning the policies of mass persecution and imprisonment, although under a dictatorial regime, can also be observed in the case of the Spanish Civil War: the prison population decreased radically within five years of the end of the war.[4]

The decrease in the population of political prisoners came as a result of the "appeasement measures" stipulated in a series of laws between 1950 and 1952. These laws gave political prisoners convicted by special courts-martial the opportunity to have their cases reheard, commuted death sentences to life imprisonment, and provided for the release of political prisoners upon the recommendation of a special committee. Rehearings of sentences by special courts-martial and led to reduction of heavy sentences and often to the release of political prisoners. By 1954 about fourteen thousand sentences of special courts-martial had been reviewed.[5] The appeasement measures, according to Minister of Justice Dimitrios Papaspyrou, were a "friendly gesture to those

---

Notes for this section begin on page 235.

who have not lost their national consciousness to return to the bosom of the Motherland." The purpose of these measures was to restore "domestic normality and peace," and also to decongest prisons that had become "organized, proper 'schools' of subversive ideas."[6]

Nevertheless, "appeasement measures" that led to the release of large numbers of political prisoners did not signify a return to democracy. A whole arsenal of laws and measures that facilitated discrimination against leftists and allowed for more subtle forms of political exclusion remained in force. These laws and measures that had passed during the Civil War remained in force after its end and were not repealed after the voting in of the new constitution in 1952, not even when they were contrary to it. These laws and measures constituted a second legal body that Nikos Alivizatos calls "paraconstitution." As he points out, many of these laws featured a clause that allowed their application "for as long as the rebellion lasts." In order to maintain their force, the post-Civil War governments subscribed to the theory "of the permanent civil war." As absurd as it might seem, Greek courts up until 1962 judged on the premise that the Civil War was not yet over, since its termination had not been decreed by an official act![7] From the legal point of view, the Greek Civil War ended in 1962.

Due to the "paraconstitution" and the theory of the "permanent civil war," Law 509, which banned the Communist Party of Greece, remained in force. The Communist Party would become legal again in 1974, twenty-seven years after its ban. The government reinstated the Metaxas law of 1936 on espionage, and many members of the Communist Party coming from Eastern Europe in the 1950s, entered the country illegally to organize the underground mechanism, got arrested, and were convicted as spies. The penalty of banishment (exile) and the public security committees continued to exist (1,722 individuals were banished between 1952 and 1967). Last but not least, the loyalty certificates and loyalty boards guaranteed the monitoring of the state apparatus and the exclusion of "disloyal" citizens.

After a liberal intermission in 1964-1965, the military dictatorship in 1967 launched a new campaign of terror, arrests, prosecution, torture, and imprisonment of leftist political opponents. Articles of the constitution concerning fundamental democratic rights were suspended. The civil service, the universities, the judiciary and the army were thoroughly purged, and special court-martial took over the administration of justice. Within the first days of the colonels' "national revolution" on 21 April 1967, eight thousand persons were arrested and about seven thousand of them were interned at the camps on the island of Giaros. More than eighty thousand persons were arrested for political reasons between 1967 and 1974, of whom ten thousand were banished and 1,700 were sentenced to various prison terms.[8] So much for democracy in Greece during the quarter-century between the end of the Civil War and the restoration of democracy in 1974.

In this epilogue I shall discuss the impact of the Civil War and of the experience of imprisonment on political prisoners after their release. More specifically, I shall discuss the experience of release in the politically suffocating atmosphere of Greece in the 1950s, where political prisoners had to readjust themselves to the "free" society under the burden of their defeat in the Civil War. Then, I shall turn to the re-elaboration of prison experience in memory, as it is impressed on political prisoners' memoirs published in the 1980s and 1990s.

A Subject under Change

These are not the streets we knew
An alien crowd crawls now in the avenues
They changed the names of the suburbs
Asylums are erected in the fields and the squares.
Who is waiting for your return? Here the descendants
Throw stones at strangers, make sacrifices to effigies,
You are a stranger within an unknown congregation
And from the pulpit they excommunicate strangers
They curse at those who speak another tongue.
Manolis Anagnostakis, "These Are Not the Streets …," 1954[9]

This poem captures the loneliness and estrangement felt by a political prisoner after his release in post-Civil War Greece. He is free, but feels like a stranger who recognizes neither the city nor the people, a stranger who speaks another language and is not able to communicate. This unintelligibility silences the political prisoner; indeed, silence and memory are two themes that frequently recur in Manolis Anagnostakis' poems. The poet himself was involved in the resistance, and was arrested during the occupation. He became a member of the Communist Party and was arrested again in 1948, expelled from the party, and sentenced to death in 1949 at the age of twenty-four. Two years later he was granted amnesty. What is so devastating, what casts such a heavy shadow over the assumed happiness of being free again? The agony of the political prisoner, implicit in the question "Who is waiting for your return?" is all the more eloquent, given its rhetorical tone.

For many political prisoners, release was the moment of realization of the impact of imprisonment and civil war. For some, the network of relationships that sustained the individual before imprisonment had been dissolved. Many friends, relatives, and family members had been killed or had fled to Eastern European countries. For some others, the political prisoner was an awkward figure from a past they wanted to forget. The first concern of the released prisoners was to reconstruct their personal lives. This was not easy. Some of them had been so traumatized by the experience of imprisonment that they could not overcome it. In the following letter, Niki Nifakou, the wife of a political prisoner who spent two and a half years at the Makronisos camps, describes the change in her husband and asks for the help of their foreign friend from the British solidarity organization "League for Democracy in Greece":

> A few months ago they released my husband. When he left he was very healthy, but now that he has returned he is washed out, his health is irreparably damaged, he has a weak heart because of his depression. (…) In the past, at the time they took him away from us, he was lively and full of vigor. When he returned, he was someone else. Pessimism and gloom had seized him, and it is difficult for me, a simple woman, to try to instill in him a sense of optimism. For that reason, when you write again to us, write him something—he speaks French and he could write to you in this language—on top of that, he doesn't have proper clothes to go out for a walk and unwind.[10]

The deconstruction of subjectivity after the ordeal of internment at the Makronisos camps had consequences for both the detainee himself and his family. The pessimism and change (after the release "he was someone else") acknowledged by the wife of this political detainee are but some of the consequences of the internment. Another is the additional financial difficulty that the internment caused to a poor family, which forces Nifakou "to ask from a stranger an old dress or coat."[11]

The society prisoners left before entering prison was not the same as the one they faced upon their release. Time did not "freeze" during their imprisonment. Postwar Greece was a country under reconstruction, under change. That's how a political prisoner described his first days of freedom in a letter to a cadre of the same solidarity organization:

> I would like to thank you for your loving interest. I live in a hotel. Relatives—here in Athens—I don't have. After my release, my health is not that good. What first impresses me is the amount of traffic and how fast people move. The amount of traffic made me feel dizzy in the first days. There is a certain indifference of the people towards one another; perhaps this is a result of a long-lasting narrow life and the fact that I don't have an intimate environment. For some days, in the mornings when I woke up I thought that I was in prison—this of course only for a few seconds. I might spend Easter with my Mother.[12]

In this letter, like in Manolis Anagnostakis' poem, the feeling of loneliness and estrangement is salient. Prison life is present as a contrast to his life as a citizen. Prison is a domain of sameness and repetition, whereas society is marked by change. The quickness of city life is implicitly contrasted with the slow rhythms and monotony of prison. The close relationships between prisoners are contrasted with the free citizens' individualism. The letter is tinged with a certain nostalgia for prison, as a world of familiarity and solidarity. There is something more than mere readjustment in the process of leaving institutionalized life. The former prisoner must also cope with the disruption of social relationships and private life. The broader social network appears to have dissolved (no friends or comrades are mentioned) and is replaced by the smaller world of kinship. His last resort is the past, his personal past, and the emblematic figure of the Mother as the past.

One might think that the pessimism and gloom can be attributed to the readjustment process following the release of a prisoner. The very fact of being free again after having spent years in prison is somehow a shock to the prisoner. Then, institutional routines provided a pattern for everyday life, however monotonous and restricted it was. Release requires adjustment to the needs of a citizen's everyday life. Erving Goffman, in his study of total institutions, suggests that inmates' sense of bitterness and alienation due to their internment weakens upon the release and that ex-inmates tend to forget what life was like on the inside.[13] This holds true for former political prisoners because they face a strong disjunction of cultures between the inside and the outside prison. Despite the ordeal of prison life, the prisoners' collectivity was characterized by strong bonds of solidarity and commitment, and a culture based on these. Even the reconstruction of one's personal life was a collective task in prisons, no matter how ambiguous the intentions were. This led to an idealization of certain aspects of prison life, as we shall see below. The experience of community and collectivity, however, contrasts sharply with life outside. The reconstruction of personal life is an individual task. The culture of solidarity and commitment had to be confronted with the values of individualism and competition that prevailed in free society.

The loneliness and estrangement of ex-political prisoners had also to do with the defeat in the Civil War and its consequences on a both personal and collective level. The defeat is a turning point, the moment of recapitulation of the past. The questions political prisoners ask themselves—"What happened?" "Was it worth it?"—are imminent and pressing. This sense of estrangement, pessimism, and loneliness, which recur in the remembering of release in prisoners' writings is connected with the realization of the deconstruction of one's personal and social life. And it is just one of the consequences of defeat that the political prisoners faced after their release. These feelings were accentuated because of the position of the former political prisoner in post-Civil War Greece and the consequences of defeat for communist identity.

An additional reason for the ex-political prisoners' sense of estrangement was their marginalization in post-Civil War society. The polarization of the Civil War was institutionalized after its end in the form of the construction of an anticommunist state, that is, a state that operated along the distinction between citizens who were "nationally minded" (*ethnikofrones*) and those who were not. The latter became targets of state policies of systematic repression and discrimination, which rendered extremely difficult the incorporation of former political prisoners into post-Civil War society as full citizens. Ex-political prisoners, like any leftist in general, lived with "the fear of the gendarme," as people said at the time. Ex-political prisoners were "second class citizens": their rights could be arbitrarily suspended, they had to report to the police regularly, they were excluded from any employment whatsoever in the public sector and easily fired from their jobs upon police request, their everyday life was closely monitored by the police, and so on. Harassment by the local police and right-wing people forced many ex-political prisoners to leave their hometowns and villages for the city, where there was greater anonymity and more job opportunities.

The defeat in the Civil War had grave consequences for the collective subject. Perhaps the single most important effect was that a large number of communists were forced to leave the country. After the defeat, about fifty-seven thousand people fled to Eastern European countries. The rest, who remained in Greece, were either in jail or, if they remained politically active, involved in the reconstruction of the Left in Greece (through the party of the EDA or the maintenance of the underground mechanism of the Communist Party). The Greek communist movement was split into two parts: those who lived in Greece and those who fled abroad, who would not be allowed to return to Greece until the mid-1970s. The forced migration of guerillas and their families after the end of the Civil War deprived the movement from perhaps its most militant part, and rendered impossible its future reorganization. Forced to migrate and become political refugees behind the "Iron Curtain," those people faced a quite different social reality in these countries and had a particular relationship to Greece, one closely monitored by the Communist Party apparatus. They therefore developed a different identity from those who stayed in Greece.[14]

The defeat had repercussions for the leadership as well. It raised many questions about the responsibility for and correctness of the decisions of the party leadership with regard to the Civil War. The faction around the secretary general of the Communist Party, Nikos Zachariadis, in order to maintain its power, launched an attack against other leading cadres who criticized the leadership and challenged its authority. The result of this attack was the expulsion from the party in 1950 of many leading cadres and members of the Politburo, who were accused of being stool-pigeons, Titoists, antiparty, and so on. A series of internal conflicts (often involving physical violence), expulsions and heated debates was generated in the first half of the 1950s. In 1957 the party leadership, after the dramatic changes that followed the twentieth congress of the Communist Party of the Soviet Union, was overthrown and replaced by a "non-Stalinist" one. Finally, in 1968 the divergence and the different priorities between the party mechanism abroad and the other inside Greece would lead to the split of the Communist Party into two parties. These political developments in the Communist Party, which I have roughly outlined, were accompanied by certain important changes in the identity of the subject.

The defeat opened a period of crisis, the main aspect of which was the reevaluation of the past. After the *Dekemvriana* events in 1944 and the Varkiza agreement, the leadership of the party was criticized for its decisions but the problems and questions regarding the party line were left unanswered. After the defeat in the Civil War, however, the leadership, in order to avoid the mounting criticism, put forward a radically different conceptualization of the past. Nikos Zachariadis, though he had held the post of secretary general during the occupation, was not responsible for the party line because he was interned in a German concentration camp. To discredit his party opponents, he accused the occupation party leadership, for the bad turn of events which led to the defeat in the Civil War. As he himself bluntly put it, comparing the party line in the period of occupation with the one in the Civil War: "In the first period our line was basically wrong. In the second period our line was basically right."[15] Starting from the party line during the occupation, the reinterpretation of the past resulted in the construction of a disputed past—or, as some would have it, a silenced past

> The nearly three and a half years of armed struggle [in the Civil War] was an incessant hard struggle, full of self-sacrifice, heroism, and grandeur. Despite our military defeat, these three and a half years, together with those of 1821 [the war for national independence], are the most glorious from all the years of Greek people's struggle for national and social liberation.[16]

In this new genealogy, something had been omitted: the years of the resistance. Participation in, or some sort of affiliation to, the resistance organizations was constitutive of the identity not only of the political prisoners but of all those who had fought in one of the two camps of the Civil War. People who were proud to have fought in the lines of the ELAS, were now being told that among the ELAS cadres, "agents of the enemy dominated".[17] Already during the Civil War the ELAS model had been seen as an impediment to the development of the Democratic Army of Greece because the former was heavily influenced by bourgeois conceptions and ideas. Resistance politics during and after the Civil War were criticized as not "people's republican," that is revolutionary, enough. The general hypothesis that can be put forward is that during the Civil War the Communist Party sought to "bolshevikize" the resistance movement, and more revolutionary in this case meant more disciplined and closely controlled by the party apparatus.

Political events and developments have a major impact on political identities—political prisoners' identity was not an exception. The defeat was a sudden "disenchantment of the world" that urged an understanding of the past and a reorientation towards the future. The defeat in the Civil War was followed a few years later by disclosures about the crimes of Stalin's regime. The *doxa* of the subject was shattered, and unity gave way to criticism. Improvement of the living conditions in prisons also helped. The numerous restrictions and prohibitions imposed in the late 1940s were relaxed after the end of the Civil War. Correspondence and visits were more frequent, the prison administration unofficially recognized political prisoners' representatives, political prisoners' activities were tolerated, and newspapers were allowed in prisons. Also after the changes in the Greek Communist Party leadership in 1956-1957, the new leadership in prisons took the initiative to organize political prisoners' collectives in a more democratic and participatory way.[18] The *doxa* was transformed into clashing heterodoxies and orthodoxies, and different approaches to the past and interpretations of the current situation were put forward. The conflict between "revisionists" and "Stalinists" led to the destabilization and questioning of previously sacred truths. Needless to say that the disputes and conflicts became even more heated and far-reaching in 1968, when the Communist Party split into two.[19] All these developments and changes led many prisoners to a critical self-reflection and a certain distancing from the collective subject.

The defeat in the Civil War, the experience of prison or refuge, the breakup of the Communist Party, the Socialist Party's accession to power in Greece in 1981, and the collapse of the communist regimes in Eastern and Central Europe in 1989 created new conditions and posed new questions. The self-reflection (the process of making sense of the past in order to reorientate oneself to the future) and the shifting position (not identification but distancing) that these developments stimulated, placed many former political prisoners in an awkward situation. They found themselves dislocated: inside and outside at the same time, attached to the generation that fought in the resistance and the Civil War, but distanced from the political agent (the Communist Party) to which they belonged at that time. We still have to ask, commitment to what, and why? I think the memoirs of former political prisoners can give us some clues.

Detached Commitment

> Then—do you remember?—you say to me: The war is over!
> But the war hasn't finished yet.
> Because no war has ever finished.
> Manolis Anagnostakis, "The War," 1945[20]

When is a war over? Or, rather, when was the Civil War in Greece over? For the defeated, the hardships did not stop in 1949. The experience of pain, loss, separation did not cease with the end of the war on the battlefield, but continued into the 1950s and 1960s, in prisons, in political refugees' communities, in the suffocating atmosphere of post-Civil War Greece and under the colonels' dictatorship. Greece was divided into two camps, the national-minded and the communists, the victors and the defeated. This perpetuation of the Civil War created a deep division between the Left and the Right that dominated all aspects of social, political and, cultural life. Well in the 1970s, the official state considered the communists traitors and bandits, and the Civil War was still referred to as the "bandit war." The accession of the Socialist Party to power in 1981 represented a decisive break with decades of state anticommunism. The Socialist Party government put forward an inclusive policy and reinterpretation of the past. The contribution of the leftist resistance organizations to the struggle against the occupation was officially acknowledged in 1982, though at the same time in the newly fabricated narrative of "National Resistance" the most troubling aspects of the period of the occupation, such as collaboration and the civil war of 1943-1944, were conveniently silenced. After the "National Resistance," the moment of "National Reconciliation" had to come. Ironically, this happened in 1989, the year the communist regimes in Europe collapsed, by a coalition government of communists and the right wing. This government passed a law recognizing that the war after 1944 had been a Civil War, not a "bandit war," and that the defeated had not been "bandits" but the Democratic Army of Greece. Now that the country had come into terms with its past and had finally managed to reconcile its two parts, it was time to get over that unsettling past. Recognition became condition for forgetfulness.

It was against this background that leftists' memoirs concerning the 1940s proliferated. First, in the 1970s and the 1980s, came the memoirs of leading personalities of the Left who had played significant roles in the resistance and the Civil War. These memoirs read more like historical narratives of political and military events that addressed the persistent questions of the reasons and the responsibility for the defeat, while at the same time their authors also settled old scores with each other or between the two communist parties. Then, from the mid-1980s and mainly in the 1990s, a new kind of memoirs appeared. The authors this time were the rank and file, they were men and women who had been involved in the resistance, been imprisoned during the Civil War, or fought with the Democratic Army of Greece. They focused not on the crucial events, but rather on the personal experience, on their relations with their fellow combatants or inmates, on the mundane. The narrative framework also changed: the clear-cut antithesis "us" versus "them" (the prison administration and the state) was accompanied by the self-referential relation "us/us."[21] The turning point in political prisoners' memoirs was Chronis Missios' ... *kala, esy skotothikes noris* (... luckily, you were killed early), published in 1988. It very quickly became a best seller, perhaps because it was very unconventional. In very strong language, it focused on the experience of political prisoners with a working-class or rural background, relentlessly criticized the party leadership inside and outside prisons, and highlighted the multiple contradictions underlying the subjectivity of communist political prisoners. After Missios' book, more and more former political prisoners decided to write about the experience and memory of prison, and dozens of these memoirs were published in the 1990s.

Political prisoners' autobiographical writings and memoirs are differentiated from the conventional rules of autobiography. In the genre of the autobiography, the emphasis is on the development of the individual through the successive stages of the formation of one's personality.[22] However, in political prisoners' autobiographical writings, as Mary Jo Maynes points out for working-class autobiographies, the "individual is enmeshed in the collectivity."[23] The autobiographical "I" in these writings and memoirs is replaced by the plural self, the "we." The authors are not professional writers (or at least they make clear that they do not have literary intentions), and the narrative has a certain linearity (from their arrest to their release).[24] The authors want to bear testimony to what happened, and they emphasize that the historical significance of their testimony is that it is not an individual experience but rather an experience of thousands of individuals. Through their testimonies, former political prisoners reclaim the right to write the history of a subject that has already been "written." The autobiographical writings of political prisoners are attempts to reconstruct the self as well as the collective subject, which was stigmatized, distorted, and silenced for many years by the regime, the press, legislation, declarations of repentance, and official anticommunism. By publishing their stories, former political prisoners reclaim the "power of writing" that for decades was monopolized by the regime.[25]

The very fact of writing a prison memoir illuminates the mark that the experience of imprisonment has impressed upon the author and exposes the way that experience is interpreted. To begin with, it is a traumatic experience. A general sense of disillusionment and loss is salient in political prisoners' memoirs. Disillusionment stems from their political or party experience inside and outside prisons. The defeat in the Civil War was the turning point. The defeat, Missios wrote, left the rank and file "without perspectives, without myths, without ideology, without hope."[26] Furthermore, the "need that every man has to live his own experience,"[27] was suppressed, denied, and twisted by the party leadership. Discipline, prohibitions, and self-censorship were not simply imposed but internalized as well. In their memoirs, political prisoners explicitly reclaim a subjectivity that was repressed for many years due to party or self-discipline.

The subjectivity that is reclaimed bears the marks of loss, absence and death. Personal lives and family ties were fractured, often irreparably, during these harsh years. Fani Manolkidou-Vetta wonders in her memoirs about the experiences of the children who were raised in orphanages or by relatives or who grew up in the "people's republics" because their parents were killed or imprisoned. Her bitterness originated in her own personal life: even her daughter once told her "People like you, communists, should never have children."[28] Pagona Stefanou refers in her memoirs to the same people, the "invisible" people: mothers who lost their children who fought as guerillas in the Civil War; and also other, younger women who were married to guerillas and, after the end of the war, were left alone with a child. "Who is going to talk about them?" Stefanou asks, about all these women and children who were left behind. And, when she reflects upon her own prison experience, the concept of loss acquires an additional dimension: the loss of youth. She contrasts her experience of youth with that of others, especially children of later generations. When she and her old friends talk about their youth, they speak not of studies, loves, or travels, but rather of executions, prisons, battles and transfers.[29] These traumatic and violent experiences made her strict and rigid at that time. But with the passage of years, "it seems to me," she writes, "painful and absurd. Did we spend our youth, our adolescence in prison?"[30]

In 1948, Pagona Stefanou, age seventeen, was sentenced to fifteen years' imprisonment and transferred to the Averof women's prison, where she spent most of the four years she stayed in prison. The only things she has kept from her prison years were notebooks from her mathematics classes. The reason she kept them was that her mathematics teacher, Ismini Sidiropoulou, was executed on 26 August 1948—a day she can not forget. She writes in her book:

> The first night after the execution I believed that there was not enough air in the dormitory. With my eyes open I was seeing nightmares. I was trying to remember who I was. I had forgotten even the name of my mother; my head was like a wide hole, full of darkness. I believed that I could never laugh again, but I couldn't even cry. They took our teacher, they shot dead our friend. Death had come inside me.[31]

Half of a century later, death still resides inside political prisoners. Executions are the most painful memory from the prison years. For the authors of these memoirs, the death of a fellow-inmate in front of the firing squad was a heroic death, a sacrifice that should not pass into oblivion. Their memoirs are testimonies, accounts that constitute historical evidence. To write about the executed political prisoners, to record their names and their deeds, is part of the duty of the living: to ensure that their sacrifice was not in vain, and will not be forgotten.

However, when Stefanou recollects her release in 1952, she writes "I am not happy, I don't feel free, half of me stays inside. My sisters."[32] It is a sense similar to the "nostalgia and bitterness" of Chronis Missios.[33] Both narratives are characterized by the coexistence simultaneously of nostalgia and pain, attachment and distance. The contradiction between these emotions and positions makes one wonder what had been so particular in the experience of prison, what had counterbalanced the pain and trauma in their memory.

Carlo Ginzburg has written about "prison communism."[34] The solidarity, egalitarianism, and commitment of the political prisoners in communal life was a unique experience that was never repeated in their later lives again as free citizens. It was this kind of "moral communism," which cultivated the values of comradeship, that characterizes the remembered experience of prison. In political prisoners' memoirs, especially those written by women, the remembering of the collective life is at the core of the narrative. The collective organization of their everyday life—the choir, dances, classes, chores, theatrical performances—is a commonplace in the memoirs. This way of life, something like "communism in practice," and these values were in deep contrast to their individual lives after release, in politics and in society in general. But also part and parcel of this collective life was the sharing of the traumatic experience of prison and of the cruelty of the state. Death, executions, torture and refuge created bonds of solidarity among the people who found themselves on the side of the defeated. The perpetuation of the deep rupture between the winners and the losers of the Civil War created a strong sense of commitment among the latter.

Detachment and commitment occur simultaneously. Detachment takes the form of criticism—of the Communist Party and its authoritarian leadership inside and outside prison—and disillusionment due to the defeat in the Civil War with all its grave consequences for the individuals. Temporal distance, the decades elapsed since the Civil War years, and the individual trajectories of the authors, allow them to reassess their personal experience in the light of a critical examination of the politics and ideologies of the Civil War. Nonetheless, detachment is accompanied by a commitment to the collective subject that was formed through the ordeal of prison. With their associations, annual gatherings, visits to places of internment, and publications, as well as more informal personal networks, former political prisoners forge bonds between them and shape the individual and collective memory of the Civil War years. This commitment does not concern only the past, it does not only stem from a sense of duty to their executed or killed comrades. It also addresses questions of the future. Former political prisoners seek what they call the "restoration of historical truth," a re-writing of the history of the Greek Civil War in the face of public silence or indifference.

Detached commitment refers to this process of remembering prison experience, it is a result of thinking and reconstructing the past in the self-reflective act of writing. We do not remember the past, rather, we think the past.[35] Takis Benas talks about the memories of prison years as "[s]edate memories, without the passion of the time. Perhaps for that reason I put some of them on paper, to go away from me, to go and bury themselves in the pages of a book."[36] But the world of the past never dies; it lives with us as long as we live. From the vantage point of the present, one tries to grasp his or her past and establish a continuity between the past and the present. Memory is apt to construct continuity, a normal succession of different phases in one's life, in order to provide the sense of a stable and coherent self. Memory strives against changes, ruptures, vicissitudes—in short, the discontinuities of the individual experience. This does not call for the prioritization of experience over memory as more authentic or objective—Joan Scott has perceptively illuminated the pitfalls of this approach.[37] It rather points out that both memory and experience are sites of subjectivity, that both are constitutive of and constructed by the subject. And for that reason perhaps, "no war has ever finished."

Notes

1. NARA 868.00/11-949, Athens to Department of State, 9 November 1949; Averof-Tositsas agrees with these figures (he claims that 12,777 soldiers and 36,839 guerilllas were killed) and adds that 1,579 gendarmes and 4,123 nationalist civilians were also killed. Averof-Tositsas, *Fotia kai tsekouri*, 474; D. Zafeiropoulos, estimated that 651 officers, 7,789 soldiers and 38,421 guerillas were killed. Zafeiropoulos, *O antisymmoriakos agon*, 670. Giorgos Margaritis suggests that a number of 25,000 killed guerillas would be more reasonable. Margaritis, *Istoria tou ellinikou Emfyliou Polemou*, 50-51.
2. There were no other executions of political prisoners after October 1949, with the exception of the execution of Nikos Belogiannis and his three comrades in March 1952, and the execution of Nikos Ploumbidis in August 1954.
3. Koundouros, *I asfaleia*, 153, 160.
4. In 1939, the prison population in Spain was 270,719, and in 1944 there were 54,072 prisoners. See Stanley G. Payne, *The Franco Regime 1936-1975* (Madison, 1978), 223.
5. The most important among these laws were Law 1504 in 1950 and the Law 2058 in 1952. See Koundouros, *I asfaleia*, 143.
6. Konstantinos Oikonomopoulos, *Nomothesia peri metron eirinefseos* (Athens, 1952), 28, 31.
7. Alivizatos, "The 'Emergency Regime' and Civil Liberties, 1946-1949," in Iatrides, ed., *Greece in the 1940s*, 220-228. See also idem, *Oi politikoi thesmoi se krisi*, 525ff.
8. Alivizatos, *Oi politikoi thesmoi se krisi*, 601ff.; Koundouros, *I asfaleia*, 19-40.
9. Manolis Anagnostakis, "Aftoi den einai oi dromoi …," in *Ta poiimata 1941-1971* (Athens, 1995), 105.
10. MGA/LDG, Info XI, Individual dossiers, Letter of Niki Nifakou to Josephine Adebari, 24 March 1952.
11. Ibid.
12. MGA/LDG, Info XI, Individual dossiers, Letter of Giannis Palavos to Dianna Pym, 4 April 1966.
13. Goffman, *Asylums*, 70-74.
14. Ioanna Papathanasiou estimates that 56,981 individuals fled to Eastern European countries. One-third of them were boys and girls under seventeen years, whereas the adults were mainly men (60%), peasants (58%) and had only primary education (89%). See Ioanna Papathanasiou, "Contribution à l' histoire du Parti Communiste Grec, 1949-1951" (Thèse de doctorat, Université de Paris X, Nanterre, 1988), 212-232. Papathanasiou argues, however, for the trisection of the rank and file of the Communist Party: into political refugees, political prisoners, and free members. Cf. ibid., 209-211.

15. Nikos Zachariadis, "Deka chronia palis. Proto meros," *Neos Kosmos* 8 (August 1950): 397-433.
16. Dimitris Vlantas, "Triamisi chronia palis tou Dimokratikou Stratou Elladas," *Neos Kosmos* 9 (September 1950): 596-640.
17. Giorgos Gousias, "To ideologiko mas metopo," *Neos Kosmos* 9 (September 1950): 580-595.
18. Nikos Gourgiotis, *Dekaochto chronia me allo onoma* (Athens, 2001), 154-164.
19. One cannot help but notice the top-down pattern in these changes: changes in the leadership are the catalyst for changes in the rank-and-file, not vice versa.
20. Anagnostakis, "O polemos, " in *Ta poiimata*, 36.
21. Papathanasiou Ioanna, "Vioma, istoria kai politiki: I ypostasi tis prosopikis martyrias," *Ta Istorika* 13, vols. 24-25 (1996): 253-266.
22. Philippe Lejeune, *Le pact autobiographique* (Paris, 1975).
23. Mary Jo Maynes, "Autobiography and Class Formation in Nineteenth-Century Europe: Methodological Considerations," *Social Science History* 16, no. 3 (1992): 517-537.
24. Morand, *Les écrits des prisonniers politiques*, 44-45
25. Paul Gready, "Autobiography and the 'Power of Writing': Political Prison Writing in the Apartheid Era," *Journal of Southern African Studies* 19, vol. 3 (1993): 489-523.
26. Missios, *... kala esy skotothikes noris*, 108.
27. Ibid., 11.
28. Manolkidou-Vetta, *Tha se leme Ismini*, 59. On the question of political prisoners' children, see Mando Dalianis and Mark Mazower, "Children in Turmoil during the Civil War: Today's Adults," in Mazower, ed., *After the War Was Over*, 91-104.
29. Stefanou, *Ton afanon*, 77.
30. Ibid., 80.
31. Ibid., 84-85.
32. Ibid., 112.
33. Missios, *... kala, esy skotothikes noris*, 221.
34. Carlo Ginzburg, "Comunismo di carcere," in *Il Registro. Carcere politico in Civitavecchia 1941-1943*, ed. A. Natoli, V. Foa and C. Ginzburg (Rome, 1994), 45-50.
35. Allan Megill, "History, Memory, Identity," *History of the Human Sciences* 11, no. 3, (1998): 37-62.
36. Benas, *Tou emfyliou*, 87.
37. Joan W. Scott, "'Experience,'" in *Feminists Theorize the Political*, ed. Judith Butler and Joan W. Scott (New York and London, 1992), 22-40.

Bibliography

PRIMARY SOURCES

Unpublished

Interviews

Andreadis Spyros, 2, 3, and 6 April 1998
Aronis Panagiotis, 20 February 1998
Barbatsi Stamatia, 20 February 1997
Benas Takis, 24 February and 10 March 1998
Chatzisavva Cleopatra, 3 July 1998
Chatzisavvas Savvas, 25 February 1997
Mendrakou Kalliopi, 17 February 1997
Mouratidis Dimitris, 20 and 27 February 1998
Zamanos Stelios, 1 July and 9 September 1998
Zamanou Aristea, 15 February 1997

Archives

Greece

Archeia Synchronis Koinonikis Istorias (Contemporary Social History Archives)
KKE Archives: Boxes 421, 422, 423
EDA Archives: Box 252 (Archive of National Resistance), Box 226 (Archive of "Phoenix"), PEOPEF File

Aegina Prison Archives

Archives of the Ministry of Justice:
Register of decrees of special courts-martial

Averof Prison Archives (Korydallos Prison):
Register of convicts of Averof Prison

Great Britain
Public Records Office
Foreign Office: 371 General Correspondence (Greece)

Modern Greek Archives / League for Democracy in Greece
Info: I, II, IV, V, X, XI, XIV, XVI

United States of America
National Archives and Records Administration
State Department Records
868.00 Correspondence (Greece)
868.00B Correspondence (Greece - Communism)

United Nations Archives
United Nations Relief and Rehabilitation Administration
PAG 4/3.0.12.2.0.
PAG 4/3.0.12.2.3.

Published

Official publications

Government Gazette
Report of the British Legal Mission to Greece. London, HMSO, 1946
Ypourgeion Dikaiosynis. *Egkyklioi kai ypourgikai apofaseis, 1945-1953.* Athens, 1954
Ypourgeion Dikaiosynis. *Syllogi ton ishyouson diataxeon "Peri ekteleseos poinon klp." kai ton pros ektelesin auton diatagmaton, ypourgikon apofaseon kai egkyklion.* Athens, 1937.

Newspapers and reviews

Acropolis, Deltio Eidiseon tou Dimokratikou Stratou Elladas, Dimokratikos, Dimokratikos Typos, Elefthera Grammata, Eleftheri Ellada, I Kathimerini, Kommounistiki Epitheorisi, Neos Kosmos, Pros ti niki, Rizospastis, Skapaneus, Sofronistikai Pliroforiai, To Vima.

SECONDARY SOURCES

Select Bibliography

Alexander, George. *The Prelude to Truman Doctrine. British Policy in Greece,* 1944-1947. Oxford, 1982.

Baerentzen, Lars, John O. Iatrides, and, Ole Smith, eds. *Studies in the History of the Greek Civil War, 1945-1949.* Copenhagen, 1987.

Bauman, Zygmunt. *Mortality, Immortality and Other Life Strategies.* Cambridge, 1992.

Berger, Peter, and Thomas Luckmann, *The Social Construction of Reality. A Treatise in the Sociology of Knowledge.* London, 1971.

Blasius, Dirk. *Geschichte der Politischen Kriminalität in Deutschland 1800-1980.* Frankfurt a. M., 1983.

Bourdieu, Pierre, *Outline of a theory of practice*, Cambridge,1977.

Burks, R.V. "Statistical Profile of the Greek Communist." *The Journal of Modern History* 27, no. 2 (1955): 153-158.

Butler, Judith. *Gender Trouble. Feminism and the subversion of identity.* New York and London, 1990.

Calhoun, Craig. "Social Theory and the Politics of Identity." In *Social Theory and the Politics of Identity,* ed. Craig Calhoun, 9-36. Oxford and Cambridge, 1994.

Chartier, Roger. "The Chimera of the Origin: Archaeology, Cultural History and the French Revolution." In *Foucault and the Writing of History,* ed. Jan Goldstein, 167-186. Oxford and Cambridge, 1994.

Close, David H. *The Origins of the Greek Civil War.* London, 1995.

_____, ed. *The Greek Civil War, 1943-1950. Studies of Polarization.* London, 1993.

Cohen, Stanley. *Visions of Social Control. Crime, Punishment and Classification.* London, 1985.

Dal Pont, Adriano. *I lager di Mussolini. L'altra faccia del confino nei documenti della polizia fascista.* Milano, 1975.

de Villefosse, Louis. "Makronissos, laboratoire politique.", *Les Temps Modernes* 51 (January 1950): 1287-1299.

Deleuze, Gilles. *Michel Foucault.* London, 1988.

des Pres, Terrence. *The Survivor: An Anatomy of Life in the Death Camps.* New York, 1976.

Dodds, Norman, Stanley Tiffany, and Leslie Solley. *Tyranny and Terror: The Betrayal of Greece.* New York, 1946.

Flax, Jane. "Multiples: On the Contemporary Politics of Subjectivity." *Human Studies* 16 (1993): 33-49.

Foot, John. "The Tale of San Vittore: Prisons, Politics, Crime and Fascism in Milan, 1943-1946." *Modern Italy* 3, no. 1 (1998): 25-48.

Foucault, Michel, *Discipline and Punish: The Birth of the Prison.* London, Penguin, 1991

_____. "The Subject and Power." In *Michel Foucault: Beyond Structuralism and Hermeneutics,* ed. Hubert L. Dreyfus and Paul Rabinow, 208-226. Brighton, 1982.

Franco, Jean. "Gender, Death and Resistance: Facing the Ethical Vacuum." In *Fear at the Edge. State Terror and Resistance in Latin America*, ed. J. Corradi, P. Fagen, and M. Garreton, 104-118. Berkeley, 1992.

Garland, David. *Punishment and Modern Society. A Study in Social Theory.* Oxford, 1990.

Garland, David and Peter Young. "Towards a Social Analysis of Penality." In *The Power to Punish. Contemporary Penality and Social Analysis*, ed. David Garland and Peter Young, 1-36. London, 1983.

Ginzburg, Carlo. "Comunismo di carcere." In *Il Registro. Carcere politico in Civitavecchia 1941-1943*, ed. A. Natoli, V. Foa and C. Ginzburg, 45-50. Rome, 1994.

Goffman, Erving. *Asylums.* New York, 1961.

Goldstein, Robert J. *Political Repression in 19th Century Europe.* Totowa, 1983.

———. "Political Repression in Modern American History (1870-present): A Selected Bibliography." *Labor History* 32, no. 4 (1991): 526-550.

Gross, Jan. "War as Revolution." In *The Establishment of Communist Regimes in Eastern Europe, 1944-1949*, ed. Norman Naimark and Leonid Gibianski, 17-40. Boulder, 1997.

Gready, Paul. "Autobiography and the 'Power of Writing': Political Prison Writing in the Apartheid Era." *Journal of Southern African Studies* 19, no. 3 (1993): 489-523.

Gsovski, Vladimir, and Kazimierz Grzybowski, eds. *Government, Law and Courts in the Soviet Union and Eastern Europe.* New York, 1959.

Hahn, Alois. "Contribution à la sociologie de la confession et autres formes institutionalisées d'aveu: Autothematisation et processus de civilisation." *Actes de la recherche en sciences sociales* 62-63 (1986): 54-68.

Hall, Stuart. "Introduction: Who Needs 'Identity'?" In *Questions of Cultural Identity*, ed. Stuart Hall and Paul du Gay, 1-17. London, 1996.

Hammond, John L. "Organization and Education among Salvadoran Political Prisoners." *Crime, Law and Social Change* 25, (1996): 17-41.

Harlow, Barbara. *Barred: Women, Writing and Political Detention.* Hanover and London, 1992.

Hebrard, Jean. "La lettre representée. Les pratiques épistolaires populaires dans les récits de vie ouvriers et paysans." In *La correspondance. Les usages de la lettre au XIXe siècle*, ed. Roger Chartier, 279-365. Paris, 1991.

Henriques, J., W. Hollway, C. Urwin, C. Venn, and V. Walkerdine. *Changing the Subject: Psychology, Social Regulation and Subjectivity.* London and New York, 1984.

Herring, Gunnar. *Die politischen Parteien in Griechenland 1821-1916.* Munich, 1992.

Herzfeld, Michael. *Portrait of a Greek Imagination: An Ethnographic Biography of Andreas Nenedakis.* Chicago, 1997.

Higham, Robin, and Thanos Veremis, eds. *Aspects of Greece 1936-1940: The Metaxas Dictatorship.* Athens, 1993.

Hondros, John Louis. *Occupation and Resistance. The Greek Agony 1941-44.* New York, 1983.

Huyse, Luc. "La reintagrazione dei collaborazionisti in Belgio, Francia e nei Paesi Bassi", *Passato e Presente* 16, no. 44 (1998): 113-126.

Iatrides, John O., and Linda Wrigley, eds. *Greece at the Crossroads: The Civil War and Its Legacy*. University Park, 1995.

Iatrides, John O., ed. *Greece in the 1940s: A Nation in Crisis*. Hanover and London, 1981.

Ingraham, Barton L. *Political Crime in Europe: A Comparative Study of France, Germany, and England*. Berkeley, 1979.

Johnson, Robert, and Hans Toch, eds. *The Pains of Imprisonment*. Beverly Hills, 1982

Jones, Howard. *"A New Kind of War". America's Global Strategy and the Truman Doctrine in Greece*. New York and Oxford, 1989

Kenna, Margaret E. "Making a World: Political Exiles in 1930s Greece." *Cambridge Papers on Modern Greek* 2, (1994): 21-45

_____. "The Social Organization of Exile: The Everyday Life of Political Exiles in the Cyclades in the 1930s." *Journal of Modern Greek Studies* 9, (1991): 63-81.

Kirchheimer, Otto. *Political Justice. The Use of Legal Procedure for Political Ends*. Princeton, 1961

Kofas, Jon. *Intervention and Underdevelopment: Greece during the Civil War*. University Park and London, 1989.

Kousoulas, D. George. *Revolution and Defeat: The Story of the Greek Communist Party*. London, 1965.

Matlock, Jann. "Doubling Out of the Crazy House: Gender, Autobiography, and the Insane Asylum System in Nineteenth-Century France." *Representations* 34, (1991): 166-195.

Mavrogordatos, George. *Stillborn Republic. Social Coalitions and Party Strategies in Greece, 1922-1936*. Berkeley, 1983.

Mayer, Arno J. *Dynamics of Revolution and Counter-Revolution in Europe, 1870-1956*, New York, 1971.

Maynes, Mary Jo. "Autobiography and Class Formation in Nineteenth-Century Europe: Methodological Considerations." *Social Science History* 16, no. 3 (1992): 517-537

Mazower, Mark, ed. *After the War was Over: Reconstructing, the Family, Nation and State in Greece, 1943-1960*. Princeton, 2000.

_____. "Policing the Anti-Communist State in Greece, 1922-1974." In *The Policing of Politics in the Twentieth Century*, ed. Mark Mazower, 129-150. Providence and Oxford, 1997.

_____. *Inside Hitler's Greece. The Experience of Occupation 1941-1944*. New Haven and London, 1993.

Megill, Allan. "History, Memory, Identity." *History of Human Sciences* 11, no. 3 (1998): 37-62.

Mellor, Philip A. "Death in High Modernity: The Contemporary Presence and Absence of Death." In *The Sociology of Death*, ed. David Clark, 3-30. Oxford, 1993.

Morand, Bernadette. *Les écrits des prisonniers politiques*. Paris, 1976.

Ortner, Sherry B. "Resistance and the Problem of Ethnographic Refusal." *Comparative Studies in Society and History* 37, (1995): 173-193.
Papadatos, Pierre. *Le délit politique. Contribution à l'étude des crimes contre l' état.* Geneva, 1954.
Papathanasiou, Ioanna. "Contribution à l'histoire du Parti Communiste Grec, 1949-1951." Thèse de doctorat, Université de Paris X, Nanterre, 1988.
Passerini, Luisa. "Lacerations in the Memory: Women in the Italian Underground Organizations." In *Social Movements and Violence: Participation in Underground Organizations*, ed. Bert Klandermans and Donatella della Porta, International Social Movement Research, vol. 4, 161-212. Greenwich and London, 1992.
Perrot, Michelle, ed. *L' impossible prison*. Paris, 1980
―――. "Délinquance et système pénitentiaire en France au XIXe siècle." *Annales ESC* 30, no.1 (1975): 67-91.
Peters, Edward. *Torture*. Philadelphia, 1996.
Richter, Heinz. *British Intervention in Greece. From Varkiza to Civil War*. London, 1986.
Rodocanachi, C. P. *A Great Work of Civil Readaptation in Greece*. Athens, 1949.
Rose, Nikolas. "Calculable Minds and Manageable Individuals." *History of the Human Sciences* 1, no. 2 (1988): 179-200.
Rothman, David J. *The Discovery of the Asylum: Social Order and Disorder in the New Republic*. Boston, 1971.
Rusche, Georg, and Otto Kirchheimer. *Punishment and Social Structure*. New York, 1939.
Samatas, Minas. "Greek McCarthyism: A Comparative Assessment of Greek Post-Civil War Repressive Anticommunism and the U.S. Truman-McCarthy Era." *Journal of the Hellenic Diaspora* 13, nos. 3-4 (1986): 5-76.
Sampson, Edward E. "The Deconstruction of the Self." In *Texts of identity*, ed. John Sorter and Kenneth J. Gergen, 1-19. London, 1989.
Sawicki, Jana. "Feminism, Foucault and 'Subjects' of Power and Freedom." In *The Later Foucault*, ed. Jeremy Moss, 93-107. London, 1998.
Scarry, Elaine. *The Body in Pain: The Making and Unmaking of the World*. New York and Oxford, 1985.
Scott, James C. *Domination and the Arts of Resistance: Hidden Transcripts*. New Haven and London, 1990
Scott, Joan. "'Experience'." In *Feminists Theorize the Political*, ed. Judith Butler and Joan Scott, 22-40. New York and London, 1992.
Sewell, William H., Jr. "How Classes are Made: Critical Reflections on E.P. Thompson's Theory of Working-class Formation." In *E.P. Thompson. Critical Perspectives*, ed. Harvey J. Kaye and Keith McClellan, 50-77. Cambridge, 1990.
Sfikas, Thanasis. *The British Labour Government and the Greek Civil War. The Imperialism of "Non-Intervention."* Staffordshire, 1994.
Simmons, Anthony, ed. *They Shall Not Die: The Trial of Greek freedom*. London, n.d.
Smothers, Frank, William Hardy McNeill, and Elizabeth Darbishire McNeill. *Report on the Greeks. Findings of a Twentieth Century Fund Team which Surveyed Conditions in Greece in 1947*. New York, 1948.

Sorokin, Pitirim A. *Man and Society in Calamity: The Effects of War, Revolution, Famine, Pestilence upon Human Mind, Behavior, Social Organization and Cultural Life*. New York 1942; reprinted Westport, 1973.
Sykes, Gresham. *The Society of Captives*. Princeton, 1958.
United Nations and International Labour Office. *Report of the ad hoc Committee on Forced Labour*. Geneva, 1953.
Vimont, Jean-Claude. *La prison politique en France. Genèse d' un mode d' incarcération spécifique XVIIIe-XXe siècles*. Paris, 1993.
Vlavianos, Haris. *Greece 1941-49. From Resistance to Civil War*. Basingstroke, 1992.
Wittner, Lawrence. *American Intervention in Greece 1943-1949*. New York, 1982.
Woodbridge, George. *UNRRA. The History of the United Nations Relief and Rehabilitation Administration*. New York, 1950.

Select Bibliography in Greek

Akronafplia – Dialexeis. Athens, 1945.
Alivizatos, Nikos. *Oi politikoi thesmoi se krisi, 1922-1974. Opseis tis ellinikis empeirias*. Athens, 1995.
Antoniou, Konstantinos. *Istoria Ellinikis Vasilikis Chorofylakis 1833-1965*. Athens, 1965.
Antoniou, Nikos, and Eleni, Skarpeti-Tsali. *Apofasi 225A/1948*. Athens, 1989.
Averof-Tositsas, Evangelos. *Fotia kai tsekouri*. Athens, 1975.
Balta, Nasi. *O ellinikos emfylios polemos (1946-1949) mesa apo to galliko typo*. Athens, 1993.
Benas, Takis. *Tou Emfyliou*. Athens, 1996.
Bourlas, Moysis Michail. *Ellinas, Evraios kai aristeros*. Skopelos, 2000.
Bournazos, Stratis. "O anamorfotikos logos ton nikiton sti Makroniso." *Dokimes* 6, (1997): 101-134
Chatzivasileiou, Chrysa. *To KKE kai to gynaikeio zitima*. Athens, 1947.
Drosos, Giannis. *Dokimio ellinikis syntagmatikis theorias*. Athens and Komotini, 1996
Elefantis, Angelos. *I epaggelia tis adynatis epanastasis*. Athens, 1979
Ethniki Allileggyi Elladas. *Sta xeronisia tis Elladas*. Athens, 1947.
Fleischer, Hagen and Nikos Svoronos, eds. *Ellada 1936-1944. Diktatoria-Katochi-Antistasi*. Athens,1990.
Fleischer, Hagen. *Stemma kai svastika. I Ellada tis katochis kai tis antistasis*. Athens, 1995.
Flountzis, Antonis. *Akronafplia kai Akronafpliotes, 1937-1943*. Athens, 1979.
_____. *Sto kolastirio tis Makronisou*. Athens, 1984.
Gavriilidou, Nitsa. *O pateras mou Kostas Gavriilidis*. Athens, 1988.
Giannogonas, Vasilis. *Akronafplia*. Athens, 1963.
Giannopoulos, Giorgos. *Makronisos. Martyries enos foititi*. Athens, 2001.
Glykofrydis, Stylianos. *Fylakai*. Athens, 1932.
Gourgiotis, Nikos. *Dekaochto chronia me allo onoma*. Athens, 2001.
Gregoriadis, Foivos. *Istoria tou emfyliou polemou (1945-1949). To deftero antartiko*, Athens, n.d.

I komodia tis dikis ton dosilogon, Athens,1945.

I trichroni epopoiia tou Dimokratikou Stratou tis Elladas. Athens, 1998.

Istoriko topio kai istoriki mnimi. To paradeigma tis Makronisou. Proceedings of the conference, *Istoriko topio kai istoriki mnimi. To paradeigma tis Makronisou.* 6 and 7 March 1998, Athens.

Kamvysis, Dimitrios. *I Sofronistiki metaheirisis ton egklimation.* Athens, 1949.

Karanikas, Dimitrios. *Sofronistiki.* Salonica, 1948.

Karra, Maria. *Emeis oi ap' exo. PEOPEF: 1948-1954. Mia mikri epopoiia.* Athens, 1995

Katopodis, Georgios. *Fylaki. Esoteriki leitourgia, sofronistiki metaheirisis.* Athens,1947.

Kommounistko Komma Elladas. *Episima Keimena*, vol. 6 (1945-1949). Athens, 1987.

Kordatos, Giannis. *Ta simerina provlimata tou ellinikou laou.* Athens, 1945.

Kostis, Konstantinos. *Ermineia tou en Elladi ishyontos Poinikou Nomou.* Athens, 1928.

Kotaridis, Nikos."Oute 'atimos' oute 'ntropiasmenos'. Antistasi kai emfylios sto idioma tis syggeneias kai tis axies tis androprepeias." *Dokimes* 6, (1997): 75-100

Koundouros, Roussos. *I asfaleia tou kathestotos.* Athens, 1978.

Kyrkos, Michalis. *Piso apo ta kagkela.* 1961, reprinted Athens, 1995.

Lambropoulou, Dimitra. *Grafontas apo ti fylaki. Opseis tis ypokeimenikotitas ton politikon kratoumenon.* Athens, 1999.

Linardatos, Spyros. *4 Augoustou.* Athens, 1988.

Loverdos, Andreas. *Gia tin tromokratia kai to politiko egklima.* Athens, 1987.

Magkriotis, Dimitrios. *Thysiai tis Ellados kai egklimata Katochis 1941-1944.* Athens, 1949.

Manolkidou-Vetta, Fani. *Tha se leme Ismini.* Athens, 1997.

Manousakas, Giannis. *To chroniko enos agona. Akronafplia 1939-1943.* Athens 1986.

Mara-Michalakea, Dimitra. *Gynaikeies Fylakes Averof. Athina, 12-13 Apriliou 1949.* Athens, 1995.

Marantzidis, Nikos. *Oi mikres Mosches. Politiki kai eklogiki analysi tis parousias tou kommounismou ston elladiko agrotiko choro.* Athens, 1997.

Margaris, Nikos. *Istoria tis Makronisou.* Athens, 1966.

Margaritis, Giorgos. *Apo ti itta stin exegersi. Ellada: anoixi 1941-fthinoporo 1942.* Athens, 1993.

_____, *Istoria tou ellinikou Emfyliou Polemou*, Athens, 2001.

Mastroleon-Zerva, Marigoula. *Exoristes. Chios, Trikeri, Makronisi.* Athens, 1986.

Matomeni Vivlos, n.p., 1949

Missios, Chronis. *... kala, esy skotothikes noris.* Athens, 1988.

Nefeloudis, Vasilis. *Achtina* θ, Athens, 1974.

Nenedakis, Andreas. *Apagorevetai.* Athens, 1964.

Nikolakopoulos, Elias. *Kommata kai vouleftikes ekloges stin Ellada, 1946-1964.* Athens, 1985

Oikonomopoulos, Konstantinos. *Ektakta stratodikeia kai nomothesia aforosa tin dimosian taxin kai asfaleian.* Athens, 1951.

_____. *Nomothesia peri metron eirinefseos.* Athens, 1952.

Papathanasiou Ioanna, "Vioma, istoria kai politiki: I ypostasi tis prosopikis martyrias," *Ta Istorika* 13, vols. 24-25 (1996): 253-266.

Panteleimon, Metropolitan bishop of Chios. *O kommounismos.* Athens, 1950.
Papadouka, Olympia. *Gynaikeies Fylakes Averof.* Athens, 1981.
Pikros, Petros ,ed. *Kalpaki -Fylakes-Xeronisia.* Athens, 1978.
Politikos Synaspismos ton kommaton tou E.A.M. *Lefki Vivlos. Paravaseis tis Varkizas (Flevaris-Iounis 1945).* Athens,1945.
Pos prepei na doulevei I gynaika sto Ethniko Apeleftherotiko Metopo , n.p., 1943.
Prokos, Aristeidis. *Symvoli eis tin organosin tou sofronistikou systimatos en Elladi.* Athens, 1936.
Sideri, Maria. *Dekatessera chronia.* Athens, 1981.
Skourtis, Stamatis. *Aftoi pou dropiasan to thanato.* Athens, 1996.
Somateio Lazareto. *Geia sas adelfia. … Fylakes Kerkyras 1947-1949 – Martyries.* Athens, 1996.
Stefanou, Pagona. *Ton afanon.* Athens, 1997.
Sti mnimi Dimitri A. Glinou, Athens,1946.
Ta thymata tou monarchofasismou kataggeloun, n.p.,1951.
Theodorou, Victoria, ed. *Stratopeda gynaikon.* Athens, 1976.
Tsakiris, Kyriakos. *Vourla. I megali apodrasi.* Athens, 1994.
van Boeschoten, Rikki. *Anapoda chronia. Syllogiki Mnimi kai Istoria sto Ziaka Grevenon, 1900-1950.* Athens, 1997.
Vardinogiannis, Vardis, and Panagiotis Aronis, eds. *Oi misoi sta sidera.* Athens, 1996
Vardinogiannis, Vardis. *Makronissos, Octovris 1948-Mais 1949.* Athens, 1983.
Vasikoi kanones epagrypnisis, Athens, 1947
Vasileiou, K. S. *I dioikitiki ektopisi stin Ellada.* London, 1974.
Vervenioti Tasoula. *I gynaika tis Antistasis. I eisodos ton gynaikon stin politiki.* Athens, 1994
Ydraios, Thodoros. *Grammata apo ti fylaki.* Athens, 1984.
Ypomnima kratoumenon pros ton Ypourgo Dikaiosynis tis kyvernisis Plastira,1951. (published, Athens, 1984).
Zachariadis, Nikos. *O kommounistis, laikos agonistis, melos tou KKE.* Athens, 1946.
_____. *Provlimata kathodigisis sto KKE.* n.p., 1953.
Zafeiropoulos, Dimitrios. *O antisymmoriakos agon 1945-1949.* Athens, 1956

Index

A
Aegina prison, 109, 119, 146, 148, 152, 166, 190, 191, 194-196, 214
Agios Efstratios, 41, 43, 92, 93, 95, 105, 125, 146, 188
Ailianos, Michael, 65, 152
Akronafplia prison, 41-43, 82, 99, 109, 125, 146, 150, 164, 171, 189, 191, 194-196, 206, 215
Alexandrou, Aris, 218
Alexandroupolis, 97
Alivizatos, Nikos, 224
Alonisos, 92
Amfissa, 146-147
Amnesty, 56, 65, 67, 96, 177, 188-189, 225
Amorgos, 41
Anafi, 35, 41, 43, 92, 93, 94
Anagnostakis, Manolis, 225, 226, 230
Anticommunism, 4, 5, 28, 35, 38, 39, 65, 78, 102, 126, 227, 231, 232
Army, 4, 5, 33, 34, 38, 52, 55, 56, 57, 58, 60, 64, 80, 100-106, 107, 108, 137, 170 174, 185
Asia Minor, 2, 34, 101, 223
Athens, 52-53, 97, 104-105, 134, 138, 145, 149, 170, 174, 177, 178, 186, 189, 191, 192, 200, 210,213, 216, 226
Austria, 22
Averof prison, 36, 99, 118, 121, 124, 126, 138, 139, 152, 153, 155, 165, 171, 173, 174, 187, 189-190, 193, 194, 195-196, 199, 201, 204, 206, 211, 214, 216, 233

B
Bairaktaris Georgios, 105, 149
Balas, Stelios, 193
Balkan Wars, 2, 101
Bandits, 2, 33, 58, 66, 85-86, 150, 151, 231
Beikos, Georgoulas, 118
Belgium, 55, 91
Benas, Takis, 234
Boer War, 100
Bolshevik revolution, 3, 21, 22, 35, 100, 172; Bolshevikization, 201, 217, 218, 229
Bourdieu, Pierre, 218
Bouzakis, Emmanuel, 109
Braziotikos, Nikos, 154
Brigands, see bandits
British Military Mission, 105
British Police and Prisons Mission 55, 57, 85, 96, 97
Bulgaria, 3, 28, 29-30, 44, 47, 103
Bulkes, 218
Bureau, 42-43, 83, 125-126, 157, 167, 168, 189, 192-194, 208-212, 214-217
Burks, R.V., 201
Butler, Judith, 11

C

Calhoun, Craig, 11
Cephalonia prison, 98, 109, 152, 154, 156, 192-194
Chaidari camp, 43, 47, 132, 135
Chania prison, 182
Charalambidis, Evgenios, 216
Chatzikosta prison, 170, 187
Chatzivasileiou, Chrysa, 127, 203
China, 60, 173-174
Chios, 77, 100, 106-107, 167, 170, 207
Church, 76-78, 169, 177, 188, 207
Collaborators, 28, 55-56, 57, 67, 91, 97, 105
Colonels' dictatorship, 63, 134
Communist Party of Greece (KKE), 5, 8, 10, 12, 35, 37, 40, 42, 44, 53, 58-59, 60, 62, 63, 65, 66, 79-83, 84, 92, 96, 99, 126, 133, 140, 150, 156, 163, 171, 178, 183-185, 193, 200, 202, 203, 205, 208-209, 215, 217-218, 224, 228-230, 234
Concentration camps, 2, 6, 23-24, 26, 40, 47, 105, 132, 165, 229
Corfu prison, 41, 42, 43, 99, 121, 125, 139-140, 174, 194, 216
Crete, 39, 101, 163, 182
Criminal prisoners, 7, 20, 27, 57, 91, 109, 152, 156, 176, 189, 212-214

D

Daily Mirror, 85
Death sentence, 55, 56, 58, 61-62, 63, 65, 66, 67-68
Declarations of repentance, 8, 40, 42, 68, 101-102, 107, 130, 135, 140, 149, 157, 174, 176, 184-185, 209, 211, 216, 232; see also chapter 4
Dekemvriana, 53-57, 64, 194, 200, 229
Deleuze, Gilles, 12
Democratic Army of Greece, 60, 67, 103, 126, 174, 183, 193, 204, 217, 219, 229, 231
Devreki, Loula, 204
Dogkas, Makis, 80

E

EA, 44, 96, 101, 177, 178
EAM, 44-47, 52-53, 55, 56, 57, 58, 60, 61, 63, 66, 74, 77, 83, 101, 172, 174, 186, 191, 200, 203, 219
EDA, 178, 228
EDES, 45-46, 61, 83
EKKA, 45-46
ELAS, 44-47, 53, 55, 56, 170, 174, 218, 219, 229
Eleftheri Ellada, 186
Eleftheriadou, Koula, 184
Emergency laws, 39-40, 58, 62-64, 65, 66, 95, 98, 138, 151, 178, 189, 208, 209, 224, 229
EPON, 44, 83, 101, 166-167, 172, 205
Eptapyrgio prison, 97, 152
Escapes from prison, 150, 175, 183, 213
Estonia, 22
Executions, 2, 3, 27, 47, 58, 78, 99, 151-157, 172, 182, 184, 189-190, 192, 193-195, 213-216, 223, 233-234

F

Feidaris, Takis, 193
Finland, 4, 22
First World War, 2, 20-21, 33, 100
Folegandros, 35, 41, 92, 94
Forced labor, 24, 26, 27, 29-30, 110-111
Foucault, Michel, 6-8, 78, 86, 123
France, 19, 20, 45, 55
French Committee for Aid to Democratic Greece, 177

G

Gakis, Thanasis, 215
Gavdos, 35, 41, 92
Gendarmerie, 4, 42, 46, 47, 55, 57, 59, 94, 107, 147, 150, 191
Georgantis, Konstantinos, 210
Germany, 3, 4, 20, 22, 23-25, 26, 28, 30, 44, 46-47, 63, 91, 132, 172, 191
Giannopoulos, Giorgos, 119
Giaros, 98, 100, 108-111, 117, 125, 132, 140, 141, 147, 213, 224
Gini, Eirini, 151
Ginzburg, Carlo, 233
Glastras, Georgios, 109
Glezos, Manolis, 202
Glinos, Dimitrios, 125, 156, 206

248   Index

Glykofridis, Stylianos, 37, 140
Goffman, Erving, 227
Government-in-exile, 45, 46, 52
Great Britain, 5, 20-21, 36, 45-46, 53, 58, 59, 61, 85, 86, 100, 141, 148, 151, 152, 165, 171, 185, 187
Gross, Jan, 3
Gytheio prison, 150, 183

H

Hall, Stuart, 8, 10
Hebrard, Jean, 123
Hungary, 4, 22, 23, 24, 28, 29, 178
Hunger strike, 149, 182, 183, 188, 192-196, 213

I

Idionymo, 34, 35-36, 39, 41, 58
Ikaria, 92, 94, 95, 141, 169
Ioannidis, Giannis, 215
Italy, 2, 3, 4, 20, 22-26, 39, 43, 44, 45, 91, 139, 150, 169
Itzedin prison, 98, 152, 170, 182, 187, 194, 195

J

Jews, 47, 165

K

Kafantaris, Georgios, 54
Kafetzis, Vasileios, 156-157
Kalamata prison, 109, 150
Kalemis, Georgios, 151
Kalpaki, 35
Kapenis, Thanasis, 215
Karagiorgis, Kostas, 81
Kassaveteia prison, 141
Kastor prison, 168
Kastoria, 137
Katsareas, Captain, 150
Kifissia prison, 134, 213
Kilkis, 151
Kimolos, 35, 41, 92
King Constantine, 33
King George, 38, 39, 45, 59, 104, 185
Kirchheimer, Otto, 25, 65
Kokkas, Lambros, 84
Kondylis' dictatorship, 37
Kordatos Giannis, 52

Kouderi, Anastasia, 116
Koutsonikou, Georgia, 83
Kyparissia prison, 36, 191
Kyriacopoulos, Vasileios, 199
Kyrkos, Michalis, 186
Kythira, 92, 150
Kythnos, 94

L

Ladas, Christos, 81
Lakonia, 150
Lambou Alexandros, 46
Lamia, 109, 118
Larisa camp, 43, 101, 170
Lazaretto, 43
League for Democracy in Greece, 177, 226
Leeper, Reginald, 199
Leros, 92
Liberal Party, 37; see also Venizelos, Eleftherios
Limnos, 92, 95, 218
Lippincott, Richard, 169
Lithuania, 22
Loulis, Alkiviadis, 186
Loyalty certificates, 40, 62, 224

M

Machi, 84
Makridis, Orestis, 155
Makronisos, 36, 63, 64, 77-78, 79, 80, 81, 84, 92, 100-105, 106, 107-108, 110-111, 116, 117, 119, 132, 133, 134, 141, 146, 148-151, 157, 173-174, 184, 223, 226Maltezos, Christos, 140
Mamali, Zoe, 174-175
Maniadakis, Konstantinos, 75
Manolkidou-Vetta, Fani, 232
Mara-Michalakea, Dimitra, 154
Margaritis, Giorgos, 59
Maurois, André, 166
Mavrogordatos, George, 34
Mavros, Georgios, 58
Mayer, Arno, 21
Maynes, Mary Jo, 232
Megali Idea, 34
Mesologgi prison, 210
Metaxas dictatorship, 38, 39-40, 41, 43, 47, 53, 59, 65, 75-76, 79-81, 94, 99, 134, 164, 170, 174, 200, 201, 215, 224

Middle East, 53, 96
Military Police, 101, 102, 108, 135, 141, 149, 186
Missios, Chronis, 140-141, 231-232, 233
Moutsogiannis, Stratis, 81
Muslims, 203
Mylonas, Konstantinos, 54

N

National Guard, 4, 53, 55, 56, 57.
National Schism, 33, 34, 38
Naxos, 35, 92
Nefeloudis, Vasilis, 139
Netherlands, 55
Newton, W.E., 182
Nietzsche, Friedrich, 86
Nifakou, Niki, 226
Ntakou, Koula, 121

O

Omades symviosis, 42, 94, 99, 167, 168, 208

P

Pangalos dictatorship, 46
Panteleimon, metropolitan bishop, 77
Papadimitropoulos, Ioannis, 109
Papadouka, Olympia, 171, 174
Papageorgiou, Andreas, 80
Papagiannopoulos Vrasidas, 105
Papandreou, George, 45
Paparigas, Dimitris, 215
Papaspyrou, Dimitrios, 223
Paros, 35
Passerini, Luisa, 216
Patras prison, 97, 109, 146
Pavlos Melas camp, 204-205
PEOPEF, 177-178
Peters, Edward, 130
Petroulaki, Eirini, 175
Pipinelis, Panagiotis, 104
Plastiras, Nikolaos, 54, 55
Poland, 22, 28, 30, 178
Police, 4, 5, 35, 39, 40, 41, 55, 57, 95, 97, 101, 131, 132, 133, 135, 150, 176, 215
Politis, Giannis, 135
Portugal, 22
Procopios, Father, 77
Psaromytas, Taxiarchis, 184

Public security committee, 33, 41, 64, 66, 92, 93, 106, 224
Pylos prison, 41, 99, 150

R

Rallis, Ioannis, 46
Rankin, Karl, 63
Red Cross, 27, 96, 177
Rightist bands, 4, 45, 47, 53, 56-57, 58, 59, 60
Rizospastis, 36, 41, 81, 166, 178, 215
Romania, 22, 28, 29, 30, 121, 178
Rotas, Vasilis, 170, 207

S

Salonica, 47, 80, 97, 101, 109, 151, 152, 174, 177, 205,
Samothraki, 92
Santas, Apostolos, 202
Sapranidis, Theocharis, 151
Scapaneus, 80, 103
Scarry, Elaine, 131
Schmitt, Karl, 39
Scobie, Ronald, 45
Scott, Joan, 235
Security Battalions, 45, 46, 56, 67
Sewell, William, Jr., 10
Sideri, Maria, 136
Sidiropoulou, Ismini, 233
Sifnos, 41
Sikinos, 41, 92, 168, 210
Skaloumbakas, Giannis, 102
Skarpeti, Eleni, 138, 214
SK-ELD, 84, 184
Slav Macedonians, 203
Socialist Party, 230-231
Sofoulis, Themistocles, 54, 60, 61
Soliotis, Sotirios, 188
Sorokin, Pitirim, 3
Sotiropoulos, Dimitris, 173
Soviet Union, 4, 22, 26-27, 28, 29, 178, 206, 214, 215
Spain, 4, 22, 23, 24, 25, 174, 223
Sparta prison, 150, 183
Special courts-martial, 61, 62, 63, 64, 68, 138, 176, 223, 224
Stalin, Joseph, 27, 166, 199, 229
Stavridis, Pavlos, 42
Stavropoulos, Ioannis, 83
Stefanou, Pagona, 233

Strangeways, D.I., 105, 185
Stratos, Georgios, 185
Svorou, Elli, 155
Swedish Committee for Aid to Democratic Greece, 177
Swiss Committee for Aid to Democratic Greece, 177
Syros, 108, 111

T

Tavoularis, Anastasios, 46
Themistocleous Street prison, 98, 191
Thompson, E.P., 10
Timogiannakis, Panagiotis, 147
Tolstoy, Leo, 166
Trikala prison, 97, 146; camp, 43
Trikeri, 92, 95, 100, 105, 106-107, 108, 141
Tripolis prison, 97, 150
Truman, Harry, 59-60
Tsaldaris, Konstantinos, 61, 96
Tsouderos, Emmanuel, 54

U

United Nations, 176, 177, 188
United States, 2, 5, 61, 62, 63, 101, 138, 139, 152, 189, 203
UNRRA, 44, 54, 92, 93, 94, 97, 146, 178

V

Vardinogiannis, Vardis, 104
Varkiza agreement, 53, 55, 56, 96, 229
Varnalis, Kostas, 213
Vasilopoulos, Antonios, 149
Vasilopoulos, Theodoros, 175
Velouchiotis, Aris, 86
Venizelos Eleftherios, 33, 38; Venizelists, 34, 37
Vidalis Panagiotis, 132
Vizirtzis, Ioannis, 193
Volos prison, 98, 192
Vonitsa, 43
Votanis, Kostas, 215
Vourla prison, 175, 183
Voutsinos, Stylianos, 190

W

Wickham, Charles, 55
Woodhouse, Chris, 199

Y

Yugoslavia, 22, 24, 84, 204, 218; Kingdom of Serbs, Croats and Slovenes, 24

Z

Zachariadis, Nikos, 41, 155, 205, 215, 218, 228, 229
Zakynthos prison, 92, 98, 166, 205; exile, 98
Zervas, Napoleon, 61, 85
Zevgos, Giannis, 171